The Food Lover's Companion to Tuscany

The Food Lover's Companion to
TUSCANY

Carla Capalbo

CHRONICLE BOOKS
SAN FRANCISCO

Tuscan maps based on Touring Club Italiano's Toscana: 1:200,000, by kind permission.

The author and the publisher have taken due care to ensure that all the information in the book is correct at the time of going to press. They cannot be held responsible for any errors or inaccuracies. Readers' comments and suggestions for further editions will be welcomed. Write to the author care of the publisher, or e-mail: capalbo@voyager.archi.it.

Printed in the United States of America.

Library of Congress Cataloging-in-Publication Data:

Capalbo, Carla.
      The food lover's companion to Tuscany / by Carla Capalbo
      p. cm.
      Includes index
      ISBN 0-8118-1209-X (pb)
      1. Food—Guidebooks. 2. Grocery trade—Italy—Tuscany—Guidebooks. 3. Restaurants—Italy—Tuscany—Guidebooks. I. Title.
        TX354.5.C37 1998
        381'.4564'025455—dc21   97-36633
                              CIP

Book and cover design: Margery Cantor
Composition: Margery Cantor
Cover illustration: Marco Ventura

Distributed in Canada by Raincoast Books
8680 Cambie Street
Vancouver, B.C. V6P 6M9

10 9 8 7 6 5 4 3 2 1

Chronicle Books
85 Second Street
San Francisco, CA 94105

Web Site: www.chronbooks.com

For Sandro

and

*for Dr. Martha Skinner and Dr. Raymond Comenzo
and the brilliant team of doctors and nurses at Boston University Medical Center
who saved my sister Isabelle's life*

Acknowledgments

It has taken me two full years to research and write this book. I spent months at a time on the road, driving alone in my van from one end of Tuscany to the other. Many people, most of whom I did not know at the outset, helped me along the way, offering everything from a bed for the night to much-needed moral support. Each of them made this fascinating but complex project a little bit easier and a lot more enjoyable.

Thank you all—I couldn't have done it without you.

In Tuscany:

MASSA CARRARA: Mauro and Eugenia Giannarelli, Michele and Gabriella Giannarelli, Avvocato Carletti, Lilia Borghetti and family. LUCCA: Fabio Tognetti, Andrea Bertucci, Enzo Petreschi, Gabriele Bertucci, Gabriele Mazzei, and Arnaldo Poli. PISTOIA: Giannina Verreschi, the Montecatini APT, and Paolo Bresci of the Pistoia APT. FIRENZE: Maresciallo Rovida of the Carabinieri, Franca Michon Pecori, Aldo and Grazia Capobianco, Vito Lacerenza. PISA: Carlo Gazzarrini, Walter Surbone, and Diliano Stefanini. LIVORNO: Ernesto Gentili, Claudio Mollo, Ulisse Mibelli of the Livorno APT. ELBA: Donatella Moro and Gherardo Frassa, Fabio Picchi. CHIANTI: Leo Codacci, Ladislas Rice, Sylvie Haniez and Roberto Melosi, Bernadette and Renzo Bolli. GROSSETO: Roberto Santini and Carlo Pascini of Grosseto Export, Antonio Perico, Rita Presenti and Attilio Barbero, Alberto Pellegrini and Nolberto Palla. AMIATA: the two Paola Coppis of the Amiata APT, Claudia Perguidi and Valentina Perguidi of the Heimat Cooperative. MONTALCINO: Franco Biondi Santi, Roberto Cipresso. AREZZO: Barbara and Julian Sachs, Burton and Nancy Anderson, Silvio Ristori and the Arezzo chapter of the Sommeliers d'Italia, Massimo Rossi, Pietro Bartoli and the AICOO, Luca Fabbri, Dott. Baldesi of the Arezzo APT, Marco Noferi.

Beyond Tuscany:

MILAN: James Siddall, Paola Bonfanti at the Touring Club, Giorgio Albonetti at Techniche Nuove, Carlo Galante, Ermanno Tritto, Alessandra Zucchi, Giacomo Ghidelli, Aldo Petillo. POLLINO: Luigina and Giulio Aiello, Christa

and Mike Irdmann. LONDON: Carole Clements and Tim Garland,
Wallace Heim, Mary Fedden, John Hubbard, Eileen and Tim Tweedy.
NEW YORK: Douglas Harry Elliott, Beth Gerowitz, Donna Gorman,
Dianne Janis, Joni Hughes and Antoine Bootz, Carla and Eddie Bigelow,
and Tracy Tynan McBride.

I am very grateful to Dott. Roberto Melis at the Touring Club
Italiano for allowing its excellent map of Tuscany to be used as the basis for the
maps in this book.

Dott. Luciano Panci of the Regione Toscana offered early
assistance with the project. Piero Pesenti of the Amiata APT was an eager host
in his area. Many thanks go to Stefano Campatelli and Marta Ripaccioli at
the Consorzio del Vino Brunello di Montalcino for their willing cooperation,
and to Ursula Thurner at the Consorzio di Chianti Classico for her invaluable
organizational help and good cheer.

My literary agent Colleen Mohyde's enthusiasm for this project
was immediate; I am also grateful for her sensitivity and support as a friend
during the writing of this book. The book's early editors at Chronicle, Bill
LeBlond and Sarah Putman, were encouraging from the start; Karen Silver,
who took it over, was remarkably patient (and diplomatic) in the face of an
overabundance of text, as was Joni Owen, who steered us through the final
stages. Thanks also to Margery Cantor, the book's designer, and Jeff Campbell,
its copy editor.

Special thanks go to Maria-Teresa Giannarelli for being my first
Tuscan friend and for getting me through the first day; Anna and Fabrizio Galli
for endlessly putting me up; Sophie and Valdo Verreschi and Giuliana and
Enrico Galli for their generous hospitality; Franco Guerrieri for keeping my
VW on the road; Bruno, Elyane, and Booboo Moos and the *club des cinq* for
sharing their house and everything else; Graziano Mannozzi for the anemones
and for his extraordinary support during my sister's illness. Judy and Nino,
Cosmo and Toto MacDonald gave me a home away from home on many
occasions; Harriet Shapiro was in on it from the beginning; Harvey Sachs
was my first friend in Tuscany and my first editor; Alberto Biagetti and David
Zuman were cheerful and tireless map-men. Thanks go to Mark Edmonds at
the London *Daily Telegraph* for being instructive about "color" in writing; to
Anne Mendelson for being the book's fairy godmother and to my uncle,
Leonard A. Stevens, for introducing me to her.

The idea for this book came out of a conversation with
Henrietta Green, whose *Food Lover's Guide to Britain* has been an inspiration
throughout. My brother-in-law, Adam Sodowick, helped change the course
of my sister Isabelle's life and thus my own. I am grateful to my sister Sandra
Lousada who took my photograph for the cover. Thanks to my brother,

Sebastian Lousada, for setting an example to us all by being an organic grower, and to my 102-year-old grandmother, Marie McBride (née Giuditta Camera) for her support and faith in me. The late Gary Nikolis, who had long been my champion, was an enthusiastic fan of the project. Lauren Crow has been a welcome friend and helpful early reader of the manuscript. A very special thank you to my father, Carmen Capalbo, who read almost every word of the text and offered an infallible ear for languages, a wealth of bookish wisdom, and quite a few laughs.

I almost invariably dined alone when reviewing the restaurants for this book, but I amused myself by taking along a group of "virtual" companions whose opinions I liked to "consult": Peter Frank lent me his fine eye for detail at all of the grandest restaurants; Elizabeth Heyert brought her sensitive appreciation and her exceptions to many dietary rules; my mother, Patricia Lousada, was everpresent with her standards of excellence in cooking and her discerning (but not uncritical) palate. My sister Isabelle Lousada was always with me, bringing her joy of eating out and her sense of style; so was my brother Marco Capalbo, with whom I first learned to love eating in Tuscany.

Two people followed the course of the making of this book on a daily (and usually distant) basis: my loyal friend and unofficial editor Nicola Rudge Iannelli, whose intelligent attention and solidarity helped me to get through it, and Alessandro Guerriero, whose love, generosity of spirit, and faith in me were the gifts that left me free to go off alone and take on the world of Tuscany.

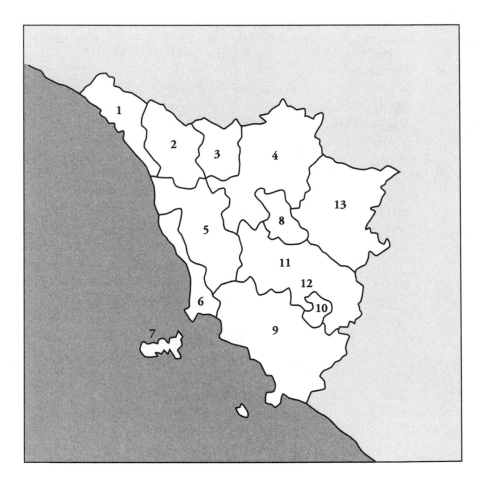

Contents

Introduction

*P*icture yourself in Tuscany. You are in the heart of Italy, surrounded by medieval hill towns, gray-green olive groves, and sloping vineyards. You appreciate good food, and you are in the mood to cook or to enjoy a leisurely lunch in the country. But where should you go to buy the finest bread or cheeses, extra-virgin olive oil, or estate-bottled wine? When is market day in the nearest village? And which are the nicest family-run trattorias?

The Food Lover's Companion to Tuscany tells you. This practical guide leads you to the best foods and wines in Tuscany. It suggests what products to buy, explains how they are made, and tells you where to find them. And it offers an insight into the complex gastronomic culture of one of Italy's most fascinating and varied regions.

To research this book I drove thousands of kilometers, on and off the beaten track. I interviewed hundreds of people: shepherds in the Maremman hills, mushroom-gatherers in the mountains above Carrara, fishermen along the Mediterranean coast. I visited historic wine castles in Chianti as well as tiny vineyards in less famous locations whose wines are just as noteworthy. I searched for unpretentious trattorias serving genuine home-cooking and more ambitious restaurants whose chefs are reinterpreting Tuscany's culinary traditions. To uncover the best food products I sampled dozens of gelati and chocolates, *salumi* and cheeses, baked goods and bottled preserves. Along the way, I learned a lot about the people who make them.

This book is a love letter to Tuscany's food artisans—to the bakers and cheesemakers, wine producers and *salumieri* who have devoted their lives to doing one thing and to doing it with passion and pride. They are as much a part of Italy's cultural heritage as the Duomo in Florence or Botticelli's *Venus*. But many of them are fighting to survive in a world of convenience foods and one-stop shopping. And sadly, the elderly *salumiere* in his medieval village or the dedicated young couple producing handmade goat's cheeses in the Apennine mountains are not only countering the evils of mass marketing. They may also be battling overzealous bureaucracies intent on industrial standardization, whose respect for the "little man" is often not what it might be.

Luckily, there still are people who understand the difference between a loaf of bread that is factory-made with bleached flours and preservatives and one crafted of stone-ground grains, leavened with natural yeasts, and baked on chestnut leaves in a wood-burning oven. These foods still exist, although they often qualify as "endangered species."

Like most Italians, the Tuscans treasure their "secret" food sources. As a sign of hospitality they proudly offer guests slices of hand-cured local prosciutto, a glass of a favorite estate wine, or a taste of freshly pressed olive oil bought at a nearby *frantoio*. These precious resources have been carefully sought out, tried, and tested. They are valued for their genuine quality and for the link they maintain with the honored traditions of the past. Often they are to be found within a stone's throw of a town or supermarket. You just have to know where to look.

An early morning outing to a fish market or a tour of the cellars of a stately wine *castello* may be as memorable an experience as a trip to a landmark frescoed church. They represent complementary aspects of Italian culture: one frozen in time, the other still very much alive today.

With this *Companion* in your pocket, your visits to Tuscany should be full of pleasurable, delicious, and informative gastronomic adventures. Mine certainly have been!

How to Use This Book

For the sake of this book, I have divided Tuscany into thirteen sections (and chapters): most correspond to official province boundaries (such as Pistoia or Livorno), but in three (Lunigiana and Versilia, Chianti Classico, and Mount Amiata) entries belonging to more than one province are grouped together for greater consistency of subject matter or ease of travel. The island of Elba, belonging to the province of Livorno, has a chapter of its own, as does the town of Montalcino.

The Maps

Each chapter begins with a map showing the area's key towns. Wherever an entry appears, the town's name is printed in boldface. These maps are intended to help you organize your visits to foodmakers, but I strongly recommend obtaining Touring Club Italiano's Toscana 1:200,000 (green cover) map for anyone planning to do much driving in rural Tuscany. It is readily available and is the only map I have found that shows the smaller roads in enough detail to be useful.

The Entries and Their Categories

Towns and villages containing entries are listed alphabetically within each chapter. Within each town, the entries are grouped by category—by food type (bread, cheese, olive oil, wine) or establishment type (bar, olive mill, restaurant)—and within these categories, the listings are arranged alphabetically by key words. Some entries have more than one category. Others may suggest additional products within the text: for instance, most wineries also produce fine olive oil.

How to Read an Entry

After the town and category, each entry begins with the full NAME AND ADDRESS of the business, including the postal code. (When writing, always add the town and province name after this code. For example: Macelleria Marini. Via Selva, 313. Ferruccia. 51030 Agliana. Pistoia.) Note, too, that in Italy, house numbers are written after the street name.

OPENING HOURS are given, but these may vary by season or whim: if you are planning a long trip, phone first to check whether the establishment will be open. Many wineries and other private artisan producers are only open by appointment; phone before going to confirm that they are visitable. Meals served, rather than open hours, are given for restaurants.

CLOSING DAYS are given whenever possible; holiday closures, when known, are indicated by month, although the establishment may not be closed for the entire month.

MAIL ORDER is included for those companies who provide this service for their products.

If an establishment takes CREDIT CARDS, these are indicated: Visa, MasterCard (MC), American Express (Amex), and Diner's Club (DC).

DIRECT SALE is included for farms and estates that sell directly to the public. When direct sale is not possible, a nearby stockist is given.

Each entry also tells WHETHER ENGLISH IS SPOKEN or not.

FEATURES, such as "summer garden terrace," apply mainly to restaurants, so you can see at a glance if outdoor dining is possible.

RESERVATIONS applies only to restaurants, indicating when reservations are required. However, it is always best to reserve.

The PRICE CATEGORY is also used only for restaurants, and it gives the average cost per person of a four-course meal without wine, beverages, or service and cover charges (prices accurate as of summer 1997). Here are the ranges used:

$	up to 25.000 lire
$$	25.000-40.000 lire
$$$	40.000-65.000 lire
$$$$	65.000-90.000 lire
$$$$$	90.000-120.000 lire
$$$$$$	120.000 and over

These price ranges should be used as a guide only. Meals may cost less, if fewer courses are ordered, or they may cost more, depending on the wines you choose.

The "OTHER" category indicates aspects of an establishment that are not directly connected to food, such as apartments for holiday rentals or museums on the grounds.

DIRECTIONS are given to help you locate the entries, and they should be used in conjunction with a good road map. In rural Tuscany, few roads have names (and fewer still have signs telling what their names are). The most important visible indicators are the blue-and-white signs pointing to the next town or village. When an entry's directions say "go toward" a village, I am referring to these signs. They are usually the only way to know that you are going in the right direction. All distances are given in kilometers. When a direction states "in the town center," it means within the *centro storico*, or historic center. This is always indicated from the outskirts of town by the symbol of black concentric circles on a white ground; they are easy to find. Within large towns or cities, cross streets or nearby landmarks are given, but almost every village has a large map in the main square showing its landmarks and streets. In Firenze and other large towns, I suggest buying a map with a street index. They are sold at every newspaper stand or bookstore.

What You Will Find in the Entries

I have personally visited every address of the over 450 that are included in this book (with one noted exception), looking for the best in each category. I tried to choose places that are fun to visit—where the food is great, the people are charming, and the locations are lovely. The entries include food and wine producers, restaurants, food shops, and table crafts.

The Food Entries

These entries describe fine food producers and some of their products. I have included information about how these products are made and descriptions of those foods I was able to taste or liked best. Other products are also often available.

The Wine Entries

This book describes over ninety-five quality wine estates throughout Tuscany—many more exist, far too many for any one book. No matter how detailed the tasting notes on a particular wine may be, they rarely offer much insight into the personality of the winery that produced it. I felt it was more important to bring out the characteristics of the winemakers and their estates than to analyze their wines. After all, you will have a chance to visit some of these wineries and judge their products yourself; read about the estates listed here and visit those that sound most interesting. There is no substitute for the experience of tasting a fine wine in the cellars that made it.

Wines may be bought directly from most estates at prices that are the same or slightly lower than nearby wine shops. It is best to phone ahead to arrange a visit at all but the biggest wineries (who may have permanent staff on hand to show you around). All are hospitable and keen on receiving interested visitors—novices and experts alike—so don't miss out on this wonderful, fascinating opportunity.

In the listings, the wine entries are alphabetized by the key word in their company titles: Castello dei Rampolla is under R.

The Restaurant Reviews

I have reviewed restaurants offering well-cooked food in all price ranges and styles. Some specialize in traditional Tuscan cuisine, others take a more modern approach. Since seasonal foods are not always available, I mention the time of year I visited.

This book does not give scores or grades; the restaurants were not visited anonymously. I describe a meal in each restaurant rather than list its complete menu: these necessarily subjective accounts should help visitors choose the restaurants best suited to their tastes.

Boxed Inserts

These offer detailed information about some of Tuscany's most important foods and wines.

Also

These are shorter mentions following at the end of a town's entries; the reduced length does not imply that the products are less interesting.

Tuscan Market Days (see p 349)

An alphabetical list, divided by chapter, of the towns and villages, giving their weekly or monthly market days.

Glossary (see p 355)

This provides translations for Italian (and some French) food and wine words commonly used in Tuscany and in this book. It will also help in translating menus written in Italian.

Index (see p 363)

At the end of the book you will find a comprehensive, general index listing the entries and their foods by category. For example, you can see where chocolate is made throughout Tuscany, and thus read about the chocolate makers before deciding which to visit.

PART ONE

THE FOODS OF TUSCANY

Tuscany's food is rooted in *cucina povera*, poor or peasant cookery, a rural cuisine based on available natural ingredients: olive oil, unsalted bread, vegetables and pulses, wild leaves and mushrooms, and salt-cured or simply cooked meats. Many dishes are purely seasonal, looked forward to and eaten only when their ingredients make their annual appearance. But Tuscany's noble families also favored elaborate dishes of Renaissance origin.

Tuscan antipasti include *crostini* (canapés topped with chicken livers or vegetables), *salumi* (salt-cured pork meats such as prosciutto and *salame*), and *bruschetta* (grilled bread topped with olive oil or tomatoes). *Primi*, first courses, feature hearty soups more than pasta, like the two popular bread-thickened *zuppe: la ribollita* and *pappa al pomodoro*. Each province's favorites are discussed in the entries. *Secondi*, main courses, include grilled meats, game, country rabbit stewed with olives, and fish on the coast. *La Fiorentina* is the Tuscan T-bone steak, served rare and best made from Chianina beef. Vegetarians will find stewed or sautéed vegetables, salads, and egg dishes like frittata. Desserts are simple: Vin Santo with *cantucci* cookies is a classic, but there are often rather dry cakes, gelati, or the ubiquitous tiramisù. Locally grown fruit and berries are always good options.

Much of this book is devoted to Tuscany's artisan food producers. Many still work using traditional methods—water-powered stone mills for grinding, or hand-stirred milk for cheesemaking—adapted now to a modern world dominated by industry and impersonal production regulations.

The quality of these foods sets them apart from their industrial counterparts. Only the experience of a perfectionist (and all the artisans are that) can judge whether the meat for *salame* has been kneaded enough or the dough for an organic loaf needs more time to rise. These artisans are justly proud of their work. Many sell directly from farms and workshops, and welcome visitors. If possible, phone before you go, especially if you are interested in seeing how they work: they may otherwise be in the fields or barns.

RESTAURANTS AND EATING OUT

Tuscany offers many options for eating out. A *bar* sells drinks, coffee, and snacks; some even serve several courses at lunchtime. *Enoteche* are wine bars; many also serve food. *Trattorias* and *osterie* are similar: they feature rustic home cooking and are often family-run. *Ristoranti* (restaurants) are usually well appointed and include world-class establishments. I have grouped them all under the category "restaurant."

Mealtimes in Italy respect a well-defined timetable. Lunch is normally served from 12:30 to 14:30 and dinner from 19:30 to 21:30. Some kitchens may stay open later, but they are the exception, especially in the country. Do not expect restaurants to serve a meal in midafternoon, though a simple *panino* (sandwich) can usually be found in a bar.

Italians traditionally eat three or four courses at each meal: antipasto (hors d'oeuvres), *primo* (pasta or soup), *secondo* (meat or fish main course with a *contorno* of vegetables), and *dolce* (dessert). These habits are changing, and it is now usually acceptable to have just two or three courses. Some restaurants may not look favorably on those wanting only a pasta and salad, but others understand that not everyone eats as many courses as the Italians. Those restaurants that require diners to order a full four-course meal are indicated.

Not all restaurants have printed menus; in some the proprietor recites the day's offerings. If you want a full meal, many restaurants offer a *menu degustazione*, or tasting menu. In a good restaurant, this can be a good value, offering a chance to taste dishes in each category at a predetermined price.

To avoid disappointment it is always advisable to make a phone reservation: popular restaurants may be fully booked, and country trattorias sometimes close off-season if no customers have reserved.

FOOD MARKETS

Most villages and towns in Tuscany host a weekly market in addition to any permanent market structures they have. These are great to visit not only for shopping—prices are usually lower than in the supermarkets, and the produce is fresher—but also to see what is in season. Vegetables and fruits are sold and priced by weight: either by the kilogram (2.2 lbs) or the *etto* (100 grams, or 3.5 ounces). Any item sold and priced singly will be marked *cadauno* or *cad.* (each).

For a listing of Tuscany's principal market days, see p 349.

FOOD FESTIVALS

At least once a year, almost every village in Tuscany holds a food fair, which may be called a *sagra* or *festa*, and be big or small. On summer weekends many villages hold fairs on the same day. *Sagre* are usually dedicated to one particular food or dish: *sagra della bistecca* (steak festival), *della fragola* (strawberry), *del cinghiale* (wild boar), *del pecorino* (sheep's cheese), and so on. They range from elaborate events with costumes, music, and a rich assortment of foods to very local village affairs with a few tables set up in the main square. Whatever their size, they are usually fun to attend and offer an insight into rural life in Tuscany.

Usually local cooks prepare the village's specialties using the seasonal ingredient the fair is dedicated to. Visitors pay a modest fee and sit at large communal tables for their meal.

The best way to find out about food fairs is to look for posters a week or two before the fair. If attending a fair involves much traveling, phone the commune or the local Azienda Promozione Turistica (APT) that is holding it to make sure it is really happening. I once drove three hundred kilometers to attend an onion fair I saw advertised, only to discover it had been canceled!

TABLE CRAFTS AND KITCHEN SHOPS

For those who collect handmade table crafts—ceramics, baskets, and linens—Tuscany has some to offer, though there are fewer artisans now than in the past. Several Tuscan towns (Montelupo Fiorentino, Monte San Savino, Impruneta) produce ceramics using local clay and traditional and Renaissance designs. Be careful in souvenir shops, however, which often sell hand-painted ceramics signed underneath with the name of their town. Most of this pottery is made semi-industrially in Deruta (in Umbria) or in Italy's south: there is nothing wrong with it, but it probably was not produced where it is being sold. Unless you see the potter sitting at the wheel, the pieces may have been factory made elsewhere.

I found some fine Tuscan linens (at Arezzo and Anghiari), hand-woven baskets for drying figs or picking olives (San Gimignano), and beautiful alabaster objects (Volterra). See the index under individual crafts if you are looking for something specific.

Well-stocked kitchen shops offer good presents to take home: individual espresso makers, olive-wood cutting boards or cheese graters, wedges for dividing Parmesan, or any of the modern design objects the Italians are brilliant at producing.

OLIVE OIL

The olive tree is a bushy evergreen with pointy gray-green leaves. It lives to a great age when not attacked by disease or severe cold. Until recently the Tuscan landscape was characterized by enormous, sculptural olive trees over a hundred years old. The freak winter of 1985, with heavy snow and temperatures of -20°C/-4°F in areas accustomed to only light frosts, killed the majority of Tuscany's oldest olive trees. The great trunks, many measuring several feet across, were cut down. Luckily, the olive tree sends up new shoots if its roots are not dead. Look carefully at the olive trees now growing in Tuscany, and you will often see two or three young plants growing around a large cut stump.

The olive is a fruit. At its purest and best, olive oil is the "juice" of this fruit—just crush and press the olives and it will drip free. Unfortunately, the process is rarely kept this simple. There is a world of difference between industrial extra-virgin olive oil and estate-bottled oil made from homegrown, hand-picked olives. The latter will more than repay itself in quality. An aromatic, fruity oil can turn a good meal into a great one.

It is worth knowing that industrial extra-virgin oil is bought as "crude extra virgin" from many Mediterranean countries, regardless of where the bottler is located. It is always a blend, often including seed oils—though companies are not obliged to declare this on the label. Industrially refined "virgin olive oils" and "light" olive oils have been stripped of their taste and defects by chemical solvents.

Tuscany is one of Italy's most important producers of high-quality extra-virgin olive oil. Like all natural products, each oil's particular characteristics are determined by plant type, climate, and geography. Lucca's coastal oils, like Liguria's, are light in color and sweet in taste; they go well with seafood. Oils from Tuscany's central hills are more decisive in flavor, with a peppery aftertaste and agreeable bitterness; they are best on salads and vegetables, or drizzled on grilled bread.

Reputable small producers are attentive to each stage of the (necessarily costly) process. To make the best oil, healthy olives are hand-picked early in the season, before they are ripe enough to fall to the ground. (Falling means bruising, and the likelihood of rotting or fermentation.) They are carried in airy crates to the *frantoio*, or mill, and preferably milled within thirty-six hours of being picked. There are currently two nonindustrial systems for extracting the oil: the traditional stone mill and the modern continuous cycle plant.

"Until recently everyone agreed that stone-ground oil was the finest," explained Marco Chiletti, a Tuscan oil producer. "It certainly is the most picturesque system—nothing could be more dramatic than to watch the great round stones as they crush the olives, with the air full of a fine mist of aromatic olive oil."

The washed olives are ground to a dark brown pulp. This is usually heated very slightly, or it would not release its oil, and kneaded before being spread onto circular woven mats. These are stacked onto a steel pole, sandwiching the paste between them. A hydraulic press squeezes the mats together, forcing the oil out. A final spin in a centrifuge separates the oil from its accompanying vegetal water. The residue of the paste, a hard brown substance that looks a bit like cork, is called *sansa*. This may be burned as a fuel or sold to refineries that extract more oil from it using chemical solvents. This Olio di Sansa should be avoided.

"The modern 'continuous cycle' system is increasingly popular," continued Chiletti. "It has several advantages. It is more hygienic: the olives and pulp are worked entirely in stainless-steel containers, which are easily cleaned and reduce the risk of contamination from one batch of olives to the next. Each client can tailor the machinery to his needs, as it is temperature controlled at every stage. In some types the olives are not crushed but cut with a series of fine blades, enabling the oil to drip away by gravity. This is definitely the way of the future."

Many fine wine producers also make olive oil: the terrain required is similar and the harvesting seasons are staggered, the grapes being picked in September and October, the olives from late October through December.

There has been a lot of talk about acidity levels and cold pressing in olive oils. Although an oil must have less than 0.1 percent acidity to be considered extra virgin, low acidity levels alone do not guarantee good flavor (industrial oils may be manipulated chemically to "correct" acidity), and some experts claim that the difference between 0.02 and 0.06 percent acidity cannot even be distinguished by the tongue. Even the word "cold" is relative: unless the olive paste is at least 15°C/59°F, little oil can be extracted; below 8°C/46°F, the oil freezes. The most important factor for the layperson is the reputation of the producer—all the rest is personal preference.

Buying a bottle of artisan-made, pure extra-virgin olive oil may seem expensive, but used sparingly, its wonderful fresh flavor will enhance any meal, lasting much longer than a comparably priced bottle of wine.

How to Store Your Oil

Pure extra-virgin olive oil is a delicate natural product. Keep it away from its principal enemies, heat and light. Oil is also easily contaminated by bad odors, so never refill your oil cruet unless it has been perfectly cleaned and dried. Even a little oxidized residue is enough to ruin the taste of fresh oil.

Unlike wine, oil does not improve with age. Use it within a year of being made.

There are now several associations dedicated to the appreciation of fine olive oils that organize tastings and publish literature. Contact Associazione Italiana Conoscere l'Olio d'Oliva (AICOO), tel/fax 0577 40334.

WINE

Tuscany is one of Italy's most important wine-producing regions, and its best wines are among the world's finest. Tuscany contains many subzones that have been granted a nationally recognized wine-making status: DOC (*Denominazione di Origine Controllata*) or the more recent and more stringent DOCG, which adds *e Garantita* to the DOC. These denominations are similar to France's *appellation* system: wines made within a circumscribed area must comply to set standards in order to be accredited with the DOC or DOCG label. Grape varieties, a maximum grape yield per hectare (2.47 acres), and vinification and aging specifications are established for each type of wine. Ideally, these are strict enough to keep standards high and to discourage fraud while affording producers some flexibility of interpretation.

Winemakers within a DOC region may make wines outside of these regulations, but they may not be classified as DOC or DOCG wines. Indeed, in the last twenty-five years there has been a revolution in Tuscany's winemaking as progressive estates have created new wines outside the DOC categories. At first, these wines had no official name, so they adopted the simple "table wine" description given to Italy's humblest wines. These new *vini da tavola* have since been christened "super-Tuscans" (see below, p 30). These powerful, *barrique*-aged, expensive wines are modeled on the great wines of Bordeaux and have gained an international following. The Tuscan wine that sparked this revolution was Sassicaia (see Tenuta San Guido, p 146).

Vin Santo, or Holy Wine, is a Tuscan specialty, the perfect ending to any meal. This amber dessert wine ranges from dry and sherrylike to sweet and opulent. It is made of white grapes partially dried on cane mats or hung from wires or rafters. After several months, when their sugars have been concentrated, the grapes are pressed and sealed into *caratelli*, small wooden casks, for three years or more. The kegs are stored in the *vinsantaia*, a room under the roof where the wine's temperature may rise and fall with the seasons. Vin Santo is traditionally dunked with *cantucci* biscuits; the finest Vin Santi are complex, rich wines better savored alone.

But What Is Wine?

I recently heard a foreign visitor ask a winery owner: "So what is in this wine, aside from grapes, sugar, and water?" The question was fair, but it clearly surprised the winemaker—he assumed everyone knew that wine was made only from grapes. So, for those new to winemaking, here is a simplified description of the process.

Wine is an alcoholic drink made from fermented grape juice—ideally without water or sugar. Red wine is made from red grapes, getting its deep color from the skins (the pulp of red grapes has little color): red grapes are fermented with their skins, white grapes are usually not. The stalks and seeds contain bitter tannins, and while red wines need some tannins to help them age and give them character, too many are not good, so the stalks are removed. In Tuscany, where most grapes are picked by hand, a machine that looks like a giant corkscrew presses the pulp, skins, and seeds through, leaving the stalks behind; what comes out is called "must."

The must is pumped into large tanks of stainless steel, vitrified cement, or wood, where it begins to ferment. Yeasts (either naturally present or added) heat the mass as they convert the grapes' natural sugar into alcohol, giving off carbon dioxide. The heat must be controlled and should not exceed 25°C to 32°C (77°F to 89°F). (Tanks used to be cooled by being hosed over with cold water, but modern steel tanks have built-in coolers.) As the gas rises to the top of the tank, it pushes the skins up into a thick layer called the "cap." This should be pushed back down to the bottom of the tank, usually twice a day, to keep the skins in contact with the fermenting juice. This is now done by pumping juice up from below and over the cap, forcing it back down. This fermentation process "on the skins" may last from one to several weeks depending on the style of wine being made. For red wines that are intended to be drunk young, and not requiring excessive tannins, the fermenting juice may be separated from the skins and seeds after just a few days and put into another tank to finish its fermentation.

At this point, a second, "malolactic" fermentation may occur naturally or be induced—a bit of ambient heat starts the wine fermenting again. *La malolattica*, as it is called in Italy, transforms malic acid (as in apples) into lactic acid (as in milk) and the result is a more mellow, softer wine. The wine may then be kept in steel vats until bottling or aged in wooden barrels, large or small. Large Tuscan casks (*botti*) were often made of chestnut but are now usually Slavonian oak. Large casks hardly impart any of the wood's character to the wine, as the wood to liquid ratio is very low. Modern-style wines such as the super-Tuscans are usually put in small French oak barrels called *barriques*. These do affect the wine's flavor and structure, giving it added tannins and a woody flavor.

Wine may be aged for anything from a few months to one hundred years—depending on the grape type and structure—in steel, old or new wood, glass, or a mixture of them all. The aging process continues in the bottle, which is why many "big" red wines need prolonged cellaring to give their best.

Dry white wine (which may also be made from red grapes) is made somewhat differently, as contact with the skins (and their tannins) is not usually desirable. Here the grapes are softly pressed to separate the juice from the skins and seeds. The juice is filtered before being fermented at slightly lower temperatures than red wine in order to keep their flavors fresh and aromatic, usually for ten to fourteen days. The wine is then run off the sludge of dead yeasts; it may or may not undergo the secondary malolactic fermentation. Some modern-style Tuscan Chardonnays are fermented in *barriques* to give them more complex flavors and the ability to age longer than normal white wines.

WHAT ARE THE SUPER-TUSCANS?

"The original super-Tuscan was Sassicaia," explained Burton Anderson, an American wine expert who has lived in Tuscany for many years. "When in 1968 Mario Incisa put that wine on the market, and it was a big success, it inspired the use in Tuscany of Cabernet, which in turn inspired Piero Antinori in 1975 to make a wine from Sangiovese and Cabernet, Tignanello. Giacomo Tachis, the enologist for both Antinori and Sassicaia, was the prime mover."

This revolution came about because most Sangiovese vines planted in Tuscany in the sixties and seventies were inferior clones grown in the wrong way: too few vines per hectare, too much growth per vine. "The result was that Chianti was basically a wishy washy wine by the end of the 1970s, with very few exceptions. It was pale not only because of the added white grapes but because the Sangiovese was inferior." Some producers familiar with the great red wines of Bordeaux felt that Tuscany ought to be capable of producing wines of similar intensity and style.

Sassicaia also inspired the use of *barriques*, the small barrels of French oak, for aging the wine. "If you start with the right wine, *barriques* are a way of making it more appealing to the so-called international market. And not just because of the wood: if it has the right structure, a wine in *barriques* matures to become more complex and interesting," Anderson said.

"The first pure Sangiovese super-Tuscan was Sergio Manetti's Le Pergole Torte, which also started a school. Before that people believed that without Cabernet, their wines would not have enough to them. But Sergio proved that Sangiovese did have enough to it to benefit from the *barriques*." Most super-Tuscans are now made primarily from Sangiovese, often blended with Cabernet or Merlot, or even Syrah.

"Super-Tuscan can be a confusing concept: these are wines that have no status other than of table wine, *vino da tavola*, yet they are some of the country's greatest and most expensive wines. They will inevitably have to be classified, if nothing else, under the DOC for Tuscany."

PART TWO

CHAPTER 1

The Lunigiana and Versilia

*D*riving into Tuscany from Parma you come across the Apennines into the Lunigiana, on what was the CISA—one of the earliest roads through these imposing mountains. The Lunigiana was named for Luni, a Roman town now in neighboring Liguria. The *autostrada* curves down past the rustic villages of Pontremoli, Aulla, and Bagnone before straightening out along the sea. There it runs a spectacular course between the dramatic marble mountains of Carrara, the Apuan Alps, and the Mediterranean coast, known here as Versilia. The most famous Riviera town is Viareggio; it hosts an elaborate winter carnival.

Carrara's quarries have for centuries provided Italy's sculptors and architects, including Michelangelo, with marble; the extraction of the monumental blocks is now mostly mechanized. Years ago it represented one of the hardest and most dangerous manual jobs. This part of Tuscany may be less "typically Tuscan"—there are few cypresses, vineyards, or olive groves—but it is a fascinating area combining the cultures of mountain and sea.

The foods, of course, reflect this. If the Lunigiana still offers an authentic country cuisine based on wild herbs, mushrooms, chestnuts, and other "land" ingredients, Versilia's beach resorts boast some of the region's best fish restaurants.

Azienda Promozione Turistica
Lungomare Vespucci, 24
54037 Marina di Massa, Massa
0585 240063, fax 0585 869015

Viale Carducci, 10
55049 Viareggio Lucca
0584 962233, fax 0584 47336

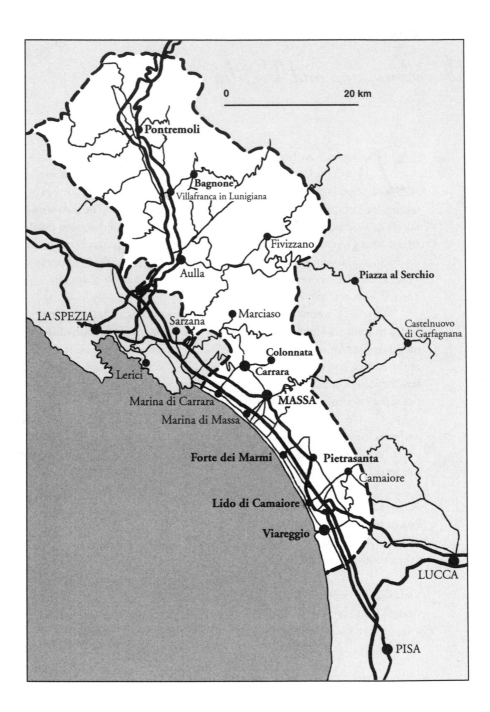

Town names in **bold** indicate towns that are included in this chapter.

BAGNONE

I FONDI   Borgo della Repubblica, 26   Bagnone   Massa
RESTAURANT   TELEPHONE   0187 429086   OPEN Lunch and dinner
                       CLOSED Tuesday; January   CREDIT CARDS None
                       ENGLISH SPOKEN A little   RESERVATIONS Recommended
                       PRICE $$ DIRECTIONS On Bagnone's main street

I Fondi are "the depths" of a fifteenth-century building in this Apennine hillside village. Enter the restaurant down a tunnel staircase that seems carved out
of the rock. Its dining rooms and terrace overlook Bagnone's namesake (the
word means "large bath"): a cascading river with waterfalls. The kitchen is
Signora Batilla's, a small, energetic woman with a friendly manner. The food
is country fare: seasonal antipasti include local *salumi* and savory vegetables.
Testaroli, pastalike pancakes with garlic and basil pesto, are specialties; this
area borders with Liguria, where pesto originates. Tagliatelle are homemade
and substantial. The local *bomba di riso*, rice with pigeon sauce, can be
ordered in advance. The unpretentious menu contains simply cooked meats
and fresh pizzas.

CARRARA

BAR GARIBALDI   Piazza Battisti, 1   54033   Carrara   Massa
BAR   TELEPHONE   0585 777611   OPEN 6:00-20:30   CLOSED Sunday
                       in winter   CREDIT CARDS None   ENGLISH SPOKEN No
                       DIRECTIONS Beside the Animosi Theater in the town center

In the odd-shaped piazza, next to the refurbished Animosi Theater, once an
Anarchist stronghold, is the Bar Garibaldi—as much a landmark as its the-
atrical neighbor. Fortunately, it has not been modernized. Through the rose-
covered arch, past the summer terrace, is the personal world of proprietor
Alfonso Pollina. Every inch of the high room is hung with photographs of
theater people, individually dedicated to Alfonso, or "Crosta" (a Carrarese term
for a Genovese miser).

    "They teased me because I complained if someone left some
milk or took too much sugar, so the locals started calling me Crosta!" explained
Alfonso, a sweet-tempered elderly gentleman who looks more like a Frank
Capra angel than a scrooge. He and his wife stand behind their small marble
bar and serve the quarry workers playing cards at the tables, drinking local
wine and "corrected" coffees.

DROGHERIA RIACCI
GROCERY STORE

Via Rosselli, 1   54033   Carrara   Massa
TELEPHONE 0585 71936   OPEN 7:00-13:15, 16:30-20:00
CLOSED Wednesday afternoon; Sunday   CREDIT CARDS None
ENGLISH SPOKEN No   DIRECTIONS In the town center

This general grocery store, or *drogheria*, still has its *Liberty*-style (Italian for art nouveau) interior, unchanged since the early 1900s. The walls are lined with carved wood and glass cabinets with handsome iron detailing. The long marble counter had a zinc bar for serving liqueurs (a *drogheria*'s licence enabled it to sell spirits), but now it holds an espresso machine. *Drogherie* once carried exotic spices and products like Turchetino—a bluish powder rinse added to white washing for a fresh blue sparkle (when ash was used instead of soap for washing)—and black dye, for women having to attend a funeral who had no black dress. Times have changed, and sadly shops like this have all but disappeared.

Also

Bar Gelateria Tognozzi. Via Verdi, 6. 0585 72850.
    This place definitely has some of the best gelati in the area: not sickly or cloying, but deeply flavorful with a good clean texture. The less-common fruit flavors, like the tangy blood orange when it is in season, are fresh-tasting and creamy, and there is an interesting selection of nut flavors: almond, *pinoli*, and walnut as well as the ubiquitous hazelnut.

"DA OMETTO"—
CIRCOLO ARCI & ANPI
RESTAURANT

Via Martiri del Lavoro   Bedizzano   54033   Carrara   Massa
TELEPHONE 0585 768211   OPEN Lunch and dinner   CLOSED Some
Sundays in summer   CREDIT CARDS None   ENGLISH SPOKEN No
FEATURES Summer terrace   RESERVATIONS Recommended in
summer   PRICE $ DIRECTIONS From Carrara go towards
Colonnata; Da Ometto is after 3 kms, on the right before Bedizzano.

The sign outside this trattoria reads: *Da Ometto tutto è perfetto* (everything is perfect at the "little man's"). Perched breathtakingly high in Carrara's marble mountains, this is officially a "circolo ARCI e ANPI"—a recreational bar for members of the worker's and Italian partisan associations: before dinner the dining room is filled with quarry workers and aging partisans, smoking, drinking, and playing cards.
    There is a small chance you may be refused admission: technically, the restaurant is not licensed for the general public. The "Ometto," seventy-five-year-old Francesco Farsetti, is free to choose whether to bend the rules or not. This area was a partisan stronghold during World War II, and the stark dining room's only decoration is a framed panel of photographs of the 360 local resistance fighters who died defending the mountains against the occupying German forces.

If the Ometto is in a welcoming mood, you will have an unpretentious but very good dinner. The cook does justice to the local specialties: her excellent *pasta e fagioli* is a herbed bean soup with homemade *tagliolini* noodles; the popular tripe is well stewed in a piquant tomato sauce. There are mountain *salumi*, rabbit, and seasonal game. Wines are local. In summer you eat outside at monolithic marble tables on the breezy terrace, amid the high quarries.

COLONNATA

VENANZIO
RESTAURANT

Piazza Palestro, 3   Colonnata   54030   Carrara   Massa
TELEPHONE/FAX 0585 73617   OPEN Lunch and dinner
CLOSED Thursday; Sunday evening; December 20 to January 20
CREDIT CARDS Visa, MC   DIRECT SALE *Lardo* may be bought from
Alimentari Cattani, Piazza Palestro, 2   ENGLISH SPOKEN A little
RESERVATIONS Necessary   PRICE $$$ DIRECTIONS Colonnata is
signposted from Carrara (7 kms). Park in the car park on the left
upon entering Colonnata and walk up stairs to the square and restaurant.

Driving from Carrara to Colonnata is exciting: the road winds steeply up through the imposing, cavernous quarries that for centuries have given the world its finest marble. Even Michelangelo got his stone here. It is overwhelming to think of the human labor that has gone into taming these monumental mountains. The tiny stone village of Colonnata is tucked into this dramatic landscape. Its only restaurant is now synonymous with a special food: *lardo di Colonnata*, salt-cured pork fat from the animal's back.

"Our *lardo* is as old as the quarries," explained Venanzio Vannucci, who brought Colonnata's *lardo* into the gastronomic spotlight. "For a thousand years this village has conserved slabs of *lardo* in *conche*, troughs or bowls carved in marble. Recipes for the *salamoia*—curing salt, herbs, and spices—are generations old." Using this *salamoia* for six months in the marble results in a pure white, aromatic *salume*—nothing like its yellowed, rancid, and tough air-dried counterpart.

Venanzio's is exquisite. My February lunch began with pieces of hot bread topped with fine, ribbonlike slices of *lardo*, with only a tiny streak of pink meat within the white. A sprig of fresh rosemary lay on the piping hot plate; its warmed, aromatic perfume hit me first. The heat of the bread, the light, buttery softness of the *lardo*, its delicate yet exotic fragrance and perfectly balanced seasonings were unexpected and extraordinary. An unusual carpaccio followed: a fillet of Chianina beef was marinated in the *lardo's salamoia* for three days, then sliced paper thin. The tender coral meat, whose delicate flavor just hinted at the spices and herbs it had been kept with, came surrounded by *mentuccia*—a vibrant wild mint. These pure foods had the clarity of birdsong.

A freshly-made omelette was filled with just-picked sprigs of fragrant *vignalba*, a wild clematis, and topped with slivered gray truffle. The truffle's heady perfume complemented the herb's sweet bitterness. A sensual, brilliant dish. Tender ravioli with a light meat stuffing came in a fresh tomato and basil sauce. Sliced *tagliata* of beef arrived on a searingly hot plate and cooked as I watched, with an intense sauce of soy and truffle. A frozen chocolate dessert was decorated with flowers Venanzio had gathered himself. There are wonderful wines (Sergio Manetti's ladies smiled down from his Pergole Torte labels) and a relaxed atmosphere in this small room, where quarry workers eat alongside foreign visitors. After lunch Venanzio showed me his garden. I left with my hands full of wild herbs and violets.

FORTE DEI MARMI

LORENZO
RESTAURANT

Via Carducci, 61   55042   Forte dei Marmi   Lucca
TELEPHONE 0584 84030, 89671   FAX 0584 84030
OPEN Lunch and dinner; dinner only in July and August
CLOSED Monday in winter; December-January   CREDIT CARDS Visa,
MC, Amex   ENGLISH SPOKEN Yes   RESERVATIONS Recommended,
especially in summer   PRICE $$$$ DIRECTIONS Via Carducci runs
parallel to the sea, a few blocks inland, by Piazza Marconi.

Lorenzo's is a great restaurant—the kind you enjoy immediately and look forward to returning to. It has all the right elements: unbelievably fresh ingredients (especially fish) cooked deliciously yet simply, a lively atmosphere that is elegant but not stuffy, an award-winning wine list, and an owner-host with a rare talent for his calling.

"I choose and buy my fish every day," explained the charming Lorenzo Viani, who personally visits local fishermen and Viareggio's auction in his quest for the freshest seafood. "A fish has twenty-four virtues—but loses one with each hour that passes."

The *cernia di fondale* (stone bass), *gallinella* and *capone* (both in the gurnard family), do not lose many of theirs before becoming a tartare of deep-water fish. This meltingly soft, cool patty of ground raw fish is subtly enhanced with lemon, herbs, fruity olive oil and tomato. The *fritto di mare* is the best I have ever had. The fish seem Lilliputian: tiny *rossetti* (transparent goby) the size of minnows, colorless despite their Italian name; slender shrimp no longer than a bay leaf, so tender you eat them whole; miniature *calamaretti* (squid), fine-skinned and delicate. They are dipped into a light batter and quickly fried, a far cry from mundane deep-frying.

Natura di totanini al forno is equally unusual: small flying squid (Alan Davidson explains in *Mediterranean Seafood* that they do not fly, but propel themselves out of the water) are baked whole, partially gutted, with just their own liquids to stew in. If at first they are a bit disconcerting—the transparent "quill" is still inside the sac—they have remarkable intensity of flavor. Sautéed red mullet topped with tomato, celery and raw fava beans is fresh, light and Mediterranean.

Lorenzo's best-loved pasta dish is *bavettine sul pesce*, thin linguini with seafood. Its secret is that the pasta is cooked along with the fish— shrimp, squid, *calamaretti*—with water added gradually as for risotto. The result is more fish than pasta, which has good biting texture and a depth of flavor boiled pasta rarely attains. At Lorenzo's shellfish are alive until they are prepared, either raw or cooked simply so as not to lose their character. Fish are lightly baked, poached, or grilled over a wood fire with Mediterranean aromatics. A parallel "land" menu also exists. "It is important to eat well," asserted Lorenzo," but just as important to feel well afterward."

Also

Gastronomia "dei Parmigiani". Via Mazzini, 1/B. 0584 89496.

Forte dei Marmi is one of the coast's fanciest resorts. If you are planning an elegant picnic on the beach, stock up at this *gastronomia*. It offers Italy's top cheeses—including truffle-scented *crutìn* and rare pit-matured *formaggio di fossa*—*salumi* (prosciutti from Parma, San Daniele, and Tuscany), prepared rice salads, pasta dishes, cooked vegetables, wines... everything you'll need for your epicurean feast.

Magazzini del Forte. Via Carducci, 19. 0584 89542.

This housewares store's stylish displays are arranged by ex-fashion buyers Raoul and Amanda Doni. The Magazzini once sold fittings for sailboats and fishermen; now it carries everything from fine linens to designer kitchen gadgets, cookbooks to cutlery, tapestry wools to tabletop objects.

LIDO DI CAMAIORE

GASTRONOMIA/
ENOTECA GIANNONI
SPECIALTY FOODS:
DELICATESSEN

Viale Colombo, 444   55043   Lido di Camaiore   Lucca
TELEPHONE 0584 617332   FAX 0584 981791   OPEN 7:30-13:30,
16:30-20:00 in winter; till 20:30 in summer   CLOSED Wednesday
afternoon, Sunday in winter, Sunday afternoon in summer; October
CREDIT CARDS Visa, MC, Amex   ENGLISH SPOKEN A little
DIRECTIONS Viale Colombo is the main road along the coast, running
parallel to the sea.

I haven't given awards in this book, but I would give one to this handsome gourmet shop, located unexpectedly on a busy road near the coast. It would not be out of place in the world's fanciest shopping streets. The big, high-ceilinged room is lined with attractive wood-and-glass cases displaying beautiful food.

A long counter features selected Italian cheeses and a few international stars. So alongside fresh and smoked *bufala mozzarella* delivered from Campania or Tuscan pecorini of varying ages are Stilton and chèvre. *Salumi* are excellent: the brothers Giuliano and Sauro Giannoni mature selected prosciutto hams near Parma for up to two years, far longer than usual. There is also wonderful *lardo di Colonnata*, which is cured in marble containers (see p 37).

The Giannonis also cook vegetables, pasta, sauces, main courses, desserts, and pastries of a very high standard, that are sold to take out. Individual "soufflés" are made of artichoke hearts or spinach; the pesto is of fresh basil; the apple tarts are as good as they look. The brothers' passion for fine foods extends to wines; they feature the top Tuscans and import French wines and Champagne *crus*. A really great store.

MASSA

ALIMENTARI CECCARELLI SPECIALTY FOODS: SALT COD AND STOCKFISH	Piazza Guglielmi, 9 (La Conca) 54100 Massa TELEPHONE 0585 42094 OPEN 8:00-13:00, 17:30-21:00 in summer; 8:00-13:00, 16:00-20 in winter CLOSED Wednesday afternoon, Sunday CREDIT CARDS None ENGLISH SPOKEN A little DIRECTIONS In the town center, near Piazza degli Aranci

At Massa, Ceccarelli's has been synonymous with *baccalà* and *stoccafisso* since the 1930s, when Dante Ceccarelli began importing the cured North Sea fish, which were first brought to Italy by the Vikings. Once a staple in households where women had the time to devote to its preparation, the well-flavored fish is now competing with its frozen counterparts. Ceccarelli offers free local recipes to stimulate interest in this popular Italian food: deep-fried in *fritelle* or stewed in a spicy tomato sauce, *in umido*.

Baccalà is cod fished in winter (from mid-January onward, when the fish is oiliest). It is cleaned aboard ship, processed on land in brine with 20 percent salt for five days, dried for twelve hours, then layered with more salt. It must be soaked, preferably under running water, for at least twenty-four hours before cooking. *Baccalà* is sold in different grades; the finest comes from Norway, Iceland and the Faeroe Islands. *Stoccafisso*, or stockfish, is also cod, but air-dried, not salted, in the Arctic for 60 days at an optimal outdoor temperature of 0° or 1°C. When properly dried, the fish should have almost no odor. Stockfish must be soaked for forty-eight hours before cooking.

The store, now run by Marilisa Ceccarelli and her husband, Antonio, has elegant marble baths with wrought-iron animal's head spouts for soaking the fish, which can be bought *bagnato*, ready to cook. The shop's recent renovation has retained the feel of an old-fashioned store. Other products include selected local *salumi* and cheeses, Tuscan olive oils, grains, chick-pea flour for *farinata*, and Carrara marble mortars and pestles.

**DROGHERIA
"GLI SVIZZERI"
SPECIALTY FOODS**

Via Cairoli, 53   54100   Massa
TELEPHONE 0585 43092   OPEN 7:00-13:00, 17:00-20:00 in summer;
7:00-13:00, 16:00-19:30 in winter   CLOSED Wednesday afternoon,
Sunday   CREDIT CARDS None   ENGLISH SPOKEN None
DIRECTIONS In the town center, near Piazza degli Aranci

"Gli Svizzeri" is one of Massa's oldest stores, named for the original Swiss pro-
prietors who came to the Lunigiana in the 1850s. It changed from a *speziale*, or
spice shop (the pharmacies of that time), to a *liquoreria* at the end of the 1880s,
before becoming a *drogheria* in the 1920s. *Drogherie* were general grocery stores
stocking everything, including products not easily found: oriental spices, medicinal teas, imported extracts, and tinctures.

The Belatti family's shop remains a "colonial" treasure trove,
selling China Yerba tea and Argentinian maté, whole Indian spices, sacks of
aduki beans and basmati rice (hard to come by in Italy), flavored extracts
for home-blending triple sec or vermouth, loose candied fruits for making
mostarda, imported North Sea herring, and local *lardo di Colonnata* displayed
in carved marble troughs. There is even a small bar at one end of the counter
where you can stand for a coffee and let your mind wander—to spice routes
and camel trains.

Also

Il Pane. Via Mura Nord, 8.

Massa's best bakery makes assorted unsalted Tuscan breads and
focaccia—made in a wood oven and brushed with a little oil before baking.
Excellent focaccia is topped with soft cooked onions subtly tasting of vinegar.
Alfio Morandi sells an aromatic *torta d'erbi* brought in from Villafranca in
Lunigiana. *Torta di riso*, Massa's favorite Easter dessert, is made to order.

PIETRASANTA

**L'ENOTECA MARCUCCI
WINE BAR, RESTAURANT**

Via Garibaldi, 40   55045   Pietrasanta   Lucca
TELEPHONE/FAX 0584 791962   OPEN Wine bar 10:00-13:00,
17:00-1:00 a.m.; dinner 20:00-24:00   CLOSED Monday in winter
CREDIT CARDS Visa, MC   DIRECT SALE Yes
ENGLISH SPOKEN A little   RESERVATIONS Necessary on weekends
and in summer   PRICE $$ DIRECTIONS In the town center

Pietrasanta (holy stone) is a sculptor's haven: near Carrara's monolithic marble
quarries, it is bursting with artisanal *botteghe*, or well-equipped workshops where
sculptors may carve the stone. Sculptures adorn every public space, making it a
nice cultural outing for anyone interested in three-dimensional art.

The *enoteca* opened in 1988. A friend described its style as *chic
povero*—poor chic. It is a great space: a high-vaulted room lined with tall

shelves of wine bottles, like "stacks" in a library, with whites on the right, reds on the left. Long stone-topped tables are used for tasting by day, dinner by night. There are Italian and international wines, including Tuscany's stars and a good range of the best local producers. The young Marcucci brothers are enthusiastic and very knowledgeable. Wines may be bought to take out or drunk at the *enoteca*.

For dinner (the only meal served), the Marcucci parents do the cooking. The menu is easy-going and the prices reasonable. There are hearty soups and pastas and some less usual starters: herrings with steamed potatoes, small peppers stuffed with anchovies (a Piemontese specialty), and a "salad" of boiled meat with capers and olives. Main courses feature meats, including duck and ostrich (*struzzo*), grilled over wood embers (*alla brace*), and seasoned with herbs grown by Signor Marcucci. Vegetable dishes are interesting, and desserts homemade. The kitchen is open till late, but reservations are necessary at this "in" spot.

PONTREMOLI

SALUMERIA	Via Garibaldi, 11 54027 Pontremoli Massa
OSVALDO ANGELLA	TELEPHONE 0187 830161 OPEN 8:00-12:45, 16:00-19:30
MEAT: SALUMI	CLOSED Wednesday afternoon CREDIT CARDS None
	ENGLISH SPOKEN No DIRECTIONS The shop is on the corner of
	Via della Bietola, near the Duomo.

Armando Angella is one of Tuscany's finest *salumieri,* if not its most senior. After over forty years of work, this sprightly artisan is still passionate about his art. In his small workshop he personally "transforms" over two hundred quality local pigs per year. The *salumi* mature in tiny cellars beneath the quaint shop.

Spalla cotta con l'ossa, or cooked cured shoulder on the bone, is his specialty. An unusual halfway house between boiled ham and *prosciutto crudo,* the pork shoulder is salted and hung for four months before being simmered in several changes of fresh water for five to six hours to draw off some of the salt. It is a deep dusky pink, darker than normal boiled ham, and retains the marked flavor of its cure. Sliced off the bone by hand, it is eaten with peas or mashed potatoes in sweet counterpoint to its salt. Angella's other specialties include: Lunigiana *mortadella nostrana,* a spiced salami bearing no resemblance to its large Bolognese cousin; *tartaruga,* a cured and wrapped *culatello* (rump); and *lardello,* a lean salami to which only 5 percent white fat, salt, and peppercorns are added.

Sadly, Armando Angella has no one to carry on the business begun in the 1850s by his grandfather. His daughter has another career, and he is pessimistic about finding an apprentice able to maintain his high standards. European Union laws are hard on small *artigiani* who have made excellent products for decades without knife-sterilizers or walk-in refrigerators. To have had to buy them now or be faced with closure has been demoralizing for the independent-minded Signor Angella. "I will keep going as long as I can," he confided, "and hopefully I'll find a way to keep my family's artistry alive."

IL FUNGO
PRODUCE: MUSHROOMS
Via 1 Maggio, 14   54027   Pontremoli   Massa
TELEPHONE 0187 832574   FAX 0187 830418   OPEN 7:30-12:30,
16:00-19:30   CLOSED   Wednesday afternoon, Sunday
ENGLISH SPOKEN No   DIRECTIONS On the town's southern outskirts,
southwest of the river

Being an early bird is the best way to find mushrooms, assuming you know where to look. It also guarantees you get them before anybody else. The *contadini*, or peasants, living around Pontremoli are rewarded in cash for their early morning searches, and Il Fungo gets the freshest supply of the wood's harvest. The prized porcini *(Boletus edulis)* grow under the sweet chestnut trees, but other varieties include chanterelles, *galletti*, and *Volvaria volvacea*.

The Giumellis trade in the offerings of the woods and fields: mushrooms are sold fresh, sun-dried and *sott'olio*—under oil. The porcini season begins in June, then tails off until September and October, but preserved mushrooms are usually available. The attractive store sells produce all year, including wild salad greens popular in Tuscany and wild strawberries, blueberries, and raspberries.

DA BUSSÉ
RESTAURANT
Piazza Duomo, 31   54027   Pontremoli   Massa
TELEPHONE 0187 831371   OPEN Lunch Saturday-Thursday, dinner
Saturday and Sunday   CLOSED Friday; July   CREDIT CARDS None
ENGLISH SPOKEN A little   RESERVATIONS Recommended at weekends
PRICE $$ DIRECTIONS Near the Duomo

When Da Bussé opened in 1930, Pontremoli was a popular stopping point on the CISA, the main road cutting through the mountains from north to south. The family-run trattoria became known for its unpretentious Pontremolese cuisine and for the intimacy of its dining rooms—small interconnecting parlors on the ground floor of a house. Despite the modern *autostrada*, which now bypasses Pontremoli completely, things haven't changed much.

Da Bussé does a brisk lunch trade, and you may find yourself sitting near local lawyers or councilmen who have been coming here for years. The mercurial Signora Antonietta knows them all, and keeps up a steady banter as she flashes in and out of the rooms bearing the fruits of the kitchen's labors.

Local *testaroli,* pancakelike pasta rectangles served with *pinoli*-less pesto, are aromatic but oily; eat them for lunch or as a half portion. Vegetable tarts reflect the local passion for wild greens: in spring *erbadela* has polenta-flour pastry and a quichelike filling of scallions and potatoes, with a note of anise from the wild fennel. *Secondi* often include stewed rabbit, boiled veal, or meatball-stuffed *involtini*: meat rolls in light tomato sauce, served in a terra-cotta dish.

Nut tarts are classic desserts, as is the Sunday *torta al mascarpone.* In season *frutti di bosco,* wild berries from the local woods, are exquisite.

TRATTORIA "DEL GIARDINO" DA BACCIOTTINI RESTAURANT	Via Ricci Armani, 13 54027 Pontremoli Massa TELEPHONE 0187 830120 OPEN Lunch and dinner CLOSED Wednesday evening, Thursday; two weeks in June CREDIT CARDS None ENGLISH SPOKEN A little RESERVATIONS Recommended PRICE $$$ DIRECTIONS On the town's central street

Bacciottini's restaurant is one of Pontremoli's best-known; begun by the present owner's parents, it specializes in traditional Lunigiana foods. After Signor Bacciottini died, his son Rafaelo reopened with his young wife, Clara, who has a fine repertoire of local recipes. The trattoria occupies a large vaulted room reached by a passageway from the town's main street. The atmosphere is informal but friendly.

Clara is a natural cook, especially with vegetable-based dishes. The area's famous *testaroli*—flat rectangles of a pancakelike pasta cooked on cast-iron *testi,* or molds—are here served with an easily digestible light herb pesto infused with garlic. Stockfish and salt cod are regular features on the menu, in the local tradition. Stockfish cooked with Mediterranean eggplant, capers, olives, and yellow peppers is delicious, offering a sweet contrast to the intense fish. Spring *minestre* (soups) and *torte* (savory tarts) use wild herbs. *Erbadela* features wild fennel; *torta d'erbi* contains beet and other greens, potatoes, and onions in a light crust. Autumn wild mushrooms are served many ways, including deep-fried. Meats here tend to be cooked simply: grilled, fried, or stewed.

Also

Pasticceria Aichta "Degli Svizzeri." Piazza della Repubblica, 21. 0187 830160.

If you are in the mood for a sweet treat, stop in here, at the town's best dessert bakery and bar. Good local pastries include *baci di dama,* chocolate-filled cookie sandwiches, and *Amor,* crisp wafers or butter cookies with a thick *crema* filling.

VIAREGGIO

ROMANO Via Mazzini, 120   55049   Viareggio   Lucca
RESTAURANT TELEPHONE/FAX 0584 31382   OPEN Lunch and dinner
CLOSED Monday; January   CREDIT CARDS   Visa, MC, Amex
ENGLISH SPOKEN Yes   RESERVATIONS Recommended
PRICE $$$$ DIRECTIONS Via Mazzini runs perpendicular to the sea
from Piazza Mazzini.

"When we opened here, over thirty years ago," recounted Romano
Franceschini, "I was twenty-two years old and my wife, Franca, was sixteen.
Then lunch cost 1.000 lire [less than one dollar]." Today, Romano is famous
for his fine fish cookery. The current restaurant, on a busy street near the market, is comfortable and well appointed in a late seventies style: clean-lined
black Thonet chairs, black lacquer dressers, modern pictures, and potted
plants. The food is distinctly Mediterranean and includes some meat. There
is an extensive wine list.

My spring lunch began with *dentice* (dentex, a fish in the porgy
family) served with tangy fresh tomato sauce, puréed green radicchio, and fine
mayonnaise. *Insalata di mare*—tender squid, shrimp, crayfish, and sliced octopus tossed with oil and herbs—was accompanied by Tuscan *fagioli* (white
beans) and good olive oil. A striped, silver-skinned fillet of *ombrina* (ombrine)
on a bed of julienned carrots and zucchini was flavored with balsamic vinegar
and chives. Olives and capers added sharper accents. Giant mussels were garnished simply with lemon.

The *calamaretti ripieni* were excellent: miniature squid stuffed
with finely ground vegetables and breadcrumbs. *Spannocchi* (the local word for
mazzancolle, large shrimp) came with an unusual piquant warm honey sauce
and fried artichoke slices that were cold and crunchy. The squid reappeared
in a *zuppa*, an herbed broth with fresh tomato; toasted Tuscan bread and fruity
oil completed this rustic dish. In *bavette con scampi*, pasta was rich with shrimp
in a light tomato and herb sauce—a classic Riviera dish. Fish are fried, poached,
or grilled. Desserts include sorbets, mousses, and Viareggio's characteristic
seasonal carnival pastries.

PUNTODIVINO Via Mazzini, 229   55049   Viareggio   Lucca
WINE BAR/ TELEPHONE 0584 31046   OPEN Lunch and dinner, till 1:00 a.m.
RESTAURANT CLOSED Monday; January   CREDIT CARDS Visa, MC, Amex
DIRECT SALE Yes   ENGLISH SPOKEN Yes   RESERVATIONS For weekend
dinner   PRICE Restaurant $$$ DIRECTIONS The *enoteca* is seven
blocks inland from the sea.

Keith Haring's images set the tone in this lively wine bar. It is a place designed
for young people, with a serious wine collection and an appetizing menu.

Prices are affordable, the hours are flexible and late. It is a nice place to sit and drink a bottle of wine or to buy some to take home.

The owners, Roberto and Cristina Franceschini, are no strangers to the restaurant business. Their parents run Viareggio's most renowned restaurant, Romano (see page 45), across the street and down the road. Despite some parental guidance the two establishments are separate entities, Roberto assured me.

Also

La Bottega di Mamma Rò. Via Fratti, 284. 0584 31192.

"Humble materials in tasteful contexts" is this store's subtitle. Its bright, earthy objects fit well with today's notions of country style. A large range of glazed terra-cotta objects includes bowls and vases, plates and cookpots; the colors are pretty, though I wish more were made without logos. There are rough-weave cotton fabrics, chunky colored glasses, kitchen utensils and chopping boards—all reasonably priced. This store belongs to a Lucca-based franchising network with branches in the United States.

CHAPTER 2

Lucca and the Garfagnana

*L*ucca is one of Tuscany's most fascinating towns. An independent city state until the nineteenth century, Lucca's wealth and power was based on commerce. Historic walls enclose an active center of medieval streets, Romanesque churches, and stately palazzi. Lucca's rich silk merchants and noble families summered in villas built in the gentle hills around the town. These villas, often Baroque with formal gardens, are surrounded by olive groves: the area is known for its mild, almost sweet, extra-virgin olive oil.

To Lucca's north the hills steepen as the River Serchio traces a course between the Apuan Alps and the Apennines known as the Garfagnana. Here the summers are cool and breezy, with forests of pine, beech, and chestnut. Stone houses cluster in villages surrounded by mountain pastures for sheep and goats.

The cooking of the Garfagnana is hearty, with thick soups of *farro*—the locally cultivated spelt wheat—chestnut flour, and pulses. There is game and mutton, sheep's cheese and wild mushrooms. If this mountain fare represents *la cucina povera*, Lucca's classic dishes reflect the city's wealth: *torta di erbe* is a Renaissance vegetable pie studded with pine nuts and raisins, fragrant with spices only the rich could afford.

Azienda Promozione Turistica
Piazza Guidiccioni, 2
55100 Lucca
0583 491205, fax 0583 490766

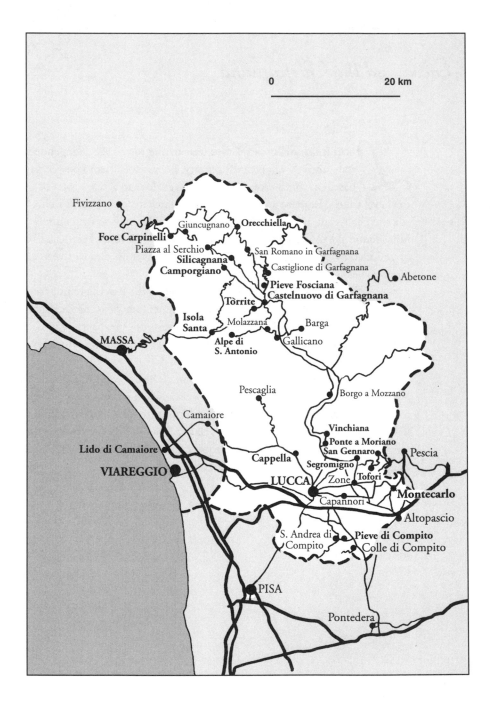

Town names in **bold** indicate towns that are included in this chapter.

ABOUT FARRO

Farro is the Italian name for one of the world's oldest grains, *Triticum dicoccum*. Its earliest citings date to 6000 B.C.; it was cultivated in Syria and Palestine, and by the Ancient Egyptians who used it for soups and rudimentary breads. It spread to other Mediterranean countries and by the third millennium B.C. was known as *oliria*, for its pure white flour. The Greeks brought it to Italy. In the Roman Empire, *farro* symbolized honor and glory; it was awarded to heroes. Pliny called it *primus antiquis latio cibus*, "the primary food of Ancient Rome."

    Farro is often called spelt wheat in English, though this is not completely accurate: spelt is *Triticum spelta*, not *Triticum dicoccum*. The *farro* kernel is protected by a thin dark outer skin that may be polished away to facilitate cooking or grinding. It is now cultivated in only several hundred hectares in Italy, of which one hundred are in the Garfagnana. The plant thrives in poor soils at altitudes of 350 to 1,000 meters (1,000 to 3,200 feet). Most Garfagnana *farro* is organic. A consortium has recently been formed to safeguard and market the grain.

What to Look For

Ideal *farro* grains are an elongated oval, split along one side into two parts. If they have been polished (*brillato*) the color will be mottled, the tan outer skin partially rubbed away to reveal the bright white interior. *Farro* of this type needs no presoaking, though it may be rinsed briefly in warm water before cooking. Unpolished grain needs pre-soaking and longer cooking. Poor quality spelt has no floury interior: it is all dark without the white, needs long cooking, and lacks the plump starchiness of fine *farro*. Break a kernel in half crosswise. If it is white inside, it is *farro;* if the outer husk seems empty and dark, it is grain of little culinary interest.

    Farro is a whole grain rich in fiber and starches, wonderful in soups or stews. Boiled and cooled it forms the basis of salads, replacing rice or other grains. Ground into flour it goes into pasta and bread, alone or with other flours. Some desserts are even made with it.

ALPE di S. ANTONIO

LA BETULLA
RESTAURANT

Via Peritano Sotto, 3   55020   Molazzana
TELEPHONE/FAX 0583 760052   OPEN Lunch and dinner
CLOSED Monday; March   CREDIT CARDS None
ENGLISH SPOKEN A little   RESERVATIONS Always recommended, necessary on weekends   PRICE $ DIRECTIONS From Castelnuovo follow signs for Monte Perpoli and Molazzana, then Alpe di S. Antonio. At the top of the mountain, signs lead to the restaurant.

Nestled near the mountaintop, this unpretentious restaurant has a curious history. In 1987 Stefano Bresciani and his sister, Lia, decided to open a restaurant in their village. No suitable buildings were available and construction was impossible. By chance they learned that prefabricated buildings once used to house earthquake victims were to be sold off. "Large houses were going for a song," recounted Stefano, "you just had to go and get them. We paid less than five dollars for ours." They dismantled it, trucked it to Tuscany and up the mountain, reassembled it—and their restaurant was born. On a clear day the views are spectacular as you drive up the winding roads to the village.

In autumn a cheery fire burns in the fireplace. Unusual homemade antipasti include local "*grifoni*" mushrooms preserved in oil, looking like pale coral; *pomodori acerbi*, pickled green-gold tomatoes; *baccalà sott'olio*, deep-fried salt cod put "under oil"; sliced herbed tongue; and home-cured *salumi*. *Primi* are hearty: flat pasta sheets sauced with light meat *ragù;* and fresh ricotta and spinach ravioli. *Sformato di cavolfiore* was a savory cauliflower bake.

Rosticciana coi rapini are roast pork ribs served over stewed turnip greens. Veal slices come topped with juicy chunks of porcini. Sheep's cheeses are made by the family, who also grow much of the restaurant's produce. Up on the mountain the atmosphere is informal—after meals the long wooden tables are used for card games or conversations to while away the mountain evenings.

CAMPORGIANO

MULIN
DEL RANCONE
RESTAURANT, BAR

55036   Camporgiano
TELEPHONE/FAX 0583 618670   OPEN Restaurant for lunch and dinner; bar; 8:00-24:00   CLOSED January and February
CREDIT CARDS Visa, MC   DIRECT SALE Yes—shop for specialty foods
ENGLISH SPOKEN Yes   FEATURES Eight rooms; mountain refuge; camping; horses; river swimming   RESERVATIONS Recommended
PRICE $$ including wine   DIRECTIONS The mill can be reached from both sides of the Serchio River: from Camporgiano or from San Romano. There are signs.

Mulin del Rancone is a hub of Garfagnanan activity. Down by the river the rural stone buildings of the former mill house a myriad of activities: besides a lively restaurant there is a bar, a shop selling local specialty foods, rooms to rent, horses to ride, river pools to swim in...the list is endless.

The restaurant offers a chance to taste genuine Garfagnana cuisine. Mixed antipasti include excellent homemade *sott'olii* and *sott'aceti,* vegetables preserved in oil or vinegar; well-seasoned local *salumi;* and savory tarts and *crostini.* In the earthy *zuppa di funghi,* sliced porcini mushrooms float in a flavorful broth over a slice of dark country bread. Tortellini are made of whole wheat and *farro* flour, filled with meat and served in broth. Mulin del Rancone has been active in the rebirth of *farro* as one of the area's most important ingredients (see p 49).

Gabriele Bertucci explained why Garfagnana has a large repertoire of *primi* (first courses) like soups and pastas, corn polenta, chestnut-flour polenta and *farro.* "Up here in the mountains the people were very poor," he recounted, "and winters were cold. These simple foods were calorific and kept them warm. Meats were harder to come by." Meat is no longer scarce, but main courses here reflect their humble origins: rabbit is stewed with bitter olives, chicken is fried, and pies are made of vegetables.

Pastries are baked in-house by Enzo Petreschi, the area's best-loved *pasticciere.* He makes biscuits with chestnut, corn or *farro* flours. The menu at the mill changes daily, depending on the offerings of fields and woods and the whims of the charming cooks.

CAPPELLA

LE MURELLE   Ponte del Giglio   55060   Cappella
WINE   TELEPHONE 0583 394487, 394055 FAX 0583 394487
OPEN Sales and visits by appointment only   CREDIT CARDS None
DIRECT SALE Yes   ENGLISH SPOKEN Yes   DIRECTIONS Le Murelle is
on the main Lucca-Camaiore road, about 8 kms from Lucca.

Le Murelle is a family-run winery that has been gaining recognition for its modern-style white wines. "When my grandfather bought the property in 1929 as an investment," explained Giampi Moretti, the young man now running the winery, "it was still cultivated under the *mezzadria,* or sharecropping, system. The land was terraced for growing grains, olives, and grapes."

This area has always produced some wine, since before the 1861 unification of Italy wine could not easily be imported from outside of the independent republic of Lucca. "Each state had its own customs point," continued Moretti, "and was tied to its own traditions. And tradition often leads to stagnation." Since there was steady local demand for unbottled wines, nobody bothered to improve them. Moretti emphasized that Buonamico (see p 59) was the first winery to make any big changes in the area.

When his grandfather died in 1984, Moretti took over. His first task was to oversee the harvest, and he watched in horror as grapes both ripe and rotten were thrown into decaying wooden barrels. "The grapes were squashed semimanually," he recalled, "and it all began to boil away down there. I was appalled. 'Can it be that in this day and age we are still making wine like this?' I asked myself."

He took courses and met a few key people who encouraged him to start from scratch. "From Silvano Formigli, who was responsible for launching Ama (see p 179), I learned there could be nothing accidental about it. Changes had to be programmed and prepared." With winemaker Maurizio Castelli's help, they did experimental planting to decide which grapes would do best. The answer was clearly whites, so in 1990 they began planting Chardonnay and Sauvignon. "We decided to go for quality, and there was no risk with these internationally popular varieties."

The first bottled vintage was 1993, with immediately encouraging results. The well-balanced 1993 Chardonnay, which spent some time in *barriques,* has good structure and a pleasant taste of honey to it. The fine Sauvignon is not matured in wood. "Our terrain seems to be giving the grapes enough acidity to be able to benefit from a little aging," he concluded. "But it's still early days for us to have all the answers!"

CASTELNUOVO DI GARFAGNANA

CASEIFICIO BERTAGNI CHEESE   Via Provinciale, 9   Pontardeto   55036   Pieve Fosciano   TELEPHONE 0583 62723   FAX 0583 62846   OPEN 8:00-12:00, 15:00-19:30   CLOSED Never   CREDIT CARDS None   DIRECT SALE Yes   ENGLISH SPOKEN A little   DIRECTIONS From Castelnuovo go toward San Romano. After about 2 kms, the *caseificio* is signposted on the left.

This small cheese factory makes both sheep's and cow's milk cheeses using local and Tuscan milk. "My grandfather had his own herd, my father made cheeses, and I followed on from him," explained the soft-spoken young Verano Bertagni. "Though we don't have our own herds anymore."

A range of cheeses is sold in the small shop beside the house, including 100 percent sheep pecorini, mixed sheep's and cow's milk cheeses, and fresh cow's milk *caciotta.* The well-matured pecorino called Tuada, which means "aging cellar" in the local dialect, has a hard grayish surface and a close inner texture with small air bubbles. Its flavor is piquant, almost spicy, with a strong character of sheep's milk. The *semi-stagionato,* aged for sixty days, has a golden yellow exterior and paler interior—compact and smooth, with a faint sharpness to its taste.

OSTERIA	Via Vittorio Emanuele, 12 55032 Castelnuovo di Garfagnana
VECCHIO MULINO	TELEPHONE 0583 62192 FAX 0583 65063
WINE BAR,	OPEN 7:30-20:00 CLOSED Sunday in winter; holidays variable
SPECIALTY FOODS	CREDIT CARDS Visa, MC DIRECT SALE Yes ENGLISH SPOKEN Yes
	DIRECTIONS In the town center

Andrea Bertucci is a guiding force of Garfagnana gastronomy. A large jovial young man with the personable character of a natural host, he has for years been an active promoter of the traditional foods of this distinctive mountain region. His small but lively wine bar is one of the key addresses in the area: nobody travels up or down the mountain valley without stopping in for a glass of wine, a sandwich, or a chat.

His sandwich stuffers are legendary, beginning with the humongous Bologna mortadella (the real bologna) that occupies center stage on its purpose-built trestle. This he hand slices to accompany crisp local focaccia or the excellent potato bread made at Tòrrite (see p 66). There are great cheeses, Italian and French, and Andrea's personal pick of Tuscan *salumi.*

Wines are sold by the glass or bottle. The wine list is eclectic: hard-to-find local labels stand beside their better known Tuscan cousins. Wine tastings and courses are enthusiastically organized by the untiring Andrea. This is a good place to buy the Garfagnana's foods: *farro* wheat, chestnut flour, mushrooms under oil or dried, mountain honey, and local olive oil.

Also

Caffè Ariosto. Piazza Umberto I, 2. 0583 62647.

If you are hankering for an American-style cocktail, this bar is for you. Walter Borelli is an expert at all the classics, and he has even concocted a few brightly colored specials of his own. Many are fruit-based, with or without alcohol. On Friday and Saturday nights the bar jumps with prediscotheque action, but during the day it functions like every other Italian bar, serving coffee, drinks, snacks, and sandwiches.

FOCE CARPINELLI

AZIENDA AGRICOLA	Via Statale, 60 55030 Carpinelli
GABRIELE DAVINI	TELEPHONE 0583 611239, 611044 OPEN 8:00-13:00, 15:00-20:00
FARM PRODUCE	CLOSED Never CREDIT CARDS None DIRECT SALE Yes
	ENGLISH SPOKEN A little DIRECTIONS On the main road between
	Castelnuovo di Garfagnana and Aulla, 27 kms from Castelnuovo, 30 kms
	from Aulla.

This wonderful farm sells all its own produce: fresh vegetables and fruits, homemade preserves, cheeses, *salumi,* and fresh meats. It is a family-run business, as Gabriele Davini explained. "We do everything ourselves, from rearing the animals to butchering and preparing the meats. We grow grain, grind flour, and bake breads in our wood-burning oven. We have done this all our lives, trying to keep it all on a human scale, our scale." He added with a chuckle, "Our dream is to be completely self-sufficient, and I guess we have come close."

Situated at 840 meters, the farm overlooks the surrounding mountains and valleys. There are vegetable patches, chicken coops, cow stables, orchards—the classic vision of a real working farm. In autumn the farm shop is fragrant with locally gathered dried mushrooms. Many varieties—with local names such as *grifoni, famigliole,* and *galletti*—are preserved in oil. Signora Luciana explained that sixty-eight varieties of chestnuts grow in the Garfagnana woods. Wooden boxes, or "safes" as they are know in dialect, store the farm's flours: chestnut, corn, wheat, and *farro.* There are baskets of flat little pink-red apples, *mela casciana* or *rosina,* that last through winter if kept in straw. Despite their irregular shapes, their perfume is exceptionally fragrant. The Davini's daughter makes beautiful fruit jellies and the best wild blueberry jam I've tasted.

Of the pork *salumi,* a favorite is the *mortadella nostrale,* or *mondiola,* whose ends are tied around a bay leaf. The deep pink shoulder meat is lean, tender, and well seasoned. It is matured for three months, hanging near a warm fireplace to dry out.

ISOLA SANTA

DA GIACCÒ
RESTAURANT, BAR

Via di Valdarni, 2   55030   Isola Santa
TELEPHONE   0583 667048   OPEN Restaurant for lunch and dinner; bar open all day for snacks   CLOSED Tuesday; for dinner in winter if there are no bookings; two weeks in November   CREDIT CARDS Visa, MC   ENGLISH SPOKEN Yes   FEATURES Outdoor terrace RESERVATIONS For dinner, necessary in winter   PRICE $$ DIRECTIONS From Castelnuovo di Garfagnana go toward Arni and Pietrasanta. After 13 kms, the restaurant is on the left.

Isola Santa, the holy island, is a tiny village of gray stone buildings and roofs now perched at the edge of a lake formed by one of the area's many hydroelectric dams. When the valley was flooded the village was abandoned: its population fell to two. Despite this exodus, its restaurant has remained.

Gabriele Mazzei took it over in 1994. "I wanted to serve real local food, as I remembered it from my grandmothers," the soft-spoken chef explained. "Our cuisine used ingredients grown in the mountain fields or foraged from the woods. Simple but wholesome food, without pretensions." Gabriele is recreating this culinary atmosphere. He serves mountain cheeses, game and country meats, and wild mushrooms and greens.

An autumn lunch in the cosy dining room began with antipasti which included *fettunta*, fragrant toasted bread rubbed with garlic and drizzled with olive oil; truffle-scented coarse-grained pork *salame;* and corn-yellow grilled polenta with sharp goat's cheese. Homemade tagliatelle were nicely elastic, sauced with woodsy wild mushrooms *in bianco* (no tomato). Soft stone-ground polenta was dressed with melted butter and truffle shavings.

Gabriele explained that grazing in mountain pastures produces more flavorful cheeses and meat than lower altitudes. Chops of young goat and lamb came sizzling hot, grilled over a chestnut wood fire, their flavor intense without being gamey, accompanied by thick slices of deep-fried porcini. For dessert there are home-baked tarts of *ricotta* or of the sweet walnuts which were once pressed for oil in this region.

LUCCA

FORNO AMEDEO
GIUSTI
BREAD

Via Santa Lucia, 18-20   55100   Lucca
TELEPHONE 0583 496285   OPEN Summer: 8:00-13:00, 16:45-19:45; winter: 8:00-13:00, 16:30-19:30   CLOSED Sunday; Wednesday afternoon in winter; Saturday afternoon in summer; July
CREDIT CARDS None   ENGLISH SPOKEN Yes
DIRECTIONS Near the Duomo

You can buy a slice of this bakery's delicious focaccia right from the street through the shop's sliding window. At *merenda* time (midmorning or afternoon break) schoolchildren line up with their 1.000 lire notes to buy a slice. In addition to the usual salted and olive-oiled version, Giusti makes them olive-studded, topped with onions, and unusually sweet with sugar and raisins. The focaccia is baked fresh every two hours: it is so crisp, crunchy and warm, you'll end up eating it as you walk home. So buy a little extra, or try some of the bakery's sixty types of bread.

CIOCCOLATERIA
CANIPAROLI
CHOCOLATE

Via San Paolino, 96   55100   Lucca
TELEPHONE 0583 53456   OPEN Summer 9:00-13:00, 16:00-20:00; winter: 9:00-13:00, 15:30-20:00   CLOSED Monday in summer; Sunday afternoon and Monday in winter; August
CREDIT CARDS None   ENGLISH SPOKEN Yes
DIRECTIONS On the street between the Duomo and Piazzale Verdi

A must for chocolate-lovers, this austere, stylish little shop opened in 1994 and makes the town's best chocolates. Young chocolate-maker and pastry chef Piero Caniparoli trained in France, Belgium, and Switzerland before coming home to set up shop. Using primarily Belgian *couverture*, with 55 percent to 70 percent cocoa solids, he specializes in filled chocolates—with a nice range of centers.

His ganache fillings are delicate and meltingly creamy: the truffles have an intense richness of flavor; an unusual *fondente al tè* is unmistakeably perfumed with Earl Grey. "I aim for chocolates with clear, decisive flavors," he explained. A range of milk and white chocolates complements the dark.

Don't expect to find them in June or July, however. In the summer months Italians switch their passion for chocolate (it's too hot to make them) onto cakes and *semifreddi,* frozen desserts. In winter, the shop's cake range is limited to a few delicious but decadent creations.

MARIA PACINI FAZZI   Piazza San Romano, 16   Casella Postale 173   55100   Lucca
COOKBOOK PUBLISHER   TELEPHONE 0583 55530   FAX 0583 418245   OPEN Not open to
the public   MAIL ORDER Yes   DIRECT SALE All of Lucca's bookstores
carry the books   ENGLISH SPOKEN Yes

Being a cookbook collector, I spotted Maria Pacini Fazzi's little colored paperback cookbooks as soon as I moved to Italy. They present unusual, genuine local recipes, nicely printed and illustrated; they are not expensive, and several have been translated into English. Maria Pacini Fazzi started publishing thirty years ago. Her subjects include gastronomy, folk culture, philosophy, local history, literature, and Lucchese guides.

"I have always been fascinated by this area's culture," she confirmed. "Our cookery books research authentic recipes from historical documents, and from the people who still carry on these traditions."

English language titles include *Traditional Recipes of Lucchesian Farmers, Traditional Recipes from Florence,* and *Cooking With Olive Oil,* plus numerous guides to Lucca's culture and countryside. The Italian selection is much wider.

"A people is judged by its food," she observed. "It all depends how you look at what is around you. *La cucina povera* is only poor when made by poor people. Here many people were rich with refined tastes, and were able to turn this simple cuisine into something of quality."

PASTICCERIA   Piazza San Michele, 34   55100   Lucca
TADDEUCCI   TELEPHONE 0583 494933   OPEN Summer 8:00-20:00; winter:
PASTRY   8:00-13:00, 15:00-20:00   CLOSED Thursday; ten days in summer
CREDIT CARDS None   ENGLISH SPOKEN A little
DIRECTIONS   In the town's central square

Right behind Lucca's Duomo is Taddeucci's bakery, a Lucchese cornerstone since 1881, when the present owner's great-grandfather founded it. The beautiful wood-paneled and mosaic-tiled shop offers a piece of Lucca as it once was, as well as two of its great pastry specialties.

The most famous is the *buccellato*. Traditionally sold in a round
ring (but also baked in a long loaf), this antique sweet yeast bread is flavored
with aniseed and golden raisins. Its hard chestnut-brown crust is brushed with
sugar syrup before baking. A card suggests how to stuff, toast, top, fry, or steep
your *buccellato! Torta di erbe* is a tasty sweet spiced vegetable pie, its speckled
green filling studded with pine nuts and raisins. It calls for beet greens and
parsley, eggs, sugar, spices, and pepper.

Other pastries include seasonal *fave dei morti:* almond-paste
confections shaped like fava beans for All Saints' Day. Taddeucci also makes
panforte and *cantucci* biscuits—good presents to take home.

BUCA DI	Via della Cervia, 1/3 55100 Lucca
SANT ANTONIO	TELEPHONE 0583 55881 FAX 0583 312199 OPEN Lunch and dinner
RESTAURANT	CLOSED Sunday evening, Monday CREDIT CARDS Visa, MC, Amex
	ENGLISH SPOKEN Yes RESERVATIONS Recommended PRICE $$$
	DIRECTIONS Near the Duomo

This is Lucca's oldest and best-known restaurant, originating in 1782 as an inn.
Being close to the Duomo, it is used to dealing with foreigners. The attractive
dining room is well appointed, with wooden beams hung with copper pots and
walls adorned with spare architectural prints. The service is fairly formal, professional, and fast. Sample the Lucchesia's culinary specialties here: vegetable
and grain (especially *farro*) soups, tarts and pastas, wild mushrooms, and grilled
meats and game.

Zuppa di farro alla Garfagnina, a substantial soup, features locally
grown *farro* (see p 49) in a vegetable and bean base with ham and cinnamon;
it is very good. *Tortina di funghi,* a puff pastry tartlet, has a salty filling of ricotta
and porcini mushrooms. Its flavor is delicately earthy, though my pastry was
not quite cooked through. *Tordelli Lucchesi,* handmade pasta cushions, are
stuffed with pork, beef, and sausage, beet greens, and borage and seasoned with
nutmeg. Main courses include thick T-bone steaks (*la Fiorentina*) grilled over
a wood fire: split one between two. Seasonal porcini mushrooms are stewed,
fried, or baked in paper, *al cartoccio.*

The restaurant has interesting desserts. Stewed fruit is a mixture
of pear, apple, and semidried grapes. Lucca's special *torta di erbe* is surprisingly
green, with a sweetly spiced beet-green filling reminiscent of pumpkin pie.
Chef Giuliano Pacini said "you would need a book" to list all its ingredients.

**DA GIULIO
IN PELLERIA
RESTAURANT**

Via delle Conce, 45   Piazza San Donato   55100   Lucca
TELEPHONE/FAX 0583 55948   OPEN Lunch and dinner; and third
Sunday of each month for the antique market   CLOSED Sunday and
Monday; one week in August   CREDIT CARDS Visa, MC, Amex
ENGLISH SPOKEN Yes   RESERVATIONS Recommended
PRICE $ DIRECTIONS In the town center, near the San Donato gate
in the city wall

This large bustling restaurant serves wholesome food at wholesome prices, and
it is always packed with locals, students, and travelers. The service is fast, with
the cheery atmosphere special to big busy restaurants.

Try one of Lucca's rustic soups, of *farro* or beans, or *ribollita*—
mixed pulses and vegetables soaked up with bread. These are well-cooked, substantial dishes. The *farro*, spelt wheat, in vegetable broth with lentils and potatoes is rich and peppery. A warming dish of loose yellow corn polenta comes in
broth with vegetables. The Lucchese's characteristically sweet olive oil is
brought separately. Pastas can be ordered as a *tris*—a sampling of three.

Winter main courses are fish or meat based. (Summer features
more seafood and salads.) Stockfish topped with stewed sweet onions, and beet-
greens cooked with squid are served with soft-centered fried polenta. Meats are
roasted or stewed with olives. Many are quite salty, as is customary in Tuscany.
Desserts include creamy tiramisù, Vin Santo with *cantucci* biscuits, or Lucca's
torta di erbe—spiced vegetable dessert tart. There are Chianti flasks on each
table (pay for what you drink) plus selected Lucchese and Tuscan wines.

**ANTICA BOTTEGA
DI PROSPERO
SPECIALTY FOODS:
PULSES, SEEDS
& GRAINS**

Via Santa Lucia, 13   55100   Lucca
TELEPHONE 0583 91198 (home number)   OPEN 8:00-13:00,
16:00-19:30   CLOSED Sunday; Wednesday afternoon in winter;
Saturday afternoon in summer   CREDIT CARDS None
ENGLISH SPOKEN A little   DIRECTIONS Near the Duomo

This old-fashioned shop started out so long ago (it has been in the Marcucci
family for over three hundred years) it has ended up selling the oddest assortment of dried goods—everything from lentils to daffodil bulbs. It is a great
source of edible legumes and grains, rices and dried herbs. Sacks of beans,
seeds, flours, and nuts line one side of the simple, stylish shop. Goods are sold
by weight, scooped out and measured by the friendly staff. Cooking hints are
exchanged freely with people waiting to be served. There are pink marbled *bor-
lotti* beans, white *cannellini*, and the rarer *Sorana* and *zolfino* varieties (see pp 78
and 345): expensive but worth trying to see just how tender and delicate beans
can be. Those with vegetable gardens will find seeds for red radicchio, arugula,
fennel, and wild field chicory.

Also

Ferramenta Barzanti, Via San Paolino, 88.

This hardware store stocks a few hard-to-find kitchen items, such as the shallow copper rounds for baking *castagnaccio,* chick-pea flour *farinata,* and the pierced pans used to roast chestnuts over a fire.

Il Trifoglio. Via Elisa, 31. 0583 493122.

This good-sized health food store sells organic produce and dried goods, organic dairy products and tofu, which is hard to find in Italy. It also carries natural cosmetics, macrobiotic ingredients, and freshly baked whole-grain breads.

MONTECARLO

FATTORIA
DEL BUONAMICO
WINE

Via Provinciale di Montecarlo, 43   55015   Montecarlo
TELEPHONE/FAX 0583 22038   OPEN Monday-Friday 8:30-12:30, 14:00-19:00; Saturday: 8:30-12:30. Saturday afternoon and Sunday by appointment; tastings and cellar visits by appointment
CLOSED Sunday   CREDIT CARDS None   DIRECT SALE Yes
ENGLISH SPOKEN Yes   DIRECTIONS From Montecarlo, go toward Altopascio; the Fattoria is on the left after 1 km.

A trip to the hill town of Montecarlo with its tiny wooden 1790s theater should include a visit to its wine producers. The area's wines have been noted for over a thousand years; its white wines were popular during the Renaissance. In the 1850s French grape varieties were introduced here by Giulio Magnani; these are now included in Montecarlo Bianco, granted DOC status in 1969.

Fattoria del Buonamico, with its personable director, Vasco Grassi, has recently enlarged its modern *cantine* with the sophisticated equipment required for good white wines. The estate has twenty-four hectares (sixty acres) of vineyards. Its white Montecarlo DOC is a blend of 50 percent Trebbiano grapes, with white and gray Pinots, Sauvignon, Sémillon, and Roussanne making up the rest. Other whites, of selected grapes, are Cercatoia Bianco and Vasario, a Pinot Bianco fermented in small oak *barriques.*

The Fattoria's best red wine is a modern-style *vino da tavola* called Cercatoia Rosso, made only in very good years. Of selected grapes— 40 percent Sangiovese, with Canaiolo, Syrah, Cabernets Sauvignon and Franc—it is a full-bodied wine aged in *barriques.* Il Fortino, of Cabernet and Merlot, has also been well received by Italian critics.

TRATTORIA "DA BAFFO"
WINE, RESTAURANT

Fuso Carmignani   Via della Tinaia, 7   55015   Montecarlo
TELEPHONE 0583 2238   OPEN Restaurant May-September for dinner
only; winery open by appointment   CLOSED Monday
CREDIT CARDS None   DIRECT SALE Yes   ENGLISH SPOKEN A little
FEATURES Outdoor dining garden   RESERVATIONS Suggested
PRICE $$ including wine   OTHER A few rooms to rent
DIRECTIONS From Fattoria del Buonamico go towards Montecarlo.
Turn left onto Via Cercatoia Alta. Turn left on unpaved road marked
Via Tinaia to sign for Fuso Carmignani.

Gino Carmignani is an eccentric character. He and his parents live on a country farm, make wine, and in summer run a small rustic trattoria serving three home-cooked dishes each evening. "My philosophy has been to bring the world into my back garden," he asserted. "It's the opposite of traveling. People come from all over to eat with us or to buy my wines, especially For Duke."

A major jazz fan and keen winemaker, Gino dedicated his pure Sangiovese wine to Duke Ellington. Believing that great wines are made in the vineyard rather than the cellar, he has invested heavily in intensive plantings.

"I'll never use technology to make wines," he added. "We are the last of the artisans. I vinify in wood, using what I call my 'acoustic' method." Whatever that is, he has earned himself a following—and an evening spent eating and drinking under the Carmignani's medlar tree will never be dull.

ORECCHIELLA

LA GREPPIA
RESTAURANT

Orecchiella   55038   San Romano
TELEPHONE/FAX 0583 619018   OPEN Lunch and dinner
CLOSED Tuesday in winter   CREDIT CARDS Visa, MC, Amex
ENGLISH SPOKEN A little   RESERVATIONS Always recommended
PRICE $$ DIRECTIONS From Castelnuovo follow signs to Corfino
(via Castiglione). The restaurant is signposted from there, about 7 kms
from Corfino.

This restaurant is high in the Garfagnana mountains, beside a large nature reserve. The views are expansive. In summer you eat in the garden, with space for children to play. Phone before going up: the restaurant sometimes closes for private functions.

Talented owner-chef Mariano Rapaioli makes rustic local fare with a refined touch. *Manafregoli con panna* is a thick soup of chestnut flour, sweet yet smoky from the chestnuts' drying, with liquid cream on top. An individual quiche is given a decisive, salty flavor by *prosciutto Toscano* in fine, well-baked pastry. *Zuppa di farro*, local spelt wheat, is deliciously aromatic: a fine purée of beans is the base for a soup containing plumped *farro* grains, whole beans, and herbs. In autumn, mushrooms, rather than meat may star as a main course, arriving in a puffed cushion of silver foil—*al cartoccio.* This seals in all the flavor; the thickly sliced mushrooms stew in their juices with oil, garlic, and wild herbs. Other specialties are grilled meats and game. Desserts are elaborate and well made. The restaurant is nicely appointed without being too formal, as befits a mountain refuge.

PIEVE DI COMPITO

FRANTOIO
SOCIALE
DEL COMPITESE
OLIVE MILL

Via del Tiglio, 609   55065   Pieve di Compito
TELEPHONE/ FAX 0583 907898   OPEN Shop 10:00-12:30, 15:30-18:30;
mill November and December   CLOSED Sunday
CREDIT CARDS None   DIRECT SALE Yes   ENGLISH SPOKEN A little
DIRECTIONS   The *frantoio* is set back from the ss 439 Bientina to Lucca
road, between San Leonardo in Treponzio and Colle di Compito.

This large *frantoio,* or olive oil mill, is housed in a modern building with light green trim clearly visible from the main road. It was built in 1994 by a cooperative of olive growers in the Compitese area. During the season (November and December), growers bring their olives to be milled. Some oil is left to be sold in the mill's large shop, which is also set up for tastings. Visitors are welcome.

This *frantoio* operates using the modern stainless-steel "continuous cycle" system, generally agreed to be more hygienic and versatile than the old-fashioned method. The olives, in airy crates, are brought in as soon as possible after picking. They are weighed, washed, and ground between grooved stone cylinders. The pulp is gently heated (indirectly) to 30°-35°C/86-95°F and churned before being spun in a centrifuge with some added water: the oil and water mixture are separated from the ground pits and pulp (*sansa*). In the final procedure, the oil and water are spun in a cold vertical centrifuge, separating the vegetal waters from the finished oil. Filtering is optional.

PIEVE FOSCIANA

MOLINO
ERCOLANO REGOLI
FLOUR MILL

Molino di Sotto   55036   Pieve Fosciana
TELEPHONE 0583 666095   OPEN 8:15-12:30, 15:00-19:00
CLOSED Wednesday afternoon, Sunday   CREDIT CARDS None
DIRECT SALE Yes   ENGLISH SPOKEN No   DIRECTIONS Ask anyone
in Pieve Fosciana. Eveyone knows the miller and can point the way.

Every so often you step into a building and have the sensation of stepping out of time present and into time past. It is a moving experience—but also a little sad. For all the progress that is being made, so much is still being lost, and the hard-won experience of our ancestors is slipping away.

"There used to be many water-powered mills in this area," recalled Ercolano Regoli, the miller. "Each little stream had its own. In those days chestnuts were the staple food. Now our mill is the last one remaining. Since my wife and I have no children, I expect this tradition will end when we retire."

When I was there, in early November, the chestnuts were still in the smokehouses, not yet ready for milling. But the great pairs of horizontal stone wheels were turning, each in their private cubicle. In one, bright yellow corn was being ground for polenta; in another, white-centered *farro* grains were yielding a flecked flour. The soft-spoken miller moved from one to the other, turning hand wheels to adjust the force of the sluices. The narrow room was alive with the hum of rushing water and spinning stones, filled with a clean, wholesome smell. "When the chestnut season starts we'll work twenty-four hours a day," he confided. "There's quite an art to grinding them: unless they are completely hard and dry their paste clogs between the stones and burns with the friction. The water is important—we also have electricity here—but water power is slower, it heats less, so the flour remains sweet, not bitter." At the beginning of each season the massive stones are slid apart, their grooves cleaned out, and if necessary, recarved.

The Regoli mill supplies local bakeries with flour. Wheat flours of various grades are for sale, as well as *farro,* chestnut, and yellow corn flours—in large or small quantities. Visitors are welcome, but only a few at a time. The centuries-old building wasn't built with modern tourism in mind.

PONTE A MORIANO

LA MORA
RESTAURANT

Via Sesto di Moriano, 1748   55029   Ponte a Moriano
TELEPHONE 0583 406402   FAX 0583 406135   OPEN Lunch and dinner   CLOSED Wednesday; October 10-30
CREDIT CARDS Visa, MC, Amex   ENGLISH SPOKEN Yes
FEATURES Garden terrace   RESERVATIONS For dinner   PRICE $$$
DIRECTIONS At Ponte a Moriano cross the bridge toward Sesto di Moriano. The restaurant is signposted.

La Mora is an easy drive from Lucca up the valley of the Serchio. It is one of the area's finest restaurants, and worth the detour for its genuine Lucchese cuisine. With its two fixed-price tasting menus—regional or seasonal—and an à la carte selection, it is good value for money. The tasting menus provide seven dishes, plus desserts. If you are planning one special meal in the area, you won't be disappointed here.

The main dining room is an inside-outside kind of space—a large glassed-in cube situated in a verdant garden that backs enigmatically onto a train line. In summer there is a trellis-covered patio. The restaurant is owned and run by Sauro Brunicardi. A tall, distinguished man, he explains the menu and takes the orders. A sommelier serves the wines from a fine selection in all price ranges which are also sold at retail in the restaurant's shop. The service is gracious and efficient.

Antipasti include a coral unmolded *budino,* or custard, of red peppers with a light Gruyère-flavored béchamel and a vegetable-stuffed puff pastry with a light herb sauce. A pure cool salad of plump *farro* grains is tossed with outstandingly fruity Lucchese olive oil (characteristically sweet), finely minced fresh green olives and tiny tomato chunks; its success is entirely a result of the fine local ingredients.

The inspired *pan di fagiano,* literally pheasant "bread," is adapted from Pellegrino Artusi's *La scienza in cucina e l'arte di mangiar bene* ("science in the kitchen and the art of eating well"), his classic cookbook of 1891. A scoop of the warm *pan*—finely minced pheasant, its juices beaten into a stiff béchamel—is served on a little toast with a tangy salad of grated carrots, green tomatoes, and red radicchio.

Of the *primi,* ricotta and spinach-filled ravioli with a sauce of fresh marjoram are light and aromatic. The fine pasta is still cranked by hand by the elderly Signora Brunicardi. *Risotto sulla pernice,* a creamy partridge risotto is enriched with pieces of meat and the bird's pan juices. Autumnal main courses in Tuscany often feature game. A hearty stew of wild boar is set off by sweet and sour green olives and served with fried polenta wedges. Delicious desserts end the meal.

SAN GENNARO

FATTORIA DI FUBBIANO
WINE, OLIVE OIL

55010 San Gennaro
TELEPHONE 0583 978011, 978311   FAX 0583 978344   OPEN Visits and tastings by appointment only   CLOSED Saturday and Sunday   CREDIT CARDS Visa, MC   DIRECT SALE Yes   ENGLISH SPOKEN Yes   OTHER Vacation houses available   DIRECTIONS From the main SS 435, follow the yellow signs from either Lappato or Gragnano.

Lucca is better known for its oil than its wine. If the nearby town of Montecarlo is noted for its whites, the Colline Lucchesi are associated with a Chianti-like red that gained early DOC status in 1968.

Anyone interested in how the old-fashioned *governo Toscano* works should visit this estate in autumn. In this largely outmoded winemaking technique, selected grapes are picked before the main harvest, hung indoors on racks to dry for several weeks, and then added into the newly fermented wine to induce a secondary fermentation. "By mid-November the dried grapes are ready to use," explained Sauro Corsini, the farm's long-standing manager. "They are destalked and stirred into the new wine, in a ratio of 4 kgs/8.8 lbs of grapes to 100 liters/26.6 gallons of wine. The *governo* makes the wine ready to drink sooner. It is costly and difficult, but it can add perfumes to the wine if aromatic grapes are used." The fermentation is slow, lasting until mid-February. When the wine is decanted, a thick layer of sediment remains. Fubbiano makes several wines this way.

The Fattoria, with a beautiful 1700s villa at its nucleus, now belongs to Giampiero de Andreis, a Milanese medical publisher. He and his wife are enthusiastically restoring the estate, modernizing the winemaking, and producing good olive oil.

SEGROMIGNO MONTE

FATTORIA MANSI Via di Valgiano, 34   55018   Segromigno Monte
BERNARDINI TELEPHONE 0583 928014   FAX 0583 929701   OPEN 8:30-17:30
OLIVE OIL CLOSED Saturday and Sunday   MAIL ORDER Possible for large orders
CREDIT CARDS None   DIRECT SALE Yes, by appointment
ENGLISH SPOKEN Yes   OTHER Vacation houses for rent
DIRECTIONS From Segromigno's old church, go west past Bar Puccini for 200 meters. At T-junction turn right, go over a small hill then turn right again. The Fattoria is after about 500 meters. Or ask at Bar Puccini.

Lucca's historic country villas are famous. Many make fine olive oil, as the hills are well suited for it, positioned between the sea and the mountains. The Mansi Bernardini estate is no exception. Its olive groves are among the best-tended I have seen, with rows of healthy young plants growing out of a perfect green lawn. "We keep grass in our olive groves partly for aesthetic reasons," explained Marcello Salom, the estate's owner, "and partly because the European Community gives incentives for banning weed-killers. It certainly looks nicer this way."

The estate has modernized its olive-picking techniques. High hand-held "combs" driven by compressed air coax the olives from the trees, dropping them into nets stretched below. Few trees are worked at a time, so the olives are milled as quickly as possible at the Vinchiana *frantoio* (see p 67).

Lucca's oil is considered among Tuscany's best. Its sweetness places it between the lighter Ligurian oils and the more intense, fiery oils from farther south. I was lucky to sample Salom's oil freshly milled. A bright yellow-green (oils lose some of this vividness after a few months), it has a clear, fresh perfume of freshly cut grass, a sweet fruity taste and only a light pepperiness in the finish.

SILLICAGNANA

ANGELA PIERONI Via Provinciale per Sillicagnana   55038   Sillicagnana
HONEY TELEPHONE 0583 62944   OPEN Saturday and Sunday, or
by appointment   CREDIT CARDS None   DIRECT SALE Yes
ENGLISH SPOKEN A little   DIRECTIONS Look for the sign on main road
between Sillicagnana and San Romano.

Angela Pieroni makes honey because she loves bees. "I was a housewife, but I
had always been fascinated by bees," the vivacious Angela told me. "The hardest
part was convincing my husband to help me—he was afraid of the bees at first.
But I won him over." They started in 1983, using positioned hives (unlike the
"nomadic" system in which hives are moved to flowering areas). Angela produces a prize-winning pure acacia honey containing over 90 percent of that
flower's nectar. The acacia is in bloom for fifteen to twenty days; when the
blossoms fade, the hives are emptied.

"With acacia it is easy to tell," she confided. "No other honey is
as clear or as light in color." Hers is a pale watery yellow, with the consistency
of thick corn syrup and a remarkably subtle taste, not overly sweet, with a wonderfully delicate sensation of flowers. By contrast, *castagne* (chestnut) is much
more forceful, deep in color and in taste. Other varieties include *erica* (broom),
and *mille fiori*—literally, a thousand flowers.

Also

Garfagnana COOP. Via Provinciale, 9. 0583 613242.

This cooperative was formed in 1994 to reclaim the increasing
number of abandoned fields in the Garfagnana. "Well-cultivated land in our
grandparents' day was now overgrown with weeds," explained Lorenzo Satti.
"So we planted spelt wheat, *farro,* the Garfagnana's special grain." They registered with AIAB, the Italian organic growers' association. Other products use
wild fruits and berries, mushrooms, and chestnuts from the woods. The cooperative's *farro* and fruits can be bought in Castelnuovo.

TOFORI

FATTORIA VILLA 55010   Tofori
MAIONCHI TELEPHONE 0583 978194   FAX 0583 978345   OPEN Sales: summer
OLIVE OIL, WINE 8:00-12:00, 14:30-18:30; winter 8:00-12:00, 13:30-17:30; cellar visits
and tastings by appointment only   CLOSED Sunday
CREDIT CARDS Visa, MC   DIRECT SALE Yes   ENGLISH SPOKEN Yes
OTHER Weekly rentals available   DIRECTIONS Tofori is not on the
Touring Club map, but it is located off the SS 435 between San Gennaro
and Zone. The Fattoria is well signposted in the area.

The seventeenth-century Villa Maionchi has everything: frescoed interiors,
great views of Lucca's plain, a formal garden, landmarked farm buildings,

wonderful olive oil, underground wine cellars—even a ghost. "He's called the Colonel," volunteered Maria Pia Maionchi. "And after I experienced him for myself I named our grappa after him!" Maria Pia's husband, who looks as if he stepped out of a Renaissance painting, smiled and shrugged.

The farm produces a range of wines from 11 hectares (27 acres) of vineyards, improving now with a winemaker. The unusual Rubino di Selvata is of pure Muscat of Hamburg grapes. Collegrosso is a Sangiovese, while Toforino is a fragrant white of Vermentino and Malvasia.

Their olive oil is wonderful, made of hand-picked olives stone-ground in an old-fashioned *frantoio* at San Gennaro and extracted in a stacked "castle" press. The oil, which is sold in half-liter bottles, is fresh and fruity, with a delicacy and sweetness that is special to Lucca's hills. The family is active in promoting tourism in the area and offers various kinds of visits and tastings.

TÒRRITE

PANIFICIO
RENATA GINESTRI
BREAD

Via del Bagno, 3   Tòrrite   55032   Castelnuovo di Garfagnana
TELEPHONE 0583 62613   OPEN 7:00-13:00, 15:00-19:00
CLOSED Wednesday afternoon, Sunday; June or July
CREDIT CARDS None   ENGLISH SPOKEN A little
DIRECTIONS The shop is at the far end of Tòrrite, coming from Castelnuovo, by the river, off the main road.

Renata Ginestri makes one of Tuscany's best breads. Know as *pane scuro, pane rustico,* or *pane di patate,* it is a dense, moist bread with a nicely chewy nut-brown crust. The loaves are round or oval, and as you cut into them the aroma is like old-fashioned sourdough. It is made in two versions: with white 'O' flour or with deeper-toned stone-ground grain.

"This type of bread was typical here," Signora Renata explained from behind her flour-dusted counter, "but we are the only ones still baking it in the traditional way. The secret of its moistness is in the mashed potato that is added to the flour, giving the bread its faint sweetness and keeping it fresh for days. It requires long rising using natural yeasts." Her focaccia and *pasimata,* the local Easter bread, are also excellent.

VINCHIANA

FRANTOIO BIANCHI   55050   Vinchiana
OLIVE MILL   TELEPHONE 0583 965276   OPEN Mid-November to mid-January; sales
by appointment   CREDIT CARDS None   DIRECT SALE Yes
ENGLISH SPOKEN No   DIRECTIONS From Ponte a Moriano go straight
toward the Garfagnana. Just after the sign into Vinchiana, turn right on
the small road immediately past the small bridge on the right, at a curve.
The *frantoio* is on the left after the road curves to the right.

This small private *frantoio* processes some of the area's best olives, including
Mansi Bernardini's (p 64). It operates traditional-style *macine* (stone wheels)
for grinding. After washing, the olives are ground to a pulp; the paste is
churned as it is heated slightly and indirectly before being spun in a centrifuge
to separate the oil and vegetable water from the mass. A final spin separates the
oil from the water. You can visit the *frantoio* during the season. If you phone
ahead, it is also possible to buy oil directly.

CHAPTER 3

Pistoia and Mount Abetone

*P*istoia is one of Tuscany's better kept secrets. Its walled center, with the handsome medieval *piazza del Duomo* at its heart, is lovely—yet it is less visited than Arezzo or Pisa. I like its human scale: you can walk comfortably from one side of town to the other. Beside the Duomo are interesting narrow streets, with the small marketplace, known as La Sala, selling foods of all kinds.

Pistoia is set against the Apennines, the mountain range that divides Tuscany from the north of Italy. Its highest mountain resort, on Mount Abetone (1,388 meters/4,555 feet), is popular for winter skiing. It is reached by a curvy road that was built in 1777 to link the territories of the Grand Dukes of Tuscany and Modena. In summer and fall the majestic forests are full of wild berries, mushrooms, and chestnuts: the area's most typical cuisine makes use of these "spontaneous" foods.

Anyone interested in spa towns should visit Montecatini Terme, a rather grand turn-of-the-century town built to accommodate those who "took the waters." The mineral salt-rich water's effects are (rapidly) purgative. To compensate, the town offers a host of biscuit, pastry, candy, and ice cream shops, restaurants, and wine bars.

Azienda Promozione Turistica
Piazza Duomo, 4
51100 Pistoia
0573 21622, fax 0573 34327

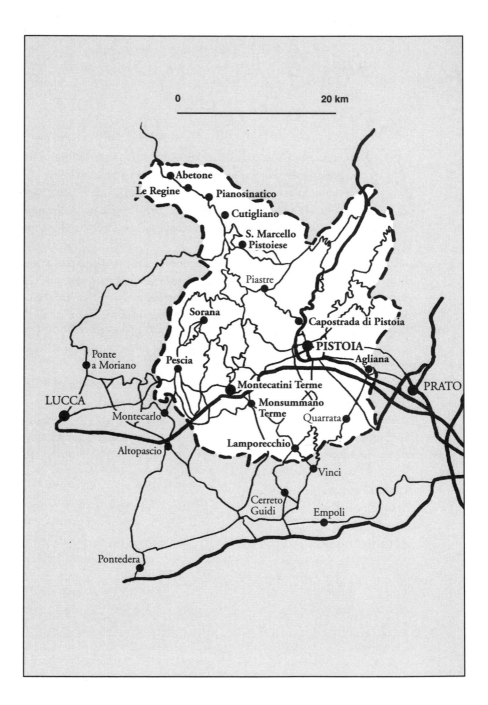

Town names in **bold** indicate towns that are included in this chapter.

ABETONE

IL CHICCO
PASTRY

Via Brennero, 494   51021   Abetone
TELEPHONE 0573 606869   OPEN 7:00-20:00   CLOSED Tuesday;
May, June, and October   CREDIT CARDS None
ENGLISH SPOKEN A little   DIRECTIONS The shop is on the lower level
of Via Brennero in the center of town.

This *pasticceria* is the young skiers' favorite. In winter, *bomboloni,* deep-fried
pastry balls, are filled with jam, chocolate, or custard and served piping hot.
In summer, the *gelato al cartoccio* is served with a fragrant hot fruit sauce.

AGLIANA

ROBERTO CATINARI
ARTE DEL
CIOCCOLATO
CHOCOLATE

Via Provinciale, 378   51031   Agliana
TELEPHONE 0574 718506   OPEN 8:00-13:00, 15:30-19:30
CLOSED Sunday; Monday in summer; Monday morning in winter;
August   CREDIT CARDS None   ENGLISH SPOKEN A little
DIRECTIONS The shop is on the main provincial Pistoia-Prato road
at Agliana.

Roberto Catinari is one of Tuscany's leading chocolate *maestri.* With his long
gray beard and twinkling eyes, he might have stepped out of the chocolate factory in a child's fairy tale. Trained in Switzerland, he started his own business in
Italy in 1974. He currently makes over one hundred different *cioccolatini,* filled
chocolates.

Catinari also specializes in liqueur- and wine-filled chocolates,
including Vin Santo and Chianti Classico. As you bite into them the sugar
crystal lining gives way to a warm, heady fullness that complements the dark
chocolate casing. Just be sure to bite on them once they are completely in your
mouth, not before!

Catinari starts with high-quality *couverture* chocolate from
Belgium, Switzerland, or France, with a cocoa solids content of up to 85 percent. He blends this with cocoa solids from the Ivory Coast or Ecuador for his
finest bitter chocolate. Milk chocolate comes from Lindt in Switzerland. Fine
Piemontese hazelnut paste is used in his *gianduja.*

I particularly liked Catinari's *torta di Bardalone*—a dense, rich
chocolate paste with an almost smoky depth to it, studded with almonds,
hazelnuts, and tangy candied orange and citron peel. This tribute to *panforte*
comes in discs of 500 grams, wrapped in crisp red cellophane.

At Eastertime, sculpted eggs can be commissioned to enclose a
surprise gift of the customer's choosing. The shop is inhabited by endearing
chocolate animals and unlikely "rusty" tools.

MACELLERIA   Via Selva, 313   Ferruccia   51030   Agliana
SALUMIFICIO MARINI TELEPHONE/FAX 0574 718119   OPEN 8:00-13:00; also Friday
MEAT: SALUMI   16:30-20:00 in summer; Friday and Saturday 16:30-19:30 in winter
                        CLOSED Sunday; two weeks in August   MAIL ORDER Yes
                        CREDIT CARDS Visa, MC ENGLISH SPOKEN A little
                        DIRECTIONS From the Prato Ovest exit on the A11 *autostrada*, go toward
                        Quarrata and Ferruccia 3 kms, then follow signs.

Marini's is the quintessential butcher's shop: spotlessly clean, odorless, with
walls of cheerful red and white tiles, and handsome marble counters. *Salumi*
are handmade: "There must be a separate room for each stage of the curing
procedure," explained Adriano Marini, "with designated temperature and
humidity levels. The freshly butchered meat goes in one end and travels
through them as it is 'transformed'—cut, salted, spiced, and dried."

Using local country pigs, the Marini family produce many
regional specialties. The refined prosciutto is aged for twelve months; a deep
salmon pink, it is only a hint saltier than its Parma cousin. The coarse-grained,
fennel-scented *finocchiona* is made of lean shoulder meat and fat from the jowl.
It is eaten very fresh. Many of Marini's *salumi* are available vacuum-packed for
easy transportation. The fresh meat counter showcases excellent beef, corn-fed
free-range Comet chickens (*pollo nostrale*), and tender milk-fed lamb.

Marini supplies some of Tuscany's best restaurants, whose owners like
to come personally to select their goods and to visit the affable family. It is not
unusual to find them there, late in the afternoon, sampling *salumi* with a glass
of good wine. Adriano's brother, Claudio Marini, has a butcher's shop at Via
Statale, 317 at Olmi, with the same hours.

ENOTECA   Via Provinciale 154/G   Spedalino   51031   Agliana
CARLO LAVURI   TELEPHONE 0574 751366/751125   FAX 0574 751366   OPEN 8:30-
WINE STORE   13:00, 15:30-20:00   CLOSED Sunday; two weeks in August
                     MAIL ORDER Yes   CREDIT CARDS Visa, MC, Amex
                     ENGLISH SPOKEN Yes   DIRECTIONS Take Via Provinciale, the main
                     road from Pistoia toward Prato. The shop is on the outskirts of
                     Spedalino, before you reach Agliana. It is on the ground floor
                     of a modern building, set back from the road, on the right.

"You need to educate your vineyard, as you would a child," declared Carlo
Lavuri, this wine store's friendly owner. "Things are changing fast in Tuscan
wines. The natural conditions were always there, but we are now making the
most of their potential—and tasting the results."

Lavuri's excitement for his subject is contagious. The clean-
lined modern shop is stocked with several hundred labels, most of them Italian,
many Tuscan. Tastings are held regularly; Lavuri is happy to discuss and recommend wines from the best big and small producers. There is a fine selection of
Tuscan estate-bottled olive oils. The shop also serves excellent coffee.

Also

Gelateria Bar Anisare. Via Roma, 93. 0574 718490.

This small *gelateria* makes very fine fresh fruit ices and gelati.
It is open late and has tables out on the shady sidewalk in summer.

CAPOSTRADA DI PISTOIA

GASTRONOMIA
CAPECCHI
SPECIALTY FOODS:
DELICATESSEN

Via Dalmazia, 445   51033   Capostrada di Pistoia
TELEPHONE 0573 400208   OPEN 7:00-13:30, 16:30-20:00
CLOSED Sunday; Saturday afternoon in summer; Wednesday afternoon
in winter; August   CREDIT CARDS None   ENGLISH SPOKEN A little
DIRECTIONS From the northwest corner of the town of Pistoia take Via
Dalmazia (SS 66) north toward Abetone and Bologna for 3.5 kms until it
crosses SS 64 at Capostrada. The shop is at that junction.

This gastronomic treasure trove has been run by the Capecchi family since
1908. They make their own bread, cakes, and ready-to-eat dishes, and sell many
of Tuscany's finest artisan-made foods.

Of the founder's grandchildren, Piero is the baker, while Stefano
and Cinzia make the prepared foods. Classic Tuscan breads include a rustic
focaccia all'olio di oliva, baked on oven bricks, and excellent *cantucci* biscuits
using a nineteenth-century recipe. The prepared foods change daily, but always
include *primi*—hearty soups or pastas—and a range of *secondi,* from stewed
baccalà (salt cod) to baked chick-peas or beans.

The display cases contain yellow bags of Martelli's excellent
pasta (p 123), pasta sauces from Grosseto, Florentine oils, goat cheeses from
Ville di Corsano (p 281), ash-cured Pienza pecorini, *lardo* from Colonnata
(p 37), great *salumi* from nearby Marini (p 72), and much more.

CUTIGLIANO

DA FAGIOLINO
RESTAURANT

Via Carega, 1   51024   Cutigliano
TELEPHONE 0573 68014   OPEN Lunch and dinner   CLOSED Tuesday
evening and Wednesday in winter; November   CREDIT CARDS Amex,
DC   ENGLISH SPOKEN Yes   RESERVATIONS Recommended
PRICE $$ DIRECTIONS In the village center

Da Fagiolino has been a keystone of local mountain fare for over fifty years.
This is a good place for a rustic country lunch after a hike in the woods.
Specializing in seasonal wild mushrooms, chestnuts, and game, the menu
also offers freshwater fish from nearby streams. As antipasti, the selection of
salumi di selvaggina may include cured wild boar or venison, and the *crostini
di funghi porcini* are flavorful and hearty. Porcini appear again in soups, risotti,
polenta or pasta sauces, and they come deep-fried. Main courses include roast

lamb, rabbit, and goat. The experienced waitresses are friendly and efficient, the tablecloths perfectly pressed, and the glassed-in terrace offers views of the neighboring hills.

Also

Latteria Tiziana Pagliai. Via Pacioni, 17. 0573 68280.

This small store stocks the Pistoiese Apennine's best offerings: exceptional sheep's milk ricotta and pecorini made near the shop by Anita Fini or Giovanni Ricci, local honeys and wild berry jams, dried herbs, flavored oils, and pasta sauces.

LAMPORECCHIO

**OLEIFICIO
COOPERATIVO
MONTALBANO
OLIVE MILL**

Via Giugnano, 135   51030   Lamporecchio
TELEPHONE 0573 803210/1   FAX 0573 803216   OPEN 8:00-12:00,
14:00-18:00   CLOSED Saturday afternoon; Sunday   MAIL ORDER Yes
DIRECT SALE Yes   CREDIT CARDS None   ENGLISH SPOKEN A little
FEATURES Guided tours and tastings by appointment   OTHER The
cooperative's other mill is in Via Beneventi, Vinci TEL/FAX 0571 56247
DIRECTIONS The *frantoio* is just outside Lamporecchio on the road
toward Larciano and Montecatini Terme.

This is the modernized *frantoio*, or olive mill, of a large cooperative with 1,850 members (*partitari*), who are offered a choice between the traditional grinding stone and modern temperature-controlled centrifuge systems. The stainless-steel machinery is easily cleaned and therefore more hygienic; temperatures for each phase may also be controlled. Batches are always analyzed and tested before being bottled or blended.

Under the name Montalbano Agricola Alimentare Toscana, the cooperative sells several grades of extra-virgin oil, extracted from 100 percent Tuscan olives with an acidity level below 0.5 percent. The cooperative runs another *frantoio* in the town of Vinci. Both have shops selling members' oils and may be visited.

LE REGINE

**L'ERBOLAIO
SPECIALTY FOODS:
FRUIT PRODUCTS**

Via Brennero, 112   Cechetto   51021   Abetone
TELEPHONE 0573 60514   OPEN 9:00-13:00, 14:00-17:00 (later
in August)   CLOSED Never   MAIL ORDER Yes
CREDIT CARDS None   ENGLISH SPOKEN No
DIRECTIONS   The shop is on SS 12 from San Marcello Pistoiese to
Abetone, at Cechetto, on the right as you go up.

This enterprising cooperative was formed in 1980 to process the wild berries growing in the magnificent mountain woods. About thirty people, mostly women, pick the wild raspberries, blueberries, and blackberries. They also gather mushrooms. Strawberries come from a local grower.

"The competition is fierce," one woman explained. "You have to get up at the crack of dawn and walk for miles to find the best fruit, or your neighbor will beat you to it."

The fruit is pesticide-free; no artificial colorants or preservatives are used. The jams contain fruit and sugar in equal parts. I liked some better than others: the blueberry *confettura* is very good, with tiny whole berries in a delicately flavored jelly; the dark red *fragola* jam is sweeter and contains nice whole fruits; the puréed blackberry jam is overcooked and oversweet. *Bibita al lampone* is an intensely fruity crimson raspberry drink. It is highly concentrated, but would be refreshing diluted with water or soda.

L'Erbolaio makes an unsweetened extract of blueberries. The local *mirtilli* (*Vaccinium myrtillus*) are smaller and more flavorful than their domestic counterparts. They apparently have curative powers; this pasteurized extract is a tonic for the eyesight and circulation, taken by the spoonful. The shop also provides gastronomic souvenirs: gift packages and miniatures are sold.

IL BAGGIOLO
SPECIALTY FOODS:
FRUIT PRODUCTS

Via Brennero, 355   Le Regine   51020   Abetone
TELEPHONE 0573 606644   OPEN 9:00-13:00, 14:30-18:30
CLOSED Wednesday   MAIL ORDER Yes   CREDIT CARDS None
ENGLISH SPOKEN A little   DIRECTIONS The shop is on SS 12 from San Marcello Pistoiese to Abetone, about 3.5 kms before Abetone, on the left going up.

Like l'Erbolaio (see above), this little shop features products made from wild berries. Specializing in fruit-flavored grappe, liqueurs, and jams, they also carry a handful of other local products: honey, pecorino, fruit biscuits, and hand-made soaps. For those who enjoy novelty items, fruit alcohols come in a rainbow of colors and flavors—raspberry, blueberry, rose petal, rue, walnut—in decorative bottles.

MONSUMMANO TERME

SLITTI CAFFÈ E
CIOCCOLATO
CHOCOLATE,
COFFEE, BAR

Via Francesca Sud, 240   51015   Monsummano Terme
TELEPHONE/FAX 0572 640240   OPEN 7:00-13:00, 15:00-20:00
CLOSED Sunday; August 10-20   MAIL ORDER Yes
CREDIT CARDS None   ENGLISH SPOKEN Yes   DIRECTIONS From the Montecatini exit of A11 *autostrada*, go to Monsummano Terme, then toward Fucecchio. Slitti is 1 km out of the center of Monsummano.

Take one step into this elegant marble shop and you will be overwhelmed by the aroma of fresh coffee and chocolate. The Slitti family has made its name selling select coffees, with a penchant for 100 percent pure Arabica (which naturally contains about 50 percent less caffeine). In 1988 the talented young

Andrea Slitti devoted himself to another, complementary, passion: chocolate.
In 1994 he won first prize for artistic presentation at the Grand Prix
International de la Chocolaterie in Paris.

Slitti's chocolate creations are a delight to the senses: beautifully
presented, their heady perfume precedes a rich taste experience. Slitti starts
from a bitter paste of 70 percent Central American and 30 percent African
cocoa, making refined *cioccolatini,* nut-centered *dragees,* imaginative Easter
eggs, bitter chocolate bars (the bitterest has 73 percent cocoa solids), and his
signature bittersweet coffee spoons. A cluster of cocoa-dusted "rusty" tools is
in homage to the local *maestro,* Roberto Catinari (p 71).

Grani d'Arabica, chocolate-covered coffee beans, are excellent.
Bite down through the shiny bittersweet chocolate to a barely resistant Arabica
bean, custom-toasted to be tender and aromatic. *Crema di nocciole,* a glossy
hazelnut-cocoa spread, is Slitti's refined answer to the Italian staple Nutella.
Andrea Slitti is charming and enthusiastic; a perfectionist who loves his work.
His shop merits a detour, whether to sample the handmade chocolates, to
admire the imaginative Christmas or Easter "themes," or to enjoy a fragrant
caffè at the bar.

MONTECATINI TERME

PASTICCERIA   Viale Grocco, 2   51016   Montecatini Terme
BARGILLI   TELEPHONE/FAX 0572 79459   OPEN 8:00-13:00, 15:30-20:00
PASTRY   CLOSED Monday in winter; January   MAIL ORDER Yes
                     CREDIT CARDS None   ENGLISH SPOKEN A little
                     DIRECTIONS The shop is just off Viale Verdi, in the town center.

Le cialde are Montecatini's most popular souvenir. The sweet crunchy biscuits
are a favorite antidote to the purgative effects of Montecatini's waters. Bargilli's
has been making them since 1936, when Paolo Bargilli's father bought the business. "*Era una cosa empirica.* It was a matter of trial and error," explains Paolo.
"Over time we modified and refined the *cialde* to arrive at the present biscuit."

Cialde are made by sandwiching crushed almonds and sugar
between two host-thin wafer disks. They are fat-free, containing only sugar,
flour, milk, eggs, and top-quality almonds from Puglia. The result is a brittle
golden disk like a medallion, just an eighth-inch thick. The wafer batter is
press-molded as it cooks and heated again to bind it with the filling.

PASTICCERIA Via Gorizia, 5 (Piazzetta Bicchierai)   51016   Montecatini Terme
DESIDERI TELEPHONE 0572 71088   OPEN 8:30-13:00, 16:00-20:00
PASTRY CLOSED Monday in winter; February   MAIL ORDER Yes
CREDIT CARDS None   ENGLISH SPOKEN No
DIRECTIONS In the town center

Montecatini is famous for two kinds of biscuits, *brigidini* and *cialde*. And two *pasticcerie* in town stand out as making the best: Desideri and Bargilli.

Stefano Desideri's grandfather was making *brigidini* (also claimed by the nearby town of Lamporecchio as their specialty) before 1900, and by 1918 had won prizes with them at international fairs. Crisp, wavy wafers delicately flavored with anice, the classic *brigidini* are baked for only a few seconds and are light as air. They contain sugar, eggs, flour, and extract of aniseed. Once made by hand, they are now made on machines designed by Mr. Desideri that are so secret he did not want me to see them. If kept in airtight containers, the fragile biscuits last for several months; they are traditionally served with ice cream or soft fruit desserts. Desideri also makes a very good version of the *cialde* (see page 76), sold loose or in attractive tins with art nouveau decorations.

VINERIA DA Viale Verdi, 35   51016   Montecatini Terme
GIOVANNI TELEPHONE 0572 910300   OPEN 9:30-13:00, 17:30-1:00 a.m.
WINE BAR CLOSED Monday   CREDIT CARDS Visa, MC, Amex
ENGLISH SPOKEN Yes   DIRECTIONS On the main street in the
town center

The old-fashioned, charming Vineria was once an outlet for Fattoria Antinori, one of Tuscany's principal wine-making families. It is now run by Giovanni Rotti, a key figure on Montecatini's gastronomic scene (see next entry). Fine wines are available by the glass or bottle, plus snacks.

Also

Enoteca Da Giovanni. Via Garibaldi, 25/27. TELEPHONE/FAX 0572 71695.

Giovanni Rotti's *Enoteca* comprises a high-class restaurant with creative cooking on one side and a less formal *enoteca* serving hearty Tuscan food on the other. There are great wines to be had in both.

Pasticceria Giovannini. Corso Matteotti, 4. 0572 79848.

This great sixties-style bar is the place in town for a coffee, fine pastry, or *cioccolatino*—a filled chocolate. Signor Giovannini is one of the area's *maestri* at making beautiful chocolates.

FAGIOLI DI SORANA—TUSCANY'S FINEST BEANS

Tuscany is famous for its *fagioli* (beans), and its most celebrated are the pearly white *fagioli di Sorana.* These flat, oval, shiny beans are remarkably thin-skinned, and they have long been a favorite delicacy of the rich and famous who visit Montecatini Terme, just a few kilometers from the village for which they are named. They are thought to be descended from the *bianco di Spagna,* a larger, white, Spanish bean.

Valdo Verreschi, author of a book on the beans, explained: "The origins of our bean is shrouded in mystery. Legend has it that, centuries ago, a caravan of pilgrims was passing along this valley on its way to Rome, when a big storm broke out. A sack split, and the beans were scattered and washed up along the small River Pescia. Its silty bed proved a perfect breeding ground for the beans, which rot in heavier soils." Indeed, to this day, the *fagioli* are watered using small irrigation canals of river water, *le gore.*

Sorana is a tiny village set high up above the river valley, and today only a handful of country people still grow the beans. They are cultivated in grooves (*solchi*) and trained up high poles. The small beans are partially dried while still on the plant; the pods are then removed.

"Once, these beans were considered a *brutto legume*—the poorest of poor foods," Verreschi went on. "Today, they satisfy the most refined palates." The traditional way to cook them is in a wine flask: the *fiasco* is part-filled with beans and water, and seasoned with oil, sage, and salt. The bottle is loosely corked and placed beside wood embers for at least three hours.

PESCIA

RISTORANTE CECCO
RESTAURANT

Via Forti, 96/98   51017   Pescia
TELEPHONE 0572 477955   OPEN Lunch and dinner
CLOSED Monday; two weeks in January; July   CREDIT CARDS Visa,
MC, Amex   ENGLISH SPOKEN A little   FEATURES Outdoor terrace
RESERVATIONS Recommended at weekends   PRICE $$$
DIRECTIONS In the town center. The restaurant can be entered from the
riverfront or from Piazza Mazzini.

Cecco is a wonderful place to sample Pistoia's gastronomic specialties. The menu always includes a few hard-to-find dishes and features locally grown produce, like Pescia's renowned jumbo green asparagus. The attractive dining room has a high vaulted stone ceiling with unadorned ochre walls, and the service is great: the waiters have worked there for years and are proud of the food they serve.

Antipasti include tasty *salumi,* chicken liver *crostini,* and the exceptional *fagioli di Sorana* (p 78), fine-skinned local beans topped here with salty shavings of *bottarga di tonno*—sun-dried tuna roe.

Cecco is famous for cooking mushrooms; in early summer fresh porcini begin to appear in soups and pasta dishes, alone, or with meats. Homemade potato-herb gnocchi (*della casa*) are delicious, topped with sliced raw porcini, shaved Parmesan, melted butter, and wild marjoram. In autumn rare *ovoli* (*Amanita caesarea*) are gathered in woods nearby and served raw or with spaghetti. Winter is truffle season.

Cecco's *pollastrino al mattone* is popular: half a local chicken is seasoned, weighted with bricks to flatten it, and cooked on a griddle, giving a crispy browned exterior and moist lean meat. Cecco's *fritto misto* of deep-fried mixed meats and vegetables is prepared in a feather-light, crunchy batter—the finest I encountered. The more adventurous should try the local specialty, *cioncia alla Pesciatina:* diced beef muzzle in an aromatic tomato sauce.

Desserts are nicely presented: mixed wild berries (*frutti di bosco*) come in a little tart with a mascarpone filling or are stewed with sweetened white wine and spooned hot over ice cream. The wine list is almost exclusively Tuscan.

PIANOSINATICO

SILVIO LA STORIA A TAVOLA RESTAURANT	Via Brennero, 181-183 51020 Pianosinatico
	TELEPHONE 0573 629204 OPEN Lunch and dinner
	CLOSED Tuesday; a week in spring; two weeks in October
	CREDIT CARDS Visa, MC, Amex ENGLISH SPOKEN Yes
	RESERVATIONS Recommended, especially on weekends PRICE $$
	DIRECTIONS The restaurant is between Cutigliano and Abetone, in the village of Pianosinatico.

Eating at Silvio's merits a detour. After a steep but scenic drive up the mountain, you reach the small restaurant in the sleepy village of Pianosinatico.

Inside, in the little dining room to the right past the bar, a nice mix of local workers and visiting food lovers eat at the restaurant's few tables. The service is informal but attentive: the waiter announces each dish with pride. Silvio often comes in from the kitchen, jovial in his tall chef's hat, to confer with the customers who have traveled to eat there.

An ex-medieval history professor, culinary historian, and self-taught cook, Silvio Zanni ran a wine bar in Prato, a restaurant in Paris, and a trattoria on this mountain before opening this restaurant with his partner, Andrea Vannucci, in 1992. Working only with seasonal ingredients, Silvio offers an affordable tasting menu of five different vegetable-based *primi* each day, followed by simple meat *secondi* for those who want them. The menu changes daily. A wine connoisseur, Silvio suggests wines to accompany each dish, but there is also an excellent *carta dei vini.*

An early summer *primi* menu consisted of *passato di piselli e porcini,* a warm puréed soup of sweet fresh peas and porcini, which had a woodsy undertone from the mushrooms; handmade *ricotta tortelli,* tangy from the local sheep's cheese and set off by a salty vegetable broth and a sprig of sage; spaghetti with red onions, a deceptively simple combination of sweet and sharp tastes and textures; *gnocchi al tartuffo,* fresh potato gnocchi with some resistance to the bite, coated with a creamy sauce and slivers of pungent black truffle; and *farfalle con bietole e basilico,* pasta bows stained pink by sweet fresh beets with a peppery counterpoint in the basil leaves. Each vegetable's flavor is experienced fully, married to the pasta shape that suits it best.

The subtitle of the restaurant, *la storia a tavola,* means "history at the table," and Silvio often exploits his culinary knowledge by incorporating recipes and food combinations from past eras of Italian cooking.

PISTOIA

CONFETTERIA   Piazza San Francesco d'Assisi, 43   51100   Pistoia
CORSINI   TELEPHONE 0573 20138   OPEN 8:00-13:00, 16:00-19:00
CANDY   CLOSED Sunday; Saturday afternoon in summer; two weeks in August
    MAIL ORDER Yes   CREDIT CARDS None   ENGLISH SPOKEN Yes
    DIRECTIONS The piazza is in the northwest corner of the town, within the old walls.

No Italian baptism, christening, or marriage would be complete without *confetti,* hard white candies that are tied into tulle bundles and given away to commemorate the occasion or thrown like rice at newlyweds for good luck. This custom has very old roots: *confetti* were first brought to Venice around 1100 by Far East traders. During carnival, noble families threw *confetti* from their palace windows to the populace below. Good *confetti* did not shatter on impact.

Pistoia's *confetti* are unusual. Instead of a smooth almond shape, they have a bumpy surface, like pieces of knobbly white coral. Corsini offers *confetti a riccio* with various "souls": the hard candy exterior contains a firm core of chocolate, nuts, candied fruit, or aniseed. The coating procedure takes over ten hours and is a well-kept trade secret. They are available from the unfussy shop by loose weight or in gift boxes, and they may be custom ordered.

Corsini's expertise is well known: they were commissioned to re-create sixteenth-century blue *confetti* for the film *Casanova*. The old-fashioned laboratory and shop still houses fascinating early candy-making machinery.

Also

Pistoia, a beautiful little city, has at its heart (near the Duomo) a square called La Sala. Six mornings a week the food market is held here; there are also a number of permanent food stores in the buildings that surround the square.

SAN MARCELLO PISTOIESE

S.A.M. Piazza Cini, 10   51028   San Marcello Pistoiese
SPECIALTY FOODS TELEPHONE/FAX 0573 630535   OPEN 7:30-13:00, 16:30-19:00
CLOSED Sunday in winter; Wednesday afternoon
CREDIT CARDS None   ENGLISH SPOKEN A little
DIRECTIONS The shop is in the village's main square.

This minisupermarket stocks all the staples, but it is worth visiting for its selected artisan foods. S.A.M. stands for Società Agricola Montana, a cooperative of mountain farmers and shepherds. Fresh cheeses are exceptional, especially the pecorini and the fine-textured, fragrant sheep's ricotta. There are mountain *salumi*, local vegetables, and mushrooms and berries from the surrounding woods, plus great honeys, pasta, and herb teas.

Also

Gelateria Bar Terrazza. Via Gavinana, 7a. 0573 630150.
This ice cream parlor and bar is on the bridge in the town center. It has a large outdoor terrace and makes fresh gelati using seasonal fruits.

VINCI

Lunardi at Vinci Frantoio. Villa del Ferrale. 50059 Vinci. 0573 25285.
Lunardi, one of Pistoia's oldest olive oil establishments, has recently moved to Vinci, taking over an existing *frantoio* to produce extra-virgin oils from Tuscan olives. Lunardi also specializes in "aromatized" oils flavored with chili or green peppercorns, which are sold in decorative bottles.

CHAPTER 4

Firenze, Prato, and Their Provinces

The great Renaissance city of Firenze (Florence) should need no introduction: it is the cultural heart of Tuscany, admired by everyone who visits it. From a food lover's point of view, the city and its surrounding provinces have much to offer.

Despite mass tourism, Firenze has maintained the integrity of its food markets and grocery shops—few tourists do much cooking. There are still market stalls selling homegrown produce from the Tuscan countryside and hand-picked *erbe* (wild herbs), for adding a bitter note to salads and vegetable dishes. The city still has several *fiaschetterie*, although many have disappeared; these unpretentious wine bars took their name from the straw-covered Chianti *fiasco* and offer a glass of wine and a *panino* of locally cured salty ham or pecorino cheese. Of course, there are also grand and fine restaurants for tasting the region's best foods and wines.

Some of these great wines are produced within the province of Firenze: Chianti Rùfina is a small but excellent wine zone only a short distance to the city's east; Carmignano is another to its west. Chianti Classico, some of which is also within this province, has its own chapter (p 177).

The hills above Pontassieve contain an exceptional organic bakery; Prato is renowned for its great *biscotti;* fine extra-virgin olive oil is produced all around the area. Firenze is a wonderful starting point for exploring the foods and wines of Tuscany's varied countryside.

Azienda Promozione Turistica
Via Cavour, 1R
50129 Firenze
055 290832/3, fax 055 2760383

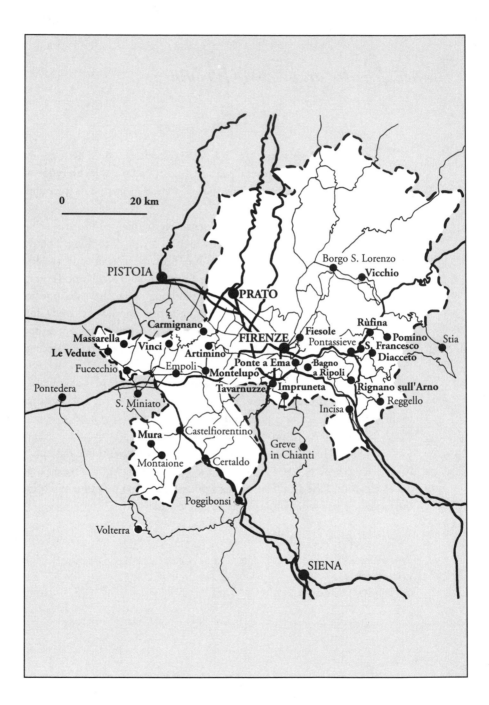

Town names in **bold** indicate towns that are included in this chapter.

ARTIMINO

DA DELFINA
RESTAURANT

Artimino 50042 Carmignano Firenze
TELEPHONE 055 8718119, 8718074   FAX 055 8718175   OPEN Lunch
and dinner   CLOSED Sunday for dinner; Monday; August
CREDIT CARDS None   ENGLISH SPOKEN Yes
FEATURES Outdoor terrace   RESERVATIONS Necessary
PRICE $$$ DIRECTIONS The restaurant is at the entrance to Artimino,
before the villa.

Da Delfina's summer terrace overlooks the beautiful Medicean villa Artimino and its vineyards. The restaurant offers some of the most wonderful and authentic food in Tuscany. "There is an increasing demand for a return to the simple rustic dishes of our past," explained Carlo Cioni, the restaurant's owner. "We have always tried to keep these peasant dishes alive." Ingredients and produce are local or wild, gathered in the woods and fields.

When I arrived in early spring, the elderly Signora Delfina was hunched over the kitchen table, painstakingly cleaning freshly picked wild herbs. Lunch began with a bright green *sformato di rapa*—unmolded rape soufflé. It was soft and light and came with a sage-scented purée of beans. I tasted crisp fried *malva* (mallow) leaves, a *crostino* of strong liver, polenta topped with cheese, and a *Parmigiano* of eggplant and herbs. But the most unusual, most exceptional dish was a Florentine Renaissance recipe of baby goats' tongues cooked in *agro dolce*—a sweet and sour sauce with pine nuts and raisins. The meat was tender and delicate, the sauce complex and intriguing. I can think of no other restaurant that would have proposed such a dish, nor pulled it off with such artistry.

Homemade *taglierini* were thin noodles dressed with an egg sauce of wild asparagus tips. Delfina's *ribollita* is recooked in a frying pan: the substantial vegetable and herb soup thickened with bread is browned at the edges and drizzled with fragrant green oil. A stew of veal and potatoes was ochre, the potatoes a reddish orange. Young lamb chops were grilled over a wood fire, topped with bay leaves, and accompanied by white beans that had been fried or roasted—they were as crunchy as soft nuts.

Dessert was a soft cream mousse and a slice of *ghirighio*, a thin cake of chestnut flour studded with pine nuts and rosemary that was the finest I have had. A thoughtfully selected Tuscan wine list completes this feast of the senses.

ARTIMINO
WINE

Viale Papa Giovanni XXIII, 1   50040   Carmignano   Firenze
TELEPHONE 055 8792051/2   FAX 055 8718080   OPEN Visits by appointment only   CLOSED Weekends   DIRECT SALE No STOCKIST Artimino's wines are available from shops in the village of Artimino: Via Cinque Martiri, 3   ENGLISH SPOKEN Yes OTHER Hotel, restaurant, convention center   DIRECTIONS The villa is at the top of the hill, clearly visible. The *cantina* is below the town.

Artimino is called the "Villa of the Hundred Chimneys," for the late sixteenth-century Medicean villa is adorned with a vast collection of them. The villa, whose interior is not open to the public, is part of a large estate: 730 hectares (1,800 acres), of which 80 (197) are vineyards. The villa is rather grand and impersonal, but worth seeing—and it offers great views.

The winery has recently invested in modern cellars located at the bottom of the hill. "These *cantine* may not be very poetic—we have enough poetry up on the hill—but better wines are certainly made this way," affirmed Giuseppe Poggi, Artimino's director. Artimino's first vintage using the new equipment was 1993, and the recent wines are already showing improvement. The most important wine is Carmignano DOCG Riserva Medicea, which is only made in great years. It contains 65 percent Sangiovese, with 15 percent each of Cabernet and Canaiolo, the remaining divided between other red grapes. It spends two years in wood. Other wines include the reasonably priced Barco Reale (Carmignano's "younger brother"), and Carmignano's unique rosé, Vin Ruspo. See also Carmignano, p 87.

BAGNO A RIPOLI

CENTANNI
RESTAURANT

Via di Centanni, 7   50012   Bagno a Ripoli   Firenze
TELEPHONE 055 630122   FAX 055 630533   OPEN Lunch and dinner CLOSED Saturday for lunch, Sunday; August   CREDIT CARDS Visa, MC, Amex   ENGLISH SPOKEN Yes   FEATURES Summer terrace RESERVATIONS During summer and on weekends   PRICE $$$ OTHER Apartments available for holiday rentals DIRECTIONS Centanni is clearly signposted from Bagno a Ripoli. Look for the yellow signs.

Silvana Bianchi is a lovely woman who started her restaurant over thirty years ago. Centanni is situated in the hills outside Firenze, amid silvery green olive groves. A large dining room has tall picture windows. Signora Bianchi sees to the flowers and plans the daily menu. Everything, from the bread sticks to the pasta, is handmade by local women who work in the kitchen; if you arrive early for lunch, you can watch them fill the ravioli.

Cappelletti di piccione are pasta ovals stuffed with subtly flavored minced pigeon. Spinach and ricotta ravioli, of the same fine pasta, are topped with a savory meat sauce. They also serve several fresh country soups.

Centanni's signature main course is not particularly Tuscan. *Pollo Centanni* is a breaded chicken breast topped with porcini mushrooms, prosciutto, and cheese. There are grilled steaks and chops, assorted fried meats, and a good range of vegetable dishes. Desserts, too, are homemade. I sampled a rich pineapple upside down cake and a warm apple tart that was thankfully not too sweet. The well-priced wine list is highly informative; there is a good group of Tuscans and drinkable house wines.

CARMIGNANO

TENUTA DI CAPEZZANA WINE, OLIVE OIL

Via Capezzana, 100   Seano   50040   Carmignano   Firenze   TELEPHONE 055 8706005, 8706091   FAX 055 8706673   OPEN 8:30-12:30, 14:30-18:30; *cantina* visits and tastings by appointment only   CLOSED Saturday and Sunday   CREDIT CARDS Visa, Amex   DIRECT SALE Yes   ENGLISH SPOKEN Yes   OTHER Holiday apartments for rent; cooking courses for professionals   DIRECTIONS From the Prato Ovest exit on A11 *autostrada*, go toward Seano and Carmignano. The winery is signposted from there.

Located in the hills between Firenze and Prato, Tenuta di Capezzana is synonymous with one of Tuscany's smallest but most distinguished wine denominations, Carmignano DOCG. "Carmignano's history is fascinating: wine was made here by the Etruscans," recounted Ugo Contini Bonacossi. "And in 1396 Ser Lapo Mazzei (p 188), a notary, documented paying a high sum for it." The Medicis were also fond of Carmignano's wines, and in a 1716 decree they delimited the boundaries of its production area. "Under Fascism, estates were pressured to produce quantity rather than quality," he continued. "And even in the fifties and sixties our wines were lumped in with the surrounding Chianti producers. The unique qualities of Carmignano's wines were being lost in the shuffle." After a long, almost single-handed battle, Contini Bonacossi was able to reestablish an autonomy for his area's wines, gaining DOC status in 1975 and DOCG in 1990. They were also the first Tuscan denomination to allow what the locals called "the French grape"—Cabernet —in the blend of Carmignano Rosso DOCG. Cabernet had been planted here since the time of Caterina de' Medici, who brought it from France.

Carmignano is an elegant, well-balanced red wine made in "normal" and reserve versions. Barco Reale has the same grape varieties, but is made to drink young, as its tannins are not bitter. Contini Bonacossi described it as "never too young, never too old." Ghiaie della Furba is Capezzana's acclaimed super-Tuscan of 70 percent Cabernet and 30 percent Merlot. Other wines include Vin Ruspo—Carmignano's particular rosé—Chianti Montalbano, and Vin Santo.

Capezzana is itself a beautiful villa built for one of the Medici daughters. It has a maze of underground cellars, a *vinsantaia,* courtyards of lemon trees, and a fine *orciaia*—the room in which the large terra-cotta urns of olive oil were stored. The lovely Contini Bonacossi family welcomes interested visitors by prior arrangement.

FATTORIA **IL POGGIOLO** WINE	Via Pistoiese, 90 50042 Carmignano Firenze TELEPHONE 055 8711242 FAX 055 8711252 OPEN 8:00-12:00, 13:00- 17:00; tastings and visits by appointment CLOSED Saturday and Sunday (unless by appointment) CREDIT CARDS None DIRECT SALE Yes ENGLISH SPOKEN Yes DIRECTIONS The winery is on the road between Carmignano and Seano, 1 km from Carmignano.

Giovanni Cianchi Baldazzi has one of Carmignano's larger estates, with over 30 hectares (74 acres) of vineyards. Traditional methods are used for producing Carmignano DOCG. Giovanni's son, Giuseppe, is the estate's young *enotecnico*—wine technician.

Giuseppe told the story of Vin Ruspo, a rosé made from the same grapes as Carmignano's red wine. In the days of sharecropping, the peasants used to secretly draw off a couple of demijohns of must while the grapes were being transported from the vineyards to the landowner's farm. This must was left to ferment, and the resulting wine, of a light ruby color, was called Vin Ruspo. It was traditionally drunk during the corn harvest. Vin Ruspo now forms part of the Carmignano DOC's list of wines.

DIACCETO

FORNO A LEGNA **"LA TORRE"** BREAD: ORGANIC	Via Santoni, 3 Diacceto 50060 Pelago Firenze TELEPHONE 055 8326635 OPEN Monday, Wednesday, Friday 8:00- 20:00; Thursday, Saturday 8:00-14:00 CLOSED Tuesday; Sunday CREDIT CARDS None STOCKIST La Raccolta in Florence p 93 ENGLISH SPOKEN Yes DIRECTIONS From Pontassieve take SS 70 for the Consuma and Bibbiena. Via Santoni runs parallel to the main road through Diacceto. There are signs for the bakery in the village.

In my opinion, Stefano Borselli makes the best bread in Tuscany. This remarkable young man left a career in electronics to join a Gandhian-style pacifist group in the 1980s, and he became increasingly interested in the organic and "alternative" movements.

"I thought it over," he explained simply, "and decided that the best, most useful thing I could do for my community was to bake bread. In the old days bread was the fundamental basis of everyday life. Now it has been reduced to the role of a *soprammobile*—a decorative ornament—in our society. But I believe that this can change." In 1985 he started baking, and in 1989 he opened this wonderful bakery, high on a hill to the east of Firenze. Specialist artisans built his large wood-burning oven—free of lead or iron. Borselli, who is helped by his parents and wife, studied different enzymes and their effects on flours to develop three types of natural yeasts.

The first, for use with high-fiber whole-grain flours, is made of water and rye flour. *Pane Toscano,* Tuscan unsalted bread, requires a less acid starter made from water, rye, and wheat flours. The third type of yeast, used only for sweet dough, is made from fresh fruit soaked in water for a week until it ferments. His *pasticceria* is given very long raising times (up to twenty-four hours) in order to sterilize the acids in the doughs. These yeasts also give the baked products an extended shelf life. All his flours and other ingredients are certified organic. Many of the bakery's flours are stone ground.

I sampled several of Borselli's breads—and was knocked out by them. His large round of unsalted Tuscan bread, weighing 1 kg/2.2 lbs, has a crunchy golden crust and the flavor of fresh grain; it is perfect for Tuscany's famous bread soups. The bakery also produces an interesting range of whole wheat and complex breads. One compact loaf was topped with sesame seeds and packed with olives, sweet peppers, herbs, and seeds. *Pane di S. Egidio* is delicious, a cross between a fruit cake and a savory bread, thick with figs, almonds, raisins, chopped nuts (including some wonderfully fresh walnuts), and a pinch of *peperoncino*—hot chili pepper. Borselli also makes breads for special and allergic diets. Anyone making the trip to visit this talented young baker will not be disappointed.

FIESOLE

TRATTORIA TULLIO **RESTAURANT**	Ontignano, 48 50014 Fiesole Firenze TELEPHONE 055 697354 OPEN Lunch and dinner CLOSED Wednesday CREDIT CARDS Visa, MC, Amex ENGLISH SPOKEN Yes RESERVATIONS Weekends and summer for terrace dining room PRICE $$ DIRECTIONS Go up through Fiesole and after 2 km pass Au Petit Bois. Take the next right toward Montebeni. The restaurant is signposted from there.

From Fiesole there is a picturesque drive to this restaurant through pine woods and olive groves. This country trattoria has a panoramic dining room; in summer its many windows are opened. As is often the case in restaurants popular with Italians, the simplest dishes are the best. A modest slice of Tuscan bread toasted over an open fire, rubbed with garlic, and topped with hot *cannellini* beans, fruity olive oil, and pepper is delicious. Tagliatelle with meat sauce or thick vegetable soups are good first courses.

Fritto misto—deep-fried meats and vegetables—is a trattoria favorite. Tullio's is good: in spring a light crispy batter encased sliced red onion, eggplant, and tender artichokes, as well as chunks of rabbit, chicken and lamb.

Other meats are grilled over wood embers, *alla brace.* Desserts are homemade, the house wines unpretentious, and the service experienced but not formal.

FIRENZE

FIRENZE—FLORENCE

In the city of Firenze (Florence), street addresses are numbered with two systems simultaneously—one for domestic buildings (black numbers), the other for businesses (red, or *rosso*), which have an "R" after them.

IL FORNAIO GALLI
BREAD

Via Matteo Palmieri, 24R; Via Faenza, 39R; Via Guicciardini, 3
50122   Firenze
TELEPHONE 055 2480336   FAX 055 2479705   OPEN 7:30-14:00, 17:00-19:45   CLOSED Wednesday afternoon in winter, Saturday afternoon in summer   CREDIT CARDS None   ENGLISH SPOKEN A little

This bakery, with its warm wood interior, produces and sells an extensive range of regional Italian breads at three locations, including the Cantinetta dei Verrazzano (p 91). The Galli family makes great Tuscan classics: large rounds of unsalted *pane sciocco* use selected flours and natural yeasts. The choice of flat breads, *schiacciata,* is impressive. The plain has a good crisp crust, baked until golden brown, but my favorite is the whole-wheat variety: the thin bread is bran-flecked, its crunchy crust sprinkled with coarse sea salt and drizzled with fruity olive oil. It is great with cheese or by itself and is best eaten fresh. They bake it in big slabs, and cut off and weigh as much as you want. *Pasqualina* tarts are stuffed with green, creamy spinach filling or savory ham and cheese. Pizzas also sold by weight, are topped with delicate potato and rosemary or traditional tomato. *Pan di romarino* is a glazed bread roll between sweet and salty, whose airy dough is laced with aromatic rosemary and raisins.

Desserts include biscuits, tarts, and *schiacciata alla Fiorentina,* a layer of moist, orange-flavored cake dusted with icing sugar. It is sold plain or split and filled with whipped cream, vanilla, or chocolate custard. I was impressed by the patient serving staff, who took time with tourists asking for just a handful of *grissini* or one bread roll.

CANTINETTA DEI   Via dei Tavolini, 18/20R   50100   Firenze
VERRAZZANO   TELEPHONE 055 268590; Winery 055 854243   FAX 055 295189
BREAD, WINE BAR,   OPEN 8:00-21:00   CLOSED Sunday   CREDIT CARDS Visa, MC, Amex
COFFEE SHOP, SALUMI   DIRECT SALE Yes   ENGLISH SPOKEN Yes   RESERVATIONS None
accepted   DIRECTIONS Off Via dei Calzaiuoli

The Cantinetta puts four expert producers of foods and wine under one roof—
and it works. A nicely styled ground-floor position between the Duomo and
the Ponte Vecchio gives each partner a sales point within the whole.

Savor an excellent *caffè* or centrifuged fruit juice at the Piansa coffee
counter (p 92), choose from Forno Galli's delicious breads (see last entry),
or sit and eat a piece of cake or freshly baked focaccia—I loved the one stuffed
with peas—made regularly in the wood oven.

The adjacent room features Falorni of Greve's *salumi* (p 191)
and the fine wines of Chianti's Castello di Verrazzano. From 3 p.m. until closing
there is waiter service at the tables for snacks or wines. The "Specialità Verrazzano" was a beautiful plate of open-faced sandwiches on special Galli breads
(the spiced *pandivino* was reminiscent of French *pain d'épices*). Falorni toppings
include: peppered wild boar sausage, coarse-grained *finocchiona* with fennel
seeds, *soppressata* (head cheese) flavored with lemon peel, and pecorino and pear.

If you don't have time to visit the Verrazzano Castello at Greve,
you can sample the wines here or buy them to take out. In addition to the
Chianti Classico and its powerful Riserva, there are two pure Sangiovese super-
Tuscan wines to try: Sassello and Particolare. New Yorkers will be interested to
note that the Castello was explorer Giovanni da Verrazzano's birthplace—
namesake of the Verrazzano Narrows bridge.

CAFFELLATTE   Via degli Alfani, 39R   50121   Firenze
CAFÉ   TELEPHONE 055 2478878   OPEN 9:00-24:00   CLOSED Sunday
CREDIT CARDS None   ENGLISH SPOKEN Yes
DIRECTIONS Off Via della Pergola

Six little tables, a bunch of wildflowers in a jar, a handsome old marble
counter—Caffellatte is an easy-going place to have a coffee while you read the
paper or to sit over tea with a friend. In what was once a butcher's shop and
then later a *latteria* (dairy), Eleonora and her mother, Vanna Casati, offer a
peaceful, welcoming respite from the pressures of city life.

There are organic teas to choose from and Arabica coffee from
Nicaragua sold by the CTM cooperative, bypassing the multinationals and their
markup. The women make good desserts: carrot and almond or apple cake,
Tarte Bretonne (a kind of baked custard), and some sugarless and other special-
diet cakes. The *caffellatte* comes in large bowls and is great for breakfast with
toast and jam.

CAFFETTERIA PIANSA   Borgo Pinti, 18R   50121   Firenze
CAFÉ   TELEPHONE 055 2342362   OPEN 7:30-2:00 a.m.   CLOSED Sunday;
                         August   CREDIT CARDS None   ENGLISH SPOKEN Yes
                         DIRECTIONS Off Via di Mezzo

This recently opened, handsome *caffetteria* is a good inner-city outlet for Pietro Staderini's Piansa coffee (see below). You can buy selected coffees by weight, including Piansa's pure Arabica blend, "The Magnificent Ten." The large bar serves coffee, tea, and drinks all day, plus sandwiches, salads, pastries, *primi,* and snacks that may be eaten at the tables.

MORÈ   Lungarno Archibusieri, 6R   50122   Firenze
CHOCOLATE   TELEPHONE 055 2382411   FAX 055 677559   OPEN 10:00-19:30
                  CLOSED Monday in winter   CREDIT CARDS Visa, MC
                  ENGLISH SPOKEN Yes   DIRECTIONS Along the Arno between the Ponte
                  Vecchio and the Uffizi

Chocolate is a seasonal food in Italy: once summer sets in, chocolate production ceases until autumn (a bit tough on chocoholics). So, to taste some of Firenze's best, you must come between September and May. In summer this shop sells candies, pure fruit jellies, cookies, and ice cream, which are fine, but less compelling than its chocolates.

This shop is named for Giuseppe Morè, a nineteenth-century Piedmontese baker and chocolate maker. His company in Piedmont still produces fine chocolates, supplying this and other shops. Assorted dark and milk *cioccolatini* have interesting fillings: the orange and lemon centers are refreshingly subtle; using dried fruit "powders" with a pastelike consistency, they were not over-sweet. A fresh-tasting walnut purée complemented the bitterness of its *couverture* chocolate. Morè uses high-quality Belgian and French *fondente* (dark chocolate) for the casings. As one would expect, the hazelnut fillings are excellent. The marriage between the *nocciola* and chocolate has long been a Piedmontese specialty, and their crunchy, toasted nut and chocolate fillings put commercial Baci to shame. Andrea Picconi, the shop's manager, will wrap them in pretty gift boxes or sell them loose—even just one or two—for anyone in need of a quick chocolate fix.

DROGHERIA PIANSA   Viale Europa, 126-128R   50126   Firenze
COFFEE   TELEPHONE 055 6532117, 6531987   FAX 055 645774   OPEN 8:00-
                       13:00, 16:00-20:00   CLOSED Sunday, Wednesday afternoon in winter,
                       Saturday afternoon in summer; holidays in summer
                       CREDIT CARDS None   ENGLISH SPOKEN Yes   DIRECTIONS Viale
                       Europa is south of the Arno, south east of central Firenze, near Badia
                       a Ripoli and the Firenze Sud *autostrada* entrance.

Piansa is Firenze's leading coffee roaster, with outlets all over the city. This is its "home" base and southern Firenze's favorite coffee bar. The double-fronted store has a long counter serving Piansa coffees, drinks, great sandwiches, and pastries. There are also a few tables. The other storefront carries Piansa's extensive range of coffees, roasted by Pietro Staderini in nearby Ponte a Ema. These are sold as beans or ground to order. The shop also stocks teas, candies, and assorted specialty foods.

Piansa's most popular blend is the Magnificent Ten, *I Magnifici Dieci,* blended from ten pure Arabica coffees, including Jamaica Blue Mountain, Hawaii Kona Kay, San Domingo Barahona, and Ethiopia Mocca Yrga. These and other premium coffees, including decaffeinated, are also sold singly. Piansa is one of the food artisans participating in the Cantinetta dei Verrazzano (see p 91) and has a café in Borgo Pinti, 18R.

FIRENZE'S ORGANIC PRODUCE MARKETS

La Fierucola is a large organic fair held twice yearly, in September and December, in Piazza della Santissima Annunziata. La Fierucolina is a smaller organic market held on the third Sunday of each month in Piazza Santo Spirito.

ASSOCIAZIONE CULTURALE "LA RACCOLTA" HEALTH FOODS

Via Leopardi, 10 (downstairs)   50121   Firenze
TELEPHONE/FAX 055 2479068   OPEN 10:00-14:00, 16:00-19:30
CLOSED Monday morning, Saturday afternoon, Sunday
CREDIT CARDS None   ENGLISH SPOKEN Yes   OTHER Courses and seminars   DIRECTIONS Via Leopardi is one block north of Piazza Beccaria. La Raccolta is in the cellar of a residential building. Go in main entrance and down stairs on left.

The sure measure of a health food store is the freshness of its organic produce. In Italy, where the concept of eating chemical-free foods is sadly still largely unknown, it is a struggle for those few promoting the organic cause. Sometimes the produce, necessarily more expensive than its treated counterparts, looks too worn out to buy. Not so the range of fresh fruits and vegetables on display at this cheerful shop, located in the bowels of a residential palazzo not far from the Sant' Ambrogio market. The constant turnover permits daily deliveries of certified organic foods from Tuscany and beyond.

It was a pleasure to discover that La Raccolta sells my favorite Tuscan organic breads, from Forno "La Torre" (p 88), I Pulitini (p 133), and Montegemoli, near Pisa. La Raccolta (which means the harvest or gathering), began in the late 1980s. It features selected dairy foods, herbal remedies from Aboca (p 311), a huge range of pastas, bottled vegetables, grains, pulses, seeds and all the other standard health food products. Great for macrobiotics and everyone who cares about the quality of the foods they eat.

FIRENZE'S FOOD MARKETS

Central Firenze has two major permanent food markets: San Lorenzo and
Sant'Ambrogio. Both are in covered buildings but spill out into the surrounding streets. They are great to visit—and for shopping. Most produce is
sold and priced by the kilo (2.2 lbs) or etto (100 grams or 3.5 ounces).

MERCATO CENTRALE
Monday-Saturday 7:00-14:00, Saturday 16:00-19:00
The Mercato Centrale, or San Lorenzo market, is in a large nineteenth-
century cast-iron building. It houses hundreds of food stalls of all types,
some selling ready-cooked foods to take away. Upstairs the market continues with more stalls, including some of the most interesting salad and herb
sellers. Nerbone (Tel: 055 219949), established in 1872, is a Florentine
favorite and the best place to try *trippa* (tripe), *lampredotto* (chitterlings),
and other specialties. The stall has a few tables and a take-out business; it
is run by the son of Loriano Stagi, who owns the Vecchia Bettola restaurant (p 105). Perini (Tel: 055 2398306) has a spectacular prepared food and
grocery stall, and it also caters. They sell bread baked in a wood oven.

For a real slice of Italian life, the area around the market is
fun to explore. Via Sant'Antonio has a number of cut-price food and wine
stores, some of which are old-fashioned and interesting. There is still a
friggitore at number 50R selling deep-fried doughnuts.

In Via del Melarancio, the China Foodstores stock some
international foods. Back on the other side of the marketplace, at Via

DE HERBORE   Via del Proconsolo, 43R   50122   Firenze
HERBAL PRODUCTS   TELEPHONE 055 211706   FAX 055 683207   OPEN 9:00-13:00, 15:30-
                        19:30   CLOSED Monday morning, Sunday; one week in August
                        CREDIT CARDS Visa, MC   ENGLISH SPOKEN Yes
                        DIRECTIONS Near the Bargello

Health foods, natural cosmetics, bouquets of silk flowers, dried herbs, vitamins, macrobiotic ingredients, soaps, potpourri . . . De Herbore has all this
and more. Set spectacularly in a grandiose hall on the ground floor of Palazzo
Pazzi, the shop is the brainchild of two brothers, Doctors Luciano and Arnaldo
Tanganelli, erstwhile owners of a pharmaceutical company.

Panicale, 16R, Afro Market (Tel: 055 2382694) is the place to go if you have a yen for pounded yam, green bananas, or African spices. Indian and other Far East foods can be found nearby in Piazza Santa Maria Novella, 21/22R at Asiamasala. This nice shop is run by the owners of India, the Indian restaurant at Fiesole in Via Gramsci, 43A (Tel: 055 599900).

MERCATO DI SANT'AMBROGIO
Monday-Saturday 7:00-14:00
This market is a smaller, more intimate affair. As well as indoor stalls covering the entire gastronomic spectrum, there are outside stalls grouped around the sides of the building—with small vendors coming in from the countryside to sell their home-grown produce. Look for the little bunches of *erbi di campo*—hand-picked wild field greens to cook or use in salads.

Across the street from Cibrèo, at Via de' Macci, 117R, the Pescheria Silvestri sells wonderfully fresh fish and will even give cooking suggestions to those who can muster a little Italian.

The hardware store Mesticheria-Casalinghi Mazzanti, in Borgo La Croce, 101R (Tel: 055 2480663) has a second entrance a few doors down from Cibrèo (Via del Verrocchio). It stocks lots of inexpensive items: wooden spoons of all shapes and sizes, terra-cotta cooking pots, olive-wood cheese graters, chopping boards, oil tins with spouts, rustic spatterware pottery, and more. It is fun to browse in if you are in the neighborhood.

"Nowadays the only thing that brings me joy," Luciano Tanganelli confided, "is to help people heal themselves from the problems our modern society is subjecting us to. All the unnatural hormones and additives in our foods, the pollution, the stress—they're no good for us." Dr. Tanganelli mixes individual "cocktails" of curative herbs or suggests some of the many remedies his shop is stocked with.

Even if you are feeling perfectly healthy, the shop with its extravagant displays is fun to explore: the sweetly scented lotions and potions make great presents. So treat yourself.

OFFICINA PROFUMO- Via della Scala, 16   50123   Firenze
FARMACEUTICA TELEPHONE 055 216276, 2302437   FAX 055 288658
DI SANTA MARIA OPEN 9:00-13:00, 15:30-19:30   CLOSED Monday morning in winter,
NOVELLA Saturday afternoon in summer   CREDIT CARDS Visa, MC, Amex
HERBAL PRODUCTS ENGLISH SPOKEN Yes   DIRECTIONS Near Santa Maria Novella

The Officina is an extraordinary antique pharmacy founded by Dominican friars in 1542. Inside is a timeless world devoted to the senses. The fragrance of rarified perfumes strikes you first, then the strains of meditational early music; the eye is charmed by the beauty of the interiors with their painted tiles, frescoes, sculptures, and furnishings. Rare honeys, herbal teas, and *elisirs* are sold here, and an extensive range of natural preparations and skin-care products.

Some of them seem right out of an eighteenth-century romance novel: lavender salts to prevent fainting spells, rhubarb elixir to aid the digestion, mint spirit to clean the breath. Exotic perfumes, extracts, and essences are derived from violet and verbena, acacia and amber, hay and pomegranate. There are soaps and creams, oils, astringents, and ointments. There is even something called Armenia Paper "to be burnt to scent the air"—all in all, a hedonist's haven.

YOGEN FRÜZ Via dei Pucci, 5/a   50122   Firenze
ICE CREAM TELEPHONE 055 282093   FAX 055 2343880
OPEN 7:30-19:30 or later   CLOSED Sunday; holidays in summer
CREDIT CARDS None   ENGLISH SPOKEN Yes
DIRECTIONS Via dei Pucci runs one block north of the Duomo.

Pick your favorite frozen fruit, whizz it with some low-fat yogurt, and presto! You've got Yogen Früz. I liked it a lot better than most of the *gelaterie*'s offerings, which seemed sickly sweet and artificial-tasting. You can even have a Piansa coffee or a pastry at the bar. A great idea.

MACELLERIA VIGNOLI Piazza San Pier Maggiore, 1R; Via Romana, 131R; Via Gasperi, 19R;
MEAT: BUTCHER Via Pisana, 359   50122   Firenze
TELEPHONE 055 2480436   OPEN 8:30-13:15, 17:00-20:00
CLOSED Wednesday afternoon; Sunday   CREDIT CARDS None
ENGLISH SPOKEN A little

Vignoli owns several butcher's shops in the city. In addition to its range of beef (including Chianina) and pork, it specializes in game (including wild boar) and poultry: free-range chicken and pigeon, duck and guinea fowl. Some meats are sold ready-to-cook—*involtini* stuffed with mortadella or sage leaves and stuffed chicken. There are also good *salumi.*

FIRENZE'S TRIPE SELLERS

Tripe is a popular Florentine food, and it is served in many ways. Boiled tripe was traditionally sold by vendors from stands and carts, a few of which remain in central locations, selling *la trippa* warm as a filling for crunchy rolls. They include Palmino Pinzauti, Via dei Cimatori; and Luciano Piani, Piazza Sant'Ambrogio.

DOLCI & DOLCEZZE
PASTRY

Piazza Beccaria, 8R   50121   Firenze
TELEPHONE 055 2345458   FAX 055 2346698   OPEN Tuesday-Saturday
8:30-20:30; Sunday 8:30-13:00, 16:00-20:00   CLOSED Monday
CREDIT CARDS None   ENGLISH SPOKEN A little
DIRECTIONS The piazza is at Porta alla Croce.

This pastry shop sells some of Firenze's finest and most decadent cakes. Giulio Corti was a portrait photographer who loved making desserts; his wife, Ilaria, worked in an office. They started baking cakes for friends, then just for restaurants, and they finally opened this elegant shop in 1991. The dessert counter is complemented by a small range of baked savory goods and a stand-up bar for Piansa coffee or a glass of dessert wine.

"We never had a formal *pasticciere's* training," explained Ilaria, "and that has left us free to invent our own range." The buttery pastry tarts come with various custard-cream fillings, including deep chocolate, chocolate flavored with orange zest, *gianduja* (chocolate and hazelnut), and fresh orange and raspberry in summer. There are apple or orange pies (on Saturday), rice puddings, and a good range of cakes. A provocative cake declares "I am the best chocolate cake in the world"—try one and judge for yourself!

I DOLCI DI
PATRIZIO COSI
PASTRY, BAR

Borgo degli Albrizi, 11R   50122   Firenze
TELEPHONE 055 2480367   OPEN 7:00-13:00, 15:30-20:00
CLOSED Sunday   CREDIT CARDS None   ENGLISH SPOKEN No
DIRECTIONS Near the Via Verdi post office

Walk into this narrow shop in the morning and you'll find it full of Florentines on their way to work or on their midmorning break, standing up to eat a "pasta" (here it means pastry, not noodles) with a cappuccino chaser. In the afternoon, it's the same story, different crowd: a steady flow of admirers enjoying Patrizio Cosi's freshly baked croissants and doughnuts, apple tarts and raisin twists, rice *budini* or custard-filled *bignoline* (bite-sized choux pastries), plus some savories for those not in the mood for something sweet.

CANTINETTA   Palazzo Antinori   Piazza Antinori, 3   50123   Firenze
ANTINORI   TELEPHONE 055 292234   FAX 055 2359877   OPEN Lunch and dinner
RESTAURANT, WINE BAR CLOSED Saturday, Sunday; August   CREDIT CARDS Visa, MC, Amex
DIRECT SALE Yes, for small quantities of wine or oil
ENGLISH SPOKEN A little   RESERVATIONS Recommended
PRICE $$$ DIRECTIONS On Via Tornabuoni

A high-vaulted room on the ground floor of the fifteenth-century Palazzo
Antinori is the setting for this noble Florentine family's wine bar and restau-
rant. According to its genial host, Gianfranco Stoppa, the landed gentry in
Firenze formerly sold produce and wines from their estates directly to the
public from a small window of the palazzo.

What began in the 1950s as a simple place to drink the
Antinori's wines has become a sophisticated restaurant that belies its rustic-style
interior. A large dark wood bar and wooden tables with white linen place mats
(useful for seeing the color of the wines) are the setting for an elegant menu
and a list of the family's exceptional wines.

Wine lovers can sample the current release wines by the bottle
or glass—a rare opportunity to compare Marchese Piero Antinori's ground-
breaking super-Tuscan Solaia (of 80 percent Cabernet Sauvignon with 20 per-
cent Sangiovese) with its stablemate Tignanello (the same grape varieties in the
opposite proportions), or the big *barrique*-aged Cervaro, of Chardonnay and
Grechetto, produced in the family's Umbrian estate Castello della Sala. The
extensive list includes Ornellaia and Poggio alle Gazze from brother Lodovico
Antinori's estate at Bolgheri (see p 145). Wines may be drunk at the bar with-
out food.

As for the menu, it is traditional Tuscan (where else, if not here?)
prepared with attention and style. When I visited in February, mixed *crostini*
included one toast topped with *cavolo nero*, the sweet Tuscan winter cabbage.
Salmone chiodato (salmon home-cured in salt, sugar, and cloves) was more
delicately aromatic than smoked salmon. A plate of fettucine was dressed in
a green sauce of finely puréed herbs: rosemary, sage, and parsley. *Baccalà*, an
Italian Friday special, was unusually mild and tender, cooked with tomatoes
and served with chick-peas. Chicken drumsticks were stewed with a savory
sauce of chopped black olives and onions and came with mashed potatoes—
a perfect dish to accompany the decisive red wines. Interesting salad combin-
ations offered modern accents: radicchio and pecorino cheese were served
with thinly sliced baby artichokes, as were poached shrimp and crayfish.
Much of the produce comes from the Antinori estates, some of the largest
holdings in Tuscany.

Dessert was highlighted by the aromatic late-harvest meditation
wine Muffato della Sala, also made in Umbria. It is a wine to savor and sip, and
it produced a remarkable taste contrast with a slice of warmed *castagnaccio*, the

chestnut-flour cake flavored with rosemary and pine nuts, here topped and tempered by a paper-thin layer of ricotta.

OSTERIA DELLE Via delle Belle Donne, 16R   50123   Firenze
BELLE DONNE   TELEPHONE 055 2382609   OPEN Lunch and dinner
RESTAURANT   CLOSED Saturday, Sunday; holidays in summer   CREDIT CARDS None
ENGLISH SPOKEN Yes   RESERVATIONS Recommended for dinner
PRICE $$ DIRECTIONS Behind Palazzo Antinori

This colorful restaurant's small interior is dominated by an enormous Arcimboldesque fruit, vegetable, and flower arrangement. Simple tables are topped with hand-painted tiles, butcher-paper place mats, and decorated plates; seating is on stools. The daily menu is written on a blackboard. Soups, salads and pastas are unpretentious and affordable. The place is informal and usually packed, so get there early.

IL CIBRÈO   Via de' Macci, 118R   50122   Firenze
RESTAURANT   TELEPHONE 055 2341100   FAX 055 244966   OPEN Lunch and dinner
CLOSED Sunday, Monday; August, one week in January
CREDIT CARDS Visa, MC, Amex   DIRECT SALE Selected specialty foods
on sale at restaurant during meal times   ENGLISH SPOKEN Yes
RESERVATIONS Necessary at restaurant; none accepted at trattoria
PRICE $$$$ restaurant; $$ trattoria
DIRECTIONS Near Sant'Ambrogio market

Located amid the hustle and bustle of the Sant'Ambrogio market square, Cibrèo is Firenze's most compelling restaurant. Fabio and Benedetta Picchi have enriched the whole neighborhood with their three-in-one: one kitchen positioned between two storefronts supplies both an elegant, fully serviced restaurant on one side and a casual trattoria on the other. Across the street is the charming Cibrèo Caffè where diners may order snacks and a few dishes: at mealtimes waiters scurry back and forth through the traffic carrying plates of food. At the restaurant and trattoria the food is the same (though the restaurant's menu gives more choices): the trattoria offers no trimmings but its prices are half those of the restaurant. Note that Cibrèo serves no pasta. (Fabio Picchi said: "It's easy to make, and we all eat it at home anyway. So what's the point?")

My February lunch in the restaurant began with some wonderful antipasti: thin slices of Cibrèo's deliciously moist potato bread came topped with melted *robiola* cheese and jewel-like slivers of *mostarda*, the piquant candied fruit that made the cheese seem sweet. *Sformato di ricotta* was a subtle mousse with just a hint of the milky curds' sharpness; Picchi's three-liver *crostino* topping was as light as a cloud, with none of the bitterness this dish often has. A refreshing tomato aspic was excellent: scented with basil, it was served chilled with a spoonful of the new season's oil. A room temperature "salad" of marinated tripe was spiced with crisp red onion and parsley.

Picchi's yellow pepper soup has become a classic: pure in taste and color, it exemplifies the restaurant's refined-rustic style. A potato *sformato* (which means unmolded) was creamy and delicately flavored, served with a *ragù* of white meats and enriched with butter and Parmesan.

I tried two main courses, a Swiss-style meatloaf of veal and ricotta, which was nicely herbed and served with a fine tomato sauce, and another of the restaurant's signature dishes, *calamari in inzimino*. This is the Cibrèo dish that struck me most. A traditional peasant recipe that, Picchi explained, has its origins in Turkey, it seemed to me primordial, deep, and dramatic. Dark red-stained squid is stewed with chard and spinach greens cooked down to resemble seaweed. The strong, memorable dish is highly spiced with hot chili.

Picchi's wife, Benedetta Vitali, is the dessert chef at the restaurant (and author of the *Cibrèo Cookbook*, available from the restaurant in an overliteral English translation). She specializes in cakes, and in tarts of bitter orange, summer berries, or cheese. I sampled the *torta di cioccolato amaro:* probably flourless, it was moist, rich, and buttery but lacked full chocolate depth. The fine wine list includes Tuscany's best as well as excellent after-dinner spirits. Whatever your budget, a must for interested food and wine lovers.

DEI FAGIOLO
RESTAURANT

Corso dei Tintori, 47R   50122   Firenze
TELEPHONE 055 244285   OPEN Lunch and dinner   CLOSED Sunday,
Saturday in summer; August   CREDIT CARDS None
ENGLISH SPOKEN Yes   RESERVATIONS Recommended for dinner
PRICE $$ ·   DIRECTIONS From the Uffizi take Via dei Neri to Corso dei Tintori.

This centrally-located trattoria is run by the extended Zucchini family. The father has cooked here for thirty years, creating the kind of friendly, uncomplicated place you are always happy to come back to.

The cuisine is decidedly Tuscan; the emphasis is on the simple, home-cooked dishes the region is famous for. So sample *crostini tipici* (canapés topped with chopped chicken livers), *ribollita* (bread-thickened vegetable soup), or *pappa al pomodoro* (summer tomato and bread soup).

Main courses include classic *bollito misto* (assorted boiled meats served with an intense parsley sauce), *baccalà* with chick-peas (a Friday special), or the *Fiorentina*—T-bone steak grilled over a wood fire. Try a plate of *fagioli* beans or chick-peas drizzled with new oil as a side dish. The wine list is short but drinkable. To finish the meal, Signora Zucchini uses her grandmother's recipe to make fine homemade jam *crostate* (tarts).

GAUGUIN
RESTAURANT:
VEGETARIAN

Via degli Alfani, 24R   50121   Firenze
TELEPHONE   055 2340616   OPEN Lunch and dinner
CLOSED Sunday lunch, Monday; late summer holidays
CREDIT CARDS Visa, MC, Amex   ENGLISH SPOKEN Yes
RESERVATIONS Necessary on weekends   PRICE $$
DIRECTIONS Off Via della Pergola

Gauguin is a rarity: vegetarian restaurants in Italy are often macrobiotic, serving very pure, pared-down food. When Gauguin's owners decided to feature a menu without meat or fish, they determined to make it interesting. They use the good vegetables, pulses, and cheeses Italy has to offer and assemble them decisively. The restaurant's small rooms are alive with color: an eclectic collection of paintings, *objets*, and glassware makes for a lively atmosphere.

When I visited in winter, the *antipasto misto* included light, sweet-and-sour *caponata* (the Sicilian eggplant and celery combination), truffled cheese toast, and a *crostino* topped with warm herbed lentils spiced with orange. An unusual soup of chestnut, *farro* (spelt wheat) and porcini mushrooms used smoky-sweet chestnut flour as its base; half-moon-shaped pasta had a ricotta–orange zest filling and came in an orange-scented cream sauce. Main courses featured cardoons (in a deeply bitter lemon sauce), pumpkin (in an open-faced tart with Gorgonzola and poppy seeds), artichokes (stewed with white wine), and vegetable couscous. Desserts are homemade.

"Most of our customers are not vegetarians," explained Jean-Michel Carasso, Gauguin's co-owner, "and at first it was difficult to get Tuscans used to the idea of a menu without meat. But we are succeeding."

FIRENZE'S FIASCHETTERIE

These unpretentious wine bars got their name from the flasks (*fiaschi*) Chianti was traditionally bottled in. They range from small stand-up shops selling unbottled wines and sandwiches to slightly larger bars with a few tables serving drinkable wines and a few simple dishes. They are centrally located, atmospheric, and very reasonably priced. Here are some of the best among many: La Fiaschetteria, Via dei Neri, 17R; Vecchio Vinaio, Via dei Neri, 65R; Fani, Via degli Alfani, 70R; and Antica Mescita San Niccolò, Via San Niccolò, 60R.

IL LATINI
RESTAURANT

Via dei Palchetti, 6R   50122   Firenze
TELEPHONE 055 210916   FAX 055 289794   OPEN Lunch and dinner
CLOSED Monday; two weeks in August   CREDIT CARDS Visa, MC,
Amex   ENGLISH SPOKEN Yes   RESERVATIONS Recommended for
groups   PRICE $$$ DIRECTIONS Off Via della Vigna Nuova

"Ninety percent of our customers love us to death," exclaimed Giovanni Latini, one of Il Latini's family of owners. "The rest are just not wild about this type of atmosphere." The ever-packed restaurant has an age-old, inimitable style: the large sprawling dining room is filled with refectory tables that hold at least eight. Diners are seated wherever there is a space, and often find themselves in conversation with their neighbors (part of the charm of the place). There is a mad mixture of stuff around, including prosciutto hams hanging from the ceilings, bottles of the Latini's wines, and flasks of Chianti. The half-paneled walls are thick with photographs of literary figures: the family offers an annual literary award to writers whose lives have been dedicated to their art. The prize consists of a convivial dinner at the restaurant and a prosciutto.

The menu is Tuscan-in-a-hurry: the hearty soups are simple but good, pasta dishes arrive in seconds and tend to be soft, and there are hand-cut *salumi*, ready-cooked roast meats, and stews. So go for the fun of it.

TRATTORIA MARIO
RESTAURANT

Via Rosina, 2R 50122 Firenze
TELEPHONE 055 218550   OPEN Lunch only
CLOSED Sunday; August   CREDIT CARDS None
ENGLISH SPOKEN A little   RESERVATIONS None accepted
PRICE $ DIRECTIONS Beside the Mercato Centrale

Located a few steps from the San Lorenzo market, this is a genuine Florentine gem—if you get there early enough to get a table. The kitchen takes up half of the tiny dining room and the tables are a crush, but the food and jolly atmosphere are worth it. A few *primi* are prepared each day: simple soups, like the wonderfully warming chick-pea and rice, and a couple of pastas. Then there are steaks, roasts, *baccalà* (salt cod), and *bollito* (boiled meats). *Contorni,* side dishes, include boiled vegetables to eat with a little good olive oil. You can have a glass of wine at the table or at the miniscule bar (open all day) by the front door after your meal.

MIRÒ
RESTAURANT

Via San Gallo, 57/59R   50122   Firenze
TELEPHONE 055 481030   OPEN Lunch and dinner
CLOSED Sunday; August   CREDIT CARDS Visa, MC
ENGLISH SPOKEN Yes   RESERVATIONS Recommended for dinner
PRICE Lunch $, dinner $$ DIRECTIONS Near Piazza San Marco

Anyone who is tired of restaurants with that "rustic Tuscan" look will be pleased by Mirò, which has taken a more idiosyncratic approach to its decor. An ex-theater, the restaurant's entrance has frescoed ceilings, and inside it is peopled with objects of design: Ingo Maurer's high-wire lighting, modern sofas, and an eclectic collection of dining chairs. The tables are big and well spaced—there is room to spread out.

If the interior is citified and modern, the food has remained loyal to its country roots. Mirò offers separate menus for lunch and dinner, the former being a short list of quick and very reasonably priced dishes. The evening range is larger and slightly more expensive. The *primi* always include a few humble *cucina povera* soups—chick-pea and *farro* (spelt wheat), fava bean and chicory, *pappa al pomodoro* (tomato and bread), and *cavolo nero con le fette* (Tuscan winter cabbage with sliced bread). Pastas, too, change with the seasons.

Secondi are unpretentious but tasty: lamb cooked with baby artichokes, beef stewed in red Carmignano wine, or boned rabbit in white wine. There is a good range of vegetarian main courses, including assorted cheese platters and deep-fried vegetables. Desserts are homemade, with the exception of Dai Dai's frozen *cassatina* (p 152).

LE MOSSACCE
RESTAURANT

Via del Proconsolo, 55R   50122   Firenze
TELEPHONE 055 294361   OPEN Lunch and dinner
CLOSED Saturday, Sunday; August   CREDIT CARDS Visa, MC, Amex
ENGLISH SPOKEN Yes   RESERVATIONS None accepted   PRICE $$
DIRECTIONS One block south of the Duomo

Le Mossacce is a popular, fairly priced trattoria in central Firenze. Squeeze in past the narrow entrance to the dining rooms, which are crammed with regulars and tourists at peak hours: there is always a warm atmosphere and a quick turnover.

The menu features Tuscany's unpretentious signature recipes: *la ribollita* (thick bread and vegetable soup), *pasta e fagioli* (white bean soup with pasta), and minestrone. Main courses include *spezzatino* (stew), *arista* (roast pork), *trippa* (tripe), and the celebrated Tuscan T-bone, *la Fiorentina*. There are several vegetable side dishes to choose from, a few desserts, and basic wines.

ENOTECA
PINCHIORRI
RESTAURANT

Via Ghibellina, 87   50122   Firenze
TELEPHONE 055 242777, 242757   FAX 055 244983   OPEN Lunch and dinner   CLOSED Sunday, Monday and Wednesday for lunch; August
CREDIT CARDS All   DIRECT SALE Wines are not for sale except in the restaurant.   ENGLISH SPOKEN Yes   FEATURES Summer garden dining
RESERVATIONS Necessary   PRICE lunch $$$$$; dinner $$$$$$
DIRECTIONS Near Teatro Verdi

Few places create a sense of occasion as well as grand restaurants, which are necessarily formal, polished, larger than life—anything less and we might be disappointed. The Enoteca Pinchiorri fits readily into this category, offering world-class wines, refined cuisine, and over-the-top service. So if you are in the mood to go out for a really special meal with all the attendant pomp and circumstance, reserve a table here.

The restaurant is on the ground floor of Palazzo Ciofi-Iacometti. The well-lit rooms are high and vaulted, the colors clear pastels, and the materials heavy linen, silver, and fine crystal (over seventy styles). In February, an enormous vase of white lilies and glossy-leaved magnolia branches mirrored the volume of an imposing Murano chandelier. An army of slim waiters (including a water waiter) caters to the customers' every need.

Giorgio Pinchiorri has a world-famous cellar, with tens of thousands of bottles of great wines. So, to complement its catalogues of Italian, French, and other wines, the list offers several set-price wine "combinations." The expert wine staff are happy to share their knowledge and offer advice.

As for the food, in addition to an à la carte menu, diners are offered two *degustazione* (tasting) menus: "Menu Toscano," traditional Tuscan recipes revisited, or "Menu del Giorno," creative seasonal dishes (served as a surprise). I chose the former.

Chef Annie Féolde's *pappa al pomodoro* was unlike any other. Three spoonfuls of warm spicy tomato-bread paste arranged in a row (like rosy quenelles) were topped with wafer-thin round *schiacciatine*—hot salted biscuits fragrant with olive oil. Their cold green basil sauce tasted purer than pesto. It was all delicious; if you closed your eyes, you had the essence of the humble recipe done with a pinch of humor, culture, and refinement. Steamed fillets of red mullet (shiny side up) on a pale celeriac purée looked like an abstract painting with colorful accents: fried basil, parsley, and tomato skin.

A soup of spelt wheat (*farro*) was "garnished" with jumbo shrimp roasted with stark leaves of bay. Livornese *cacciucco* was here a silk-smooth coral sauce of fish stock and tomato, with chunks of clam and lobster, sea bass and bream. Narrow *pinci*—eggless noodles—floated in this deeply flavored sauce. *Tortelloni* had mashed potato fillings and an intense dry sauce of dried porcini, tomato concassé and thyme. Smoky-sweet *necci* (chestnut-flour pancakes) were stacked with fine ricotta, toasted *pinoli*, and rosemary. Seared duck breast came with soft stewed fennel and sharp black olives.

These technically proficient, sophisticated dishes never lose sight of the taste of their *cucina povera* origins. "I always try to come back to the purity and simplicity of the ingredients," Annie Féolde explained. Pure and simple they may be, but at its best this food impresses for the clarity of its flavors, the lightness of its touch, and the style of its presentation.

ALLA VECCHIA Viale Ariosto, 32-34R   San Frediano   50100   Firenze
BETTOLA TELEPHONE 055 224158   OPEN Lunch and dinner   CLOSED Sunday,
RESTAURANT Monday; three weeks in August   CREDIT CARDS None
ENGLISH SPOKEN Yes   RESERVATIONS Recommended   PRICE $$
OTHER The house wine is included in the cover charge.
DIRECTIONS The restaurant is south of the Arno, by Piazza Tasso.

"I come from a long line of Florentine street food sellers," Loriano Stagi
explained proudly as he added a place for me at his table. "My grandmother
was well known here in the *rione* [quarter] of San Frediano for selling *capi roti*
[broken heads]—the good parts cut from bruised oranges."

Loriano opened here in 1979 with his wife, Carla Zetti. They
wanted to recreate the kind of unpretentious eating house once common in
Firenze, the *bettole*. Its interior of tiled walls, marble-topped tables, and wooden
stools is embellished with compositions of fruit and flowers, hanging salami
and prosciutti. An old-fashioned iron stove heats the room in winter. The
menu, written on ochre butcher's paper, changes daily. "It depends what's fresh
in the market," recounted the amiable Carla. "Our cuisine is based on the sim-
ple foods of *la cucina povera*: hearty bread soups, pasta, fried or roasted meats,
tripe, and other organ meats."

I sampled a series of dishes, all well flavored and delicious: *cros-
tini* toasts topped with a delicate paste of *milze* (spleen), anchovies, and capers;
baked artichokes stuffed with home-cured pancetta and herbs; *penne alla bettola*,
a spicy pasta with tomatoes, hot pepper, and vodka; cauliflower cooked with
tomatoes and fennel seeds; *fagioli* beans drizzled with fruity olive oil.
Lampredotto (chitterlings), "cooked in the manner of tripe," was sliced and
stewed until tender. The restaurant serves fine T-bone steak—*la Fiorentina*.
The *salumi* have been carefully selected: you can sample the genuine *prosciutto
Toscano* cured by Belsedere (p 280).

One of the couple's sons runs the famous Nerbone stall inside
the San Lorenzo food market, which specializes in filled rolls: a great place for
a snack when browsing through the market (p 94).

G. CIATTI Via Panicale, 19R   50122   Firenze
SPECIALTY FOODS: TELEPHONE 055 214848   OPEN 7:45-13:00, 17:00-19:30 in winter;
SALT COD & STOCKFISH 7:45-13:00, 17:30-20:00 in summer   CLOSED Wednesday afternoon,
Sunday   CREDIT CARDS None   ENGLISH SPOKEN A little
DIRECTIONS Beside the Mercato Centrale, under the arches

"There's no future for our kind of shop," Enrico Ciatti told me wistfully. "We
are the end of a long line. The supermarkets have killed us off." The Ciatti
brothers' store is, indeed, from another time. Here, in a *salumeria* that sells no
salumi, the salt-preserved foods are anchovies and cod (*baccalà*). The ceiling is
hung with stiff dried stockfish, while underneath are the original marble baths
used to soak and tenderize these once-popular fish.

"In our grandfather's day, at the turn of the century when the shop opened, *baccalà* and *stoccafisso* were regular staples in almost every household," he went on. "Of course in those days there was always a woman in the house to prepare them—because they do require preparation." The Ciattis still trade in these North Sea fish, and in loose dried chick-peas, fava beans, lentils, *fagioli*, and rices, whose sacks line the walls of their beautiful marble store. Long may they continue.

LEOPOLDO PROCACCI	Via Tornabuoni, 64R 50100 Firenze
SPECIALTY FOODS:	TELEPHONE 055 211656 OPEN 9:00-13:00, 16:30-19:30
TRUFFLE SANDWICHES	CLOSED Wednesday afternoon, Sunday; August CREDIT CARDS None
	DIRECT SALE Yes ENGLISH SPOKEN A little
	DIRECTIONS Near Palazzo Strozzi

This wonderfully old-fashioned shop is a must for epicures. At its heart a quaint glass case contains the *panini tartufati*, truffle-scented sandwiches, that have justly made it famous. Eat a couple standing at the bar as you sip a glass of *spumante* for a suggestively *grand tour* experience.

"This shop has been in our family for over III years," declared the elderly Signora from her strategic position at the cash desk. "We use only the finest local truffles, like the white *Tuber magnatum pico*. They are found in the winter months around San Miniato and San Giovanni d'Asso." The shop's elegant wall cabinets house fancy foods and wines, but the quintessential Proccaci delights are those genteel little rolls with their earthy, fragrant paste.

FORNASETTI	Borgo degli Albizi, 70R 50122 Firenze
TABLE CRAFTS	TELEPHONE/FAX 055 2347398 OPEN 9:30-13:00, 15:30-19:30
	CLOSED Monday morning; August MAIL ORDER Yes
	CREDIT CARDS Visa, MC, Amex ENGLISH SPOKEN Yes
	DIRECTIONS Near Palazzo degli Albizzi

That enigmatic smile, those black-and-white eyes . . . are unmistakably Fornasetti. They look out (or is it in?) from teapots and dinner plates, chair tops and clock faces, hand trays and vases.

This jewel of a shop, sister to the store in Milan's Via Manzoni, is a window into the late Piero Fornasetti's personal world. The great designer's timeless objects are still fresh, still amusing, still desirable.

DINO BARTOLINI	Via dei Servi, 30R 50122 Firenze
TABLE CRAFTS:	TELEPHONE 055 211895 FAX 055 289223 OPEN 9:00-12:30, 15:30-
KITCHENWARES	19:00 CLOSED Monday morning and Saturday afternoon in summer;
	Monday in winter; three weeks in August MAIL ORDER Yes
	CREDIT CARDS Visa, MC ENGLISH SPOKEN Yes
	DIRECTIONS Via dei Servi runs north-east from the Duomo.

This is one of the best kitchen supply shops in Firenze, if not in Tuscany. They carry (a lot of) everything, from pasta pots to Alessi's copper pans, cheese graters to *mezzaluna* (half-moon) choppers, espresso pots to prosciutto stands, gelato scoops to oil cruets. There are departments for fine china, crystal glassware (including Riedel sommelier wine glasses), chef's knives, baking pans . . . and much more. They even stock cork stoppers in all shapes and sizes—so measure your topless jars or bottles before you go. Bartolini holds its annual sale for three weeks from the end of January—a winter's treat!

MARCHESI DE'
FRESCOBALDI
WINE

Via Santo Spirito, 11   50125   Firenze
TELEPHONE 055 27141, 2381400   FAX 055 280205, 211527
DIRECT SALE No   ENGLISH SPOKEN Yes

The Frescobaldi head office is in Firenze, and appointments may be made at the above numbers to visit the family's Tuscan wineries. (For visiting information and groups, speak with Cristina Rinaldi). Or see Rùfina (p 114) for the Castello di Nipozzano and Pomino estates; Montalcino (p 293) for the Castelgiocondo estate. For Laudemio oil see p 116.

PITTI GOLA &
CANTINA
WINE STORE

Piazza Pitti, 16   50100   Firenze
TELEPHONE/FAX 055 212704   OPEN 10:00-13:00, 15:00-19:00
CLOSED Monday morning; Sunday in winter; August
MAIL ORDER Yes   CREDIT CARDS Visa, MC, Amex
ENGLISH SPOKEN Yes   OTHER English-language cookbooks sold
DIRECTIONS Across the street from the Pitti Palace

This attractive, interesting wine store is situated in an elegant position overlooking the Pitti Palace. The high-ceilinged room is lined with wine bottles and jars of artisan-made foods. Since the shop opened in 1995, its young owners, Andrea Poli and Cecilia Bandinelli, have devoted themselves to seeking out Tuscany's best wines (and some foods). They also (intelligently) sell books about food and wine, some of which are in English. The shop has quickly gained a following, and its downstairs room has become a center for wine tastings and courses.

Poli has hand-picked his wines and oils to include many small but interesting wineries. He is a soft-spoken young man who is knowledgeable and passionate about his subject. I wish them well.

Also

Pasticceria Robiglio. Via dei Servi, 112R. 055 214501; and Via de' Tosinghi, 11R.

Robiglio is a Florentine institution favored by the city's well-to-do. Pastries can be eaten at the bar with a coffee or bought in a *vassoio* (tray). There is also a good range of savory snacks.

Caffè Rivoire. Piazza della Signoria, 5R. 055 214412 .

After an exhilarating (but exhausting) visit to the Uffizi, un-
wind in the old-worldliness of the Rivoire tearooms. The cakes and pastries are
fresh and good, and the *cioccolata con panna*—Italian-style hot chocolate with
whipped cream—is sinfully rich. You won't need dinner afterward!

Bar Hemingway. Piazza Piattellina, 9R.

On the south side of the Arno, this is a great place for chocolate-lovers. This recently opened bar runs a chocolate association, stocking
chocolates from many of Tuscany's *maestri,* including de Bondt (see p 128)
and Slitti (see p 75).

IMPRUNETA

**FATTORIA LA
QUERCE**
OLIVE OIL, WINE

Via Imprunetana per Tavarnuzze, 41   50023   Impruneta
TELEPHONE/FAX 055 2011380   OPEN 10:00-13:00, 15:00-19:00; wine
visits and tastings by appointment only   CLOSED Second half of July
CREDIT CARDS None   DIRECT SALE Yes   ENGLISH SPOKEN A little
DIRECTIONS From Impruneta go toward Tavarnuzze. The farm is on the
left after 1,200 meters.

Massimo Marchi's estate produces wine and olive oil. La Querce, a modern-
style red table wine of 90 percent Sangiovese and 10 percent Canaiolo, uses the
traditional *governo Toscano* method, in which semidried Colorino grapes are
added to the wine after the first fermentation to provoke the second.

"The concentration of these added grapes gives the wine more
intense color and *profumi,*" explained Marco Ferretti, the estate's young manager. The wine matures for two years in large casks, with part being finished
in *barriques* for La Querce's Selezione Speciale del Proprietario.

The estate is also known for its oil. Marchi prefers the traditional
stone-grinding system. "When used properly, it makes the oil less bitter," continued Ferretti. "Tuscan oil can initially be difficult for foreigners to appreciate,
with its strong, decisive flavors, artichoke bitterness, and peppery finish. But
given time, it grows on you."

MARIO MARIANI
TABLE CRAFTS:
POTTERY

Via Cappello, 29   50023   Impruneta
TELEPHONE 055 2011950   OPEN 8:00-12:00, 14:00-19:00
CLOSED Saturday, Sunday, except by appointment
CREDIT CARDS None   ENGLISH SPOKEN A little
DIRECTIONS From Impruneta's central square go down toward Ferrone
until the road to Ferrone turns left. Go straight toward Vanni. After 200
meters Mariani's gate is on the left.

"What you need to make these pots," exclaimed the vivacious Mario Mariani,
"are fire, earth, water, and elbow grease!" His human-size terra-cotta urns are

indeed handmade from local clay and fired in a wood-burning kiln as big as a
room. To see the kiln loaded with mountains of logs, ready to be lit, is a specta-
cle. Urns may not be easy to carry home (some smaller objects are produced),
but anyone interested in original artisan crafts should see these. They even
adorn the Presidential palace in Rome.

LE VEDUTE

LE VEDUTE
RESTAURANT

Via Romana Lucchese, 121   50050   Fucecchio
TELEPHONE 0571 297201, 297498   OPEN Lunch and dinner
CLOSED Monday; August   CREDIT CARDS Visa, MC, Amex
ENGLISH SPOKEN A little   FEATURES Summer terrace
RESERVATIONS Recommended on weekends and for terrace
PRICE $$$$ DIRECTIONS On main road from Fucecchio to Altopascio

The ample menu in this well-groomed restaurant is divided between "land"
and "sea" and changes daily. This is a family-run restaurant with professional
service and a certain style; the spacious indoor rooms are comfortable, with a
vine-covered terrace for summer meals. Many customers are tannery managers
from nearby Santa Croce.

My autumn meal celebrated wild mushrooms and truffles.
From a piping hot dish came a startling, intense perfume: white truffle shavings were scattered onto sizzling stewed leeks—the earthy aroma was remarkable. Warm butterflied shrimp came with arugula and sliced yellow-gilled *ovoli,*
delicate wood mushrooms that resemble eggs before they open.

Straccetti all'aragosta, a "sea" pasta, had irregular "rags" of vivid
green pasta tossed in a coral lobster sauce; the fine-flavored fish married well to
its light cream binding. Other *primi* included risotto blackened by squid ink,
linguine with shellfish, and tagliatelle with mixed mushrooms.

As main courses, mushrooms came grilled, fried, stuffed—alone
or with veal, lamb chops, or stewed kidneys and potatoes. Fish and shellfish
were paired with olives and capers, steamed vegetables, or rosemary and oil.
Some were cooked *in cartoccio*—packets of foil to seal in the cooking juices.
A well-stocked dessert trolley was irresistible. The wine list has a good selection
of Tuscans and a fair selection of prices.

MASSARELLA

IL CACCIATORE
RESTAURANT

Via delle Cerbaie, 36/38　Massarella　50054　Fucecchio
TELEPHONE 0571 296238　OPEN Lunch and dinner
CLOSED Monday evening, Tuesday; August　CREDIT CARDS No
ENGLISH SPOKEN A little　RESERVATIONS Recommended on weekends
PRICE $$　DIRECTIONS Massarella can be reached from the
Montecatini-Fucecchio road.

This is a classic Tuscan-style trattoria serving local specialties, including home-made pastas and soups, like the thick vegetable and bread *ribollita*. Main courses feature meats and game grilled on the big wood barbecue, *alla brace*. In autumn and winter there is wild boar, hare, and local duck cooked simply but well, and there is a nice choice of Tuscan wines and local oils.

MONTELUPO FIORENTINO

ND DOLFI
TABLE CRAFTS:
POTTERY

Via Tosco Romagnola nord, 8　50056　Montelupo Fiorentino
TELEPHONE 0571 910116, 51264　FAX 0571 910116　OPEN 9:00-20:00
CLOSED Monday　MAIL ORDER Yes　CREDIT CARDS Visa, MC,
Amex　DIRECT SALE Yes　ENGLISH SPOKEN No
DIRECTIONS From Montelupo take the SS 67 towards Firenze;
the pottery is on the left after 3 kms.

This artisan pottery has been in the Dolfi family for three generations, but there has been a tradition of fine hand-painted ceramics at Montelupo since 1500. In the 1800s local clay pits were rediscovered; the town now boasts a ceramics museum. Many historic designs use only blue and white, but more recent Montelupo motifs—such as courtiers with daggers—are featured on a distinctive yellow background.

　　　Some of the deeper colors used on decorative plates, tiles, and vases contain lead, but all plates destined for the table are guaranteed to be lead-free. In addition to classical medieval and Renaissance patterns, the Dolfis' handsome showroom features colorful modern designs painted on tiles, urns, candlesticks, platters, and wall ornaments.

MURA

**CASAMASI-
TRATTORIA TOSCANA**
RESTAURANT

San Benedetto Mura　50050　Montaione
TELEPHONE 0571 677170　FAX 0571 677042　OPEN Lunch
and dinner　CLOSED Monday　CREDIT CARDS Visa, MC
ENGLISH SPOKEN Yes　RESERVATIONS Recommended for dinner
PRICE $$　DIRECTIONS From Mura, go down toward San Miniato;
after 2 kms, turn left just before the small bridge. Follow the unpaved
road to the restaurant.

Casa Masi is located in a large stone barn in a shady garden. Alessandro Masi and his wife, Luciana, have adorned the walls nicely with baskets, old cutting boards, wooden tools, and other collectibles. Within a few months of opening there was already a lively, convivial atmosphere.

The food is good country fare, *alla Toscana.* "We want to bring back the flavors of foods we knew as children," explained the attractive Luciana. "Some of these recipes were my grandmother's—and they are wonderful." The menu marks "old Tuscan" recipes with an asterisk.

Autumn antipasti included artisan-made *salumi,* mixed *crostini, salame* with fresh figs, and fried polenta wedges topped with stewed leeks and sausage. *N'cavolata nera* was a rustic soup of finely chopped vegetables, beans, and Tuscan black winter cabbage. Another satisfying soup featured chick-peas and beet greens. *Gnuddi* of spinach and ricotta were little green dumplings nicely flavored with sage.

Stewed rabbit was tender, as was guinea fowl cooked with Vin Santo and served with onions and field mushrooms, in earthy contrast to the sweet sauce. Pecorino was grilled and served hot with aromatic truffle oil. Desserts were well made and showed some northern influence in their finesse. A tart of thinly sliced apples was served with a lustrous *crème anglaise.* A rich chocolate tart had good depth of flavor and a fudgelike consistency. The wines are local, the service friendly, the place fun.

PONTE A EMA

CASA EDITRICE "IL FIORE" BOOK PUBLISHER

Via B. Fortini, 124/1   50125   Ponte a Ema
TELEPHONE 055 643288   FAX 055 641554   MAIL ORDER Yes
DIRECT SALE No   ENGLISH SPOKEN Yes

Aldo Capobianco's independent publishing house, Il Fiore, has produced some authoritative books on Tuscan gastronomy. The biggest and most complex is *Vino e Olio in Toscana—Wine and Oil in Tuscany.* The comprehensive book includes essays by experts, and a comprehensive list, zone by zone, of Tuscany's key wineries. One label from each estate is reproduced in color.

Other books include historical and cultural treatises on Firenze and Tuscany. *Carmignano: L'Arte del Vino* is a fascinating book in Italian on this small but historic wine-producing area near Firenze. Il Fiore's books may be ordered directly from the publisher or through bookstores in Firenze.

PRATO

**BISCOTTIFICIO
ANTONIO MATTEI
PASTRY**

Via Ricasoli, 20   50047   Prato
TELEPHONE 0574 25756   FAX 0574 36650   OPEN 8:00-13:00,
15:30-19:30 in winter; 8:00-13:00, 16:00-20:00 in summer
CLOSED Sunday afternoon and Monday in winter; Sunday and Monday
in summer   MAIL ORDER Yes   CREDIT CARDS None
ENGLISH SPOKEN Yes   DIRECTIONS Near Piazza San Francesco

Seekers of the true *cantucci* should make a pilgrimage to Prato, home of the
original *biscotti di Prato*—better known (everywhere but in Prato) as *cantucci*.
Near the imperial castle is the marvelous old bakery that first created these
almond-studded biscuits; with Vin Santo they are the quintessential ending to
a Tuscan meal. The bakery's store is handsome: a large lofty room with a marble counter displays cobalt blue biscuit packages printed with gold. A glass case
contains cookies, cakes, and Antinori Vin Santi and wines (the companies have
a mutual admiration society).

     The bakery was founded in 1858 by Antonio Mattei. Today
the crunchy, almond-studded *biscotti* (meaning twice-cooked) are made to his
original recipe, using the same ingredients. "Only the finest almonds, freshest
eggs, sugar, and flour are used," explained one of the founder's granddaughters.
"Thirty years ago some procedures were mechanized, so biscuits that were once
hand-sliced are now cut by machine."

     Mattei produces a few other baked goods: *brutti ma buoni* (ugly
but good) are chunky, coarse-grained macaroons with a rich nut flavor; *il filone
candito* is a low cake of brioche-type pastry studded with liqueur-soaked cher-
ries and covered with crunchy marzipan; and *la Mantovana* is a moist yellow
cake topped with almonds and icing sugar.

     As I entered the shop, my eye was caught by the unusual win-
dow displays of old handwritten postcards from the 1950s and 1960s. The
senders were given a multiple-choice question: Were the cookies bad, good, or
excellent (*ottimi*)? You can guess the results . . . *ottimi, ottimi, ottimi!*

**GASTRONOMIA/
ENOTECA BARNI
SPECIALTY FOODS:
DELICATESSEN, WINE
BAR, RESTAURANT**

Via Ferrucci, 24   50047   Prato
TELEPHONE 0574 33835, 607845 *enoteca*   FAX 0574 33835
OPEN Shop: 7:00-14:00, 16:30-20:30; restaurant: Monday lunch only;
Tuesday-Friday lunch and dinner; Saturday dinner only
CLOSED Sunday; shop: Wednesday afternoon in winter, Saturday
afternoon in summer; August   CREDIT CARDS Visa, MC, Amex
ENGLISH SPOKEN Yes   RESERVATIONS For dinner at restaurant
PRICE $$$ for dinner

This double-fronted shop is a delicatessen on one side and a wine bar and
restaurant on the other. The shop, in the same family for sixty years, began as a

flour mill and bakery. The *gastronomia* sells fine cheeses, *salumi*, breads baked in their wood oven, pastries, oils and preserves, but it is also known for its freshly cooked foods. There are pasta specials and rustic vegetable soups to start. Main courses include tripe, roasted pig's liver, roasted meats, and *baccalà alla Livornese* (salt cod) on Fridays.

Go in the other door for the *enoteca*. Here well-selected wines may be bought to go, or drunk at the bar by the glass or bottle. At lunchtime the back rooms serve as a *tavola calda* restaurant with ready prepared dishes; at night they function as a full restaurant with a full menu.

RIGNANO SULL'ARNO

FATTORIA IL POGGIO
OLIVE OIL: ORGANIC

Il Poggio, 60   50067   Rignano Sull'Arno
TELEPHONE 055 8348346   FAX 055 8348562   OPEN Always, but best to phone first   CLOSED Never   CREDIT CARDS None DIRECT SALE Yes   ENGLISH SPOKEN Yes   OTHER Holiday apartments available   DIRECTIONS From Rignano go toward Incisa. After 1.5 km turn right toward Troghi. The farm is on the right after 1.5 km.

Enrico Brambilla and his wife run a biodynamic farm (under the auspices of Demeter) producing organic olive oil, grape juice, and grains. When they took over the farm, chemical pesticides and fertilizers were still being used.

"The land was ruined," explained Enrico. "So we joined the Set Aside European Union program and left the land alone for five years, as a kind of purge." Having no animals to produce manure, they buy organic manures and use biodynamic and homeopathic preparations to accelerate growth and improve the soil's fertility.

Their extra-virgin oil is obtained in a traditional stone mill at low temperatures. It can be bought from the farm or in Firenze at La Raccolta (see p 93). In summer they grow their own organic vegetables which visitors can purchase when available.

RÙFINA

FATTORIA
SELVAPIANA
WINE

SS 67   50065   Pontassieve
TELEPHONE 055 8369848   FAX 055 8316840   OPEN 9:00-12:00, 13:00-19:00; visits, sales, and tastings by appointment only CLOSED Sunday   CREDIT CARDS None   DIRECT SALE Also from farm shop "Torracino" on the main SS 67   ENGLISH SPOKEN Yes DIRECTIONS Selvapiana is east off the main road SS 67 between Pontassieve and Rùfina.

Chianti Rùfina has steadily been gaining recognition as one of Tuscany's most interesting, albeit smaller, wine producing zones. This is primarily thanks to Francesco Giuntini of Selvapiana, whose long-standing belief in the area's

potential, his considerable personal charm, and his fine wines convinced
the wine world of Rùfina's quality. He now also makes wine for Fattoria di
Petrognano at Pomino: the tiny Pomino DOC is above Rùfina and comprises
two producers, the other being Marchesi de' Frescobaldi (see below). Pomino
wines are characterized by their French grape varietals, planted there in the last
century. Cabernet and Merlot form part of the Pomino Rosso blend with
Sangiovese; Chardonnay goes into the white.

　　　Working with his adopted son, Federico Masseti, and winemaker
Franco Bernabei, Giuntini produces classic Sangiovese-based wines that conform to Chianti specifications—without the optional white grapes. From 30
hectares (74 acres) of vineyards, they produce Chianti Rùfina DOCG, its Riserva,
and *crus* Vigneto Bucerchiale and Fornace. These are well-structured, warm,
and elegant wines that only improve with age. The estate's best white is Borro
Lastricato, a blend of Pinots Bianco and Grigio.

　　　I was impressed by the atmosphere of culture at Selviapiana,
a handsome seventeenth-century villa with a formal garden. Giuntini and
Masseti offer a "complete and generous education" to interested visitors,
showing them the vineyards and explaining the winemaking process. Tastings
are guided. As many winery visitors are not experts, this openness encourages
further interest. It is no wonder that Rùfina's winemaking is rapidly improving,
for many smaller estates have seen this magnanimity and are now following suit.

**MARCHESI
DE' FRESCOBALDI
WINE**

Castello di Nipozzano　SS 70 della Consuma　50060　Pelago
TELEPHONE　Nipozzano: 055 8311325; Pomino: 055 8318810; group
appointments call Cristina Rinaldi 055 27141　FAX　055 280205
OPEN　9:00-12:00, 14:00-18:00 Monday-Saturday, one Sunday per month
Guided tastings by appointment only.　CLOSED　Three Sundays a month
CREDIT CARDS　None　DIRECT SALE　Yes, from Nipozzano
ENGLISH SPOKEN　At Nipozzano　OTHER　Frescobaldi listing in
Firenze (p 107)　DIRECTIONS　Nipozzano is signposted off the SS 70
west of Diacceto.

"When you write the word Rùfina," urged Marchese Ferdinando Frescobaldi,
"please put the accent on the u." For Rùfina denotes the area northeast of
Firenze where this noble family has some of its biggest estates. The Frescobaldi's epithet, "castles and vineyards since 1300," suggests how central a role
this family has played in Tuscan winemaking. The present-day directors of the
company are three brothers, Vittorio, Ferdinando, and Leonardo; they have
been responsible for bringing the family's traditional-style wineries up to date.

　　　On a sunny winter's day I visited two important estates with
Ferdinando Frescobaldi: Nipozzano and Pomino. The large holdings—Nipozzano has 180 hectares (445 acres) of vineyards, Pomino has 100 (247)—are
beautifully positioned in the foothills of the Apennines. "Being on high ground
[between 350 and 700 meters/1,150 and 2,300 feet] our vines experience greater

extremes of temperature than those lower down," he explained. "But the wines are more perfumed and *fruttato*."

The estates' *cantine*, dating back to the fifteenth century, epitomize the recent changes to Tuscany's wineries: rows of small *barriques* now stand in cellars built to accommodate enormous wooden *botti*. Many Frescobaldi wines reflect this marriage of the traditional with the new.

The Pomino estate, cradled high on a south-facing slope of Mount Pomino, has produced wines for centuries. Chardonnay, the primary grape in the white Pomino Il Benefizio DOC, was first planted there in the 1850s; the vast Benefizio vineyard, 23 hectares (57 acres) at 700 meters, was replanted with selected Chardonnay clones in the 1980s, when the *barriques* were introduced. The elegant modern-style wine is fermented and aged in these small oak casks; it has a full perfumed bouquet, with a fine balance between fruit and wood. Other Pomino DOC wines include Pomino Rosso, the nonreserve Pomino Bianco, and Vin Santo.

The nearby eleventh-century Castle of Nipozzano produces Chianti Rùfina DOC wines Castello di Nipozzano Riserva, and Montesodi, from a single vineyard of Sangioveto grapes; they are both elegant, drinkable wines of good structure. Like these, Mormoreto, a Cabernet Sauvignon *cru*, is aged mainly in *barriques*.

See also Castelgiocondo at Montalcino (p 293) and Laudemio (p 116) for their extra-virgin olive oil.

PULITI **"GRANDI VINI"** WINE STORE	Viale Duca della Vittoria, 15 50065 Rùfina TELEPHONE 055 8397081, 8397251 FAX 055 8397081 OPEN 9:00-13:00, 15:30-20:00 CLOSED Wednesday afternoon, Sunday CREDIT CARDS Visa ENGLISH SPOKEN No DIRECTIONS On the main road through Rùfina

You would be forgiven for not immediately understanding that this store sold fine wines: the front part sells loose candies and *bomboniere* (candy souvenirs), while the "stacks" are at the back—industrial shelving holds an amazing range of 974 wines and 76 types of whisky. This is a no-frills wine store with a lower than usual mark-up.

Silvano and Fernanda Puliti run a cheerful business. "It started back in the sixties, when our customers began asking for bottled wines," explained Silvano as he tied a pink bow onto a candy dish. "Before that it was mostly *sfuso*—unbottled. I became increasingly interested in quality wines, and now you could say I was hooked!"

On Saturday, which is market day in Rùfina, wine tastings are held regularly for interested buyers—but everyone is welcome. The Pulitis stock the fine local Rùfina and Pomino wines and selected Tuscan and other Italian wines. Extra-virgin olive oils complete the range. "I only sell good wines," he declared simply. "And I'm glad young people around here are now switching to wine. They are the future, and they'll be a lot better prepared than we were."

LAUDEMIO: A NOBLE OIL

"Laudemio is both the definition of a territory and a philosophical concept," explained Marchese Ferdinando Frescobaldi, one of its creators. "Laudemio denotes the hills of central Tuscany: extra-virgin olive oil bearing this name above the producer's is guaranteed to come from olives of this area. A group of producers set up guidelines for the oil: each estate makes oil under its own label but adheres to common principles.

"Every stage, from the growing of the plants to the picking and pressing of the olives, is rigorously controlled. A deadline of December 15 has been set for the picking—to exclude overmature olives. Olives must be picked from the trees, not be so ripe as to fall to the ground. The extraction must be at low temperatures, by whichever process is preferred.

"A special bottle was designed for Laudemio extra-virgin oils. I hope other geographical areas will follow suit—only then can customers be assured of what they are buying."

Other members of the Laudemio group include Marchesi Antinori, Riccardo Falchini, and Fattoria di Bossi. As with fine wines, the quality and taste vary with each producer and *terroir* of production; Laudemio's prices, however, are consistently high.

For further information contact Bona Frescobaldi or Dr. Piero Tesi, 055 2336565, Consorzio Olivicoltori della Toscana Centrale.

SAN FRANCESCO

Gelateria Sottani. Via Forlivese, 93. 055 8368092.

This *gelateria* is on the SS 67 between Firenze and Rùfina, north of Pontassieve. Giancarlo Sottani specializes in fruit gelati, with exotic summer flavors like papaya, pineapple, watermelon, and pomegranate. He favors natural dyes like beets rather than artificial ones. The *creme* range includes a fine *nocciola* made with pure crushed hazelnuts, *castagne* (chestnut), and a group of invented flavors with fanciful titles.

TAVARNUZZE

Macelleria Tognaccini. Via della Repubblica, 17. 055 2374544.
    This small, family-run butcher's shop has a good range of fresh
meats and home-cured *salumi*. *Arista salata sull'asse* is a specialty: boned pork
fillet cured on a wooden board; it makes a lean meat to eat, thinly sliced, as
an antipasto.

VICCHIO

IL FORTETO
CHEESE, MEAT,
PRODUCE

SS 551   50039   Vicchio
TELEPHONE/FAX 055 8448183   INTERNET www.Forteto.com
E-MAIL forteto@ats.it   OPEN Monday-Friday 8:30-13:00, 15:30-19:30;
Saturday, Sunday 8:00-20:00   CLOSED Monday-Thursday in July
CREDIT CARDS Visa, MC   ENGLISH SPOKEN Yes
DIRECTIONS From Dicomano take the SS 551 toward Vicchio. Il Forteto
is on the main road after 4 kms.

Il Forteto is a cooperative of cheese makers, cattle breeders, and vegetable
growers. Since 1977 it has expanded to include a modern supermarket featuring
the members' products. Its specialties are sheep's and cow's cheeses and beef of
the acclaimed Chianina breed. Farm produce is also available.
    Cheeses are made from Tuscan milk: fresh creamy ricotta;
pecorini, fresh and matured; even a cow's milk mozzarella. I particularly liked
the Riserva del Casaro, a crumbly well-flavored pecorino matured for five
months with an olive-oiled crust.
    Il Forteto is a leading Tuscan producer of Chianina beef. These
pale-colored animals with large dark eyes were once used primarily for farm
work. "The politics of beef-raising has changed," explained Mauro Vannucchi,
responsible for the farm's Chianina. "Ten years ago they were practically
extinct." In recent years demand for their meat has increased: the best *bistecche
alla Fiorentina*, or T-bone steaks, call for them. The meat has less fat and more
protein than other beef, and the pure breed animals are raised and butchered
under strict controls of the European Union and the breeders' consortium. In
Italy, hormones are forbidden by law, and all meat is rigorously tested.
    At Il Forteto the animals are raised in large barns, spending
some of their lives outdoors (a rarity in Italy). They are fed only hay and grain
produced on the farm. Its mountainous show bull and cows may be visited,
just a few steps from the store.

LA CASA DEL Via Ponte a Vicchio, 1   50039   Vicchio
PROSCIUTTO TELEPHONE 055 844031   OPEN Bar and shop 8:00-15:00, 17:00-19:30
RESTAURANT, (till 20:00 in summer); trattoria for lunch only   CLOSED Monday;
DELICATESSEN holidays in July and January   CREDIT CARDS Visa
ENGLISH SPOKEN No   RESERVATIONS Recommended, especially on
weekends   PRICE $ DIRECTIONS From the SS 551 at Vicchio go
toward Ponte a Vicchio. The restaurant is across the narrow bridge.

This little trattoria-delicatessen-bar is atmospheric, with hams hanging from
the ceiling. The loyal clientele stand at the counter for coffee or a sandwich and
glass of wine. Lunchers can sit in the dining room, choosing from a menu of
moderately priced rustic country dishes.

The "ham house," on the site of an inn dating back to 1400, is
named for its fine home-cured prosciutti and other *salumi*—everything from a
fennel seed–studded *finocchiona* to the head cheese, *biroldo* or *soppressata*, that
is so popular in Tuscany. Worth sampling are its excellent farm-produced local
pecorini and ricotta cheeses, made by a local woman from Santa Agata. The
cheeses and cured meats may be bought to take away, or in sandwiches.

CHAPTER 5

Pisa and Its Hills

*P*isa's Piazza dei Miracoli—Place of Miracles—seems aptly named
and is one of the world's most spectacular. The beautiful square
contains not only the famous Leaning Tower, but the white marble
Romanesque Duomo and its Baptistery. Pisa was once a strategic seaport, positioned at the mouth of the river Arno. By the sixteenth century, however, the
river had silted up, and Livorno became the area's most important harbor.

Pisa is lovely to walk in, with the river Arno weaving a picturesque course through its center. It contains great foods, a charming marketplace, and interesting restaurants. Beyond the Arno's valley, the Pisan hills, *le
Colline Pisane*, are some of Tuscany's most unspoiled. Small rural villages are
surrounded by patchwork fields of olives, vineyards, and crops. Further inland
is Volterra, one of the Etruscan civilization's most important cities. It is a
remarkable place, positioned high on a flat hilltop. It is famous also for
alabaster—the translucent white stone worked then as now by skilled artisans.

The province of Pisa contains a handful of top food producers
and winemakers—including fabulous handmade chocolates, one of Italy's oldest pasta factories, and a producer of organic sheep's cheeses.

Azienda Promozione Turistica
Piazza Arcivescovado
56126 Pisa
050 560464, fax 050 40903

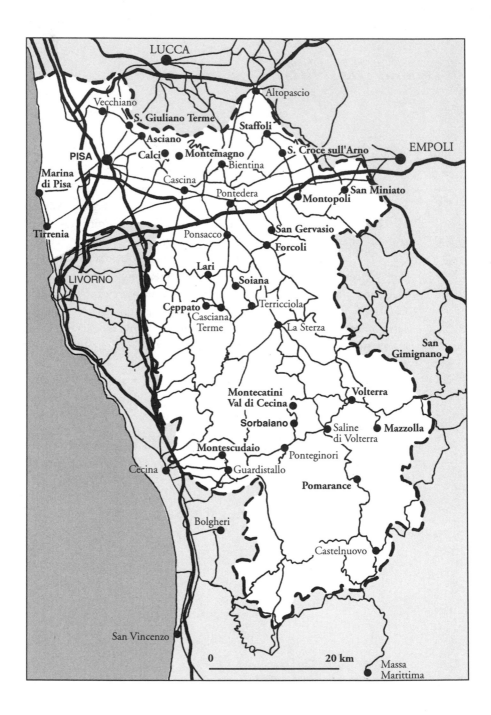

Town names in **bold** indicate towns that are included in this chapter.

ASCIANO

FATTORIA DI
ASCIANO
OLIVE OIL

Villa Scerni   Via Trieste, 8   56010   Asciano Pisano
TELEPHONE/FAX 050 855924   OPEN Sales all year, by phone
appointment only   CREDIT CARDS None   DIRECT SALE Yes
ENGLISH SPOKEN A little   OTHER The villa is available for functions.
DIRECTIONS Facing the church in Asciano, Villa Scerni is the
large villa to its left. Ring the bell on the right.

This distinguished sixteenth-century villa produces one of the area's finest olive oils. It has 39 hectares (96 acres) of olive groves around Asciano. Their position, shielded from northerly winds by the hills and facing the warm sea breezes, saved the trees in the devastating winter of 1985. The steep terraced groves are inaccessible to tractors, but the Marchesa Angelica Raggi de Marini Scerni has found a picturesque solution for keeping the grass down and the land fertilized: she has enlisted the help of a troop of horses. The animals roam the olive groves and do a fine job of organic recycling.

The Fattoria's stone grinding mill and old-fashioned press may be visited in November and December when the hand-gathered olives are being processed. At other times oil may be bought directly from the farm manager (by appointment only). It is sold bottled or unbottled, *sfuso*. The rich golden oil is a cross between light Ligurian oil and the intense, *piccante* oils of Tuscany's hills, with some of the sweetness and fragrance characteristic of Lucchese oils.

CALCI

AZIENDA AGRICOLA
IL COLLETTO
OLIVE OIL

Par di Rota   56010   Calci
TELEPHONE 050 938320   OPEN By appointment only
CREDIT CARDS None   DIRECT SALE Yes   ENGLISH SPOKEN Yes
DIRECTIONS The small farm is difficult to find. Marco Chiletti will meet
clients in Calci and lead the way.

This organic olive oil producer's groves are high on a hillside above the sea. A narrow winding road climbs up through steep walled terraces of olive trees. Chiletti hand picks his olives early in the season, taking each batch quickly to be milled in a "continuous cycle" *frantoio* nearby. He believes that the future belongs to these hygienic modern steel systems.

"When my oil is fresh, it's so green it hurts your eyes!" exclaimed Marco Chiletti, the farm's young owner and oil expert, who has produced a CD-ROM about oil making. His fine Olio del Par di Rota is fiery and full of character, with a nice bitterness and decisive "pepperiness" to it. It is also sold from his wife's restaurant at Montemagno Calci (see p 125).

"The biggest problem facing olive growers at low altitudes is the olive fly, *dacus oleae*," he explained. "It is more prevalent in humid areas near the sea. We have developed a complicated defense system that does not rely on chemicals." The critical period is from July to October. By setting traps to attract the males and taking samples from many trees, Chiletti can monitor the fly's behavior. Insect predators and bitter herb solutions sprayed on the trees help ward off attack.

CEPPATO

LA FRATTINA
RESTAURANT

Via Pisana, 22   Ceppato   56034   Casciana Terme
TELEPHONE   0587 649233   FAX 0587 979046   OPEN Dinner only;
Sunday lunch and dinner   CLOSED Tuesday; variable winter holidays
CREDIT CARDS Visa, MC   ENGLISH SPOKEN Yes
RESERVATIONS Recommended   PRICE $$$ including house wine
DIRECTIONS From Casciana Terme, follow signs for Ceppato. Look for
the fork-and-knife restaurant symbol.

This friendly *osteria* is in a miniscule village in the Pisan hills. In hot weather you eat out on the shaded terrace; in winter the warm dining room has a log fireplace. In this family-run restaurant, the home-cooked dishes change daily. If there is a written menu, we never saw it. The all-inclusive price fluctuates with the cost of ingredients; it includes house wine and is a good value. Lino and Elisabetta serve two *primi* and two *secondi* daily, depending on the season. Mixed antipasti precede them and a simple dessert ends the meal. Despite this system, the kitchen was flexible enough to accommodate a vegetarian without advance warning.

Our mid-September, Sunday lunch began with assorted *crostini* canapés, local *salumi*—including well-flavored *prosciutto Toscano*—onion frittata, (Italian omelette), and crunchy deep-fried bread dough. Pasta dressed with pumpkin and yellow pepper sauce followed a rustic dish of *pappardelle con la lepre,* wide ribbon noodles with hare. Tender roast pheasant was served with hot grapes and a creamy sauce of mascarpone. Rabbit was stewed with small olives and herbs. A refreshing plate of sliced peaches sprinkled with lime rounded the meal off nicely.

FORCOLI

SAVITAR
SPECIALTY FOODS:
TRUFFLE PRODUCTS

Strada Comunale Palaiese, 34   53060   Palaia
TELEPHONE   0587 629339   FAX 0587 629739
OPEN 9:00-13:00, 15:30-19:00   CLOSED Saturday afternoon, Sunday
CREDIT CARDS Visa, MC   ENGLISH SPOKEN Yes   DIRECTIONS From
Forcoli take the road up toward San Gervasio and restaurant Belvedere.
Turn left at T-junction. Savitar is immediately on the right.

This artisan company prepares foods using truffles, including the highly prized white San Miniato truffle, *Tuber magnatum pico.* In this area the truffles, a type of fungus, are routed out from under trees by specially trained dogs that have been weaned on truffles. The white variety, to which San Miniato dedicates an annual fair (p 137), is found in late autumn and winter.

Savitar's unique truffle-scented honey offers an unusual taste sensation: sweet from the honey and earthy, almost pungent from the truffle. They sell it in tiny jars (as with all truffle products, a little goes a long way); it makes an affordable present for adventurous food lovers. Other truffle-flavored products include: pâté, anchovy paste, pasta, cheese spreads, pecorino cheese, truffle butters, pastes, and oils. Fresh truffles only last a few days, but these products preserve the truffle sensations long enough to get them home! The small shop's staff are friendly and knowledgeable, and they are happy to explain more about this exquisite (and expensive) wild food.

LARI

MARTELLI FRATELLI ARTIGIANI PASTAI PASTA

Via San Martino, 3   56035   Lari
TELEPHONE 0587 684238   FAX 0587 684384   OPEN 8:00-12:30, 14:30-19:00 but best to phone first   CLOSED Wednesday, Sunday
DIRECT SALE No   STOCKIST Shops in Lari sell the pasta.
ENGLISH SPOKEN Yes   DIRECTIONS The factory is at the top of the village, below the castle.

Martelli's pasta is some of Italy's finest, and its sun-yellow packages are the best harbingers its friendly makers could have. A visit to their tiny factory is a memorable event—especially on Tuesday or Friday when spaghetti is being made. It is a thrill to see it "raining" down in long hairlike strands from quaint 1960's machinery. "We are the opposite of the big pasta companies," laughed Mario Martelli, one of two brothers who, with their wives and children, run the business. "They are afraid of industrial espionage. But we love showing visitors how our pasta is made—it says so on our packages."

The Martellis use only top-quality Canadian durum wheat. The flour is mixed with cool water—as opposed to industry's hot water—which maintains its fresh wheat flavor, though it lowers yields. "Our pasta is still made in the traditional way," his brother, Dino, explained enthusiastically. "We don't overcompress it when forcing it through the bronze dies, so its surface is not too smooth." The pasta is dried slowly (at 30°c/86°F) in wooden drying cupboards for up to two days. It is packed by hand. The pasta comes in just four shapes: spaghetti, spaghettini, penne and *maccheroni*. Its texture is softer, more elastic, and more porous than its industrial counterparts. The Martellis advise using a greater quantity of water when cooking it.

Everything in both the village and the 1870 factory is on a reassuringly human scale, and it only takes two steps to reach the family's dining room. "The big industries may have a point," Mario concluded, as he twirled his fork in a steaming bowl of spaghetti. "After all, they produce as much pasta in eight hours as we make in a year! *Buon appetito!*"

MARINA DI PISA

GASTRONOMIA MANZI Via Maiorca, 43/45   56013   Marina di Pisa
SPECIALTY FOODS: TELEPHONE/FAX 050 36647   OPEN Summer 7:30-14:30, 17:00-21:00;
DELICATESSEN winter 8:00-13:30, 16:30-19:30   CLOSED Sunday afternoon and Wednesday in winter   CREDIT CARDS Visa, MC, Amex   ENGLISH SPOKEN Yes   DIRECTIONS On the main road as you enter Marina di Pisa from Pisa

This excellent *gastronomia* is the Italian equivalent to a deli, selling a range of specialty foods: fruit and vegetable preserves, pasta (Martelli's), honey, olive oil, and wine. Fresh foods include cheese, homemade *salumi*, and breads. Cooked dishes to take out change daily: soups or pastas, roast meats, seafood, plus freshly made pasta sauces. The multitalented Manzis also bake cookies. Their unusual *cantucci* are excellent: rich and soft, with the consistency of macaroons, and enriched with honey and sweet almonds from Puglia. All in all, a great place for foods to take home or to eat on the beach.

Next door, the family's *gelateria* makes great ice creams, too.

MAZZOLLA

VIVAIO VENZANO Mazzolla   56048   Volterra
PLANT NURSERY: TELEPHONE/FAX 0588 39095   OPEN Thursday-Sunday from mid-
HERBS February to mid-December   CLOSED Monday-Wednesday   CREDIT CARDS None   ENGLISH SPOKEN Yes   DIRECTIONS From Volterra go toward Colle Val d'Elsa and Siena. After4 kms turn off toward Mazzolla. Follow signs to Venzano.

The Mediterranean garden has long held a fascination for northern Europeans and Americans. The vivid colors and exotic perfumes of jasmine, bougainvillea, lemon, hibiscus, and lavender trigger memories of warm nights by the sea, of physical and spiritual well-being, of Baudelaire's (or Matisse's) *luxe, calme et volupté*.

Creating a garden in the hot arid land, however, is not always easy. Water in rural Tuscany is often scarce; the earth is poor, rocky, and intractable. Donald Leevers and Lindsay Megarrity, in their extraordinary nursery at Venzano, concentrate on scented and herbal plants (over twelve hundred species), many of which survive quite readily in this habitat. Donald Leevers described a mixed border they have created using only indigenous flowering plants: "These wild Mediterranean plants: rosemaries, *Romneya, Cistus*, and lavender—require no watering, yet provide color and interest almost all year."

Venzano is a place of almost mystical allure. Set high above Volterra's round hills, it was built around a natural spring in a grotto existing since Roman times. It feels like an oasis: the crumbling thirteenth-century monastery buildings are set among terraced, walled gardens of simplicity and beauty. Fragrant plants are everywhere. Many culinary herbs may be bought, including thyme, savory, aliums, and *Balsamita major*. There is even the autumn-flowering crocus, *Crocus sativus*, whose precious stigma are saffron.

MONTECATINI VAL DI CECINA

FATTORIA SORBAIANO
WINE

Via Provinciale Tre Comuni   56040   Montecatini Val di Cecina
TELEPHONE/FAX 0588 30243   OPEN 9:00-12:00, 14:00-17:00; *cantina*
visits by appointment only   CLOSED Saturday afternoon, Sunday
CREDIT CARDS Visa, MC   DIRECT SALE Yes   ENGLISH SPOKEN Yes
OTHER Sixteen apartments available for short rentals
DIRECTIONS From Montecatini Val di Cecina go toward Ponteginori.
After 1 km turn right to Sorbaiano. Turn left down a hedged road,
passing the villa to reach the winery.

This large farm commands spectacular views across the wide river Cecina valley to Volterra. Sorbaiano is one of the area's up-and-coming wineries. The estate has 16 hectares (40 acres) of vineyards under the Montescudaio DOC. The Picciolini family have worked with one of Tuscany's top winemakers, Vittorio Fiore to improve their wines.

Four wines and Vin Santo are made: Rosso delle Miniere is a full-bodied red of primarily Sangiovese grapes. It is aged for one year in *barriques*, small oak casks, and is improved by further cellaring. Lucestraia, of selected Trebbiano and Vermentino grapes, also spends time in small wood. The red and white Montescudaio DOC are very affordable—this winery offers good value for your money.

MONTEMAGNO CALCI

TRATTORIA DI
MONTEMAGNO
RESTAURANT

Piazza Vittoria Veneto, 2   56010   Montemagno Calci
TELEPHONE 050 936245   OPEN Dinner only; Sunday lunch only
in winter   CLOSED Monday; Sunday dinner in winter
CREDIT CARDS None   ENGLISH SPOKEN A little
FEATURES Outdoor summer dining   RESERVATIONS Necessary in
summer and on weekends   PRICE $ DIRECTIONS The village is 1 km
beyond the Certosa di Pisa. Park in the car park to the left just before
entering Montemagno (signed with a P). Walk up through the village to
the square.

Montemagno is beyond Pisa's Certosa, the seventeenth-century Carthusian monastery with its splendid façade. The center of this tiny village is a tiny square: the trattoria's outdoor tables nearly fill it. This relaxed restaurant is a favorite with Pisa University students. The food is fresh, appetizing, and very affordable. A set-price menu includes antipasto, *primo, secondo*, side dish, and dessert, with water, service, and cover charge thrown in. Wine and other beverages are extra. There is a daily choice of first and main courses, written on a blackboard. There are two women owners, Mariella and Laila; Mariella is married to the organic oil producer Marco Chiletti at Calci (p 121). Mariella and Laila have earned a loyal following with their delicious home cooking.

Autumn mixed *antipasti* included: onion frittata; *crostini* of *peperonata,* stewed peppers, and basil-cheese paste; a salad of *nervetti,* boned calf's trotters; and fragrant herbed olives. Lasagne layered with pesto, string beans and bechamel was unusual and good; a rustic soup of mixed legumes and grains was satisfying, drizzled with their fiery oil. Main courses were roast pork with vegetables, stuffed cabbage leaves, and *piccante* tender squid stewed with beet greens—the most interesting of the three.

One homemade dessert complemented artisan gelati from Lucca: a well-filled strudel of pears and *amaretti.* The house wines were Vernaccia and Chianti.

MONTESCUDAIO

FATTORIA POGGIO GAGLIARDO
WINE, OLIVE OIL

Poggio Gagliardo   56040   Montescudaio
TELEPHONE 0586 630661, 630775   FAX 0586 685960
OPEN 8:30-12:30, 15:00-19:00; group visits and tastings by appointment
CLOSED Sunday   CREDIT CARDS None   DIRECT SALE Yes
ENGLISH SPOKEN A little   OTHER Summer apartments available
for rent   DIRECTIONS From Cecina go toward Guardistallo; go under
the *superstrada,* and after 200 meters turn right toward *zona artigianale,*
with many company names signposted. The farm is at the end of that
road, past the warehouses.

Poggio Gagliardo is in the low rolling hills just inland from the coast. This is a real working farm, the farmyard a hive of activity: crops are cultivated and barns filled with beautiful Chianina cattle. Once bred here for beef, they now are used for showing. Visitors are welcome to see them.

When Walter Surbone bought the farm in 1968, it was run down. He came from Piemonte's Monferrato, a winemaking center, and developed the farm's energies in that direction. "We spent years flattening the earth to create these large, even vineyards," he explained as we toured them. "I was interested in engineering a system of underground irrigation, and we now have over 22 kilometers (14 miles) of pipeline buried under our 50 hectares (123 acres) of vineyards." The estate's wines are improving steadily. Grape yields have been reduced and sophisticated equipment installed for the vinification—like the white wines' soft presses.

Poggio Gagliardo falls within the Montescudaio DOC established in 1977; Walter Surbone is president of its consortium of thirty-four

producers. His estate's twelve wines include the economical *podere* line
Montescudaio DOC Rosso and Bianco, and top-of-the-line *barrique*-aged white
Vignalontana and red Rovo. Of Sangiovese with some Colorino and Malvasia
Nera, Rovo is a concentrated, well-structured modern-style wine admired by
Italian critics. An extra-virgin olive oil is also available. The friendly farm is
well organized for tastings, group visits, and sales.

Also

Logica Tre. Via della Libertà, 25. 0586 655355.
    This small shop in Montescudaio's center sells a good selection
of Montescudaio DOC wines, plus organic oils, honeys, and preserves.

MONTOPOLI IN VAL D'ARNO

QUATRO GIGLI
RESTAURANT

Piazza Michele, 2   56020   Montopoli in Val d'Arno
TELEPHONE 0571 466940, 466878   FAX 0571 466879
OPEN Lunch and dinner   CLOSED Monday; holidays variable
CREDIT CARDS Visa, MC, Amex   ENGLISH SPOKEN Yes
FEATURES Summer terrace   RESERVATIONS Recommended, especially
at weekends   PRICE $$ OTHER Quattro Gigli is a three-star hotel.
DIRECTIONS In the village center

Anyone interested in the history of Tuscan food will appreciate this attractive
restaurant. Its seasonal menus include recipes from the fifteenth to the eigh-
teenth centuries. Many seem remarkably modern. "We have always loved
adapting recipes from old cookbooks," confided Fulvia Puccioni, the talented
chef. "They readily fit into today's fresh, flavorful cuisine: combinations like
chicken with pomegranate or perch with orange sound new, but are not!"
    Fulvia and her husband, Luigi Bacchini, have also created a complex
personal style in the restaurant's look, layering warm colors, decorative paint-
ings, and unusual traditional Montopoli ceramics (see below). A romantic
summer terrace with nice views is adorned with flowering vines and painted
flowerpots.
    Our late summer lunch began with *antipasto fantasia*. A beige-
toned salad of raw field mushrooms, pine nuts, and pecorino had a wonderfully
woodsy flavor; *sformato di carote* was a coral pudding of carrot; saffron-yellow
crostini toasts were topped with egg yolk paste; well-salted *prosciutto Toscano*
was perfectly paired with fresh fig purée. For *maccheroncini di pane,* a rustic
fourteenth-century *primo,* day-old bread was soaked in broth, squeezed, mixed
with flour and oil, and formed into pasta strips. They were boiled and served
with fragrant oil, fresh herbs, and pecorino. Fifteenth-century "gnocchi" of
pecorino and egg were dense corn-yellow little dumplings with a fresh cheese
flavor, their sauce of herbs and finely ground walnuts. Main courses included

loin of pork with honey and walnuts, cod with fresh tomatoes, and boned guinea fowl with prunes (from the sixteenth century).

For dessert there was Vin Santo with *cantucci* cookies, ice cream–filled meringue with chocolate sauce, or fresh fruit *bavarese*. The wine list is extensive, the service efficient but personalized.

TERRECOTTE DI   Piazza Michele, 10   56020   Montopoli in Val d'Arno
MONTOPOLI   TELEPHONE 0571 466940   FAX 0571 466879   OPEN The Quattro
TABLE CRAFTS: Gigli staff will open the shop by request   CREDIT CARDS Visa, MC,
POTTERY   Amex   ENGLISH SPOKEN Yes   DIRECTIONS Across the street from
the Quattro Gigli hotel

This small artisan pottery shop is run by the Quattro Gigli hotel's owners (see above). They hope to keep Montopoli's antique ceramics tradition alive, as long as the one remaining craftsman is willing to continue.

Gino Fossetti is very old now, but he still works hard, decorating beautiful plates and vases in this village's style. Plates are made of local red and white clays on a potter's wheel and dried before being decorated. His designs date to the fourteenth century, when Montopoli boasted five pottery workshops.

Very old stencils, *spolveri*, are used to mark out the designs. A central motif—a stylized peacock, heraldic figure, or flower—is surrounded by an elaborate decorative border in a graphic, semigeometric style. There are two stages: the outlines are traced with a shallow groove, and the plates fired for the first time. Colored glazes are then applied in the warm earth-tones that characterize Montopoli's ceramics before a second firing.

PISA

DE BONDT   Via Turati, 22 (Corte San Domerico)   56100   Pisa
CHOCOLATE   TELEPHONE 050 501896   FAX 050 506302   OPEN 10:00–13:00,
16:00–20:00   CLOSED Monday; Sunday afternoon
CREDIT CARDS Visa   ENGLISH SPOKEN Yes
DIRECTIONS The Corte may also be reached from Corso Italia, 131.

Paul de Bondt and Cecilia Iacobelli are an interesting young couple. He, a brilliant chocolate maker, and she, a designer, got together a few years ago and opened a shop to showcase the talents of each. "Our idea was to make chocolates of very high quality," explained Cecilia, "and to display them in an unusual way." They have amply succeeded in both. As far as the aesthetics go, the chocolates are presented in a spare, clean-lined environment softened by Cecilia's lovely still-life arrangements; they are sold in attractive geometric boxes.

Paul de Bondt is Dutch. After training as a pastry chef in Holland, he dedicated himself to chocolate. "I was looking for a simplicity, a purity of taste and texture," he explained. "Molded and filled chocolates are never very fine as the outer chocolate casing is always thick, thus interfering with the sensation of the filling."

De Bondt's coverings are almost imperceptibly thin—with just enough chocolate to protect the fillings and allow them to be handled. The chocolates, nearly all with chocolate-based ganache fillings, are deliciously rich and clean-flavored. Each offers a unique taste experience, with a balance of sweet and bitter, soft and hard, to complement the subtle fillings: lemon, tea, chestnut honey, nut. The coffee-scented ganache is so finely flavored you sense the coffee rather than taste it, without its usual acidity. "Each filling has its own character," continued Paul, "and I try to match it with its covering—I work with eight dark chocolates from France and Belgium, so there is a lot of scope."

Milk chocolates are available for those who prefer them; chocolate novelty shapes make affordable presents. Custom cakes and chocolates may be ordered. If you are a chocolate-lover and in Pisa anytime but summer, when the chocolates are not made, don't miss out on these—they are the finest Tuscany has to offer.

As we went to press, de Bondt was considering moving the shop to Via Crispi, 53. His telephone number will not change if he moves, so call to check before going.

L'ALTRA ROBA	Piazza delle Vettovaglie, 3 56100 Pisa
HEALTH FOODS	TELEPHONE/FAX 050 598987 OPEN 8:00-13:00, 16:00-20:00 (17:00-
	20:00 in summer) CLOSED Wednesday afternoon, Sunday
	CREDIT CARDS None ENGLISH SPOKEN Yes
	DIRECTIONS From Lungarno Pacinotti, take Via Vigna to the market.

Piazza Vettovaglie is Pisa's central food market. Just north of the river, it is an old porticoed square with stalls in the center and permanent shops around the edge. One of these is L'Altra Roba—literally "the other stuff." The narrow shop is crammed full of loose and packaged rices, legumes, and grains. Its owner, Berto Tessieri, told me he had "all the pulses you can find in Italy." I counted eighteen types of dried bean, including *pavoni*, a large speckled variety resembling birds' eggs and the expensive, tender-skinned *fagioli di Sorana* (p 78). Interesting mixes, like rice and orange lentils, need only twenty minutes' cooking. Many products are organic, either fresh or bottled: pasta sauces, honeys, olive oils, fruit preserves, plus seasonal fresh fruits and vegetables. I am grateful to Berto for introducing me to I Pulitini's wonderful organic breads (p 133). I first tasted them in his shop and consider them among Tuscany's best.

PASTICCERIA
FEDERICO SALZA
PASTRY, BAR

Borgo Stretto, 46   56100   Pisa
TELEPHONE 050 580244   FAX 050 580310   OPEN 8:00-20:30
CLOSED Monday   CREDIT CARDS None   ENGLISH SPOKEN Yes
RESERVATIONS Not usually necessary for the lunch room
DIRECTIONS Borgo Stretto runs north from Ponte di Mezzo.

The Salza family has run Pisa's finest bar and *pasticceria* since the 1920s. "My family came from Turin," explained Silvio Salza. "This is our eighth generation in the trade. It passes from father to son, from Silvio to Federico, and back to Silvio again. Ours is a family of male children, and we always use the same names."

The double-fronted shop on one of Pisa's principal streets is instantly inviting, with a delicious aroma of freshly roasted coffee, pastries, and chocolate. On the right a long display counter of cakes and chocolates features excellent *pasticceria mignon,* bite-size pastries to eat there or buy by the trayful. Their pastry, custards, and glazes are refined in flavor and execution. Salza makes soft *panforte,* a spicy rich confection studded with fruit and nuts. Even the chocolates (often disappointing in *pasticcerie*) are of good quality.

On the other side is the large bar and sandwich counter, serving over forty types of sandwiches, savory tarts, and snacks to eat at the bar or take away. At lunchtime hot sandwiches and pasta are available; a waiter-served luncheonette is in the back. The company also runs a large catering facility. Signor Salza, a spruce gentleman of the old school, is a perfectionist; he believes great service and quality are imperative, whether he is preparing a society wedding banquet or one of his delicious cappuccini.

OSTERIA DEI
CAVALIERI
RESTAURANT

Via San Frediano, 16   56100   Pisa
TELEPHONE 050 580858   FAX 050 581259   INTERNET http://www.nsm.it
OPEN Lunch and dinner   CLOSED Saturday lunch, Sunday; August
CREDIT CARDS Visa, MC, Amex   ENGLISH SPOKEN No, but there is an
English menu   RESERVATIONS Suggested for dinner   PRICE $$
DIRECTIONS Off Piazza dei Cavalieri, north of the Arno

This *osteria* (between a trattoria and a *ristorante*), in the university section of the town, is a nice place for a simple lunch or dinner. The atmosphere is relaxed, children are welcome, and the menu offers an ample choice, from soups and pastas to vegetable plates and meats. There are reasonably priced one-dish specials like osso buco (veal shanks with risotto), or mixed grilled fish with pasta. The house wines are drinkable, and there is a list for anyone feeling more ambitious.

I liked the deep ochre soup of pumpkin with added ground almonds for texture and the mixed grilled vegetables—zucchini, eggplant, and peppers—with grilled *scamorza* cheese. The desserts look good; a frozen cream pudding, *semifreddo al zabaglione,* has a light citrus flavor and crunchy praline in it.

TAVERNA KOSTAS   Via del Borghetto, 39   56100   Pisa
RESTAURANT   TELEPHONE 050 571467   OPEN Lunch and dinner
                     CLOSED Monday, Sunday lunch; August   CREDIT CARDS Visa, MC,
                     Amex   ENGLISH SPOKEN A little   RESERVATIONS At weekends
                     PRICE $$ DIRECTIONS Via del Borghetto is off Lungarno Bruno Buozzi,
                     near the Ponte della Fortezza.

Don't be put off by this restaurant's Greek name: Kostas was its former owner.
When he sold the business to his talented chef, the menu changed completely
but the name remained. Mario Ferrò and his brother, Federico, now produce
some of the best food I have eaten in Tuscany. Their cuisine is wonderful:
uncluttered and pure in its tastes yet complex and stimulating to the senses.

Even the simplest ingredients are transformed brilliantly.
The *tortino di patate e porcini* tartlet contains a delicate custard of earthy wild
mushrooms. What seems, at first glance, to be its filo pastry is a fine "crust" of
thinner-than-paper potato slices, soft with crispy edges. *Bruschetta ai frutti di
mare* is another inspired antipasto. A round toast rubbed with garlic is stacked
beautifully with delicate slices of peeled tomato, a sweet shrimp, perfect mussels and clams, and a meltingly tender tiny octopus. Chopped parsley, a little
aromatic olive oil, and that is it. *Bruschetta* revisited.

Primi are equally interesting. The Ferròs' *pasta e fagioli* is an
island of herb-flecked noodles in a rosemary-scented sea of puréed white beans.
Dramatic black *tagliolini* flavored with squid ink are set off by tiny broccoli
flowers, wisps of red tomato, and white squid tentacle curlicues. The sauce is
enriched with finely chopped mussels and miniscule shrimp. This deeply
flavored, painterly dish has all of the poetry of the Mediterranean. Fish star
again in *gallinella all'acqua pazza*, a gurnard family fish cooked in "crazy
water," a classic recipe from the brothers' native south. "*Acqua pazza* is really
nothing," laughed Mario Ferrò. "It is a fast, simple way to cook fish. Sauté a
whole fish over high heat with tomatoes and herbs; a ladleful of water is added
and 'goes crazy' as it hits the searing metal."

The seasonal menu is very reasonably priced. Desserts include
pear Tatin, lemon tart, chocolate-orange tart, a few frozen desserts, and the Greek
favorites: cinnamon rice pudding and yogurt with honey and walnuts. Wines are
well chosen, with big names to balance less familiar local producers. The service
is attentive but informal. The blue-trimmed white-and-pink rooms overlook
a wild garden; they have the comfortable simplicity of a real Greek taverna.

Also

Melani. Corso Italia, 44. 050 502323.

This large kitchen supply shop stocks everything from pots and pans to decorative glassware and china. Its collection of designer tableware and kitchen accessories includes Alessi. Wine lovers will find tasting glasses by Bremer and Villeroy decanters.

Coltelleria Fontana. Corso Italia, 124. 050 41369.

I have always been fascinated by shops specializing in knives—a key tool for anyone who likes to cook. This recent shop has a great range. It also stocks the typically Italian equipment it is fun to bring home: ravioli cutters—both the trays used with a small rolling pin and the individual wooden-handle type—Parmesan wedges for splitting chunks of the cheese, fluted pasta wheels, meat pounders, nut crackers, and more.

Cagliostro. Via del Castelletto, 26/30. 050 575413.

This recently opened restaurant and wine bar serves lunch, dinner and drinks. The decor is striking and eclectic, and the cooking is imaginative—with a great list of cheeses to match its fine wines.

POMARANCE

MACELLERIA MARIS FROSALI

MEAT

Piazza De Larderel, 28   56045   Pomarance
TELEPHONE 0588 64611   OPEN 8:00-13:00, 17:00-20:00
CLOSED Wednesday afternoon; Sunday; early August
CREDIT CARDS None   ENGLISH SPOKEN No
DIRECTIONS In the village center

This old-style marble butcher's shop is a guaranteed source of Chianina beef—the best Tuscan breed (many claim it among the world's best). Maris Frosali belongs to the 5R association which controls Italy's five top beef breeds, of which Chianina and Maremmana are special to Tuscany.

Chianina beef is firm-fleshed and has a layer of pure white fat around it. With its high-protein, low-fat content, it is the beef of choice for the famous *Fiorentina,* the wood-grilled Tuscan T-bone steak. Anyone interested in seeing the beautiful animals on their farms may ask the butcher for a 5R leaflet, which lists them. The shop has a full range of other meats, including locally bred pigeons.

ORGANIC BREADS

Panificio I Pulitini. Via Sarzanese, 141. San Girolamo. 56045 Pomarance. 0588 64625.

Angelo and Maria Santarella make some of the most wonderful organic breads in Tuscany. Unfortunately they don't sell from their tiny farm, but you can find their breads in various shops in the area. If you can speak Italian, you can phone to find out other stockists' names. You can also special-order breads and biscuits for people with food intolerances or allergies (to wheat, dairy, and sugar).

As "I Pulitini," they are registered organic bakers, using only certified organic flours, many stone ground, and purified water. Their breads are characterized by fresh ingredients and natural yeasts.

"It was difficult for us to adjust to the association's organic requirements," confided soft-spoken Signora Maria. "But we would never go back—people feel so much better when they eat chemical-free products. It is really healing. That is what keeps us going."

From a wide range of flours, including wheat, *farro*, quinoa, kamut, and amaranth, the bakers produce white-flour breads: unsalted *pane sciocco*, plain or with walnuts; olive oil *schiacciata*, plain or with vegetables or olives; and unusual "health" breads. I liked the *farro* loaf. Oil-free, it is made from spelt wheat flour, natural yeasts, and water—without salt. With a thin crust, its café-au-lait-colored dough has small air holes, a slight yeasty sourness, and a pronounced fragrance of fields. The thin *farro* crackers are also good, topped with sesame seeds and baked in rectangular slabs.

I Pulitini's breads may be found at: COOP, Pomarance; L'Altra Roba, Pisa; Cibo Per La Pace, Livorno.

SAN GERVASIO

AZIENDA AGRICOLA   San Gervasio di Palaia   56025   Pontedera
SAN GERVASIO   TELEPHONE 0587 483360   FAX 0587 484361   OPEN 8:00-12:00,
WINE, GAME   14:00-20:00; tastings by appointment or Wednesday 17:00-18:00
CLOSED Sunday   CREDIT CARDS Visa, MC   DIRECT SALE Yes
Unbottled wine sales: 8:00-12:00 Saturday only   ENGLISH SPOKEN Yes
FEATURES Folklore Museum   OTHER Holiday apartments available
DIRECTIONS From Forcoli go up hill toward San Gervasio and restaurant
Belvedere. Turn left at T-junction at top of hill; San Gervasio is on left
after 1.3 kms.

San Gervasio is a self-contained medieval *borgo*, or village, originally belonging
to the bishops of Lucca. Its circular-structured castle was the site of many battles
between Pisans and Florentines. The Tommasini family from Pontedera have
run San Gervasio since 1964. Two sons, Luca and Claudio, are now turning it
into an organic farm and improving the wines.

The estate has 11 hectares (28 acres) of vineyards. The young
winemaker, Luca D'Attoma, had just begun working at San Gervasio when
I visited. He is reducing the quantity of wine sold *sfuso*, unbottled, and improving the quality of bottled wines. Small French casks are used for aging
the white table wine, Marna (of 70 percent Trebbiano and 30 percent Chardonnay), and the red Prugnolo (of 90 percent Sangiovese and 10 percent
Cabernet). DOC wines include Chianti and San Torpè white.

San Gervasio's Museum of Rural Work and Customs features
old farm tools. The farm also has a large hunting reserve; pheasant and other
game birds are raised. It is possible to order game birds, wild boar, and hare for
the table. The *borgo* is surrounded by olive groves. The olives are milled at a
modern-style *frantoio* nearby. Here, too, the owners are switching to organic
methods of cultivation.

A final note: San Gervasio's restaurant Al Belvedere, telephone:
0587 629672, is located on the road toward Forcoli, and is independently managed. It is a pleasant place; the wholesome food is well-cooked and reasonably
priced. They also rent mountain bikes.

SAN GIULIANO TERME

**SERGIO A VILLA
DI CORLIANO
RESTAURANT,
WINE BAR**

SS 12 Pisa-Lucca   Rigoli   56010   San Giuliano Terme
TELEPHONE 050 818858   FAX 050 817790   OPEN Lunch and dinner
CLOSED Wednesday; January and February   CREDIT CARDS Visa, MC,
Amex   DIRECT SALE Yes, for wine and oil   ENGLISH SPOKEN Yes
FEATURES Summer garden terrace   RESERVATIONS Recommended
PRICE Lunch $$, dinner tasting menu $$$ DIRECTIONS From San
Giuliano Terme, go toward Rigoli (to Lucca via Ripafratta). The
restaurant is on the main road, halfway between the two towns.

Sergio Lorenzi was a leading light in Pisa's restaurant scene for years. In 1995 he
closed his exclusive city restaurant and moved to the country, opening with a
more modest formula. The current restaurant occupies the former olive oil
repository of a stately 1500s villa. In summer the tables spill out into the villa's
garden, under a four-hundred-year-old plane tree. In addition to the regular
menu, a fixed-price lunch menu includes four courses. At dinner there is a
more complex *menu degustazione*, or tasting menu.

The Tuscan cuisine bears the hallmarks of a professional kitchen.
This is particularly noticeable in the sauces and stocks for pastas and meats,
which are consistently well prepared. The thin *taglierini* noodles' well-flavored
sauce of shrimp and zucchini has a rich fish stock as its base. Sergio's signature
portafoglio, veal escalope folded around prosciutto and cheese, is nicely browned
and comes in a perfectly finished white wine sauce enriched with butter. A sliced
breast of guinea hen, *faraona*, is deliciously tender, served in a fine sauce studded
with grapes. Desserts are also very professionally made. I liked the frozen *parfait
di croccante*, a creamy *semifreddo* with crunchy caramel in it, and the intriguing
meringue textured with *amaretti* crumbs.

The dining rooms bear original painted plaques commemorat-
ing prizes the villa's oil won at the turn of the century. Two rooms have been
turned into a large wine bar and shop. Wine may be bought to take away or
drink at the wooden tables. Sergio's own oil is also on sale.

SAN MINIATO

**MACELLERIA
SERGIO FALASCHI
MEAT**

Via Augusto Conti, 18/20   56027   San Miniato
TELEPHONE/FAX 0571 43190   OPEN 7:00-13:00, 16:30-20:00; plus
Sunday in November for truffle fair   CLOSED Sunday, Wednesday
afternoon; July   CREDIT CARDS Visa, MC   ENGLISH SPOKEN A little
DIRECTIONS In the center of town, near Piazza del Popolo

This well-stocked butcher's shop sells fresh meats, homemade *salumi* (cured
meats and sausages) and a range of sauces for pasta or *crostini* toasts. Sergio
Falaschi, following his father and grandfather, makes a special salt-cured

shoulder, *spalla,* and a well-seasoned *prosciutto Toscano.* There are spicy sausages scented with truffles or hot pepper, blood sausage studded with pine nuts and raisins (*mallegato alla Sanminiatese*) and head cheese (*soppressata*).

The fresh meats include sought-after Chianina beef, which should be hung for fifteen to twenty days. It is recognizable by its fine pure white fat and firm-fleshed red meat. Ready-to-cook meats include boned rabbit scented with truffle for a quick dinner solution.

IL CANTUCCIO	Via P. Maioli, 67 56027 San Miniato
DI FEDERIGO	TELEPHONE 0571 418344 OPEN 8:00-13:00, 15:00-20:00
PASTRY	CLOSED Sunday afternoon; August CREDIT CARDS Visa, MC
	ENGLISH SPOKEN Yes DIRECTIONS The bakery is within the old town walls.

Rino Gazzarrini is a master baker (and inventor) of desserts, cakes, and biscuits. With his son Paolo, he runs a wonderful pastry shop at the edge of the old town that is worth a detour: some of the cakes were among the best I have tasted in Tuscany.

Gazzarrini specializes in sweet yeast breads, like Christmas *panettone* and Easter *colomba.* Usually produced only in traditional flavors, Gazzarrini has stretched the repertoire. His rich, buttery *colomba* (Easter dove) comes flavored with coffee, chocolate, or lemon, or made with whole-wheat flour, scented with *moscato* wine, or studded with candied exotic fruits . . . there is no limit. And they are truly delicious. *Colomba al caffè* is enriched with bitter coffee and studded with rare coffee-flavored semisweet French chocolate chips. Rino Gazzarrini called it one of his "little masterpieces."

"*Panettone* is considered a Milanese specialty," he confided, "but why should they be the only ones to have it?" He tried his hand at it, praying for guidance, and the result was a light, buttery, airy confection that is quite irresistible. He explained that the dough for *panettone* was *parecchio gentile,* pretty fine, and that part of the secret of its high raised dome was to let it cool—or "put it to sleep"—upside-down.

His son Paolo has a passion for fine wines; some are available from the bakery. He has also reinvented one of the area's sacred cows, the *brigidino.* This crunchy, wafer-thin, anise-scented biscuit originated near Montecatini Terme. It can be good (see p 77), but all too often is sold at fairs and is oversweet and artificially flavored. Not so the Gazzarrinis'! Paolo makes them in ten flavors, including one with real anise seeds and a deep dark chocolate one studded with fine crumbs of orange peel (my favorite), plus a host of other flavors. They are sold in cellophane bags to keep out the damp. A great selection of cakes and tarts (sold whole or cut in half), pastries, petits fours, and cookies are on sale from the tiny shop—at very reasonable prices.

SAN MINIATO'S TRUFFLE FAIR

Each November the town of San Miniato celebrates the season's local harvest of the *Tuber magnatum pico*, or white truffle, by hosting Tuscany's most important truffle fair—la Fiera del Tartufo—which takes place over a weekend. It is great fun to visit. The place goes truffle-mad: at the top of the lovely medieval hill town are stalls selling the precious fungus; local restaurants feature truffle-based menus; the Association of Truffle Hunters, L'Associazione Tartufai Sanminiatese (tel: 0571 418251), organizes various events; and best of all, there is a truffle-hunting contest for specially trained truffle dogs.

If it is not too cold a day, this is wonderful to watch, in a peculiarly uneventful sort of way. A group of overexcited dogs, with human trainers, are let, one at a time, into a confined area in which several small truffles have been buried (usually the children's playground). The object is to sniff out the hidden truffles in the allotted five minutes. This sounds easier than it is. When I watched, the first dog did very well and found them all, but the remaining dogs seemed more interested in the scent of the preceding dogs than in the buried treasure—much to the frustration of their owners. The prize . . . a large truffle!

Also

Enoteca "Spirito di Vino." Piazza del Popolo, 19. 0571 401059.

This is a new wine shop specializing in Tuscan wines, with an emphasis on less well known producers from the Colline Pisane. There are wines from other Italian regions and a nice group of *passiti*—dessert wines made from partially dried grapes—that Benedetto Squicciarini (of the nearby winery Tenuta di Cusignano) has chosen with Carlo Gazzarrini.

SANTA CROCE SULL'ARNO

Pasticceria Ottavio Scarselli. Via di Pelle, 1. 0571 30659.

Santa Croce is Tuscany's leather-tanning center. This large *pasticceria* and bar is a favorite of the tannery workers, who come for cups of Scarselli's home-roasted coffee. The assortment of pastries includes one that is special to the town: *amaretti di Santa Croce*. Shaped like little pyramids, these are mounds of ground sweet and bitter Sicilian almonds, sugar, and egg white, baked until golden brown on top but still nicely chewy in the center. They stand on tiny squares of hostlike rice paper. The town dedicates an annual *sagra*, or festival, to them in late autumn.

SOIANA

ELYANE AND
BRUNO MOOS
WINE

Castello di Soiana   Via Pier Capponi, 98   56030   Soiana
TELEPHONE/FAX 0587 654180   OPEN Visits, tastings and sales by
appointment only   CREDIT CARDS None   DIRECT SALE Yes
ENGLISH SPOKEN Yes   DIRECTIONS Via Pier Capponi is Soiana's
central street

You would be hard-pressed to find a couple as warm, generous, and determined to make fine wine as Bruno and Elyane Moos. Since arriving from Canada in 1983, they have practiced the art of winemaking with conscience and intelligence, and they have been instrumental in raising the viticultural standards of this previously underestimated wine zone.

The Mooses have 3 hectares (7 acres) of vineyards located on the little hills known as Colline Pisane. This is a rural area, with patches of vineyards and olive groves interspersed with orchards and kitchen gardens. Bruno and Elyane do all the work in the vineyard and cellar themselves. Their *cantina* is extraordinary: a descending underground tunnel in the village. "There was once a fortified castle in Soiana," explained Bruno, an architect who worked with Marcel Breuer in New York in the seventies. "But it was razed to the ground in 1492. Somehow its network of cellars survived."

The Mooses make and age their wines in this historic *cantina*. Like many of the world's most serious winemakers, Bruno Moos is a disciple of the great Bordeaux enologist Émile Peynaud. "Peynaud has been a master of modern winemaking," he asserted. "His books have been instrumental in teaching us the methodology of making fine, concentrated wines. Many of his ideas, including reduced grape yields, go against the traditional system used by the *contadini*, or peasants."

Soianello is a red wine of 85 percent Sangiovese, with 15 percent divided between Malvasia Nera and Cabernet Sauvignon. It is matured in large wooden barrels and is fruity and drinkable. Fontestina is the Mooses' super-Tuscan: of 95 percent Sangiovese and 5 percent Ciliegiolo, it spends eighteen months maturing in French *barriques*. It is a pure, concentrated wine of intensely flavored fruit and powerful structure. Soiano Bianco is a white of Vermentino.

Bruno and Elyane have become a key point on the viticultural map of western Tuscany; their large, old-fashioned house is a welcome refuge for stray cats, dogs, and wine writers.

STAFFOLI

DA BEPPE   Via Livornese, 35-37   56020   Staffoli
RESTAURANT   TELEPHONE 0571 37002   FAX 0571 37052   OPEN Lunch and dinner
                           CLOSED Sunday evening, Monday; two weeks in August
                           CREDIT CARDS Visa, MC, Amex   ENGLISH SPOKEN A little
                           RESERVATIONS Recommended for dinner   PRICE $$$
                           DIRECTIONS On main street through Staffoli

In his restaurant, Luca Cristiani experiments with ambitious combinations of
ingredients and flavors. Like all experiments, some are wildly successful, others
are less so. The setting, too, is curiously unsettled. Mint green waxed walls are
set off by (jar with?) pink frilled curtains that border on kitsch. A mixed collection of oil paintings adorn the walls. There are vaulted brick ceilings; tables
with differently hued pink tablecloths and greenish underskirts; and unusual
fan-tined forks.

For our meal, superb handmade rolls preceded the *grande
antipasto di pesce*, which was served on a very, very large charger and consisted
of nine fish-based hors d'oeuvres. Other options included a warm salad of
oranges with river shrimp; baby squid with porcini mushrooms; stuffed cuttlefish with saffron; and several land-based choices. For *primo,* a spinach-leaf was
stuffed with barley, celery, and pieces of white fish. A dish of rice was stained
black by squid ink and contained miniscule white squid tentacles, mussels, and
tomato chunks. My companion liked it because it was sweetish and barely tasted
of squid ink. I couldn't help wondering if that wasn't what it was missing.

An adult cuttlefish stewed with beet greens and some tomato
had a strong presence of garlic, but it lacked the fiery impact this rustic dish
often has. A large fillet of sea bass was beautifully topped with row upon row
of perfect porcini slices and drizzled with garlicky green oil. The pastry chef,
who may also be the bread maker, did an excellent job baking the desserts.
Luca Cristiani is an enthusiastic man who has worked under some of Italy's
most prestigious chefs. He came back from his travels to take over what had
been his father Beppe's popular trattoria—to give it his own personal stamp.

TIRRENIA

DANTE E IVANA   Viale del Tirreno, 207/c   56018   Tirrenia
RESTAURANT   TELEPHONE/FAX 050 32549   OPEN Lunch and dinner Monday-
                           Saturday; in August, nightly for dinner only   CLOSED Sunday; lunch
                           in August; January   CREDIT CARDS Visa, MC, Amex
                           ENGLISH SPOKEN Yes   RESERVATIONS Recommended for dinner
                           PRICE $$$ DIRECTIONS Viale del Tirreno runs parallel to Tirrenia's sea
                           front, separated from the beach by a pine wood.

This well-known fish restaurant has a tranquil modern interior with soft
diffused light. The varied menu offers fish and shellfish from the Tyrrhenian

Sea as well as other varieties from farther afield. The ingredients that accompany and enhance them are Mediterranean: tomatoes, *cannellini* beans, zucchini flowers, herbs, wine, and most importantly, extra-virgin olive oil. The restaurant uses a sweet and fruity oil from nearby Buti, and it stars in many of the dishes. Dante Grassi, who runs the restaurant with his wife, Ivana Lucchesi, is an experienced restaurateur and sommelier. His extensive wine list leans toward whites, supplying information on producers and grape varieties.

My *antipasto carpaccio* of raw sea bass came on a sizzlingly hot plate, topped with arugula and peppery olive oil. A beautiful green-ribbed zucchini flower was stuffed and steamed with a compact mousse of *aragosta*—the clawless spiny lobster; it, too, was accompanied by the golden-green oil. Spaghetti was offered with clams, shellfish, or lobster (priced accordingly). A specialty from nearby Lucca were *tacconi*—egg pasta handkerchiefs richly sauced with chunks of shrimp, tomato, and arugula. *Bavettine,* like thin linguine, were great with flaked *triglie,* red mullet, sweet cherry tomatoes, parsley, and oil. Red mullet is popular along this coastline; its firm flesh and full flavor stand up well to Mediterranean aromatics.

Main courses included fresh scampi, large shrimp tossed into a colorful, crunchy salad of carrot, fennel, and radish. Here, too, the oil played its part. Chunks of filleted *orata* (gilt-head bream), were sautéed with meaty porcini mushrooms. Fish were available simply steamed or grilled. A refreshing sorbet of muscat wine and pink grapefruit finished the meal.

VOLTERRA

AZIENDA AGRICOLA 56048   Volterra
LISCHETO TELEPHONE 0588 30403   OPEN Shop: 8:00-12:30, 14:30-19:00
CHEESE: ORGANIC CLOSED Never   CREDIT CARDS None   DIRECT SALE Yes
ENGLISH SPOKEN No   OTHER Holiday apartments available
DIRECTIONS From Volterra go toward Pontedera and Montecatini Val di Cecina. The farm is signposted after about 7 kms. Follow the unpaved road to the end.

Giovanni Cannas's farm is situated in a remarkable position. Perched on top of one of the pure, treeless round hills that characterize this part of the country, its stone buildings look across a strange "moonscape" to the town of Volterra. It is a moving sight. Giovanni's father, a Sardinian shepherd, took over this land in the 1960s. "There was nothing here then, just some ruined buildings in an abandoned landscape," recounted Giovanni. "My father brought a few sheep and put in thirty years of work to turn it into a thousand-head herd."

When Giovanni decided to make cheese, his father was against it. But Giovanni convinced him both to make the cheeses and to convert the farm to organic. "That was my dream," he confided. "And this land lent itself well. It is very poor terrain, so we sow it with clover and *sulla* [*Hedysarum coro-narium*], a flowering leguminous plant. The sheep like it and it makes their milk very sweet. We are now the biggest organic cheesemaker in Tuscany— even if we are very small."

From pasteurized sheep's milk Cannas makes very mild, sweet and aromatic ricotta, *ravaggiolo* (a fresh single-curd cheese), and a range of pecorini. The small round *tomino*, a bright white fresh cheese, has a more com- pact consistency. Lightly salted, it is delicious sprinkled with good olive oil and pepper. The orange-rind pecorino is matured for two months and has a delicate tang to it. *Pecorino stagionato* is aged for six months. It has a natural brown crust, a smooth consistency, and a decisive, unmistakable flavor of sheep's milk. The farm has a small shop for selling its cheeses, olive oil (made from olives grown in Bibbona), and honey.

PASTICCERIA
MIGLIORINI
PASTRY

Via Gramsci, 21   56048   Volterra
TELEPHONE 0588 86446   FAX 0588 86946
E-MAIL migliorini@sirt.pisa.it   OPEN 7:30-13:00, 16:00-20:00
CLOSED Sunday afternoon, Tuesday; holidays in July and January
CREDIT CARDS None   ENGLISH SPOKEN A little
DIRECTIONS Off Piazza xx Settembre

This lovely pastry shop with its 1960s decor makes a fine variation on *panforte*. Torta Etruria is a dense, spiced honey confection studded with chopped toasted almonds and candied orange peel; it is topped with a nice layer of dark choco- late. Other unusual pastries include the *pane del pescatore* (fisherman's bread), a short crust pastry enriched with almonds and nuts. The *pasticceria* produces a full range of cookies, doughnuts, cakes, and *semifreddi*—frozen desserts.

ENOTECA SACCO
FIORENTINO
WINE BAR,
RESTAURANT

Piazza xx Settembre, 18   56048   Volterra
TELEPHONE 0588 88537   OPEN 12:00-14:30, 19:00-21:30
CLOSED Friday; November to March   CREDIT CARDS Visa, MC, Amex
ENGLISH SPOKEN A little   RESERVATIONS Recommended on weekends
PRICE $-$$ DIRECTIONS In the town center, near the museum

Formerly a refined trattoria, the Sacco Fiorentino has recently changed tack. Its owners have switched to a more flexible formula—a good idea, given the restaurant's location in the center of the much-visited Etruscan city, and it is being done with some style.

An ambitious wine list offers many wines by the bottle or glass. The accompanying menu includes a page of light snacks: stuffed focaccia sand- wiches, well-chosen cheese and *salumi* platters, and salads. There are *primi*— pastas and soups—and some *secondi:* egg frittatas, sausages, rabbit, chicken, and a few grilled meats. You can choose to have just a light meal, or more, with or without wine. And there are good desserts, too.

VOLTERRA'S ALABASTER

Volterra has been a center for alabaster since the Etruscans carved it for their funerary urns a thousand years before Christ. Visit the town's extraordinary Etruscan Museum to see these. The beautiful, at times translucent, stone is found all around the area, in both surface and underground mines. Over fifty varieties are known, ranging from marblelike veined dark stone to the better known powdery white version that looks like cloudy glass.

The town is full of artisan and semi-industrial boutiques selling alabaster objects, in shapes from the sublime to the ridiculous. Seeing so many all together may be a bit overwhelming, but some of the simpler objects, such as the wide shallow bowls, have a purity of line and substance that makes them worth the effort of taking home.

CHAPTER 6

Livorno and Its Coast

The great Medicean port of Livorno was heavily bombed during World War II: today little remains of the town's once grand center or fine palazzi. A pleasant but rather anonymous post-war district has replaced it. Despite this I found Livorno interesting; in 1593, Ferdinand I declared it a free port and an open city, one in which people of all religions were free to worship, and it has retained something of this atmosphere of acceptance and interchange. Its great sea dish, *cacciucco*, a mixed fish stew, is well worth experiencing.

Livorno's shore, stretching south along the Tyrrhenian Sea as far as Piombino, is known as the Coast of the Etruscans. This early Italian civilization settled here from 900 to 600 B.C., founding many towns and leaving a legacy of seaports, roads, and irrigation. Today the area is celebrated for the fine wines of Montescudaio, Val di Cornia, and Bolgheri (including Sassicaia, the legendary first "super-Tuscan"). World-class vineyards now cover hills that until recently were considered unsuitable for vine-growing. Olive oil, too, is increasingly being improved as better methods of cultivation and processing are practiced. The flat coastal strip is used for agriculture, producing wonderful tomatoes, tiny artichokes, fava beans, and fruit, and there is an amazing variety of local fish to be found in its markets and restaurants.

Azienda Promozione Turistica
Piazza Cavour, 6
57126 Livorno
0586 898111, fax 0586 896173

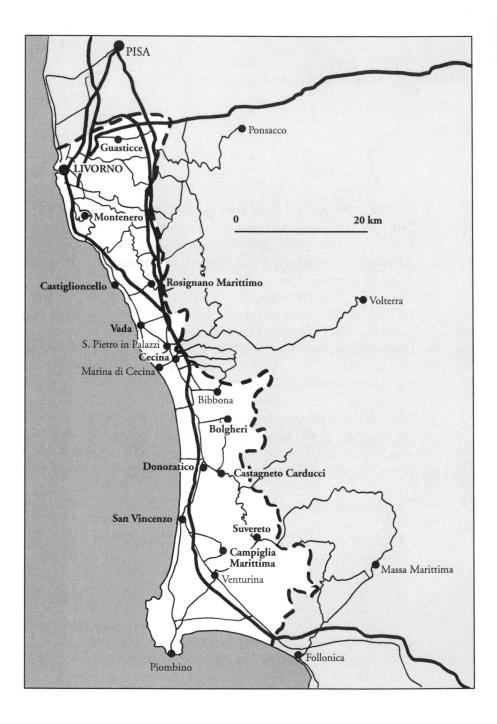

Town names in **bold** indicate towns that are included in this chapter.

BOLGHERI

LE MACCHIOLE
WINE

Le Contessine   Via Bolgherese, 189   57020   Bolgheri
TELEPHONE 0565 766092   FAX 0565 763240   OPEN Visits by
appointment only. No tastings   DIRECT SALE No
STOCKIST The wines are available from the *enoteche* at Bolgheri and
Castagneto Carducci   ENGLISH SPOKEN No
DIRECTIONS   On the road between Bolgheri and Castagneto Carducci

Compared to his neighbors Ornellaia and San Guido, Eugenio Campolmi's winery may seem small, but it has provided him with big results. "I was considered the black sheep of my family," confided the tall, broad-shouldered young man. "They had run a business for seven generations, but I had my heart set on making wine." He bought the property in 1983, and in 1984 began planting the vineyards. He now owns 10 hectares (22 acres) and rents 6 (15).

Campolmi's prize wine is his Paleo Rosso, a big, *barrique*-aged red wine in the new Bolgheri style, of 90 percent Cabernet Sauvignon with 10 percent Sangiovese. "Its first year was 1989—a terrible year. I wasn't sure what to call my wine. I looked out at the rainy vineyards high with weeds and said in our local jargon: '*che paleo che c'è quest'anno* [what high grass there is this year].' And there was the name: I wanted a short, decisive, masculine-sounding name."

The earliest vintages of Paleo had higher percentages of Sangiovese. "The Sangiovese was added because it takes the edge off the green sharpness of the Cabernet, making it rounder, mellower," he explained. Even so, this is a wine with big tannins that benefits from being cellared before drinking. After being aged in the small casks for eighteen to twenty-four months, Campolmi fines it in the bottle for eighteen months before selling it.

Working with the young winemaker Luca D'Attoma, Campolmi has brought his wines up to be competitive with those of his famous neighbors. What was the secret, I asked?

"A lot has changed here in the last twenty years," replied D'Attoma. "Italians used to think that great wines were made in the cellars, but that has changed. They recognize that the vital work is done in the vineyards. And no matter what a winemaker says, the real 'soul' of each winery is its owner."

TENUTA DELL'
ORNELLAIA
WINE

Via Bolgherese   57020   Bolgheri
TELEPHONE 0565 762140   FAX 0565 762144   OPEN Visits by prior
written request only   DIRECT SALE No   STOCKIST Ornellaia's wines
are sold in all the local wine shops, subject to availability
ENGLISH SPOKEN Yes   DIRECTIONS On the road between Bolgheri and
Castagneto Carducci

Since its first vintage in 1985, Ornellaia has been esteemed by the international wine circuit. Its wines are modern in style and have been particularly appreciated by Americans. Ornellaia's proprietor, Marchese Lodovico Antinori, studied and lived in California, and the estate's original consultant was André Tchelistcheff, the "father" of California's wine industry. Another key consultant was Michel Rolland, one of Bordeaux's leading winemakers.

Thanks to the example set by Ornellaia's neighbor, San Guido —whose Cabernet, Sassicaia, started the so-called Tuscan wine revolution—the winemaking potential of Bolgheri was recognized. Antinori also determined to produce quality French-style wines in a coastal area previously considered unsuitable for such an enterprise.

Large investments followed. The estate's 135 hectares (333 acres) of vineyards were planted with select clones of popular international grape varieties: the Cabernets Sauvignon and Franc, Merlot, and Sauvignon Blanc. Consultants Tibor Gal from Hungary and Danny Schuster from New Zealand oversee the *cantina* and vineyards. The ultramodern cellar was designed by the Florentine architect Farinelli, who was visibly inspired by the Renaissance architect Bernardo Buontalenti: the cellar's half-buried pentagonal structure recalls the Medici's fortresses.

Ornellaia's award-winning, powerful reds are Masseto, of pure Merlot, and Ornellaia, a Bordeaux-style blend of Cabernet Sauvignon, Merlot, and Cabernet Franc. Poggio alle Gazze is the estate's most popular white: of Sauvignon Blanc matured without wood, it is a fragrant, balanced wine that has earned its loyal following.

TENUTA SAN GUIDO Capanne, 27 57020 Bolgheri
WINE   TELEPHONE 0565 762003 FAX 0565 762017 OPEN Visits by prior written request only DIRECT SALE No STOCKIST Sassicaia is sold at the wine shops at Bolgheri; sales are normally limited to two bottles per person. ENGLISH SPOKEN Yes DIRECTIONS On the road from the SS1 to Bolgheri

Visiting the home of Tuscany's most famous wine is a great experience. I was pleased to discover how unpretentious, how normal, a home it is. Tenuta San Guido is, first and foremost, a working farm—albeit an exceptional one. Wine (and they make just one) is just one of its activities. Its grand old buildings, historic cypress avenue, and stately villa are imposing, but thankfully free of hype, hoopla, and PR persons. However, to visit you must write in advance to make an appointment.

Marchese Niccolò Incisa della Rocchetta, an unassuming, intelligent man with lively, attentive eyes, believes in meeting with journalists personally. The contact is direct—who better than he can explain his legendary wine, Sassicaia?

"When it all started there was no intention to sell this wine," he began as we sat in his small private office. "Sassicaia was the product of my father's passion. He was a man of culture and refinement—perhaps more so than other Tuscan landowners of his generation. He wanted to make wines of quality. This was back in 1944."

At that time most Tuscan wines were sold unbottled, or exported *en masse*, like Chianti. Marchese Mario Incisa took the radical step of planting Cabernets Sauvignon and Franc, of drastically reducing grape yields, and of following vinification principles common in France.

"My father saw it as an adventure, a challenge," he recalled. "To make a good red wine in an area with a terrible reputation. I like to think that Sassicaia was born from his hard-headedness—he was determined to prove his point." He paused to smile. "I think we can safely say he succeeded."

For almost twenty years Mario Incisa considered the wine as an experiment. It was never drunk outside of family circles. "In the late 1960s," he continued, "his experiment turned into something more important." Mario Incisa decided to sell Sassicaia, but was unsure if it would age well. It would be sold through Marchese Piero Antinori, whose winemaker was Giacomo Tachis.

"Antinori was very impressed by Sassicaia's original *impronto,* or stamp, but felt we needed help in handling its vinification and in making it more consistent. He suggested Tachis could advise us on that." A long and fruitful collaboration ensued between Tuscany's most brilliant enologist and the Incisa della Rocchetta family. Sassicaia immediately won admirers internationally; it was favorably compared to the greatest Bordeaux, despite having no official status at home beyond that of a mere *vino da tavola,* or table wine. The super-Tuscan generation had begun.

"If there is one thing that really pleases me," said Niccolò Incisa, "it is to see the way in which Italian winemaking has changed since then. Sassicaia and its success triggered a revolution from Piedmont to Sicily—one that continues today."

After an assiduous grape selection in the estate's 50 hectares (123 acres) of vineyard, Sassicaia's vinification takes place in stainless-steel vats. It is matured for twenty-four months in French *barriques* before being united in one giant vat prior to bottling. This ensures that all the wine from a vintage is the same—an important fact, given that around a hundred thousand bottles are now produced annually. It then spends six months in the bottle before being sold. Niccolò Incisa recommends ideally cellaring the wine for several years before drinking, in order to fully savor its complexity and elegance.

"Sassicaia is always liked by the people who drink it," he affirmed. "The most important thing is that it should be appreciated by normal wine lovers, not just by specialists and critics."

ENOTECA TOGNONI   Strada Giulia, 6 and 4   57020   Bolgheri
WINE STORE,   TELEPHONE 0565 762001   OPEN 8:00-23:00 in summer; 8:00-19:00
SPECIALTY FOODS   in winter   CLOSED Wednesday in winter; November
                         CREDIT CARDS Visa, MC   DIRECT SALE Yes
                         ENGLISH SPOKEN A little   DIRECTIONS On main street of village

Fabio Tognoni and his wife, Paola, run adjacent stores in Bolgheri. One specializes in wines, the other offers specialty foods—oils, local cheeses, preserved vegetables, *salumi,* pasta sauces—and snacks, which can be eaten there or bought to go. At the *enoteca,* almost all the wines of Bolgheri and Castagneto Carducci may be tasted before being bought, with the exception of Sassicaia and Ornellaia.

CAMPIGLIA MARITTIMA

IL CAPPELLAIO   Via di San Vincenzo   57021   Campiglia Marittima
PAZZO   TELEPHONE 0565 838358   OPEN Lunch and dinner
RESTAURANT   CLOSED Tuesday in winter; February, part of November
                        CREDIT CARDS Visa, MC, Amex   ENGLISH SPOKEN Yes
                        FEATURES Summer garden dining   RESERVATIONS Recommended
                        PRICE $$$ OTHER The farmhouse has six guest rooms
                        DIRECTIONS Take the San Vincenzo Sud exit from the *superstrada*
                        (SS 1); go toward Campiglia Marittima. The restaurant is on the left;
                        look for signs.

The "Mad Hatter" is a farmhouse restaurant in a pastoral setting between hills and sea. In summer you eat outside in the garden; in winter, in the large dining room—its mad collection of hats is colorful and welcoming. Denni Bruci is a well-traveled young man with fresh ideas about food. He and his mother, Michela, prepare a creative, eclectic cuisine based on local ingredients combined imaginatively. Their food is fragrant with herbs, spices, and truffles.

For *primi,* a round toast is topped with plump mussels and shrimp blanketed in a savory *zabaglione* stained yellow with saffron. A deep-fried rice-paper roll contains shrimp, basil, and shredded greens. A slice of lightly smoked sturgeon is served warm, garnished with grated zucchini and sage. *Linguine con astice* comes studded with chunks of tender lobster and fresh tomato. Green vegetable risotto is scented with earthy San Miniato truffles.

For *secondi,* rabbit is boned, braised with rosemary and served with a wonderfully delicate purée of garlic. Sea bass is grilled simply over wood embers. Desserts, too, are uncomplicated yet finely flavored: pears are poached in white wine and served with a deep chocolate sauce and toasted pine nuts; apples are stewed and married to a sweet and sharp raspberry *aspretto.* There is a well-selected wine list featuring many of the area's great wines.

CASTAGNETO CARDUCCI

GRATTAMACCO   Grattamacco   57022   Castagneto Carducci
PODERE SANTA MARIA   TELEPHONE 0565 763933   OPEN By appointment only
OLIVE OIL   CREDIT CARDS None   DIRECT SALE Yes   ENGLISH SPOKEN Yes
                         OTHER Two apartments available for holiday rentals
                         DIRECTIONS Take the road from Bolgheri to Castagneto Carducci. After
                         about 5 kms turn left at sign for *ristorante*. After 300 meters, turn left
                         on dirt road. The farm is after about 1 km, by an enormous oak tree.
                         Or follow the directions for Grattamacco (next entry) and after the
                         modern *cantina* follow the dirt road down to the next farm.

Podere Santa Maria once formed part of the Grattamacco estate. Claudio
Traini came with the Meletti Cavallaris from Bergamo when they bought it in
the late 1970s (see next entry). The farms later divided. Traini makes one of the
area's most delicious olive oils. It is produced organically from the *podere*'s
fifteen hundred trees, some of which are over five hundred years old. "We were
lucky here in 1985," Claudio Traini explained. "Being close to the sea, when the
big freeze came, our trees were barely affected.

"When we first arrived the olive groves had been abandoned. If
olive trees are not pruned regularly, they send up suckers from the roots, which
eventually overpower the main trunk. We studied and experimented with
different cultivation techniques."

New plants may be grown in either of two forms: *monocono*
(a single trunk growing upright that lends itself to mechanized harvesting)
or *cespuglio* (a wider bush with three or four leading trunks, best for hand-
picking or steep terrains). Traini favors the latter system, as his trees grow on
sloping ground.

"Pure extra-virgin oil, being a natural product, is different
every year. It's like wine; some vintages are less good due to climatic conditions. Only industrial oils can guarantee consistency, but that is because they
are chemically adjusted."

Traini's oil is very fruity, with a fabulous full perfume and a light but
pleasant bitterness to it. When I held a blind taste test with friends of a group
of Tuscan oils, Traini's won.

GRATTAMACCO   Podere Grattamacco   57022   Castagneto Carducci
WINE, OLIVE OIL   TELEPHONE 0565 763840   FAX 0565 763217   OPEN 9:00-12:00,
                       15:00-18:00 prior appointment recommended; group tastings possible by
                       prior arrangement   CLOSED Saturday, Sunday   CREDIT CARDS No
                       DIRECT SALE Yes, subject to availability   ENGLISH SPOKEN Yes
                       OTHER Apartments available for holiday rentals   DIRECTIONS From
                       Donoratico go through Castagneto Carducci. About 2 kms after the
                       village, follow yellow signs to restaurant Il Cacciatore. Follow the road
                       from here, to the right, to the *cantina* building, a modern construction.
                       Or follow directions for last entry, and after passing Podere Santa Maria,
                       continue straight to the modern *cantina*.

Piermario and Paola Meletti Cavallari produce some of Bolgheri's most interesting wines. Their estate, in the hills between Castagneto and Bolgheri,
includes 8 hectares (20 acres) of vineyards and over a thousand olive trees.
The couple are from Bergamo, in northern Italy. When Piermario decided
to change his life and leave Milan, he first opened a wine store.

"I met some of the smaller wine producers," he recounted, "and
I began to think it would be more interesting to be producing wine than selling
it." The couple bought Grattamacco and set about planting vineyards. That
was more than twenty years ago, when the Bolgheri winemaking "revolution"
had just begun.

"I have tried to apply my intelligence to this work," he explained
as we visited their new aging cellar. A large oval room with a striking night-blue
ceiling appears to have been scooped out of the hillside: cut-out "windows"
along its smooth circumference reveal bare earth and stones. "This is as natural
an environment as possible for the wine's maturation," he explained enthusiastically. "Here it can breathe." It was raining that day, and water trickled freely
down the "open" earth walls and away.

"We have everything to thank Mario Incisa for," he remarked.
"Without his intuition about making great red wines, we would all still be
making whites, no doubt lost in obscurity. He was an unforgettable man."

Piermario has maintained the practice of fermenting his red
wine in open-topped wood barrels. (San Guido's Sassicaia was originally
made this way, but later switched to closed stainless steel as market demands
increased.) "This is by far the most organic system," Piermario said of the open
barrels. "They need space, but the wood offers the wine a natural insulation,
resulting in softer tannins."

Natural is a word Meletti Cavallari likes: just as he has eliminated
chemical fertilizers and reduced fungicides in the vineyard, his new cellar mini-
mizes the use of pumps and filters. "I love the idea of letting the wine move
under its own weight. Being small," he concluded, "we are free to make the
wines we like, without having to adapt to the market's demands."

"It's true," added his wife. "People have always enjoyed our wines. They are intense yet elegant, but very drinkable." Grattamacco Rosso and Bianco, as of 1994 both Bolgheri DOC wines, are available as long as stocks last. The couple also produces excellent extra-virgin olive oil.

MICHELE SATTA
WINE

Vigna al Cavaliere   57020   Castegneto Carducci
TELEPHONE 0565 763483   FAX 0565 763894   OPEN Visits, tastings and sales by previous appointment only   CREDIT CARDS None
DIRECT SALE Subject to availability   ENGLISH SPOKEN A little
DIRECTIONS From Castagneto, take SS 329 toward Donoratico; then take Via dell' Accattapane; the *cantina* is on the left after one hundred meters.

"Wine comes from the land, not the sky!" exclaimed Michele Satta enthusiastically as he showed me his newly planted vineyards. Satta trained as an agronomist, and he loves the hands-on work of the land. "Even when the work is the most tiring or difficult," he continued simply, "I find it irresistible. For me, it is not a dream of country life that holds me here, but a physical, concrete attachment to this earth, these plants."

Michele Satta came to winemaking in Bolgheri by chance. He was vacationing when he met a local landowner looking for an assistant. "I was only twenty years old, but I couldn't wait to 'put my hands in the dough,' as we say. I worked for him while I finished my degree. I loved the job, but wanted to be my own boss."

He rented a few acres of vineyards, enough to make a serious start at winemaking. In 1988 came the next step: with winemaker Attilio Pagli, he decided to invest in vineyards to supplement those being rented. At present the winery comprises 12 hectares (30 acres). A new *cantina* is also in the works.

Satta is a warm, open young man who readily communicates his excitement for his work and its fruit. His wines, too, have a wonderful warmth to them. Vigna al Cavaliere, named for the single vineyard the grapes are picked from, is made of pure Sangiovese.

"This is a *cru* from a low, flat vineyard," he explained. "Here in Castagneto the *terroir* is unique: the ground is rich in minerals, the position very luminous and hot. The vines develop impetuously, precociously, even violently, and this enormous burst of energy makes the wines elegant and less 'tired' than the local wines traditionally have been."

Satta's other "table wine" is Piastraia, a blend of equal parts of Sangiovese, Merlot, Cabernet Sauvignon, and Syrah. This, too, is an intense, fruit-rich wine with a lively quality to it. Satta's wines are well structured, but drinkable, with balanced tannins. Diambra, his affordable "simple" red wine, is fresh and fruity and made to be drunk young. La Costa di Giulia is a white wine made from the Vermentino grapes that have long been associated with this part of the Mediterranean coast.

ENOTECA IL BORGO   Via Vittorio Emanuele, 25/27   57020   Castagneto Carducci
WINE STORE   TELEPHONE/FAX 0565 766006   OPEN 10:00-12:00, 17:30-23:00
    CLOSED Monday; November-Christmas, January-Easter
    CREDIT CARDS Visa, MC   DIRECT SALE Yes   ENGLISH SPOKEN Yes
    DIRECTIONS In the town center

Pasquino Malenotti runs one of the best wine stores in the area. It features a large selection of Tuscans, with special emphasis on the great local wines and on Chianti. Wines may be bought by the glass at the stand-up bar, along with grappa and Vin Santi. They also hold tastings and cater to groups. Snacks are available, as well as a selection of local oils. Across the street is a modest trattoria, Da Ugo (same phone), that is run by the *enoteca's* owners. I found its wine list of a higher caliber than its food. It does, however, have a fabulous view.

CASTIGLIONCELLO

DAI DAI   Via del Sorriso, 16   57012   Castiglioncello
FROZEN DESSERTS   TELEPHONE 0586 752754   FAX 0586 751653   OPEN Café: June,
    July, August: 21:30-late; winter: Friday, Saturday: 21:30-late, Sunday:
    15:30-20:00   CLOSED Café: Monday-Thursday in winter; office:
    Saturday and Sunday   CREDIT CARDS None   DIRECT SALE Yes,
    from the office, Monday-Friday 8:30-17:30 for large orders
    ENGLISH SPOKEN A little   FEATURES Café's terraced garden overlooks
    the sea   RESERVATIONS None accepted   DIRECTIONS From Castigli-
    oncello take the SS 1 Aurelia toward Livorno. Just beyond the village
    there is a small turning on the right, signposted. Go up to the top of
    the hill.

How many ice cream companies are named for the call of a cart driver to his mule? How many can claim to dip all their frozen bon-bons by hand? Or boast of having Oliviero Toscani as their photographer? I certainly can't think of another. In the world of frozen desserts, Dai Dai is unique.

"Last year we broke fifty-seven thousand eggs here," the company's spirited owner Antonio Bartoletti volunteered. "Every ingredient we use, from the Maremman cream to the Pisan pine nuts, is fresh and authentic—no artificial anything!"

The mule and cart story may seem apocryphal, but it's true— *"Dai! Dai!"* is the Italian equivalent to "Giddy up!" In the 1920s a Sicilian hawker drove his cart along the local beach, selling ice creams as he cajoled his mule; the phrase stuck. Sixty years later Bartoletti bought the recipe for his *cassatina,* and Dai Dai was born.

"We started with one product," he said, "and then added only a few more. The ice cream industry is very, very tough to crack into. The big companies can squeeze the little guys out by refusing them space in the freezers they place in almost every bar and restaurant. The only way to survive is not to compete—to make a limited range of artisan products in a different category."

Dai Dai makes *semifreddi*, not gelati. *Semifreddi* are desserts frozen after they have been made, whereas gelati, or ice creams, are frozen as they are being made. One of his most popular items is the *bocconcino*, a bite-sized chilled cream custard square, hand-dipped in chocolate and then frozen. It retains the crystalline structure of frozen, but unbeaten, whipped cream.

Dai Dai sells its geometric-shaped desserts to many restaurants and in its lovely café, perched high on the hill overlooking the Mediterranean. The range includes *pezzi duri* (hard pieces), triangles of fresh fruit sorbets made with mineral water; *tartufini*, rich chocolate truffles; *mattonella*, a *semifreddo* cream studded with pine nuts; and the original *cassatina*, individually wrapped slices of frozen cream hand-covered with a thin layer of bittersweet Pernigotti chocolate.

CECINA

MEDITERRANEA BELFIORE—FAMIGLIA CIARLO PRESERVED VEGETABLES

Via Guerrazzi   La Cinquantina   San Pietro in Palazzi   57023   Cecina   TELEPHONE 0586 620555   FAX 0586 622363   OPEN 9:00-12:00, 15:00-19:00   CLOSED Sunday   CREDIT CARDS None   DIRECT SALE Yes   STOCKIST In Cecina: Casa Belfiore, Via Turati, 11.   ENGLISH SPOKEN Yes   DIRECTIONS Exit from SS 1 *superstrada* at S. Pietro in Palazzi (just north of Cecina). Go toward Cecina Mare on Via Guerrazzi. After about 2 kms, follow green sign to Famiglia Ciarlo along an unpaved road.

This farm, located on flat land near the sea, produces wonderful bottled vegetables, sauces and preserves. The Ciarlo family began processing tomatoes in 1974, especially for *passata*—a purée of fresh, lightly cooked tomatoes—which forms the basis of many sauces.

"My father took advantage of this area's exceptional tomatoes," explained one of the three Ciarlo daughters. "He cultivated and bottled them. We only work hand-picked mature tomatoes: human pickers are able to select ripe, healthy tomatoes—machines are not." The Ciarlos make fresh-tasting, ready-made tomato sauces and bottle tomatoes for organic producers like La Selva (p 231).

Other fine products include seasonal vegetables preserved in olive oil (peppers, sun-dried tomatoes, red onions); olive, red pepper, or tuna *creme* (purées to put on pasta or *crostini*); roasted vegetables (artichoke hearts, eggplant, peppers) in olive oil; and a fresh pesto that needs refrigeration but is packed with cheese and fresh basil. All are available from the farm shop.

DONORATICO

BOTTEGA VERDE
HEALTH FOODS

Via Aurelia 1/F   57024   Donoratico
TELEPHONE/FAX 0565 775138   OPEN Summer: 9:00-13:00, 16:30-20:00;
winter 9:00-12:30, 16:00-19:00   CLOSED Sunday   CREDIT CARDS Visa,
MC   ENGLISH SPOKEN A little   OTHER Another shop in Livorno on
Via S. Gallo, 3/5/7   DIRECTIONS On the SS Aurelia just north of
Donoratico, set back slightly from the main road.

This modern health food store is one of the biggest and best I have found in
Italy, and is part of a new chain. It carries a wide selection of organic and other
natural products from Tuscany, Italy, and beyond, as well as locally grown
organic produce. There are counters of cheeses and dairy products and selec-
tions of organic olive oils and wines. There are also nonorganic wines from
the three local DOC areas: Montescudaio, Bolgheri, and Val di Cornia.

  Run by a cooperative, Bottega Verde is linked to a nearby
modern-style olive press (*frantoio*), which mills olives grown by the members.
These oils, organic and non, are sold in the shop. Of the food producers, many
are written about in this book. There is also a large *erboristeria* section, selling
herbal treatments, cosmetics, and remedies. A great store!

GUASTICCE

OSTERIA DEL
CONTADINO
RESTAURANT

Via D. Sturzo, 69   57010   Guasticce
TELEPHONE   0586 984697   OPEN Lunch and dinner
CLOSED Saturday for lunch; Sunday; August   CREDIT CARDS Visa,
MC, Amex   ENGLISH SPOKEN Yes   RESERVATIONS Recommended
PRICE $$$ DIRECTIONS Guasticce is on the main road (SS 555) from
Livorno going east. Or get off the Li-Pi-Fi (SGC) at Collesalvetti and
follow signs to Guasticce. Via Sturzo is the main road through the village.

This cheery restaurant is full of local color. Hams, flasks, dried peppers, and
garlic hang from the ceiling; pitchers are filled with flowers; and tables are
laden with cheeses, *salumi*, and breads. But don't be misled by the rustic
appearance—this is no tourist trap but a rare chance to taste Tuscany's authen-
tic country foods. Bruno Gastaldìn, its host and creator, is himself a character.
An expansive, bearded fellow with a fine sense of humor, he is very knowledge-
able about the foods and customs of the country.

  "My restaurant celebrates the simple dishes that were once
staples on farmers' tables," he explained. "It is getting harder to find good
artisan-produced ingredients, but you can sample them here." With his
talented family, Gastaldìn offers a menu that follows the seasons, as produce
is mostly home-grown.

  My autumn dinner began in the well-stocked wine room with
an *aperitivo* and a chunk of well-matured Parmesan. A selection of antipasti

included a salad of raw porcini mushrooms and flaked Parmesan; frittata of egg, leek and garlic; *sformato di funghi,* a tender custard of wild *chiodini* mushrooms; small wild boar *salamino;* butter-soft *lardo* wrapped around a fragrant Italia grape; toasted polenta topped with chopped chicken and rabbit livers; and a slice of ash-matured (by Gastaldìn) *prosciutto Toscano,* moist and not too salty. All in all, a true panoply of decisive flavors.

    Primi were equally abundant and well cooked. Noodles are handmade with eggs from the family's free-range chickens—and you can taste the difference. *Zuppa di farro* was the color of red clay from the puréed beans and had plumped grains of spelt wheat in it. The *gnocchetti al tartufo* were exceptional: these small dumplings are made from baked, not boiled, potatoes and are soft without being gummy. They came dressed with aromatic truffle-butter and sprinkled with truffle flakes.

    Main courses feature meats cooked *alla brace,* over a wood fire. There was delicious black Maremman lamb (whose flavor is more gamey than American or British lamb) grilled with garlic and rosemary; a tender pork loin slightly smoky from the embers; and medallions of pork stewed with truffle-scented white beans. Even the cheese was given an added sparkle: Amiata pecorino was matured in a barrel of ash, then heated quickly and served with two tiny fried quail's eggs. There are home baked cakes and Dai Dai ice creams (p 152) for anyone who still has room. All in all, a gastronomic feast for the hungry that merits a detour.

LIVORNO

MERCATO CENTRALE   Scali Saffi   Via Buontalenti   57126   Livorno
FOOD MARKET   TELEPHONE 0586 892188   OPEN 5:00-14:00 Monday to Friday;
5:00-19:30 Saturday   CLOSED Sunday
DIRECTIONS The landmark building is in the town center.

Livorno's large covered food market, with over 180 stalls, is well worth a visit. The historic 1895 building (identical to Firenze's Mercato Centrale) is home to vendors of fish, meat, fresh produce, grains, bread, dairy products—just about everything one could imagine to eat. The atmosphere is lively, and colorful characters abound. The market activities spill out into the surrounding streets, including Piazza delle Erbe, where fresh vegetables are sold.

    When I scouted the area in early fall, I found an old woman selling tiny skinned frogs on skewers and live crabs; a boy with a cardboard box full of bunches of scented-geranium leaves and of thyme; mounds of porcini and orange-yellow *ovoli* mushrooms; a cart laden with shiny *castagne* (sweet chestnuts), persimmons, pomegranates, fresh walnuts and *giuggiole* (jujube berries); bundles of spindly cardoons; and bunches of saffron-colored zucchini flowers.

PASTICCERIA   Via Ernesto Rossi, 25   57123   Livorno
IL GIGLIO   TELEPHONE 0586 899369   OPEN 7:00-14:00,16:00-21:00 Tuesday-
PASTRY   Saturday; 7:00-14:00, 18:00-21:00 Sunday   CLOSED Monday; mid-July
to mid-August   CREDIT CARDS None   DIRECT SALE Yes
ENGLISH SPOKEN A little   DIRECTIONS Off Via Ricasoli, in the
town center

This small *pasticceria* makes some unusual Livornese specialties in addition to a wide range of pastries. *Roschette* are bite-sized rings of dough that are baked and salted. The classic version uses plain flour, but I liked the pale yellow variety made with granular corn flour. They are deliciously crunchy and go well with a glass of wine.

Between Lent and Easter Vinicio Pinelli makes the *schiacciata Livornese,* a complex sweet Easter bread that requires three separate risings. It is flavored with rose water and anise seeds and contains a lot of eggs. Another local dessert pastry is the *torta di ricotta e cioccolato:* a short crust pastry case filled with chocolate custard and sweetened sheep's ricotta.

RISTORO DELLA   Via Don Quilici, 10   57123   Livorno
VECCHIA CASINA   TELEPHONE 0586 889007   OPEN Lunch and dinner
RESTAURANT   CLOSED Tuesday; September   CREDIT CARDS Visa, MC, Amex
ENGLISH SPOKEN Yes   RESERVATIONS Recommended for dinner and
Sunday lunch   PRICE $$ DIRECTIONS At the corner of Via della
Vecchia Casina, in the town center

In this unpretentious, moderately priced restaurant you can sample some of Livorno's favorite recipes. As in all great ports, the culinary tradition is sea-based, with many local Mediterranean fishes starring in simple but appetizing dishes once cooked by fishermen's wives.

Marisa Tronconi and her son prepare *cacciucco,* the celebrated Livornese multifish soup that is a meal in itself, by advance order only. But I was able to try *triglie alla Livornese,* the town's special way of cooking red mullet (in a tomato sauce scented with fennel seeds), with no advance warning. I also had a plate of mixed smoked fish that included swordfish, salmon, and *cernia* (grouper) which was deep pink with a more pronounced flavor than the swordfish. Shellfish were served steamed with big wedges of lemon. The popular *fritto misto* is fried in a light batter and, in autumn, comprised shrimp, cuttlefish, and little fishes.

For *primo* there was *riso nero,* black-stained from squid ink, with its characteristic intense sea flavor; spaghetti with clams tossed in oil and garlic; and round raviolini stuffed with delicately textured *grongo di mare* (conger eel) and served in a robust tomato sauce with a hint of *peperoncino.* Main courses are dominated by whatever seafood is to be found fresh in the market, though some meats are also served.

DA GAGARI   Via del Cardinale, 23   57126   Livorno
SNACK BAR   TELEPHONE 0586 884086   OPEN Summer 8:00-12:30, 17:00-21:00;
                    winter: 8:00-21:00   CLOSED Sunday; July   CREDIT CARDS None
                    DIRECT SALE Yes   ENGLISH SPOKEN No
                    DIRECTIONS Across the street from the covered Mercato Centrale

Every great city has its favorite popular foods, and Livorno is no exception. *La torta* is Livorno's answer to a slice of pizza or a hot dog. And Da Gagari is the place to get it. The tiny shop is always crammed full of locals waiting patiently for the latest panful to be pulled, bubbling hot, out of the deep wood-burning oven. Signora Fiorella, a Botero figure with a jolly disposition, stands at the ready.

Cinque e cinque! calls the first person on line. "Five and five" is local jargon for a wedge of chick-pea flour pancake sandwiched between a slice of split focaccia. Fiorella slices off a piece of the thin ochre-colored *torta*, sprinkles it with pepper, and wraps it in the bread. The cost? About the same as a cup of coffee and a doughnut. "In the old days," she explained as she waited for the next batch to cook, "it was called by this name because you would ask for five *soldi's* worth of pancake and five *soldi's* worth of bread. The prices changed, but somehow the name stuck!"

Moroccan chick-pea flour is mixed with water, peanut oil, and salt and left to rest for a couple of hours in winter—less in summer or it may *prendere forte,* or ferment. It is poured into a vast, round, shallow tin-lined copper pan and baked for about fifteen minutes. The resulting cake is crunchy on the outside and still just creamy on the inside—a bit like eating a dense purée.

Fiorella's husband, whose name is Salvatore Chiappa but who is known locally as "Gagari" (he was nicknamed after Gagarin, the Russian astronaut), has been making the *torta* in this shop for over thirty-six years. He stacks the next lot of branches neatly underneath the oven as Fiorella watches approvingly. *Si, così si fa bella figura!* "Yes," she asserts, "that's the way to create a good impression!"

CANTINA NARDI   Via Cambini, 6/8   57123   Livorno
WINE BAR   TELEPHONE 0586 808006   OPEN 8:30-20:30   CLOSED Sunday; part
                    of August   CREDIT CARDS Visa, MC, Amex   DIRECT SALE Yes
                    ENGLISH SPOKEN No   RESERVATIONS Recommended for lunch
                    PRICE $ DIRECTIONS In town center, off Via Marradi

Two rooms lined with wine bottles, a few tables inside, a few more in the garden: the Cantina Nardi has been a fixture in Livorno for over thirty years. This is a fine place for an easygoing lunch—a plate of local food with a glass of Tuscan wine (among others from farther afield). Nadio Nardi has a vast assortment of wines for sale by the bottle or glass. There is also a little marble bar for those who prefer to stand for an *aperitivo* with hors d'oeuvres.

The menu changes daily, but there are always a few *primi* and *secondi:* baked polenta with cheese, pasta with homemade sauces, salt cod (*baccalà*), tripe, egg frittata with vegetables or the humble boiled beef "redone" with onions. It is open all day for wine or snacks, so drop in anytime.

ENOTECA DOC
WINE BAR

Via Goldoni, 40/44   57126   Livorno
TELEPHONE 0586 887583   Marco Falleni   OPEN 12:00-15:00, 20:00-3:00   CLOSED Monday; August   CREDIT CARDS Visa, MC, Amex   DIRECT SALE Yes   ENGLISH SPOKEN Yes
RESERVATIONS Necessary for dinner   DIRECTIONS Off Via Mayer, in the town center

This is Livorno's trendiest wine bar, with all that the word implies. It has a really extensive international and Italian wine list, with an impressive showcase display of the bottles. A big modern-style bar serves wines by the glass as well as American-style cocktails. A few tables are scattered around for meals and snacks from an eclectic menu. This is a good after-dinner spot if you are feeling hip (and long on attitude).

Also

Cibo Per La Pace. Corso Amedeo, 69. 0586 893591.
Centrally-located Cibo Per La Pace means food for peace, and it is a fine health food store and restaurant that sells I Pulitini's organic breads (p 133).

V.A.D. Via di Franco, 38. 0586 884106.
Located a stone's throw from the covered food market, this shop is full of big wheels of Parmesan cheese. Bruno Simonini sells aged and young Parmesan as well as a small range of more typically Tuscan pecorini.

MONTENERO

MONTALLEGRO
BAR, RESTAURANT

Piazza del Santuario di Montenero, 3   57128   Montenero
TELEPHONE 0586 579030   OPEN Restaurant: lunch all year, dinner also May-September   CLOSED Tuesday in winter; November
CREDIT CARDS None   ENGLISH SPOKEN Yes
FEATURES Panoramic terrace   PRICE Lunch $; dinner $$
OTHER Montallegro is also a hotel
DIRECTIONS In Montenero's main square, beside the sanctuary

Anyone who is fascinated, as I am, by ex-voto paintings will be keen to visit the Sanctuary of Montenero, where a truly exceptional collection exists. Dedicated to the Virgin Mary, whose image was said to have appeared to a shepherd in 1345 at the site of the sanctuary, these naïf paintings offer thanks for and testimony to the miracles of everyday life of the past 250 years. For example, if a young man survived after falling badly from his horse, an ex-voto was painted of the accident in honor of his recovery. Touching scenes of disasters at sea, on land, and at home are depicted in remarkable ways, often by unschooled painters; they offer a window on the world as it once was.

The sanctuary attracts thousands of pilgrims each year, and after visiting it, many find their way to this large restaurant and bar for sustenance. It, too, is something of a reminder of times past: meals are served in a ballroom that has barely changed since 1929. The Orlandi family, the original owners of this hotel and restaurant, are a welcoming bunch. In addition to a full-service bar that is open almost all the time, they offer a set-price "pilgrim's lunch" and, in summer, an à la carte dinner menu. The outdoor terrace offers romantic views of Livorno and its coast.

ROSIGNANO MARITTIMO

LA GATTABUIA
RESTAURANT

Via Gramsci, 32   57016   Rosignano Marittimo
TELEPHONE 0586 799760   OPEN For dinner only, but also Sunday lunch in summer   CLOSED Tuesday   CREDIT CARDS Visa, MC
ENGLISH SPOKEN Yes   FEATURES Garden terrace in summer
RESERVATIONS Necessary at weekends   PRICE $$
DIRECTIONS On the main street in the lower part of the town

Under a pink neon sign and down a narrow twisting staircase is this charming little restaurant. (Even farther down is the wine cellar under a trap door, with a ladder as steep as a submarine's; the wines are brought up with a basket pulley.) In summer, tables are set out in a shady courtyard; in winter, the vaulted rooms are cozy and inviting without being claustrophobic.

Spinella Galeazzi is a natural cook, with a flair some women seem to have for turning simple ingredients into the most satisfying dishes. After working in a few local restaurants, she and her companion, Alberto Pescatori, decided to open their own.

"The menu follows the seasons," she explained. "There is no frying, no frozen fish. I make all my own pasta. I make the most of what sparks my interest at the market." Wines are Tuscan, and feature local producers, big and small. There are also estate-bottled olive oils.

On the chilly October evening when I arrived, her thick soup of mixed pulses was very welcome. Chick-peas, lentils, beans, black-eyed peas and *farro* (spelt wheat), were left whole in a puréed bean base and served with croutons, fruity olive oil, and pepper. *Pappardelle,* wide handmade noodles, came with a rich, meaty sauce with only a hint of tomato.

Main courses are divided between fish and meat, with a number of vegetarian choices and local game in fall. Wild boar was well stewed with black olives, in a fine rendering of this oft-prepared dish. The meat was neither tough nor dry but flavorful. Roast loin of pork (*arista*), was served with sweet-and-sour onions and grapes. Fish included stockfish, grilled cuttlefish, and whole *rombo* (turbot), baked with wild mushrooms. A selection of Italian and French cheeses was a nice way to finish a bottle of wine, but there were home-baked tarts and a couple of airy creams (lemon or *zabaglione*) for those who felt the need for something sweet.

SAN VINCENZO

GAMBERO ROSSO
RESTAURANT

Piazza della Vittoria, 13   57027   San Vincenzo
TELEPHONE 0565 701021   FAX 0565 704542   OPEN Lunch and dinner
CLOSED Tuesday; November   CREDIT CARDS Visa, MC, Amex
ENGLISH SPOKEN Yes   RESERVATIONS Necessary   PRICE $$$$$
DIRECTIONS The restaurant overlooks the town's small port.

It may be unorthodox, but I'm going to begin this restaurant review at the end, for at the Gambero Rosso I had one of the best chocolate desserts I have ever eaten. A cross between a soufflé and a mousse, the *biscotto soffice* is served right from the oven, scalding hot, sumptuously rich, near-black from the concentration of its chocolateness. The intensity and depth of flavor are unforgettable. Above all, it is the quality of the cocoa extract that is remarkable, and this is perhaps the best introduction for its talented creator, Fulvio Pierangelini. His almost obsessive commitment to fine-flavored, perfect ingredients has been the building block on which he has constructed his considerable reputation.

The restaurant is perfectly situated, overlooking the charming little port of San Vincenzo. The well-appointed dining room is luminous and quite romantic—with its quintessentially Mediterranean view of nothing but sea. The interior is tasteful and elegant, a tone set by Emanuela Pierangelini, who also takes the orders. There is a fine, hand-picked, reasonably priced wine list with many older vintages. In addition to the regular *carte*, a *degustazione* (tasting) menu features the "classics of the Gambero Rosso."

"Everyone who comes here wants to eat fish," admitted Fulvio Pierangelini, a mountain of a man with an uncompromising directness. "But in fact, the most interesting dishes to come out of my kitchen are the meats—like the pigeon." His *piccione in casseruola* is, indeed, legendary. (The pigeons are bred by Meleta, see p 229.)

In late February, my lunch began with a *cannellone di melanzane*—a paper-thin slice of eggplant wrapped around a warm tomato concassé. Both were lightly cooked and very fresh-tasting. It was topped with three just-cooked morsels of San Pietro (John Dory) and a jagged leaf of a local herb that tasted like grass. The eggplant was silky, the fish plump yet grainy textured; a spoonful of exquisitely perfumed olive oil (it tasted like flowers) brought it all together.

Pierangelini explained that his *passata di ceci* soup is often copied by chefs. The idea is not complicated, but to achieve equally refined results with it would be hard. The creamy, cloud-light chick-pea purée was fine enough to barely coat the back of the spoon. In it were arranged four *gamberi rossi*, red shrimp, perfectly fresh, perfectly cooked. Here again, a splash of oil rounded it off.

Striped bream (*marmora*) was treated more like game than fish. The sautéed fillet sat on silky slices of foie gras and a bed of wilted spinach and came with a robust red wine sauce; the garnish was a hot, caramelized pear. The deglazed sauce had the saltiness of soy, in contrast (or in complement) to the dessert-sweet poached fruit. A sampling of the remarkable local and French cheeses from the restaurant's selection followed.

"To create a great restaurant," Pierangelini said, "you must do everything yourself. You need culture to get beyond a certain level in cooking. I was lucky, I had no bad habits: I had never been a waiter or a cook. I have combined classical rigor with free choice and construction—consequently, only my emotions go into my recipes."

SUVERETO

AZIENDA AGRICOLA Via S. Leonardo, 29   57028   Suvereto
ORLANDO PAZZAGLI TELEPHONE 0565 829333   FAX 0565 828196   OPEN By appointment
OLIVE OIL only   CREDIT CARDS None   DIRECT SALE Yes, by appointment
ENGLISH SPOKEN No   DIRECTIONS In the town center

Orlando Pazzagli has a beautiful private *orciaia*, the room traditionally used for storing olive oil in terra-cotta urns (*coppi*), which have now all but disappeared. Some of these vast handmade pots from Impruneta have survived over a hundred years. "Every year they are cleaned out using vinegar and sawdust," explained Pazzagli, who has his own mill nearby for grinding the olives that may be visited during November when the oil is made.

OMBRONE Piazza dei Giudici, 1   57028   Suvereto
RESTAURANT TELEPHONE 0565 829336   FAX 0565 828297   OPEN Lunch and dinner
CLOSED Monday; February   CREDIT CARDS Visa, MC, Amex
ENGLISH SPOKEN A little   FEATURES Outdoor terrace in summer
RESERVATIONS Recommended in summer   PRICE $$$
OTHER The couple runs a cooking school
DIRECTIONS In the town center, near the commune

Giancarlo Bini has long been a key figure in Maremman gastronomy. An expert wine and oil taster, his Ombrone restaurants (first in Grosseto, now here) attract food and wine lovers. His wife, Lella, the restaurant's cook, runs the Caterina de' Medici cooking school.

Some years ago Bini created his Salotto—a collection of thirty-eight Italian artisan producers. "The Salotto is my personal choice of the foods and wines I like best," he explained. "It's not about business, but about the culture of food-making." It holds one or two meetings per year; foods and wines are tasted and a feeling of solidarity enforced.

This restaurant is set in a thousand-year-old ex-olive mill. A summer terrace overlooks Suvereto's medieval *comune*'s arched facade. The food is unpretentious and wholesome; Lella is a natural cook, and seems at her best working with the primary ingredients of the Maremma: wild herbs, tangy sheep's cheeses, pulses, and grains.

My early spring dinner began with piping hot *scamorza* cheese melted over spinach and salted anchovies. Some excellent *crostini* followed: a selection of savory toppings on crusty country bread. Then a soup, described by Lella as a *cacciucco* of mixed pulses and grains. This was delicious, thick, earthy, and satisfying. *"Gnuddi"* of spinach and ricotta looked like green speckled bird's eggs. In fact, they are like pasta stuffing without the pasta—cloud-light, with the perfumed accent of fresh sage. They were exceptional.

Second courses followed in the country mode: a well-done duck breast was cooked with Vin Santo. *Faraona* (guinea fowl) was simply stewed with mushrooms, carrots, and wine. Desserts are homemade.

The Binis have an interesting wine cellar and an informal room downstairs for young diners. As we concluded our visit, Giancarlo turned to me and smiled: "There you have it," he said, "this is our little kingdom."

GUALDO DEL RE	Notri, 77 57028 Suvereto
WINE	TELEPHONE 0565 829888, 829361 FAX 0565 829888
	OPEN 9:00-12:00, 14:00-18:00; tastings and *cantina* visits by appointment
	CLOSED Sunday CREDIT CARDS Visa, MC DIRECT SALE Yes
	ENGLISH SPOKEN A little DIRECTIONS Follow signs from Suvereto

The wine-producing area near Suvereto is unlike any other Tuscan wine zone. For one thing, the land is only a few kilometers from the sea and is practically flat; fields of artichokes and vegetables give way to a few acres of vineyards at the foot of big electrical pylons. The story of how a handful of local producers turned Suvereto's winemaking around and became rising wine stars is an interesting one. Gualdo del Re's young owner, Maria Teresa Cabella, explained, "At the end of the 1970s the steel factories at Piombino were feeling the effect of Italy's industrial crisis. Twenty years earlier the countryside had been abandoned in favor of the factories. But people began to have second thoughts."

Two forward-thinking men, Suvereto's mayor Walter Gasperini and a winemaker, Marco Stefanini, were convinced that the area could make good wines if the farmers would concentrate on quality rather than quantity.

They held meetings and Maria Teresa, her husband, Nico Rossi, and his parents were among the first to become interested in the idea.

"It meant changing everything," she said. "Planting new vineyards, building serious cellars—a huge investment of time and money. And we were both still working at the factory." In 1983 Gualdo del Re (the name means the king's hunting woods) bottled its first wines; they now come under the Val di Cornia DOC. By 1990 the couple had left their other jobs to run the winery.

"For us the biggest satisfaction is that our wines are liked," she asserted enthusiastically. "Wine is one of the few products that you can follow from birth to sales—we oversee the vines, follow the wine into the cellar, through its aging, and into the bottle. We even do our own sales trips." Over time the winery has increased to its current 10 hectares (25 acres) of vineyards, with 7 more (17 acres) on the way.

"We didn't want to overthrow tradition, so we planted better clones of the existing Sangiovese as the mainstay of our big red Gualdo del Re, and concentrated on Vermentino, which was once a traditional grape used along the coast, for our white Vigna Valentina." The wines have been gaining recognition, thanks in part to Fulvio Pierangelini, the chef of the nearby Gambero Rosso restaurant at San Vincenzo (p 160). "He believed in our wines right from the start, and was a big help in getting them known," added Maria Teresa. "We would like to thank him for that."

TUA RITA
WINE

Notri, 81   57028   Suvereto
TELEPHONE 0565 829237, 0360 992498   FAX 0565 829237
OPEN Visits and tastings by appointment only   CREDIT CARDS None
DIRECT SALE Yes, subject to availability   ENGLISH SPOKEN No
DIRECTIONS Follow signs from Suvereto

"You couldn't have a more direct contact with your product than we do," laughed Rita Tua, Tua Rita's owner. "We live upstairs and the wines are right under us, on the ground floor of our house."

The tiny above-ground cellar is crammed full of *barriques*, barrels, and tanks. Not the setting you would expect for some of Tuscany's most recent award-winners. But then, the Suvereto story is unusual. (See previous entry; the two wineries are next door neighbors.)

"At the outset we didn't really plan on making wine, but nothing else would grow here," confessed the lively Rita. "I suppose you could say that our situation is the opposite of the imposing French wine chateaux: they are perfect but to me lack soul. Here it is all very personal and much more homey."

She and her husband, Virgilio Bisti, began by taking winemaking courses: in 1988 they planted their first vineyards to Cabernet and Merlot and hired a professional winemaker. Giusto di Notri was the result, a well-balanced, concentrated super-Tuscan that put them on the map. The arid terrain and long hot summers give the wines great structure, yet they remain approachable. Redigaffi is a wine of pure Merlot made in tiny quantities, Perlato del Bosco is Sangiovese, while Sileno is a "curious" white, as Rita described it—a blend of Traminer, Riesling, and Chardonnay fermented in *barriques.* "The Traminer gives this wine more perfumes," she said, "but the Chardonnay makes it mellow."

The winery has grown but remains small: at present they own 2½ hectares are owned with 2 more rented nearby (a total of 11 acres). The couple even sold their weekend house on Mount Amiata to buy *barriques.*

"If we had realized what the investment in human and financial terms would be, we would never have gotten into it," confided Rita. "But now we are hooked, and there is so much demand for our wines we never have enough to go around."

VADA

IL DUCALE
RESTAURANT

Piazza Garibaldi, 33   57018   Vada
TELEPHONE/FAX 0586 788600   OPEN Lunch and dinner
CLOSED Monday; holidays in January   CREDIT CARDS Visa, MC,
Amex   ENGLISH SPOKEN A little   RESERVATIONS Recommended on
weekends and for dinner   PRICE $$$-$$$$
DIRECTIONS In Vada's main square

This restaurant has an eclectic, almost Victorian interior filled with rugs and roses, plants and antiques, lace and chintz. The rooms are lofty: they once housed the Grand Duke of Tuscany's carriages.

The kitchen features seafood only from the local Tyrrhenian Sea. No farm-raised or imported fish are used. Sample here the area's celebrated *cacciucco*—the Livornese counterpart to bouillabaisse—as only top-quality fish are used for this all-in-one dish (including lobster and shellfish); Il Ducale suggests serving it with one of Tuscany's big reds.

In *triglie con agro di limone,* red mullet fillets are cooked with garlic, parsley, and lemon. The fish is firm-fleshed under its scarlet skin. *Pesce spada con cipolle borrettane* is a delicious dish of swordfish topped with a Mediterranean stew of flat onions, potato, tomato, and rosemary. The recipe is from the sixteenth century, explained Altero Giomi, the owner. *Crostino di polpo in cacciucco* is exotic: crisp toast is topped with *piccante* but tender octopus stained a deep reddish brown.

Il Ducale offers many pasta and fish combinations. The fish are allowed to express their natural flavors without being dominated by forceful sauces. In *spaghetti con tartufi di mare,* shellfish in the clam family are simply chopped and served in a light sauce without parsley or garlic. There is a full aroma of the sea—delicate but fishy. Sea bass (*branzino*) is cooked with a little fresh tomato and tossed over *farfalle,* pasta bows. Olive oil is used judiciously; it is sensed by the palate but does not overpower. Finally, *sarago,* a local member of the bream family, is served pure—no sauce, no oil, no lemon. Its soft creamy-white flesh is clear-tasting and delicate, offering a fine contrast to the other colorful flavors. A good-sized wine list concentrates on whites from Italy and abroad.

VENTURINA

Calidario. 0565 851504, 851240.

This is my favorite thermal bath: a sulphur-free spring of blood-temperature water feeds a dramatic pool that is open all day. The restaurant and bar makes great pizzas, just what you feel like after an invigorating evening swim.

CHAPTER 7

The Island of Elba

When people think of Elba, they think of Napoleon. Although he spent only a few months there almost two hundred years ago, he has been credited with encouraging the island's viticulture and reforming its administration. He might also, it would appear, be thanked for putting it on the map.

Elba is an arid mountainous island, but it is not barren. Its lower ranges are covered by dense *macchia Mediterranea*, the bushy scrub that flowers so magically in spring and lends the summer air its aromatic *profumi*. Fennel and rosemary, prickly pear and fig grow wild. Up higher are woods of chestnut, acacia, and umbrella pines. Remarkably pure honeys ensue—there are no pesticides or pollutants in the wilderness—of thistle-flower, herbs, or *corbezzolo* (the "strawberry tree"). Read labels carefully. Unless a honey jar specifies it was produced on Elba, it almost certainly was not.

There are fewer fishermen now than there once were. And sadly, vendors no longer hawk spicy boiled *polpo* (octopus) along the beaches. But there is good fish to be found in some restaurants and fish stores. Among the species that are locally caught are the blunt-headed *gallinella* (a type of gurnard), purplish octopus the size of one's hand, slim anchovies, striped oval-bodied *sarago* (a kind of bream). In the hills, wild boar and other game forage for food. On summer nights the boar come down to feed on ripe grapes and figs, and may occasionally be seen.

A recent renewal of winemaking traditions on the island has led to some good wines, Elba Bianco and Rosso, Ansonica—all DOC—and there is the rare and highly aromatic Aleatico *passito*, an intense cherry red dessert wine, to seek out. The real thing is fairly costly, but don't be tempted by the cheap imitation labeled Aleatico "vino liquoroso"; it is produced in Sicily and thick with additives and sugars.

The best time to visit Elba is in early summer or fall; in August the island is literally overwhelmed with campers, beachgoers, and tourists.

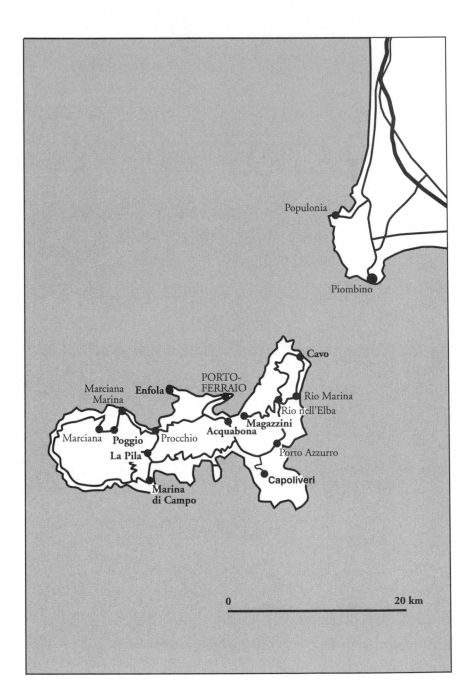

Town names in **bold** indicate towns that are included in this chapter.

Elba, which is part of the province of Livorno, is reached by ferry from Piombino (about one hour away) or by small plane.

Azienda Promozione Turistica.
Calata Italia, 26.
57037 Portoferraio
0565 91467, fax: 0565 916350
Summer hours: 8:00-20:00; winter 8:00-14:00, 15:00-18:00.

ACQUABONA

ACQUABONA Acquabona 57037 Portoferraio Livorno
WINE TELEPHONE/FAX 0565 933013   OPEN June-September 10:00-13:00, 15:30-19:30; by appointment only during rest of year. Tastings possible; *cantina* visits and groups by appointment   CREDIT CARDS None
DIRECT SALE Yes, minimum of six bottles per sale   ENGLISH SPOKEN Yes
DIRECTIONS Acquabona is on the main road from Portoferraio to Porto Azzurro, about halfway between them. It is signposted.

Acquabona is run by three friends from Milan and Florence who, in the 1980s, accepted an invitation from the estate's owners to relaunch the disused winery. Now the results are showing: Acquabona's wines are among Elba's best. It is a pretty estate, a little inland: 13 hectares (32 acres) of vineyards alongside high avenues of eucalyptus trees near the island's golf greens. The *cantina* is tiny, crammed full of vats and equipment. Capitani, Fioretti and Lucchini intend to extend it.

Acquabona makes ten wines, including two grappas. The affordable Elba Bianco DOC is a fresh, drinkable white of primarily Procanico (Trebbiano Toscano) grapes; it accounts for half the winery's sales. Elba Rosso DOC is of Sangioveto; in good years the best are kept for the Riserva Camillo Bianchi, which is aged in *barriques*—small French oak casks.

The sought-after Aleatico DOC is a rich sweet *passito* wine particular to Elba and the Maremman coast. Acquabona's is a heady wine of an intense berry red, with aromas of violets and roses. The grapes for this wine are sun-dried on racks in ventilated greenhouses before being pressed. Aleatico is best savored alone. Wonderful honey is also made on the estate by beekeeper Luciano Pasolini from "Officinalia" at San Gimignano (see p 269).

CAPOLIVERI

IL CHIASSO
RESTAURANT

Via N. Sauro   57031   Capoliveri   Livorno
TELEPHONE/FAX 0565 968709   OPEN Dinner only from Easter
to mid-October   CLOSED Tuesday in spring and fall
CREDIT CARDS Visa, MC, Amex   ENGLISH SPOKEN Yes
RESERVATIONS Always recommended   PRICE $$$
DIRECTIONS In the center of the old town of Capoliveri

This is a restaurant for people who like eating out. The atmosphere is lively and *simpatico*. The food (mostly fish) is fresh, unfussy, and delicious. It is served by agile waiters who navigate tables grouped a bit haphazardly—indoors and out—on either side of a narrow stepped alley (*chiasso* in local dialect). Il Chiasso's host, Luciano Casini, is a colorful character, warm and affable in his white linen and sandals. For twenty-five years, in these well-lit humble rooms, he has fed an international clientele of summer travelers. "The Capoliverians were dominated by the Saracens, by the Turks—by everybody," he exclaimed good-naturedly. "But we have remained welcoming. I have always wanted Il Chiasso to keep its friendly, trattoria feel."

As for the food, the aromas, colors, and tastes are pure Mediterranean. Fish of all sizes are married simply to fresh local ingredients. Mollusks are sautéed and brought to the table in copper pots, steaming and aromatic. Spaghettini are dressed with light flavorful sauces of fresh anchovies, lobster, sea bream, or tuna. There are linguine with *pesto* and rice blackened by squid ink.

Whole fish are baked to order: Casini grabs a glistening specimen under the gills and presents it to the table before cooking. Of the authentic Elban recipes, I tasted excellent *acciughe ripiene*, once a favorite dish of Casini's mother. Two fresh anchovy fillets "sandwich" a delicate ground fish stuffing; they are lightly fried then simmered in a sauce of fresh cherry tomatoes, garlic, and herbs. Elba's *cucina povera* is also responsible for *polpo con patate*. Young octopuses are boiled before being stewed with potatoes and rosemary. The result is a spicy purple mixture of succulent octopus and flavorful potatoes. "So many of the island's traditions have been lost since tourism hit," Casini said sadly.

Meat dishes and nicely grilled vegetables are available for those not wanting fish. Desserts are homemade: in the popular *misto di frutta flambé*, fresh fruits are dipped in hot caramel sauce and served over ice cream. Casini's handwritten wine list is eclectic.

CAVO

BALLINI APICOLTURA Via della Parata 57030 Cavo Livorno
HONEY TELEPHONE/FAX 0565 949836 OPEN 8:00-20:00
CLOSED Never MAIL ORDER Queen bees may be ordered by mail
CREDIT CARDS None ENGLISH SPOKEN A little
DIRECTIONS From Rio nell'Elba, take the mountain road (not the coastal road) toward Cavo. A few kilometers before Cavo there are signs for honey. The laboratory is a few meters off the road, down to the right.

Roberto Ballini was a champion bicycle racer before he took to beekeeping more than twenty years ago. An attractive man, he now works with his two sons making honey and breeding queen bees. "Making honey is an erratic business," Ballini explained. "We felt it was better to branch out and to breed queens, which can only be done in areas as geographically pure and isolated as this." The queen leaves the hive to be fertilized, and she may mate with as many as eight drones: the only way to ensure purity of breed is to be certain there are no other bees around when she comes out.

The rarest Elban honeys are *rosmarino, cardo,* and *corbezzolo.* As many as thirteen species of rosemary grow wild on the island. The light amber honey is delicate and aromatic, without being overly sugary. *Cardo* is made from the nectar of the indigenous thistle, *Galactites tomentosa.* Bright amber in color, this lustrous honey is neither too sweet nor too strong, yet has a distinctive character. The *corbezzolo* plant, *Arbutus unedo,* grows wild in the *macchia Mediterranea.* This bush (known also as the "strawberry tree") has the unusual capacity to produce its flowers and fruit simultaneously, in late autumn. The honey, a deep golden amber, is the strongest of the three. Its bittersweet and exotic taste surprised me, like incense, or resin. The aftertaste clung to the tastebuds for a long time, like a drop of perfume on the tongue.

Like every other beekeeper I have met, a lot of Ballini's time is devoted to combating varroa, the parasite now devastating the world's bee population.

"Bees have such extraordinary intelligence," he went on. "Their communication system is very sophisticated—I feel sure that once they realize they are under attack they will transmit the information to each other on how to survive."

ENFOLA

EMANUEL
RESTAURANT

57037   Enfola   Livorno
TELEPHONE/FAX 0565 939003   OPEN Lunch and dinner from Easter
to late September   CLOSED Wednesday in spring and fall
CREDIT CARDS Visa, MC, Amex   ENGLISH SPOKEN Yes
FEATURES Beachside dining garden   RESERVATIONS Recommended
PRICE $$$ DIRECTIONS From Portoferraio follow signs to Enfola.
Go all the way down to the beach.

Emanuel is situated in a romantic spot. Enfola is a cluster of houses on an unspoiled beach overlooking a bay dotted with sailboats, against a backdrop of mountains. The restaurant, with its shaded terrace, is right on the beach, with a garden for summer dining. The clean-lined dining room has picture windows framing the view. Emanuel is run by an earnest young couple, Anna Lauria and Alberto Zanoli.

This is primarily a fish restaurant, though some meats are served. The cuisine is traditional Mediterranean and Elban, with modern touches. Seafood antipasti are a specialty here and worth trying. An unusual assortment included sautéed shrimp tossed with sliced mushrooms, cherry tomatoes, arugula, and balsamic vinegar, and *totani alla diavola*—tender squid served hot with a touch of *peperoncino*. Mussels on the half shell were steeped in herbed tomato sauce and cooked on a griddle. Beaten egg was then spooned into each shell, cooked only by the heat of the mussels—a traditional Elban recipe.

I preferred the *secondi* to the *primi* in this restaurant. A delicate fillet of *rombo* (turbot) was topped by a crust of paper-thin sliced potatoes that reminded me of *pommes Anna*. *Pesce spada con capperi* was equally good. A thin slice of swordfish was dipped in egg and breadcrumbs flavored with capers and sage before being sautéed. For dessert, a *mantecato* of melon was a sorbet flavored surprisingly with white port and chili. Dai Dai's frozen *mattonella* (p 152) came with a warm *zabaglione* sauce. The wine list included a good range of whites, a few reds, and a group of meditation wines.

LA PILA

CECILIA
WINE

La Casina   La Pila   57034   Campo nell'Elba   Livorno
TELEPHONE 0565 977322   FAX 0565 977964   OPEN 9:00-12:00,
15:00-19:00; tastings possible; *cantina* visits by appointment
CLOSED Sunday; Saturday in winter   CREDIT CARDS Visa, MC
DIRECT SALE Yes, minimum of six bottles per sale
ENGLISH SPOKEN A little   DIRECTIONS Azienda Agricola Cecilia is on
the main road between Procchio and Marina di Campo, by the airfield.

Cecilia is one of Elba's most significant wine producers, along with La Chiusa and Acquabona. Housed in a large pink building, it is surrounded by flat vineyards. As the ultramodern vinification cellars reveal, the emphasis of this winery is on technology. Cecilia's owner, Giuseppe Camerini, is an engineer. He has raised the standard not only of his own wines, but also of the island's: he led the campaign to get Aleatico its DOC status, succeeding in 1994.

Coming from a winemaking background in the Veneto region, Camerini decided in 1989 to modernize and expand his family's holdings on Elba. Presently he has 5 hectares (12 acres) of vineyards but buys grapes from around the island. His cellars are equipped with sophisticated temperature controls—indispensable for making white wines in a hot climate.

Cecilia produces Elban DOCs Rosso and Bianco (with their *barrique*-aged della Casina versions), the indigenous white Ansonica, and red Aleatico—from which a highly aromatic sweet *passito* wine is made. Ansonica is particularly difficult to work: the delicately flavored, thick-skinned grapes are very low in acidity and oxidize easily. Camerini described this pale but fairly rich wine poetically: "It is ephemeral . . . it may last as long as a morning."

MAGAZZINI

LA CHIUSA Magazzini 57037 Portoferraio Livorno
WINE, OLIVE OIL TELEPHONE/FAX 0565 933046 OPEN 9:00-12:00, 17:00-19:00 in summer; 9:00-12:00, 16:00-17:00 in winter. Tastings and *cantina* visits possible. CLOSED Sunday CREDIT CARDS None DIRECT SALE Yes ENGLISH SPOKEN A little DIRECTIONS Magazzini is on the main road between Portoferraio and Bagnaia. Tenuta La Chiusa is clearly signposted.

Tenuta La Chiusa is one of Tuscany's most beautiful wine estates. From the road, an avenue of olive trees leads you gently down through ordered vineyards to the historic villa, its flower-laden gardens, and the sea. The house of a noble Florentine family twice visited by Napoleon Bonaparte, La Chiusa overlooks Portoferraio across the bay.

The winery, its atmospheric cellars, and its shop are well set up for visits. Giuliana Foresi Castelli and her husband have 8 hectares (19 acres) of vineyards. They produce Elba Bianco DOC, Elba Rosso DOC, and Rosato, a rosé. Two *passito* wines are made from Elba's most characteristic vines, Aleatico and Anzonica.

The rare Anzonica (as La Chiusa spells it) is a dessert grape formerly popular for blending with other white wines to give added body and color. The varietal known as Anzolia (or Inzolia) is still present in Sicily, and may have originated in the Middle East. La Chiusa's *passito* is like a delicate, lightly sweet sherry. It should be drunk before meals as an *aperitivo*, or afterward, but not with food.

La Chiusa makes an exceptional extra-virgin olive oil, gold-green and fresh scented. Unusually for Tuscany, the olive picking is machine-aided, as the trees are planted on flat ground. The olives are sent by boat to a *frantoio* on the mainland, returning to the island as oil.

MARINA DI CAMPO

Garden Bar. Via Venezia, 12. 0565 976036.

Right on the seafront, this large lively bar is always a crush in summertime. It makes the best *brioches*, breakfast pastries, and cappuccino in the area. Cakes and pastries may be bought to eat standing up at the counter, as most Italians like to, or arranged in a *vassoio* (tray), to take home. They also make good clean-tasting fruit gelati.

POGGIO

PUBLIUS
RESTAURANT

57030   Poggio   Livorno
TELEPHONE 0565 99208   FAX 0565 904174   OPEN Lunch and dinner
March 20-November 10   CLOSED Monday in winter season
CREDIT CARDS Visa, MC, Amex   ENGLISH SPOKEN Yes
FEATURES Panoramic dining terrace   RESERVATIONS Recommended
for dinner   PRICE $$$ DIRECTIONS From Marciana or Marciana
Marina follow signs to Poggio. The restaurant is visible as you enter
the village.

Publius is a restaurant with a view. From its perch in the unspoiled village of Poggio, it offers its guests a breathtaking panorama of Elba's mountainous seascape. An airy glassed-in dining terrace makes the most of this location, especially at lunchtime.

This restaurant's menu is now divided between meat and fish. Antipasti include homemade *funghi sott'olio* (preserved wild mushrooms), a "mousse" of local herbs, and liver-topped *crostini* flavored with rosemary, bay, and Vin Santo. Two fish-based *primi* use *tagliolini,* fine egg noodles. In one the pasta is stained with tomato, complementing the gray-green artichoke hearts and shelled clams (laudably grit-free). In the second, yellow noodles are sauced with firm-fleshed sea bream and arugula, and sweetened with mint.

Spigola (bass) fillet is wonderful baked in a *cartoccio* of foil with cherry tomatoes, olives, rosemary, and olive oil—the decisive flavors of the Mediterranean. Stockfish baked with potatoes and green olives is a rustic Elban dish. Meats are roasted over a wood fire. For dessert, Publius offers cakes and homemade *semifreddi,* or iced desserts. The wine list features the best Elban and other Tuscan wines. There is a friendly sommelier on hand to help with the choice.

PORTOFERRAIO

PESCHERIA
LA LAMPARA
FISH

Via Carducci, 174   57037   Portoferraio   Livorno
TELEPHONE 0565 914286   OPEN July and August: 8:00-13:00, 17:15-
20:00; September to June 8:00-13:00   CLOSED Sunday afternoon
in July and August; Sunday in winter   CREDIT CARDS None
ENGLISH SPOKEN No   OTHER Another fish shop, Da Cesare at
Via Carducci, 14, is owned by the same proprietor.
DIRECTIONS Via Carducci is one of the main roads into Portoferraio,
coming from the west. The shop is near the hospital.

This small fish shop is one of Elba's most reliable. It sells to the public and to
some of the island's best restaurants. The staff, a group of jolly women wearing
white coats and rubber boots, have a fast turnover of fish and shellfish. In Italy
fish is often sold ungutted, so ask for the fish to be *pulito*.

Mussels and clams arrive in net bags and are cleaned in a noisy
machine. Long-bodied flying squid (*totani*), come in varying sizes: larger for
stuffing or grilling, smaller for pan-frying. Many odd-looking sea creatures taste
delicious: *la gallinella,* a rosy-colored, square-headed fish has good flavor, as
does the beautiful speckled moray eel, *murena.*

CHAPTER 8

Chianti Classico and Its Wines

*C*hianti Classico contains some quintessentially Tuscan landscapes: medieval wine castles surrounded by gray-green olive groves and hillside vineyards, punctuated by dark cypress trees. This chapter visits twenty-six of Chianti Classico's finest wineries, as well as food producers, shops, and restaurants.

The area known as Chianti Classico is a hybrid of sections of the provinces of Firenze and Siena established from the point of view of its wine. This is the heart of Tuscany, with the Chianti hills acting as a natural boundary for a delineation first shaped in 1716 by the Grand Duke of Tuscany. The overall area for Chianti production is much larger, stretching farther into the provinces of Siena and Firenze, and into Pisa, Arezzo, and Pistoia.

If the word Chianti once conjured up the image of straw-covered wine flasks on red-and-white checked tablecloths in trattorias the world over, nothing could less represent modern Chianti's wines. Even as recently as 1967, when the area was first given its DOC status (*Denominazione di Origine Controllata*), up to 30 percent white grapes were still permitted to be blended into this professedly red wine based on Tuscan Sangiovese grapes. Since then a lot has changed.

Thanks to early dissenters with this "recipe" for Chianti—some of whom began making superior "alternative" or "super-Tuscan" wines entirely of red grapes (including the foreign Cabernet Sauvignon) and aging them in French oak *barriques* to resounding international acclaim—pressure was put on the denomination body to rethink the laws governing Chianti. In 1984 new DOCG regulations (that added stricter "guarantees" to the original laws) allowed for Chianti's wines to be made with very few white grapes (2 to 5 percent) for those who cared to reduce them. In August 1996 the decree went one step further, enabling producers to make their Chianti entirely from red grapes.

Chianti's current grape types are Sangiovese (Sangioveto) 75 percent to 100 percent; Canaiolo Nero 0 percent to 10 percent; Trebbiano and Malvasia (white grapes) 0 percent to 6 percent; other approved red grapes, including Cabernet Sauvignon 0 percent to 15 percent.

The world of Chianti production is complex: many but not all of the finest producers are part of the Chianti Classico Consortium, whose symbol is

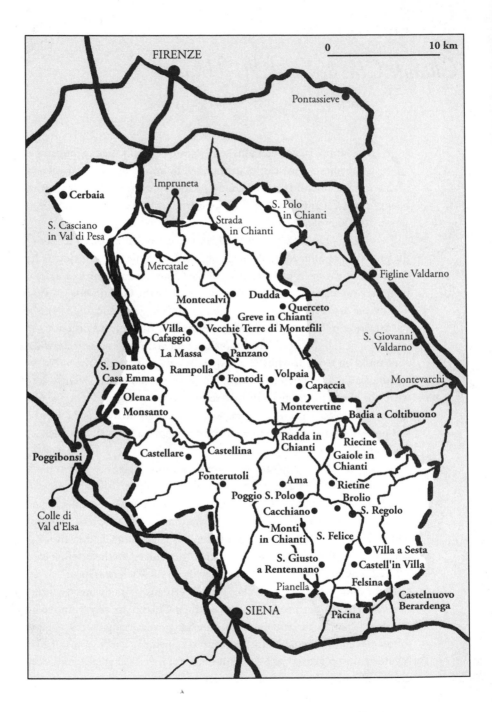

Town names in **bold** indicate towns that are included in this chapter.

the black rooster. Many also produce nondenomination *vini da tavola,* the so-called super-Tuscans, that were inspired by the great wines of Bordeaux and usually command high prices. The winemaking philosophy of an estate cannot be understood by reading its labels. The estates included in this chapter (and in the rest of the book) have been selected based on their good reputations, but the list is by no means all-inclusive. Many other fine estates exist.

Anyone interested in visiting more than one or two should get a copy of the Chianti Classico Consortium's excellent map of the area, showing all the major Chianti producers, both in and out of the consortium. It is invariably best to make an appointment before visiting a winery; many are quite small and do not have staff readily available for drop-in visitors, unless arrangements have been made. I strongly recommend visiting them; it is always an enjoyable and instructive experience, as wine producers are generous with their knowledge and passion for their wines.

Consorzio Del Marchio Storico Chianti Classico
Via Scopeti, 155
S. Andrea in Percussina
50026 San Casciano Val di Pesa
Firenze
055 8228245-6-7 fax: 055 8228173

AMA

CASTELLO DI AMA Lecchi in Chianti 53010 Gaiole in Chianti Siena
WINE TELEPHONE 0577 746031 FAX 0577 746117 OPEN Visits and tastings by appointment only CLOSED Saturday, Sunday DIRECT SALE No STOCKIST Ama's wines are sold in Lecchi and other local *enoteche* ENGLISH SPOKEN Yes DIRECTIONS The Castello di Ama is on the road between Lecchi and Radda.

The guiding force behind the successful Castello di Ama is a young woman, Lorenza Sebasti. "The vine is a plant that needs us," she explained as we viewed the vineyards from Ama's eighteenth-century villa. "Left to its own devices, it dies. Great wines require the best situation for plants—including reducing chemical treatments. We are lucky: we have the sun, the first factor for healthy plants. So you really taste the fruit in our wines."

Lorenza's family, with three others, bought the estate in 1972. Under the initial management of Silvano Formigli, modern cellars were installed and Ama began making quality wines. Eighty hectares (200 acres) of vineyards are now in production. "Ama was among the first in Chianti to apply an entrepreneurial attitude to vine-growing, winemaking and marketing," she said.

In 1982 they adopted the Bordeaux double lyre system in some vineyards: each plant is allowed two principal growing stems and attached to a wooden V structure resembling the musical instrument—giving a high-density result from less plants. "Also, our vineyards' names appeared on the labels. We said: 'Yes, this is a Chianti Classico, but that's not all!' We were stressing our grapes' provenance when most people were still cutting their wines with grapes from other regions."

Ama's name was built on its Sangiovese wines: the Chiantis, their Riservas, and *crus,* but other varietals have been successful. Vigna l'Apparita, an award-winner of pure Merlot, spends fourteen months in French *barriques* and twenty-four in the bottle. A deeply concentrated wine, it celebrates rich fruit in perfect balance with its wood. Ama impresses with its commitment to quality, its style, and its beauty. Despite its size, it produces fine wines—reds, whites, and Vin Santo—and thick green extra-virgin olive oil.

BADIA A COLTIBUONO

BADIA A COLTIBUONO WINE, RESTAURANT

53013   Gaiole in Chianti   Siena
TELEPHONE Winery 0577 749498; restaurant 0577 749424; shop 0577 749479   FAX Winery 0577 749235; restaurant 0577 749031   OPEN Winery visits by appointment only; restaurant: lunch and dinner; shop located on entrance road to Badia: 9:30-13:00, 14:00-19:00   CLOSED Restaurant: Monday, November-February; shop: Sunday, January 15-March 1   CREDIT CARDS Visa, MC   DIRECT SALE Yes, from shop   ENGLISH SPOKEN Yes   RESERVATIONS Recommended   PRICE $$$ OTHER English-language cooking school   DIRECTIONS Badia a Coltibuono is off the Chiantigiana SS 408, 5 kms north of Gaiole

Badia a Coltibuono is well known to foreigners. The magnificent villa, situated in a former abbey, is the home of the successful food writer Lorenza de' Medici Stucchi. Coltibuono includes winemaking activities, a farm shop, a restaurant, and a deluxe cooking school.

The winery is very large (producing one million bottles annually from 50 hectares/123 acres of vineyards) and has recently improved its wines, thanks to Roberto and Emanuela Stucchi Prinetti and Tuscan winemaker Maurizio Castelli. Another of the Stucchi children, Paolo, runs the restaurant, which features a fresh cuisine of traditional Tuscan dishes tailored to its international clientele. Lorenza's cooking school is very costly, but offers a unique opportunity: students live in the grand villa during the week's course, and dine in several stately homes—an unforgettable experience.

I was interested to learn of Lorenza's early career: "I wrote popular Italian cookbooks and articles for years," she recounted. "In the mid-eighties I met an American couple attending a cooking class in Firenze. They described learning to make pasta and preparing menus, and I thought: I could do that, too." Badia's cooking school was born; several stylish cookbooks have followed. Badia is now building an ultramodern *cantina* in Chianti.

BROLIO

CASTELLO DI BROLIO Brolio   53013   Gaiole in Chianti   Siena
WINE TELEPHONE 0577 7301   FAX 0577 730225   OPEN Shop: Monday-Friday 8:00-12:00, 13:00-19:00 (17:00 in winter), Saturday-Sunday 11:00-19:00. Tastings possible; *cantina* visits and guided tastings by appointment only   CREDIT CARDS Visa, MC, Amex   DIRECT SALE Yes   ENGLISH SPOKEN Yes   DIRECTIONS The shop is inside the large cellar compound down the hill from the castle.

The history of Brolio Castle is closely linked to that of Chianti wine. The Ricasolis, one of Italy's oldest winemaking families, have resided at Brolio since 1141 despite its being "destroyed a few times" over the centuries. In the 1840s, the "Iron Baron" Bettino Ricasoli began experimenting with imported French varietals. In 1874 he wrote a "recipe" for Chianti, an "important red wine," establishing Sangiovese as its primary ingredient, with a smaller percentage of red Canaiolo. If the wine was to be drunk young, he recommended adding white grapes to it, Malvasia or Trebbiano.

In 1963, almost a century later, this formula, white grapes and all, became law with the first Chianti DOC appellation. Filippo Mazzei of Fonterutoli (see p 188), Brolio's current director, sees it as a misunderstanding: "The white grapes were extraneous to Chianti if the intention was a wine fit for aging—they weakened Sangiovese's character." Other winemakers agreed and recently this "new" whiteless Chianti has finally been ratified by the DOCG body.

Since 1960 Brolio Castle's fortunes have fluctuated. Its stories of multinational takeovers, extravagant investments, near-bankruptcies, and secret coups reads like something out of the movie *Wall Street*. The fortuitous final result was that Baron Francesco Ricasoli (a former fashion photographer) and his friend Filippo Mazzei, armed with enthusiasm, quick thinking, and luck, rescued the enormous estate at the eleventh hour and now run it. "Things happened fast," explained Mazzei. "But Francesco was determined to save Brolio. We and our enologist Carlo Ferrini agree about making great wines here."

The huge industrial cellars remaining after the Seagrams take-over are now filled with *barriques*—a sure sign the shift from quantity to quality has begun. Many of the 220 hectares (540 acres) of vineyards have been replanted. Brolio now produces two lines of wines. The Castello di Brolio collection features a fine Chianti Classico with its Reserve; Casalferro, a super-Tuscan Sangiovese *cru;* Torricella, of Chardonnay grapes fermented in *barriques;* and a mature Vin Santo. The second line, Barone Ricasoli, has a wider range of improved wines at moderate prices.

CASTELL'IN VILLA

CASTELL'IN VILLA
WINE, RESTAURANT

53019   Castelnuovo Berardenga   Siena
TELEPHONE 0577 359074; restaurant 0571 359356   FAX 0577 359222
OPEN Shop: Monday-Saturday 9:00-13:00, 15:00-18:00 from Easter to November. Tastings and *cantina* visits by appointment only; restaurant: dinner only, Sunday lunch   CLOSED Shop: Sunday; December to Easter; restaurant: Monday; December to Easter   CREDIT CARDS Visa, MC   DIRECT SALE Yes   ENGLISH SPOKEN Yes
RESERVATIONS Recommended   PRICE $$$
DIRECTIONS From Castelnuovo Berardenga, go toward Gaiole. After 4.5 kms turn left. The winery is then signposted.

Castell'in Villa is an austere cluster of buildings in southern Chianti with fine views of Siena. Here Principessa Coralia Pignatelli and her late husband "came thirty years ago to put our roots together," as she explained.

The princess, a classically elegant Greek woman wearing a raw silk jacket, said her husband foretold she "would end up living in the country and producing wine. I didn't believe him then. But it turned out to be true." He was an Italian ambassador; together they lived in many countries. Since his death she has remained at Castell'in Villa, making wines and, more recently, running a restaurant.

Most of the estate's 54 hectares (133 acres) of vineyards are planted to Sangiovese, with some Cabernet Sauvignon for her "table wine," Santacroce. But her affections lie with Chianti. "I am a Sangiovese fanatic," she admitted. "I particularly like young old wines—old wines that are still young and lively. Like my 1971 Chianti Classico Riserva. Otherwise I prefer to drink them in the first year of their production." Her wines (for she is the winemaker) are the fruit of low yield, selected grapes ripened in the hot sun of Castelnuovo Berardenga—wines that are warm, rich, and balanced.

When I visited Castell'in Villa in winter, the restaurant was closed. It was beautiful, with the spare modern look that characterizes the princess' sophisticated style. Natural materials, walnut and cypress woods from the estate, are used strikingly: a long "table of life" made by the sculptor Cecco Buonanotte is the focal point. "I love the idea that people who do not know each other can sit and eat together. It creates an atmosphere of happiness. For the Greeks, hospitality is very important, complementing the activities of a farm. Here we serve simple, seasonal foods, as pure and good as the wines. That is the life-affirming message it represents."

CASTELLINA IN CHIANTI

L'ALBERGACCIO
RESTAURANT

Via Fiorentina, 35   53011   Castellina in Chianti   Siena
TELEPHONE 0577 741042   FAX 0577 741250   OPEN Dinner Monday-Saturday; lunch also Monday, Friday, and Saturday   CLOSED Sunday; November   CREDIT CARDS None   ENGLISH SPOKEN A little   FEATURES Outdoor summer terrace   RESERVATIONS Recommended in summer   PRICE $$$ DIRECTIONS Just outside the town center, going toward San Donato in Poggio

L'Albergaccio is located in a restructured stone barn. In cool weather you eat under the rafters, in summer on the garden terrace. The young proprietors have been attentive to detail—not just in material things, but in researching fine ingredients. The studied wine list features Tuscany, grouping its wines by towns.

During my February visit, coowner Francesco Cacciatori proposed home-cured *salumi* and *stuzzichini d'inverno*, winter taste-whetters, as antipasti (each season has its own). There were fried sage leaves, creamy-centered polenta topped with leeks, and *zolfino* beans (see p 345) with cured pork shoulder preserved in oil. The fine-skinned beans were wonderfully tender; the meat rather oily. The *salumi* included delicate-textured *finocchiona*, marbled head cheese (*soppressata*), and an ethereal slice of *lardo di Colonnata* (see p 37) served on warm bread.

The *primi*, which included ravioli stuffed with salt cod (*baccalà*) on puréed beans, confirmed the restaurant's commitment to unusual taste combinations. Light *gnocchetti* of ricotta came with shaved winter truffle and thyme. *Pici con digiune d'agnello* were homemade pasta with a robust sauce of lamb's intestines topped with pungent pecorino cheese. A *fagottino* (little crèpe bundle), contained diced pigeon and was sprinkled with crunchy fried leek rings. Flavorful wood pigeon (*colombaccio*) was simmered in wine, water, and vinegar, spiced with cloves, and sweetened with onion. The restaurant's desserts are a triumph of technique and taste—the pistachio tart, caramel-scented *bavarese*, and air-light ricotta mousse with orange sauce were all excellent.

ANTICA TRATTORIA
"LA TORRE"
RESTAURANT

Piazza del Comune   53011   Castellina in Chianti   Siena
TELEPHONE 0577 740236   FAX 0577 740228   OPEN Lunch and dinner   CLOSED Friday; early September   CREDIT CARDS Visa, MC, Amex   ENGLISH SPOKEN Yes   RESERVATIONS Recommended for dinner   PRICE $$ DIRECTIONS In the town center, under the commune

This popular trattoria has been the Stiaccini family's since 1895. They are generous and unpretentious, as is the food, with the simplest things being the best. The busy dining room hosts a nice mix of locals and foreigners, young and old. The menu offers a pretty standard choice with some exceptions: in winter, hot antipasti included fried polenta topped with meat sauce, spinach frittata, chicken *vol-au-vent*, and *crostini*. Assorted *salumi* were another option. *Primi* included pastas (cannelloni, *pappardelle* with wild boar or mushroom sauce,

penne piccanti) and thick Tuscan bread soups. In summer there are more
vegetable-based dishes. Roasted meats are a specialty: veal, pork, chicken, guinea
fowl, and pigeon. I tried an interesting local dish, *lesso rifatto con cipolle*. This is
a *cucina povera* recipe using leftovers from *lesso*, boiled beef. Traditionally, the
cooked meat is stewed with inexpensive ingredients: onions, tomatoes, and
herbs. It was good: the slightly stringy meat was well-flavored and nicely
spiced. Homemade desserts included *pinolata*—a pie filled with custard,
plumped raisins, a layer of cake, and toasted pine nuts. The wine list contains
some good Chiantis.

CASTELLARE   Poderi di Castellare   53011   Castellina in Chianti   Siena
WINE   TELEPHONE/FAX 0577 740490   OPEN Shop: 8:00-18:00; visits and
tastings by appointment only   CLOSED Never
CREDIT CARDS Visa, MC   DIRECT SALE Yes   ENGLISH SPOKEN Yes
DIRECTIONS From Castellina go toward Poggibonsi. After 800 meters
follow signs to the left.

Castellare is a 20 hectare (49 acre) winery owned since 1979 by Milanese jour-
nalist Paolo Panerai. Working with Tuscan winemaker Maurizio Castelli, he
produces concentrated, new-style wines that are popular in the United States.

Castellare is a pretty place, with spectacular views of the valley
above Poggibonsi. Panerai lives and works in Milan, but he has invested heavily
in the estate; modern cellars were nearing completion when I visited. Castellare's
shop sells his attractively presented wines (each year a different wild bird is featured on the labels) plus oil and vinegar produced for him at Volpaia (p 209).

Of the wines, I Sodi di San Niccolò is the best known. A super-
Tuscan of 85 percent Sangioveto with 15 percent Malvasia Nera, it is made from
grapes of mature vines and produced only in good years. The wine's lengthy
aging is in *barriques* with a year in the bottle. This well-structured, complex
wine commands high prices. Castellare's commitment to Sangiovese is also
apparent in its Chianti Classico. White grapes have been eliminated, resulting
in a rich, fruity red wine of intensity with good aging potential. For the whites,
French grape varieties have substituted the Italian: Canonico is made of pure
Chardonnay; Spartito of pure Sauvignon; and Le Ginestre is a blend of the two.

Also

On Saturday mornings at Castellina's weekly market, look out for Duccio
Fontani's unusual stall. Duccio cultivates over thirty types of aromatic herbs on
his small organic farm outside Castellina (tel: 0577 740662); he dries and combines them in wonderful ways.

CASTELNUOVO BERARDENGA

DA ANTONIO
RESTAURANT

Via Fiorita, 38   53019   Castelnuovo Berardenga   Siena
TELEPHONE 0577 255321   OPEN Lunch and dinner   CLOSED Monday;
Tuesday for lunch; when the sea is too rough to fish
CREDIT CARDS Visa, MC   ENGLISH SPOKEN Yes
RESERVATIONS Recommended   PRICE $$$$
DIRECTIONS In Piazza Matteotti, in the town center

Antonio Farina is a curious character. "I'm a man of the sea," he said, but he nonetheless opened a fine fish restaurant as far from the sea as Tuscany gets: in the heart of Chianti. Still, he cooks and sells only the freshest of each day's catch, which arrives daily from the coast's best markets. "In high seas [when no fishing is possible] my restaurant closes," he exclaimed.

Antonio's way is to prepare different fish dishes each day. Customers sit down, he cooks, and the food is brought out to them. If there is a menu, I never saw it. Anyone who is not open to this formula will probably be happier somewhere else. A treat is in store for the rest, for Antonio is a natural, talented chef; his food is wonderful.

In February, my dinner began with a quick succession of seafood antipasti. Thin slices of raw *fragolino* (a sea bream) scented with winter truffle arrived on a searing hot plate, cooking as it came. Miniscule *rossetti* (transparent gobies) were fried in a quick *frittellina*—like a small pancake; it tasted richly of the sea. Blanched *calamaretti* (young squid) were slit and opened; they looked like white rose petals and came, warm, on a green bed of peeled baby fava beans. They were unbelievably tender and silky—an early celebration of spring. A fried fillet of *nasello* (hake) was coupled with the decisive flavors of the south—cherry-tomato concassé, earthy, sharp capers—that made the fish seem sweet. Fragile wild asparagus spears were chopped and tossed with chunks of *pescatrice* (monkfish), olive oil, and lemon. Spaghetti had a light sauce of fresh tomato and flaked *triglie* (red mullet). The *fragolino* reappeared, poached and filleted without being topped and tailed, served with bitter baked radicchio. *Scampi e gamberi rossi* (pink and red shrimp) were char-broiled.

There is a detailed list of wines, its emphasis on whites from Tuscany and beyond. Indeed, the room is lined with bottles—not surprising for a seaside restaurant firmly anchored in Chianti's vineyards.

FATTORIA DI FÈLSINA Strada Chiantigiana SS 484   53019   Castelnuovo Berardenga   Siena
WINE   TELEPHONE 0577 355117   FAX 0577 355651   OPEN Shop: Easter to
October 10:00-19:00; winter: 8:00-12:30, 13:30-17:00; tastings usually
possible. Cellar visits by appointment only   CLOSED Sunday
CREDIT CARDS Visa, MC   DIRECT SALE Yes   ENGLISH SPOKEN Yes
DIRECTIONS Fèlsina is just outside of Castelnuovo Berardenga, on the road
toward Gaiole.

"To understand Fèlsina's wines is to understand its lands, its *terroir*," affirmed
Giuseppe Mazzocolin, the estate's director. Fèlsina is in a border zone at the
southern edge of the Classico denomination: it marks the changeover from
vineyards to wheat fields. It was bought in 1966 by the late Domenico Poggiali,
who first understood its potential. The large estate of 342 hectares (845 acres),
of which 52 (128) are planted to vineyards, comprises eleven farms surrounded
by woods and vineyards. At its heart is the winery, striking for the austere
grandeur of its buildings—aligned on three sides of a square courtyard, they
suggest a setting for outdoor theater. "Each *podere,* or farm, within the estate
has an identity that remains in the wines that are made there, like Rancia or
Fontalloro," explained Mazzocolin as we visited them.

    Fèlsina's wines are the fruit of a winemaking "marriage of true
minds" between Mazzocolin and enologist Franco Bernabei. They have planted
most of the estate's vineyards to Sangiovese, Tuscany's native grape variety and
the basis of Chianti Classico. Both of Fèlsina's great *crus,* Vigneto Rancia (a
Chianti Classico Riserva) and Fontalloro (a modern table wine), are of
Sangiovese. They are rich, powerful wines with an elegance that transcends
their earthy tones.

    Mazzocolin resists the idea that great modern wines must be
made from "international" (French) grape varietals. "There has to be room for
every type of wine," he asserted with the conviction of a modern-day humanist.
"You could think of it as a giant *cru* of a thousand faces! Cabernet Sauvignon is
not the only answer. We in Tuscany have Sangiovese—and we're proud of it!"

    However, Sangiovese is not all that Fèlsina produces under
its Berardenga label. Maestro Raro is deemed by some critics to be the best
Cabernet Sauvignon in Tuscany. I Sistri is a *barrique*-aged Chardonnay, while
the winery's sister estate, Castello di Farnetella, produces a delicately fruity
Sauvignon Blanc.

    "After all these years of working with it, wine remains a mystery to
me," concluded Mazzocolin, with the softness of inflection that reveals his
Venetian origins. "I may understand it from a scientific point of view, but
nonetheless each year I am amazed by the near-magical transformation of fruit
juice into wine."

CERBAIA

LA TENDA ROSSA   Piazza del Monumento, 9/14   50020   Cerbaia Val di Pesa   Firenze
RESTAURANT   TELEPHONE 055 826132   FAX 055 825210   OPEN Lunch and dinner
                        CLOSED Wednesday; Thursday for lunch; August
                        CREDIT CARDS Visa, MC, Amex   ENGLISH SPOKEN Yes
                        RESERVATIONS Recommended   PRICE $$$$$$
                        DIRECTIONS In Cerbaia's main square

La Tenda Rossa was a film, but here the movie's "red tent" has given way to a
luxurious restaurant with a shiny red door. Inside is a modern environment of
muted colors, soft lighting, potted-plant dividers, expensive *objets,* and comfort
reminiscent of the romanticism of the seventies.

The restaurant is run by three couples and their three daughters.
These young women, who dress alike, are beautiful, efficient (they are all
qualified sommeliers and serve the tables), and rather formal. Of the six parents, two host the restaurant, the others cook.

La Tenda Rossa is noted for its food and wine. The wine lists
are bound volumes filled with rare and remarkable Italian and French vintages.
As for the food, it is ambitious and adventurous: first-rate ingredients (many
homegrown) are combined in complex ways. This taste layering is reflected
in the menu descriptions: "black ravioli of pork with flowers of green cabbage
lightly scented with garlic and foie gras of goose" runs one *primo.* As a daughter
lifts the silver cloche from your dish, she repeats its title entirely.

The food is elaborately presented. Breaded fillets of red mullet
are fanned below a "flower" of black olives, asparagus, onion strips, and candied
tomatoes. Four saffron-crusted shrimp decorate a puréed soup of domestic
mushrooms, swirled with fragrant olive oil. Heart-shaped ravioli of a translucent milk-pasta are stuffed with pounded crustaceans and sauced with a delicate "mousse" of haricot beans. Thin rolls of pasta perfumed with wild fennel
come with a "white" sauce of ground guinea fowl and rosemary, the well-
flavored sauce successfully complementing the herbed pasta. Two jumbo red
shrimp are neatly wrapped with pancetta and tied with pineapple-sage on a bed
of black-edged eggplant "ribbons." A perfectly cooked lamb chop is crusted
with slivered, toasted almonds, its sweetness cut by sharp fresh goat's cheese
and beet greens.

"*La Tenda Rossa* was an adventure film," explained the restaurant's genial host, Silvano Santandrea. "We embarked on a gastronomic adventure—and we are still on it!"

DUDDA

CASTELLO DI QUERCETO WINE

Dudda Lucolena 50020 Greve in Chianti Firenze
TELEPHONE 055 8549064/9   FAX 055 8549063   OPEN 8:00-12:00,
13:00-17:00. Visits and tastings by appointment only   CLOSED Saturday
and Sunday, except by appointment   CREDIT CARDS None
DIRECT SALE Yes   ENGLISH SPOKEN Yes   DIRECTIONS The Castello is
signposted off the Figline-Greve road, near Sùgame. Follow the unpaved
road through the oak wood to the end.

The Castello di Querceto is a fairly large winery in a stately villa from 1200, set
in well-kept grounds with peacocks. The estate is owned by the François family,
who have for years produced a range of high-quality wines. Having most of its
45 hectares (111 acres) of vineyards high up in the Chianti hills gives Querceto's
wines full bouquets and elegance. "They may have less structure than wines
from lower ground, and be less masculine," Alessandro François's nephew
Paolo Zucconi told me, "but they are not lacking in *profumi.*"

In addition to its Chiantis and their reserves, the estate makes
La Corte, a single-vineyard wine of pure Sangiovese aged in *barriques.* Il
Querciolaia blends 65 percent Sangiovese with 35 percent Cabernet; it is a wine
of great character. Il Cignale is another high-profile *vino da tavola,* of Cabernet
with a touch of Merlot. The Castello is also known for its *acquavite,* distilled
from fresh *vinacce* (wine-soaked grape residues), by Nannoni (see p 218).

FONTERUTOLI

CASTELLO DI FONTERUTOLI WINE

53010 Fonterutoli Siena
TELEPHONE 0577 740476   FAX 0577 741070   OPEN Shop: 10:00-
21:00; tastings possible there; cellar visits by appointment only
CLOSED Tuesday   CREDIT CARDS Visa, MC, Amex   DIRECT SALE Yes
ENGLISH SPOKEN Yes   FEATURES The estate runs an Osteria in the
village.   OTHER Six apartments available for holiday rentals
DIRECTIONS Fonterutoli and its shop are on the main road from
Castellina to Siena.

Filippo Mazzei tells good stories about his ancestors. Ser Lapo, a fourteenth-
century gentleman, was a writer and notary and an ambassador in Florence for
Francesco Datini, a key financier of his day. "Ser Lapo was passionate about
wines," recounted Filippo Mazzei enthusiastically, "if Datini was not. One of
my favorite letters of his from 1394 reads: 'Don't worry about the price of that
wine; it may be expensive, but its goodness will restore us.'" He was also the
author of the first document citing Chianti as a wine type (see p 87 for his
connection to Carmignano). Several centuries later Filippo Mazzei (1730–1816)
took Tuscan vines and olive trees to Monticello, met George Washington, and
was present at the signing of the Declaration of Independence.

The present Filippo Mazzei's grandfather relaunched the historic *borgo* of Fonterutoli and its wines. In 1924 he was among the Chianti

consortium's founding members. "I got involved when I was still at university," explained Filippo Mazzei, who is also director of Brolio (p 181). "My father, like Sergio Manetti and the Antinoris, became interested in making new-style wines. Very early, he planted foreign vines here." Fonterutoli is a self-contained village. A modern *cantina* is in the works, but for now, each cottage houses a barrel or two of its award-winning wines.

The Chianti Classico is made entirely of red grapes, primarily Sangiovese. It is very fruity, yet mellow. Ser Lapo, a Chianti Classico Riserva, is made from grapes selected from two vineyards. Siepi is a highly acclaimed super-Tuscan of Sangiovese and Merlot in equal parts. It is aged in *barriques*. Concerto, of 80 percent Sangiovese and 20 percent Cabernet, is its equally remarkable stablemate. Filippo Mazzei, who has developed the wines with winemaker Carlo Ferrini, is justly proud of them. Brancaia (made jointly with Swiss growers) is another modern wine of 90 percent Sangiovese and 10 percent Merlot.

GAIOLE IN CHIANTI

RIECINE
WINE

Riecine 53013 Gaiole in Chianti Siena
TELEPHONE 0577 749527 FAX 0577 749098
E-MAIL riecine@chiantinet.it OPEN 10:00-12:30, 14:30-17:30: visits, tastings and sales by appointment only CREDIT CARDS None
DIRECT SALE Yes ENGLISH SPOKEN Yes DIRECTIONS From Gaiole go north towards Montevarchi. Before reaching Badia a Coltibuono, there is a small turn to the right; follow the unpaved road to Riecine.

Talking to John Dunkley, the Englishman who has created Riecine, you never lose sight of his passion for making wine. "The glory of a simple wine is like a peach still warm from the tree: it is a celebration of simplicity and purity. The further you get away from your pure, simple wine, from your 'grape juice fermented,' the more you lose. One of the exciting things about winemaking is that you don't need volume to make your mark."

Make his mark he has. With their small estate of 4 hectares (10 acres), Dunkley and his late wife, Palmina Abbagnano, were among the first foreigners (though she was Italian) to bring new blood into Chianti's winemaking. "At first, it was fun. We did it to please ourselves," he recalled. "Our first harvest, in 1972, was awful. To make good wine you need perfect grapes—but we didn't. They were mildewed from the rain. By the following year we had learned our lesson—we even won a prize."

Things became more serious: better equipment was brought in, the cellar improved. So did the wines. By the mid-seventies they had stopped adding white grapes to Chianti—way ahead of the *disciplinare* and of almost everyone else. They did all the work themselves, "me in the cellar, Palmina driving the tractor," and began making a name with their concentrated, perfumed wines. In 1982 Gioia di Riecine was born, their *vino da tavola* of pure Sangiovese. "Gioia and our Chianti come from practically the same grapes," he explained. "The Chianti is aged in big wooden barrels whose wood does not really affect it, but Gioia is put into *barriques*. This smaller wood changes the nature of the wine: it acts like putting a skeleton into the wine onto which the other things are hung. It also makes it capable of long aging." Gioia is a rich, mellow wine with "that recognizable dryness in the nose, that wonderful dustiness."

With his young partner, Sean O'Callaghan, Dunkley is now preparing for the future of Riecine. Meanwhile, he makes no bones about enjoying the fruit of his labors. "The joy of being small is that you can have a quality-control session twice a day—at lunch and dinner."

RIETINE
WINE

53013   Gaiole in Chianti   Siena
TELEPHONE 0577 731110   FAX 0577 738482   OPEN Tastings, sales and visits by appointment only   CREDIT CARDS None
DIRECT SALE Yes   ENGLISH SPOKEN Yes   DIRECTIONS From Gaiole, go south on the Chiantigiana for 2 kms. Go left over small bridge and up past *Cantina Geografica* to Rietine. The winery is just beyond the central square of the village.

Galina and Mario Gaffuri-Lazarides are a Swiss couple who in 1988 bought a 13 hectare (32 acre) vineyard just south of Gaiole. "We were lucky," explained Galina, who is of Greek origin. "We found this south-facing vineyard all in one piece." They produce an unusual "table" wine: Tiziano contains equal parts of Merlot and Lambrusco and is matured in *barriques*. The couple also produce an all-red Chianti Classico and its reserve. "I like to think of it like this," the engaging Galina admitted. "Chianti Classico is an eating wine, to enjoy every day with dinner. On Saturday you drink the Riserva. On Sunday, or your birthday, you want a special wine, like the powerful, rich super-Tuscans."

Also

Bianchi Self-Service. Via Ricasoli, 48. 0577 749501.
Bianchi's is a wonderful grocery store in Gaiole that sells everything, from great home-baked bread (including one Etruscan) to ingredients for a picnic or feast. The Bianchi family would win my prize, if I had one, for being the most patient and friendly shopkeepers with non-Italians.

Studio Fernandez (0577 749363) is on the road between Gaiole and Radda at Le Conce. This small pottery is run by Olivier Fernandez and his lovely wife, Margherita. At their farmhouse they make and sell their modern ceramics and sculptures.

GREVE IN CHIANTI

ANTICA MACELLERIA Piazza G. Matteotti, 69-71 50022 Greve Firenze
FALORNI TELEPHONE 055 853029 FAX 055 8544521 OPEN 8:00-13:00,
MEAT: SALUMI 15:30-19:30 CLOSED Wednesday afternoon, Sunday morning in winter
CREDIT CARDS Visa, MC DIRECT SALE Yes ENGLISH SPOKEN Yes
DIRECTIONS In Greve's main square

It's not hard to spot Falorni's butcher shop in Greve's market square: a stuffed wild boar stands guard outside. Inside there are baskets of *salumi*, meat counters, and pre-1914 photographs of the shop, which was *antica* even then. The current generation are active campaigners for "real" food—artisan butchers who use only quality meats from animals raised in the surrounding countryside. The interior is divided between fresh meats and the brothers' range of homemade *salumi* (vacuum packed for easy transportation). At weekends, tourists flock to it in droves (or buses), stocking up on the packages. (U.S. laws forbid the importing of meats, so Americans will have to do their tasting while in Europe).

Wild boar culled from the local woods (there is an overpopulation now) are turned into tasty little salamis joined with strings. Pork products include fennel-scented *finocchiona* (one of the fattiest of the *salumi*), and classic *salame Toscano*. "My father taught me that to make this kind of *salame* well," stated Lorenzo Bencistà, one of the Falorni descendants, "you have to spend twenty years working with someone who knows how. Everything is important: selecting the cuts of meat, dosing it with salt, garlic, and spices, and kneading the mixture."

Fresh meats include fine local Chianina beef—for the best *Fiorentina* T-bones—and the excellent organic beef from Nuova Casenovole (see p 214), as well as pork, duck, rabbit and guinea fowl. I asked whether the chickens were free-range (tough to find in Italy). "We used to keep them," admitted Lorenzo, "but we gave up—it was too costly. Now we buy battery chickens like everybody else. My advice to anyone who wants a 'real' chicken is to raise it themselves!"

MONTECALVI Via Cittile, 85 50022 Greve in Chianti Firenze
WINE TELEPHONE/FAX 055 8544665 OPEN By appointment only
CREDIT CARDS None DIRECT SALE Yes ENGLISH SPOKEN Yes
DIRECTIONS From Greve, go toward Firenze. After 1 km, Montecalvi is on the right, before the gas station.

I am grateful to Bernadette and Renzo Bolli for giving me my first official *vendemmia*—grape harvest. I volunteered, and they accepted. So for one hot October's day I joined forces with them and a group of locals and picked grapes. It was an instructive experience. I learned how to select good bunches from bad ones (rejecting the powdery blue mold that can make the wine bitter), how the grapes are destalked and crushed. It is back-breaking work, but also great fun—not for nothing is the expression: "I heard it through the grapevine." In Tuscany they call it *radio vigna*—Radio Grapevine—because being there you find out the latest gossip about everyone in the area!

When the Bollis bought their house in 1988, it was completely abandoned. The vineyards had been planted in 1932 and were overrun and diseased. The position was excellent, though, right in the heart of Chianti Classico. They decided to replant local Sangiovese using the high-density system for their delicious, drinkable wine, Montecalvi. It is matured for one year in wooden barrels and one in the bottle.

"When we started," explained Renzo Bolli, "the *disciplinare* for Chianti Classico still obliged the blending of white grapes into the Sangiovese. I had never liked those wines—they seemed astringent to me—so we decided to opt out of the DOCG and to make a 'table wine' of pure Sangiovese. The good thing about being small is being flexible."

VECCHIE TERRE **DI MONTEFILI** **WINE**	Via San Cresci, 45 50022 Greve in Chianti Firenze TELEPHONE 055 853739 FAX 055 8544684 OPEN Visits and tastings by appointment only, by phone or fax one week ahead DIRECT SALE No STOCKIST Gallo Nero *enoteca* at Panzano or Greve ENGLISH SPOKEN Yes DIRECTIONS From Panzano go toward Mercatale; the winery is on the right after about 5 kms.

Vecchie Terre di Montefili is one of Chianti's rising stars. The story of its ascent is a familiar one: Roccaldo Acuti, a successful textile industrialist from Prato with a penchant for wine, bought the run-down farm in 1979. Its vineyards were semiabandoned. He hired a winemaker, Vittorio Fiore, and invested heavily in plants and cellar equipment. Then, unusually, his young daughter, Maria, decided to run the winemaking business, which she does with her companion, Thomas Paglione, who oversees the *cantina*. The estate is still growing: its 9 hectares (23 acres) of vineyards will soon increase to 12 (30). This is a lovely setting, high in the Chianti hills, with house and farm buildings flanked by vineyards. Maria Acuti is a well-traveled, friendly young woman. Her house is tasteful and welcoming.

Vecchie Terre's big wines are its Chianti Classico (of pure Sangiovese, it is well structured, fruity, and drinkable), Anfiteatro (also of pure Sangiovese, it began as a Riserva but is now defined as *vino da tavola*) and Bruno di Rocca (a blend of 70 percent Cabernet Sauvignon with 30 percent Sangiovese, it is also a super-Tuscan). Bruno di Rocca is a powerful wine that has been put up at tastings with Sassicaia and Solaia and come away tops. I asked Maria about its name: "My father, Roccaldo, wanted to buy an estate in Montalcino. When we chose Chianti instead, he dedicated this wine to that dream: Bruno (for Brunello) di Rocca (for Roccaldo)."

ENOTECA DEL Piazzetta Santa Croce, 8 50022 Greve in Chianti Firenze
CHIANTI CLASSICO TELEPHONE/FAX 055 853297 OPEN 9:30-12:30, 15:30-19:30 (till 20:00
"GALLO NERO" in summer) CLOSED Wednesday CREDIT CARDS Visa, MC, Amex
WINE STORE DIRECT SALE Yes ENGLISH SPOKEN A little
 DIRECTIONS At the narrrow end of the town's central square

This useful shop stocks wines from the Chianti Classico consortium's members
and a good selection of nonmembers. Some space is dedicated to other Tuscan
denominations: Vernaccia di San Gimignano, Brunello di Montalcino, and so
on. Super-Tuscans from the best estates are available. The list is large, so have
an idea of what you want before going. The staff will provide information but
no tastings are allowed. Prices should be the same as at the nearby wineries.
The *enoteca* also stocks extra-virgin olive oils from many Chianti estates, Vin
Santo, grappa, and vinegar.

LECCHI

IL POGGIO Poggio San Polo Lecchi 53010 Gaiole Siena
RESTAURANT TELEPHONE 0577 746135 FAX 0577 746120 OPEN Lunch and dinner
 CLOSED Monday; November, January CREDIT CARDS Visa, MC, Amex
 ENGLISH SPOKEN Yes FEATURES Outdoor summer terrace
 RESERVATIONS Recommended in summer PRICE $$
 DIRECTIONS From Lecchi, go toward Poggio San Polo. The restaurant
 is signposted.

Il Poggio is an airy restaurant on top of a hill (*poggio* means hill). In nice
weather a large shaded terrace with climbing roses provides views of vineyards.
This busy restaurant offers many Tuscan favorites, cooked simply but well, and
made to go with Chianti.
 The mixed *antipasto Toscano* includes *finocchiona* and pro-
sciutto, and assorted *crostini*—whose chicken-liver topping comes with a
candle-warmer, a nice touch. *Bruschette di pomodoro* uses flavorful tomatoes,
crunchy bread, and just enough rubbed garlic. The *primi* are very good. Il
Poggio's kitchens are staffed by local women who handmake the pasta.
Spinach-and-ricotta-filled *tortelli* are a fresh summer choice, but there is also
a stiff *ribollita,* the peasant soup of vegetables and bread. We found a good
range of vegetable dishes at Il Poggio, enough to satisfy my vegetarian friends.
These change seasonally. The best meats are the simplest: steaks or chicken
grilled over an open fire. They are, however, highly salted—so be sure to ask
for them *senza sale* if salt is a problem. Of the desserts, some are homemade.
Of these, tiramisù is light, cool, and satisfying, while the *panna cotta* (baked
cream pudding) comes nicely balanced by a sweet strawberry sauce.

MONSANTO

MONSANTO
WINE

Castello di Monsanto   50021   Barberino Val d'Elsa   Firenze
TELEPHONE 055 8059000   FAX 055 8059049   OPEN 8:00-12:30,
14:00-18:00; visits and guided tastings by appointment only
CLOSED Saturday, Sunday; three weeks in August   CREDIT CARDS Visa,
MC, Amex   DIRECT SALE Yes   ENGLISH SPOKEN Yes
DIRECTIONS From Poggibonsi go toward Barberino. After the roundabout,
turn right toward Monsanto and Olena.

Monsanto is a stately 1700s villa set in a beautiful English-style garden. The estate, with over 50 hectares (123 acres) of vineyards, has long been in the Bianchi family, and Fabrizio Bianchi has long been a key character in Chianti. He was among the first to eliminate white grapes from the Chianti blend and to explore the use of *barriques*. His single-vineyard Chianti Classico Riserva, Il Poggio, was an early Chianti *cru*. Bianchi is a jolly, energetic man with a wry sense of humor. He is a great expert about wine and a tireless innovator. "He is the one who makes all the experiments here," laughed his charming daughter, Laura, "and I am the one who has to sell them!"

The Bianchis have created a spectacular *cantina*, with a long wide descending tunnel lined with stones retrieved from the vineyards. "The *barricaia* took three men six years to make," Laura explained. It was finished in 1992.

Monsanto's wines are concentrated and pure. The 1993 Chianti Classico Riserva is smooth and fruity, but lacks the intensity of color Chianti sometimes has. "In bad years Sangiovese has no depth of color," explained Bianchi, "which is why deeply pigmented grapes such as Colorino are often added to it." Monsanto produces no "normal" Chianti, but only the Riserva and the *cru*, Il Poggio. This comes from 5 hectares (12 acres) of vineyard positioned up at 310 meters. "This wine should stay in wood for three years," he continued. "Putting it in *barriques* for a period has the same effect but shortens the time." It spends a further year in the bottle. The estate has, in recent years, introduced some new-style *vini da tavola*. "Fabrizio Bianchi" is a wine of pure Sangiovese, mellow, structured, and rich. Tinscvil, an Etruscan word meaning "votive offering to the daughter of Jupiter," is a blend of 75 percent Sangiovese with 25 percent Cabernet Sauvignon; Nemo is pure Cabernet Sauvignon. In great years there is also a fine sweet Vin Santo.

MONTI IN CHIANTI

CASTELLO DI
CACCHIANO
WINE, OLIVE OIL

Cacchiano   53010   Monti in Chianti   Siena
TELEPHONE 0577 747018   FAX 0577 747157   OPEN 8.00-12.00,
13.00-17.00; *cantina* visits and tastings by appointment only
CLOSED Saturday, Sunday   CREDIT CARDS None   DIRECT SALE Yes
ENGLISH SPOKEN Yes   OTHER Guest apartment available for weekly
rentals   DIRECTIONS From Gaiole, take SS 408 south toward Siena
for 5.5 kms. Turn left onto SS 484 toward Brolio. After 5 kms, turn right
toward Cacchiano.

Cacchiano is an imposing, austere medieval castle commanding extraordinary
views of its surrounding countryside. It was constructed by the Ricasoli-
Firidolfis in the tenth century as part of Brolio Castle's fortifications against
the Sienese Republic, and it has been in the same family ever since.

The castle's winemaking activities are now run directly by the
Baroness Elisabetta Ricasoli-Firidolfi and her son, Giovanni, with the help of
the enologist Giulio Gambelli. Cacchiano is known for its "traditional-style"
Chianti Classico DOCG, with, in good years, the acclaimed Millennio Riserva.
A super-Tuscan called RF is made from Sangiovese and Canaiolo grapes matured
exclusively in French oak *barriques*. "RF is less nature than art," the baroness
explained. "It is a wedding between the tannins of the oak and the tannins in
the wine, and we try to control this union so that the wood does not win over
the grape."

Their Vin Santo is also of the traditional type, made from 100
percent Malvasia grapes which are partially dried on racks for four to five
months before being pressed and sealed in casks of from 30 to 200 liters. "Every
five years or so" they take it out and bottle it. The estate sells a fine extra-virgin
olive oil, pressed from hand-picked olives. "We use primarily the Correggiolo
olives with a little bit of Moraiolo and Leccino added, because the best
pollination is possible when there are several types," explained the baroness.

SAN GIUSTO A
RENTENNANO
WINE

Monti in Chianti   53010   Gaiole in Chianti   Siena
TELEPHONE 0577 747121   FAX 0577 747109   OPEN 8:00-12:00,
14:00-18:00; visits and tastings by appointment   CLOSED Sunday
CREDIT CARDS None   DIRECT SALE Yes   ENGLISH SPOKEN Yes
OTHER Several farmhouses available for holiday rentals
DIRECTIONS The winery is signposted from SS 408, the Chiantigiana,
about 12 kms south of Gaiole.

They have been called "vikings" and *capitani di ventura*—indeed, the brothers
Francesco and Luca Martini di Cigala do seem like two young men with a mission. Self-taught winemakers and hands-on farmers, they took the wine world
by storm in 1991 when their super-Tuscan of pure Sangiovese, Percarlo 1985,
went up against some of France's greatest wines in a blind tasting—and won.
But these are no Johnny-come-latelies.

For centuries Fattoria San Giusto a Rentennano belonged to the Barons Ricasoli at Brolio Castle, acting as a fortified stronghold until it was destroyed at the end of the fourteenth century. One hundred years later a country villa was built above its remaining buttressed walls. Since the early 1900s, the Martini di Cigala family has been related to the Ricasolis by marriage. Enrico Martini di Cigala inherited the property in 1957 and began improvements. Since his death in 1992, his sons have taken over. Francesco bottled San Giusto's first Chianti in 1981; Percarlo was born in 1983. Some vineyards are on tufa, which lends the wines their structure and aging power. The reds are robust and full, becoming increasingly elegant over time.

I know I am not alone in being mad for San Giusto a Rentennano's Vin Santo, but tasting it came as a revelation. Totally unlike the lean, "dry sherry" Vin Santi, the Martini di Cigala's aromatic, amber wine is sweet, rich, and seductive. "Most Tuscan Vin Santo is made from primarily Trebbiano grapes," explained Francesco, "but Trebbiano is less able to mature fully, and leads to those thin, dry wines. Ours uses mainly Malvasia grapes with a higher sugar content." The harvested grapes are dried for four months on cane racks to further concentrate their sugars. The wine is sealed into small chestnut wood *caratelli* along with the "mother" yeasts that feed the wine throughout its long fermentation. They are placed in the *vinsantaia*, usually a space under the roof where the wine can experience seasonal temperature changes. The aging lasts four to six years. Seven to 8 kg (16 lbs) of grapes are required to make each liter of Vin Santo.

OLENA

ISOLE E OLENA Via Olena, 15   Olena   50021   Barberino Val d'Elsa   Firenze
WINE   TELEPHONE 055 8072763   FAX 055 8072236   OPEN Sales, visits and tastings by appointment only   CREDIT CARDS None   DIRECT SALE Yes   ENGLISH SPOKEN Yes   DIRECTIONS From Poggibonsi go toward Barberino. After the roundabout, turn to the right toward Monsanto and Olena.

Paolo De Marchi's father bought Isole e Olena in the 1950s, and since Paolo took it over in 1976, he has become one of the most respected winemakers in Chianti, if not in Italy. The estate, with 42 hectares (104 acres) of vineyards, is located at the western edge of central Chianti Classico.

De Marchi is a young, energetic man with a refreshingly open mind. He told me that he loves having foreign students working for him, as they bring "a little of the outside world" to him. This contact with other cultures has certainly pushed him to be more adventurous with his own: De Marchi was one of Tuscany's first serious experimenters with the "foreign" grape varieties Syrah, Cabernet Sauvignon, and Chardonnay—making the decision to vinify and bottle them each separately. If the Cabernet has achieved great results, he now seems personally less convinced about the Syrah. "I now believe that Cabernet will become part of Tuscany's tradition, because it is showing excellent results here," he said.

Sangiovese is more traditionally Tuscan. From it De Marchi makes his great Cepparello, maturing the wine for fourteen months in French *barriques*, and the Chianti Classico DOCG—another great wine of primarily Sangiovese grapes. De Marchi also makes an opulent Vin Santo, of 75 percent Malvasia and 25 percent Trebbiano grapes.

Paolo De Marchi is a keen researcher into the best clones and growing conditions for his vines, as the perennial earthworks around the estate can testify. His passion for his work is apparent. I interviewed him in autumn as the *vendemmia* was due to start, with thunder and lightning crashing down around us. Each time the rain fell harder or seemed to be hail, I could feel his disappointment at the prospect of the grapes being ruined. "It only takes a few hours like this to undo a year's work," he admitted.

PÀCINA

PÀCINA
WINE

53019   Castelnuovo Berardenga   Siena
TELEPHONE/FAX 0577 359229   OPEN Sales, visits and tastings by appointment only   CREDIT CARDS None   DIRECT SALE Yes
ENGLISH SPOKEN Yes   DIRECTIONS From Castelnuovo Berardenga, go toward Pianella, then follow signs for Villa Pàcina.

Located just outside the Chianti Classico border, the stately ex-convent at Pàcina has produced wines for centuries. Since 1987, however, the winemaking has taken a more professional turn. Giovanna Tiezzi, her mother, Lucia, and their young winemaker, Giovanna Morganti, have helped Pàcina be "reborn" as an organic farm. No sulphur dioxide is used in the vinification, and only copper and sulphur are used to treat the vines.

Pàcina's red Chianti Colli Senesi is *profumato* and well structured—it needs time to evolve. It is aged in double *barriques,* twice the volume of the more commonly found small oak casks. I asked Giovanna Morganti, who is the daughter of the late Enzo Morganti (see p 207), about wines made by women: "It is lovely working with other women. I don't know if this can be felt in the wine, but there has been a change in our way of working: there is a greater sensibility in relation to the earth, and we hope this will be reflected in the wines."

PANZANO

ANTICA MACELLERIA Via XX Luglio, 11   50020   Panzano in Chianti   Firenze
CECCHINI   TELEPHONE 055 852020   FAX 055 852700   OPEN 9:00-19:00
MEAT, SPECIALTY FOODS CLOSED Wednesday, Sunday afternoon   CREDIT CARDS None
                     ENGLISH SPOKEN A little   DIRECTIONS In the town center, off
                     Piazza Bucciarelli

The first thing that strikes you in this tiny butcher's shop is the beauty of everything in it: a deep basket of rosemary, an arrangement of homegrown vegetables,
the pâtés with their jewel-like aspics, hanging garlands of peppers, hanging peppered hams . . . all have been put together with the eyes and the hands of an
artist. There is wonderful music, a wicker sofa under a shelf of cookbooks, plus
the *profumi* of herbs, spices and the salt-cured pork that is so particularly
Italian. Even the meat here is wholesomely displayed.

"What interests me," explained Dario Cecchini, as he added
spices to a batch of hand-kneaded *salsicce*, "is the authentic *cucina Toscana*. I
have spent years compiling a menu of these specialties. When you come to my
shop you can taste them." The counter is full of appetizing foods: herb-scented
lardo for spreading on hot bread, goose spiced with coriander, galantine of
duck with Marsala, pigeons stuffed with juniper, a Renaissance pâté with
prunes. There are excellent Chianina steaks and other meats.

Dario, a large, vital young man with a ready smile and large,
nimble hands, is as decisive in his ideas as he is in his work. "There are two types
of people," he asserted as he guided the sausage meat into its casings. "Those
who look for memories of their childhood in their food, and those who look for
power—eating oysters and foie gras. The only thing that upsets me," he admitted, tying off the plump sausages neatly, "are the people who come in and take
pictures here without even saying hello or tasting anything." By the time you
visit, Dario and his gentle companion Laura may have completed their extension: the little shop will be enlarged to add a tasting room "for friends."

IL VESCOVINO Via Ciampolo da Panzano, 9   50020   Panzano   Firenze
RESTAURANT   TELEPHONE/FAX 055 852464   OPEN Lunch and dinner; in February
                 lunch is by appointment only   CLOSED Tuesday; January
                 CREDIT CARDS Visa, MC, Amex   ENGLISH SPOKEN Yes
                 FEATURES Summer terrace   RESERVATIONS Recommended in summer
                 PRICE $$$ OTHER Baldi also runs a cooking school
                 DIRECTIONS From Panzano's center, go toward Panzano Alto. The
                 restaurant is at the edge of town, signposted.

Il Vescovino's summer terrace overlooks Chianti's beautiful winemaking valley,
the Conca d'Oro. "When we opened in 1987 we felt like pioneers," recounted
Mimmo Baldi, the owner and chef. "The area was still depressed and the

mayor encouraged us to open a restaurant, not a trattoria." Fresh ingredients
were hard to get: Panzano is a drive from everywhere. Baldi comes from the
Amalfi coast and wanted to cook fish, not just Tuscan "land" dishes. "We kept
to simple but good food," he explained. "Homemade pastas, fresh breads, and
terrines—a novelty here then." The menu changes with the seasons. There is
usually a choice of *primi*, and fish and meat courses, both Tuscan and original
in style. Baldi cooks with spontaneity and flair.

    In early February the restaurant was not fully open, but I tasted
tagliolini noodles with porcini mushrooms in a shallow short crust "basket."
The pasta was very fine, and the earthy mushrooms were matched with sharp,
aromatic *nepitella*—a wild herb. Pancetta bacon chunks were roasted until crisp
and served with chard stalks (*coste*), stewed with onions and spicy tomatoes.
Dessert was a deep chocolate soufflé with chocolate sauce. Not surprisingly,
Baldi's wine list features many local stars—wines are also available by the bottle
from his wine bar (see p 202).

TENUTA FONTODI   Via San Leolino, 87   50020   Panzano in Chianti   Firenze
WINE   TELEPHONE 055 852005   FAX 055 852537   OPEN 9:00-12:00, 14:00-
18:00; tastings possible; group tastings and *cantina* visits by appointment
only   CLOSED Saturday, Sunday   CREDIT CARDS Visa, MC
DIRECT SALE Yes   ENGLISH SPOKEN Yes   OTHER Four apartments
availble for holiday rental   DIRECTIONS From Panzano go toward Radda.
Fontodi is on the left after 2 kms.

The natural amphitheater surrounding Panzano is the Conca d'Oro—the
golden bowl. On its slope is Tenuta Fontodi, the vineyards and olive groves
of Domiziano and Dino Manetti. Since 1968, the Manettis have gained recognition for their fine wines and progressive management. Fontodi is a winery
worth visiting. The wines are great, the handsome buildings and *cantine* well
appointed, and the staff welcoming. A room is set apart for tasting.

    The winemaking is done by the young Giovanni Manetti and
enologist Franco Bernabei. Two wines have elicited international accolades.
Flaccianello della Pieve was one of the leaders of the new Tuscan "table wines";
of pure Sangiovese, it is matured in small French casks, or *barriques*. Vigna del
Sorbo is an elegant Chianti Classico *cru* of Sangiovese and Cabernet Sauvignon
grown in the homonymous vineyard; it, too, is matured in *barriques*. In good
years these wines rank among Tuscany's very best.

    Fontodi produces a smooth Chianti Classico and a fine Riserva,
as well as an interesting white wine, Meriggio, a blend of Pinot, Traminer, and
Sauvignon grapes matured in oak casks. The Tenuta bottles its own extra-virgin
olive oil.

LA MASSA
WINE

Via Case Sparse, 9   50020   Panzano in Chianti   Firenze
TELEPHONE/FAX 055 852701   OPEN Sales, visits and tastings by
appointment only   CREDIT CARDS None   DIRECT SALE Yes
ENGLISH SPOKEN Yes   OTHER Two apartments available for holiday
rentals   DIRECTIONS From Panzano go toward Mercatale; after 500
hundred meters, turn left; then take the right fork in the road. La Massa
is on the right down the unpaved road.

Giampaolo Motta is young, smart, funny, Neapolitan, and irrepressibly enthusiastic. He makes some of Chianti's best wine. The madcap story of how his
dream to own a winery became a reality would fill a book, but here it is in a
nutshell:

While working in his family's leather factory in Naples he had
a crisis of conscience, came to Tuscany, and encountered John Dunkley, "who
was inspirational." Then came a spell at a giant Chianti winery, "where I
learned almost nothing," paired with an old *contadino* who ate bread and
onions for lunch and spoke in monosyllables. The apprenticeship continued
at Rampolla: "Luca has a fine palate and passion for wine, but after four years
in Tuscany I still had not risked my capital."

A vast holding in the Conca d'Oro went on sale following
a bankruptcy, with 40 hectares of vineyards, "and I was looking for 4 or 5!"
After much ado, half was sold off, leaving Giampaolo Motta with 22 hectares
(54 acres) of some of the finest vineyards in Chianti.

"Our first *vendemmia* was in 1992—the worst harvest for fifty
years." With winemaker Carlo Ferrini, he decided to salvage only the best
grapes from the sodden vineyards. "We made a tiny amount of very good
wine." Motta called it Giorgio, for his grandfather who secretly helped him,
Primo, for his first wine. It is a Chianti Classico, as is his other wine, La Massa.
Giorgio Primo contains only first-choice Sangiovese grapes. "We wait till very
late to harvest when the fruit is ripe, sweet, and concentrated, so the wines are
really *morbido*, mellow. The French believe you should bottle a mellow wine,
not an undrinkably tannic one: the bottle is only a glass container—it can't
completely alter a wine's characteristics."

Motta's wines are particularly mellow, with concentrated fruit
and balanced wood. "*Barriques* are fine, but often overused. The wood should
be like a crutch under the coat—there, but out of sight." Giorgio Primo spends
eighteen months in *barriques*, old and new. La Massa, of second-choice
Sangiovese grapes, spends one year in wood and is also fruity and mellow. Both
have taken the wine world by storm. "To make wine has always been my
dream. Now that I'm doing it, I'm very happy—*felicissimo!*"

CASTELLO DEI RAMPOLLA
WINE

Santa Lucia in Faulle   50020   Panzano in Chianti   Firenze
TELEPHONE 055 852001   FAX 055 852533   OPEN 8:00-12:00, 13:00-17:00; visits, sales, and tastings by appointment only
CLOSED Saturday, Sunday   CREDIT CARDS None   DIRECT SALE Yes
ENGLISH SPOKEN Yes   DIRECTIONS From Panzano go toward
Mercatale. After 500 meters, turn left before the white church. Follow the yellow signs to Rampolla, which is at the end of the dirt road.

The Rampolla estate, with its lovely grounds and views of the Conca d'Oro valley, is one of Chianti's most striking. The castle has belonged to the Rampolla family since 1739. Until recently it was run by Matteo di Napoli Rampolla, who had taken over after his father Alceo's death, but another brother, Luca, has since taken charge. If all this change initially led to speculation about the future of Rampolla's wines, recent vintages have confirmed that the estate is definitely on an upward turn again. In part this is thanks to the renowned enologist Giacomo Tachis.

When I talked with Luca, who is a serious, gentle young man, he explained that he hoped to move the farm toward a more *biodinamico* (organic) approach, by using organic manures and as little chemical treatment of the vines as possible.

In addition to their Chianti Classico in both the "normal" and Riserva versions, the Rampollas produce one of the greatest super-Tuscans, Sammarco. Of Cabernet Sauvignon grapes with a small percentage of Sangiovese added, this full-bodied "table" wine is matured in small oak casks (*barriques*) and built to last.

VILLA CAFAGGIO
WINE

Via San Martino, 5   50020   Panzano in Chianti   Firenze
TELEPHONE 055 8549094   FAX 055 8549096   OPEN Visits and tastings by appointment only   DIRECT SALE No   STOCKIST Wines are available from the *enoteche* at Panzano   ENGLISH SPOKEN Yes
DIRECTIONS From Panzano, go toward Mercatale. After 3 kms, turn left and follow signs to the winery.

Stefano Farkas was behind the wheel of a tractor, ploughing a soon-to-be-planted vineyard. Thousands of *barbatelle,* young grape vines, had arrived from France (where they had been grafted), and were waiting under a tarpaulin in the barn. "In the next ten years there will be a giant improvement in Chianti's wines," declared Farkas, Villa Cafaggio's dynamic director and the moving force behind its award-winning wines. "Twenty years ago, when many of Chianti's vineyards were planted, no one understood about clones, or American rootstocks. Everything was very haphazard. Now those who are keeping up with the times—and the research—will be in a postion to make truly great wines here."

In 1967 Farkas's father bought the estate at the western end of the Conca d'Oro valley, one of Chianti's most perfect natural sites for vine-growing.

Today Farkas and Girelli, a wine producer from Trento, are partners. Big investments have been made, both in the planting of Sangiovese, Merlot, and Cabernet and in the modern cellar, with its temperature-controlled presses and neat rows of *barriques.* A room used to store the bottled wines was cool. "The *invecchiamento,* or aging, in bottles is just as important as that in wood," he explained. "Too high a temperature in here and the wines would age too quickly."

The estate is known for its reds: Chianti Classico Riserva and Solatio Basilica, both of pure Sangiovese; Cortaccio, of 90 percent Cabernet with 10 percent Merlot; and San Martino, of Sangiovese to which a little Merlot may be added. They are noted for their concentration of flavor, balance, and ability to age. "In making red wines," he concluded, "the most important thing is to start with perfect, ripe, and healthy grapes. If you don't, there's nothing you can do."

ENOTECA BALDI　　Piazza Bucciarelli, 25　50020　Panzano　Firenze
WINE BAR,　　　　 TELEPHONE 055 852843　OPEN 10:00-22:00　CLOSED Holidays
SPECIALTY FOODS　 in winter　CREDIT CARDS Visa, MC　DIRECT SALE Yes
　　　　　　　　　 ENGLISH SPOKEN Yes　DIRECTIONS In Panzano's central piazza

Mimmo Baldi's latest venture is this wine bar (see p 198-9). Tuscan wines are available to drink at the *enoteca* or to take out. Homemade snacks (prepared at the restaurant) are served at all hours. Specialty foods include artisan pastas, biscuits, jams, preserved vegetables, olive oils, and more.

POGGIBONSI

LA GALLERIA　　Galleria Cavalieri Vittorio Veneto, 20　53036　Poggibonsi　Siena
RESTAURANT　　 TELEPHONE 0577 982356　OPEN Lunch and dinner　CLOSED Tuesday;
　　　　　　　　 August　CREDIT CARDS Visa, MC, Amex　ENGLISH SPOKEN Yes
　　　　　　　　 RESERVATIONS Recommended　PRICE $$$　DIRECTIONS The restaurant is in an arcade between Via del Commercio and Piazza Indipendenza, in the modern area of the town to the north of the historic center.

This restaurant occupies the base of Poggibonsi's only "skyscraper," a rather unprepossessing fourteen-story 1970s construction. But don't be put off by the bland exterior. Owner-chef Michele Targi and his wife, Letizia Cappelli, opened La Galleria in 1991. Targi, a friendly, soft-spoken man, trained in some of Firenze's best-known restaurants. He inherited his passion for wine from his father, a wine and oil salesman. The interesting wine list features Tuscany, but it includes other regions. Prices are fair.

The food is refined and creative, yet recognisably Tuscan. A choice of tasting menus—including one of goat's cheeses from Ville di Corsano (p 281) served with sweet *vino muffato*—complements the seasonal à la carte selection. In early summer, antipasti included: brine-cured pork loin; imported smoked goose breast; fresh-tasting tomato *bruschetta,* and a cold salad of tripe, raw onion, potatoes, string beans, and basil that afforded a stimulating mixture of tastes and textures.

Of the *primi, taglierini alla Galleria* was fine noodles tossed with a crunchy pesto of walnuts, pine nuts, basil, and tomatoes. *Pennette* had a tangy sauce of goat's cheese and shredded arugula. *Fusilli con pomodori acerbi* was equally good, with a tart yellow-green sauce of unripe tomatoes and herbs. Fish is rare in Chianti, but Targi's was fresh and well cooked. Desserts are home-made and beautifully presented. The tiramisù is deliciously light; the unusual Medici pudding, a chilled baked custard, is studded with rice and raisins.

RADDA IN CHIANTI

**RISTORANTE
LE VIGNE
RESTAURANT**

Podere Le Vigne   53017   Radda in Chianti   Siena
TELEPHONE 0577 738640   OPEN Lunch and dinner
CLOSED Tuesday in winter; winter holidays variable
CREDIT CARDS Visa, MC, Amex   ENGLISH SPOKEN A little
FEATURES Summer garden dining   RESERVATIONS Recommended
in summer   PRICE $$ DIRECTIONS From Radda's center, go toward
Gaiole. Le Vigne is signposted on the right just beyond Radda.

This restaurant is surrounded by vineyards. Its summer terrace is tree-shaded and breezy. In cooler weather there is a large indoor dining room. Le Vigne is a good place for families: in summer children are free to play in the garden. The restaurant caters to foreign tourists and the menu is multilingual, but the young staff is spread a bit thin at peak hours.

The menu is not large, but offers Tuscan favorites. *Crostini* are topped with creamed field mushrooms; mixed *salumi* is the popular trio: *salame, finocchiona,* and prosciutto. *Primi* include *pici all'aglione,* local thick spaghetti with a garlicky tomato and leek sauce and decent pasta *al pesto.* *Secondi* are typically Tuscan: rabbit with olives, duck with rosemary, lemon-roasted chicken, and stewed wild boar, plus imaginative vegetable sides. Desserts are fairly good. The wine list features Chianti-produced wines.

CERAMICHE RAMPINI
TABLE CRAFTS: POTTERY

Casa Beretone di Vistarenni   53017   Radda in Chianti   Siena
TELEPHONE 0577 738043   FAX 0577 738776   OPEN 9.00-18.00
CLOSED Sunday   MAIL ORDER Ceramics can be shipped overseas.
CREDIT CARDS Visa, MC, Amex   ENGLISH SPOKEN Yes
DIRECTIONS From Radda go toward Gaiole. After 2 kms take the right-hand fork, toward Gaiole. Rampini's studio is signposted on the left as you go down the hill, after 1 km.

Giuseppe Rampini is a master craftsman continuing a Renaissance ceramic tradition. The powerful Medici families commissioned dinner services for ceremonial events destined to be used only once, and they had different plates designed for each season. "The Medicea plates often had simple decorations in

blue on a white ground, " explained Rampini. "This blue glaze [*blé*] was
derived from cobalt. It came from the Far East and was as costly as gold."

Working with his grown-up children, Rampini offers some of
these designs in simplified form, plus a range of elaborately decorated platters,
bowls, and pitchers, some of which recall Arcimboldi's sixteenth-century fruit
and flower compositions. All use lead-free glazes. The clay stock is found along
the Arno River.

Rampini's showroom is reached by going up the external stair-
case of the studio; it is filled with multicolored ceramics. Pieces can be bought
directly or custom-ordered. There are usually some seconds at reduced prices.

PODERE CAPACCIA   Capaccia   53017   Radda in Chianti   Siena
WINE, OLIVE OIL   TELEPHONE/FAX 0577 738385, 0574 582426   OPEN Monday-Saturday
                          9:00-12:00, 14:00-17:00; Sunday 9:00-13:00, 14:00-19:00; visits and tastings
                          by appointment only   CREDIT CARDS Visa, MC   DIRECT SALE Yes
                          ENGLISH SPOKEN Yes   DIRECTIONS From Radda, go northeast toward
                          Castello d'Albola; turn left towards Capaccia 1 km after the turning
                          for Montevertine.

Giampaolo Pacini is the Tuscan president of the Movimento del Turismo del
Vino, an association that organizes winery open days and promotes wine
tourism. His small estate is perched on a steep little hill near Radda. The road
up to the cluster of medieval buildings is not the greatest, but once there, it
feels like stepping back centuries in time. "When we bought Capaccia there
was not a roof left on," explained the hospitable Pacini. "The village was abandoned for at least seventy years. Bit by bit we are reconstructing it. As for the
vines, they had grown wild and climbed up over the olive trees!"

Working with the experienced winemaker Vittorio Fiore, Pacini
has planted mainly Sangiovese in his 3 hectares (8 acres) of vineyards. The *cantina* is squeezed into several little worker's cottages, but it includes ultramodern
equipment. A soft press for white grapes is used for Pacini's reds. Another
building serves as a tasting and sales room. Wines, fine olive oil, and homemade products are on sale. Pacini is a food historian and enthusiastic cook; he
and his wife run Tuscan food seminars.

Capaccia concentrates on two red wines: a classic Chianti
Classico, of Sangiovese with a little red Canaiolo (with its Riserva in great
years), and Querciabella, a wonderfully rich, warm, fruity super-Tuscan of pure
Sangiovese matured in small French casks for about fourteen months.

I asked Giampaolo Pacini how he had become interested in
winemaking.

"My father was a wine merchant," he recalled, "and one of my
earliest memories is of the earthy, grapey wine smell in my father's car—in

those days a lot of wine was sold *sfuso*, unbottled, so it must have spilled out. As a child I loved that smell, and I guess I still do."

FATTORIA DI
MONTE VERTINE
WINE

Monte Vertine   53017   Radda in Chianti   Siena
TELEPHONE 0577 738009   FAX 0577 738265   OPEN Visits by appointment only   CLOSED Saturday, Sunday   CREDIT CARDS None
DIRECT SALE Yes, subject to availability   ENGLISH SPOKEN Yes
FEATURES Museum of Rural Chianti   DIRECTIONS From Radda go northeast toward Albola. Montevertine is signposted from that road, on the left.

In his amusing book *Vino e Cucina,* a collection of "erogastronomic digressions," Sergio Manetti regrets the passing of the wine-drinking era of his youth. He recalls the sign posted by a bartender in Poggibonsi: If I can't sell it, I drink it. "He was right," comments Manetti. "I have admired him ever since, and I have made it my motto."

Coming from anyone else, this might seem a surprising philosophy. But Sergio Manetti is not just anyone, especially not in Chianti. For it was he, back in 1971, who thought to age his wine of pure Sangioveto (the indigenous Chianti grape) in *barriques*. He called it Le Pergole Torte ("the crooked posts" in Tuscan dialect), gave it a bold, painterly label, and launched a new era in Chianti. Le Pergole Torte revealed the potential of Tuscany's native grape, putting it alongside the so-called international varietals, Cabernet and Merlot. It is an elegant wine of concentrated fruit and flavor made to age gracefully.

Working with his trusted friend, the winemaker Giulio Gambelli, and his son-in-law Klaus Reimitz, Manetti also produces the single-vineyard wine, Il Sodaccio (Sangioveto), Monte Vertine (Sangioveto and Canaiolo), and its Riserva. "M" is a white wine aged for four years in small oak casks; Bianco di Monte Vertine is a more traditional white of Trebbiano and Malvasia; and Il Maggio is the estate's recent dessert wine, of Trebbiano and Malvasia grapes dried on the vine before being aged in small oak casks. Manetti is particularly partial to his Aqua Vitae di Pergole Torte, made for him by Nannoni (see p 218). The estate has 7 hectares (18 acres) of vineyards. Its costly wines are always in high demand, but they are not made in enormous quantities.

Monte Vertine is a place of culture: you see it in the house and sculpture garden, in the sea of vines supported by crooked wooden posts, and in the little museum of objects of everyday country life.

Also

Podere Terreno, on the road that leads to Volpaia (0577 738312), is an unusual *agriturismo*—a country house that accepts paying guests. Each night the guests dine at a long communal table presided over by the farm's owners,

Roberto Melosi and Sylvie Haniez, who are among Chianti's most hospitable hosts. The food is abundant and good, the wine flows freely, and the conversation is always multicultural.

SAN DONATO IN POGGIO

CASA EMMA
WINE

Cortine   San Donato in Poggio   50021   Barberino Val d'Elsa   Firenze
TELEPHONE 055 8072859, 8072239   FAX 0571 667707
OPEN Monday-Saturday 9:00-19:00; Sunday 9:00-12:00; tastings from April to October   CREDIT CARDS Visa, MC   DIRECT SALE Yes
ENGLISH SPOKEN Yes   DIRECTIONS From San Donato, go toward Castellina; Casa Emma is on the left after about 1 km.

Casa Emma shows what can happen when an ambitious young winery is paired with the experience of a good winemaker. In the space of a few years, Niccolò D'Afflitto, the winemaker, has transformed Casa Emma from a hard-working estate selling most of its wine unbottled, to a winery that in 1997 won a coveted "*tre bicchieri*" award—the top rating given by the Gambero Rosso-Arcigola Italian wine guide. Fiorella Lepri and family have made considerable investments in the winery, whose neat, well-exposed vineyards surround the house. "When we came in 1973 there was nothing up here but rocks and grass," she recalled. "Now we have 13 hectares (32 acres) of specialized vineyards and an efficient modern *cantina*." In addition to two types of Sangiovese, the winery has now added some Merlot. The position is high, at over 400 meters (1,300 feet), and well ventilated—which makes for concentrated wines rich in perfumes. Casa Emma makes Chianti Classico, its Riserva (the 1993 was the award-winner), and Sololo, of pure Merlot matured in *barriques*.

How does it feel to gain such recognition? "We knew we had a great product," she admitted. "But we never expected to win—the little guy rarely does. Now we will try to maintain our high standards and, who knows, we might win it again someday."

SAN FELICE

SAN FELICE AGRICOLA
WINE

San Gusmè   53010   Castelnuovo Berardenga   Siena
TELEPHONE Winery 0577 359087/8; restaurant 359260
FAX 0577 359223   OPEN Sales 9:00-12:00, 14:00-18:00; April to October wine sales from *borgo* shop 8:30-20:00; *cantina* visits and tastings by appointment only   CLOSED Saturday, Sunday
CREDIT CARDS Visa, MC   DIRECT SALE Yes   ENGLISH SPOKEN Yes
FEATURES San Felice has a relais hotel and a restaurant.
DIRECTIONS   San Felice can be reached from SS 484 (Gaiole–Castelnuovo Berardenga) or from the south. Follow signs.

San Felice is a complex of 750 hectares (1,800 acres) surrounding a lovely medieval *borgo* now owned by an insurance company. It includes one of

Chianti's most important wineries, with 220 hectares (543 acres) of vineyards. Of these, 18 (45) are dedicated to viticultural research. "San Felice has this research facility thanks to Enzo Morganti, who came here in 1968," explained Leonardo Bellaccini, the estate's young winemaker. "He was general manager until his death in 1994. He was a keen scientist and forward thinker when it came to vineyards and their problems."

Early on, Morganti created Vigorello, his first "alternative" red of 70 percent Sangiovese and 30 percent Cabernet Sauvignon, and a precursor to today's super-Tuscans. He began selecting clones of Sangiovese and other varietals that are now planted on the estate.

Morganti's fascinating experimental vineyards are called Vitiarium. He collected hundreds of Tuscany's "minor" varietals with wonderful names like Colorino, Lacrima, and Pugnitello. "The original notion was just to conserve these plants for historical reasons," continued Bellaccini, "but we realized that some had very personal qualities when made into wine."

San Felice makes three important Chianti Classicos, all Sangiovese based: the "normal," a popular wine to drink young (within two to three years); Il Grigio, a Riserva that Bellaccini called a "strategic" wine offering good value for money; and Poggio Rosso, a Riserva *cru* from vineyards that were once Morganti's, of 90 percent Sangiovese with 10 percent Colorino. It is an elegant, perfumed wine of balance and structure. The estate's list includes Ancherona (a *barrique*-fermented Chardonnay), and extra-virgin olive oil from its own *frantoio*.

SAN REGOLO

TRATTORIA	San Regolo, 33 53013 Gaiole in Chianti Siena
SAN REGOLO	TELEPHONE/FAX 0577 747136 OPEN Lunch; dinner Saturday, Sunday
RESTAURANT	and holidays CLOSED Monday CREDIT CARDS None
	ENGLISH SPOKEN A little RESERVATIONS Recommended
	PRICE $$ DIRECTIONS In the village center

San Regolo is a tiny village near Brolio Castle. The trattoria, run by the Fabbri family, has a luminous dining room overlooking the imposing castle and its vineyards. The cuisine is strictly Tuscan, beginning with a selection of assorted *crostini* or *salumi*. The seasonal homemade vegetable soups are thick and satisfying. Handmade egg noodles, tagliatelle, are served with a choice of hearty sauces: the mushroom has a deep woodsy flavor from locally-found porcini. Ricotta-and-spinach-filled *ravioli* with sage and butter are delicate despite the fairly thick pasta. At San Regolo the best main courses are the simplest: steaks and chops grilled over aromatic wood embers, *alla brace*. Roasted meats are sliced thin and served with savory gravy. A warning to the salt-conscious: the

Tuscans like their food highly salted, but the kitchen will reduce it if asked when ordering.

Desserts are homemade. The wine list reads like a local road map—Cacchiano, Brolio, Ama, San Felice, Fèlsina. The Fabbri women do the cooking, leaving the serving to Carlino and his nice son, Fabrizio. This is the kind of relaxed, friendly restaurant that it is always a pleasure to go back to.

VILLA A SESTA

LA BOTTEGA
DEL TRENTA
RESTAURANT

Via Santa Caterina, 2   Villa a Sesta   53019
Castelnuovo Berardenga   Siena
TELEPHONE 0577 359226   OPEN Lunch and dinner Saturday, Sunday, dinner only Thursday, Friday, Monday   CLOSED Tuesday, Wednesday; holidays in January and November   CREDIT CARDS None
ENGLISH SPOKEN Yes   FEATURES Outdoor dining courtyard
RESERVATIONS Necessary   PRICE $$$ DIRECTIONS The restaurant is in the village of Villa a Sesta.

This restaurant is situated in a flowery courtyard. There is no sign, and the only menu, or indication of pricing, is outside the front door. Diners are expected to eat a complete four-course meal; those not in the mood for so much food will be better received elsewhere. The long and complicated menu is recited aloud. The restaurant's chef, Mme. Stoquelet, is French, though she has lived in Italy for years. Her cooking reflects this binationalism.

The food of this fusion cuisine can be very good: antipasti feature the locally appreciated stuffed goose neck. *Primi* include celery-filled ravioli with piquant Gorgonzola sauce and subtle spinach and ricotta *malfati,* which are like the filling from ravioli without the pasta casing, set off here by shavings of pungent truffle. In the main courses the French influence is particularly apparent. Succulent duck baked slowly with wild fennel has the uncomplicated refinement of French country cooking. The boned saddle of lamb is wrapped in a crust with spinach and is of the cut and type of lamb that is rarely seen in Italy. Our "vegetarian" plate was a disappointment, as the smoky-flavored eggplant rolls contained ham.

Desserts are expertly handled with the sophistication of French *patisserie.* A delicate almond *cialde* is accompanied by a velvety white chocolate mousse, while the lemon mousse tart is cool and frothy, served with a sharp fresh strawberry sauce. Wines are well chosen. The service left much to be desired.

VOLPAIA'S ARTISAN VINEGARS

Volpaia is the only winery in Tuscany presently licensed to make vinegar. By law, winemaking facilities must be located some distance from those making vinegar. At Volpaia the traditional system is used.

"To make good vinegar, you must start with good wine," explained Carlo Mascheroni, the estate's owner, "and transform it slowly. That way its components, its perfumes, will remain in the vinegar."

Wine turns to vinegar with the help of oxygen—the vinegar-making bacteria need air to live. This good wine is impregnated with specially-grown cultures and then aerated by being pumped slowly and repeatedly through a tank containing *trucioli*—wood shavings, of oak and chestnut), and grape vine trimmings. This motion breaks up the wine and feeds the bacteria that thrive on enzymes in the woods. The pumped wine is kept at a steady temperature of 35°C/95°F. After about twenty days it will have become vinegar. A secondary fermentation may then be initiated, using a "mother" culture, to enhance the vinegar's secondary bouquet.

Volpaia's red and white wine vinegars are aged in *barriques* previously used for winemaking. The vinegar absorbs noble tannins from these oak barrels that "infuse the bouquet with extraordinary elegance." They are then given a final treatment. Five groups of *aromi*, natural flavors, are used to perfume the vinegars: groups of herbs, flowers, and spices are placed in muslin bags and left to macerate in the vinegars for about two months. The final vinegars are numbered from one to five: 1 Herbs; 2 Spices; 3 Kitchen garden; 4 Flowers; 5 Fresh. These subtle yet characterful vinegars are available at Volpaia and make wonderful additions to any creative cook's palette.

VOLPAIA

CASTELLO DI VOLPAIA
WINE, OLIVE OIL, VINEGAR

Piazza Cisterna, 1   Volpaia   53017   Radda in Chianti   Siena
TELEPHONE 0577 738066   FAX 0577 738619   OPEN Shop: 9:00-20:00; cellar visits and tastings by prior written request only
CLOSED Never   CREDIT CARDS Visa, MC, Amex   DIRECT SALE Yes
ENGLISH SPOKEN Yes   DIRECTIONS From Radda go toward Greve;
Volpaia is signposted to the right after about 4 kms.

"Wine is a food," asserted Giovannella Stianti Mascheroni. "In Tuscany it was a food you lived on, a pleasurable but vital part of daily life. What seems to be missing now is the story behind it. My wine reflects my tastes, my philosophy—that is why it takes a lifetime to make."

Everything at Volpaia—wine, oil, vinegar, even label design—was conceived with the same spirit by Giovannella and her husband. The extra-virgin olive oil, for example, is made of hand-picked, homegrown olives milled in their own *frantoio*. It uses modern Sinolea machinery that draws the oil free from the mass, ensuring that only the "*fior, fiore*," or choicest part is extracted. And it is really excellent.

"We have researched everything," continued the tall, elegant Giovannella, "and selected the best, then we have brought it to Volpaia." This has been no mean feat. For in the medieval village that is Volpaia, some rather "out of the way things" have happened. Not that you would notice from the outside, for the buildings' original exteriors have been rigorously maintained. The change is inside: open any of the small wooden doors into the village's houses and you will be confronted with an image that reminded me of the very large Alice crammed into the very small White Rabbit's house. Behind one, a stone cottage has been gutted and filled with a giant stainless steel fermentation tank, complete with overhead walkways. Behind another, a tiny church is stuffed with vast wooden barrels; another with stacks of new French *barriques*. So it goes on, each door revealing a part of the complex whole. "We had to lower the big tanks in through the roofs with a crane," laughed Giovannella as she saw my amazement. "And there are miles of underground tubing, so the wines are never transported outside."

For the winemaking, the couple are assisted by the experienced enologist, Maurizio Castelli. Their fine range includes Chianti Classico; its Riserva; Coltassala, of Sangioveto and Mammolo grapes, and Balifico, of Sangioveto and Cabernet, both of which are aged in *barriques;* the white Torniello, of Sauvignon grapes fermented in *barriques;* and Vin Santo.

CHAPTER 9

Grosseto and the Maremma

G rosseto is the capital of a large province divided between coastal
plains and the Metalliferous Mountains. Much of what is now the
Maremma, a fertile terrain favored by agriculture, was once swamp
land infested with malarial mosquitoes. Projects to drain and reclaim (*bonifi-
care*) this land were carried out by the Etruscans and the Romans, but not until
this century was the mission successfully completed.

      The coast and hills held Etruscan cities: Vetulonia, Roselle, and
Saturnia (still a renowned spa) with Tarquinia, Vulci, and Tuscania just over
Tuscany's southern border in Lazio. The tufa hills are rich in iron ore and other
metals, which the Etruscans extracted and worked. Many tomb sites still exist
in this beautiful countryside rich in ancient culture; the towns of Pitigliano,
Sorano, and Sovana are fascinating to visit.

      If the Maremma was once an untamed land of cowboys (*butteri*),
game, and natural hazards, today it offers some of the region's most glorious
countryside. In spring the gently rolling hills are full of wildflowers: small pink
gladioli, blue clouds of borage, scented wood cyclamen, rock roses and alium,
thyme and fennel. Sheep graze on aromatic grasses in hill pastures; their pecorino cheeses are sweet and fresh. Wild boar, roebuck, and smaller game live in
the woods and in the natural reserve, Parco dell'Uccellina. The local cooking is
rustic but flavorful, with peasant soups such as *l'acquacotta* and stews of game
and wild mushrooms in the hills, and spicy octopus and other appetizing
seafood on the coast. Massa Marittima, the jewel of the Maremma, is a
medieval town with a splendid Duomo; it makes the best *panforte*, Tuscany's
classic honey and spice confection.

Azienda Promozione Turistica
Via Monterosa, 206
58100 Grosseto
0564 454510, fax 0564 454606

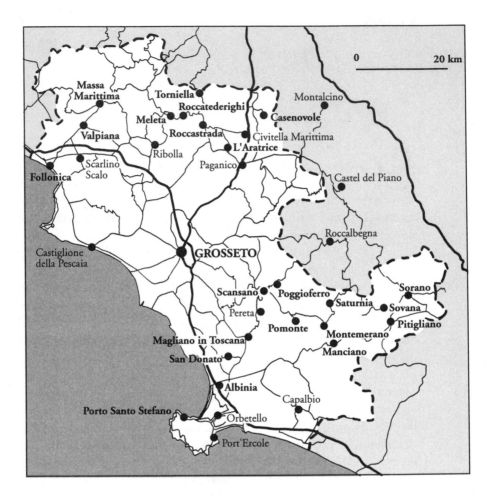

Town names in **bold** indicate towns that are included in this chapter.

ALBINIA DI ORBETELLO

LA PARRINA
CHEESE, WINE

Km 146 SS 1 Aurelia   La Parrina   58010   Albinia
TELEPHONE 0564 862636   FAX 0564 862636
OPEN Shop 8:00-13:00, 15:00-18:00 (till 20:00 in summer); farm and
cantina visits by appointment only   CLOSED National holidays
MAIL ORDER Yes   CREDIT CARDS Visa, MC, Amex
ENGLISH SPOKEN Yes   OTHER La Parrina has three shops in Rome
DIRECTIONS From Orbetello, turn right off SS Aurelia at km 146 beside
Cacciatore restaurant. After about 2 kms, turn right onto the eucalyptus-
lined dirt road leading to the farm.

La Parrina is a lovely estate. Set in the low hills north of Orbetello, the picturesque farm buildings are framed by orchards and rose-covered walls. A well-
run farm shop sells its cheeses, wine, produce, extra-virgin olive oil, and honey.
La Parrina specialises in dairy products; its cheeses are made in a converted
schoolhouse. Every day, the small dairy transforms the milk obtained from
sixty goats and six hundred sheep.

Tuscan goat's cheeses, *caprini*, are subtle in flavor; they are salted
less than their French counterparts. The *caprino nella cenere* is rolled in vegetable ash; it is very creamy—almost like fresh ricotta in its delicate sweetness.
The small round *caprino stagionato* is matured; it has a flakier consistency with
the same creaminess but no sharpness of flavor. Small *caprini*, flavored with
truffles, peppercorns or ash, also come preserved in olive oil in attractive glass
jars. They keep well and make great presents. La Parrina's range of sheep's
cheeses include the soft white spreadable *stracchinato*, the pliable, slightly sweet
cacciotte, and the piquant molded and matured *guttus*, their homage to French
Roquefort. There are thick tangy yogurts sold plain or flavored with fresh fruit.
Shoppers are welcome to sample the cheeses.

The farm is run as ecologically as possible without conforming
to the strictest organic standards; whenever possible, environmentally friendly
solutions are sought.

La Parrina started making wine in 1950, and in 1971 obtained DOC status for its red and white wines. The Riserva is a robust wine of 70 percent
Sangiovese and 15 percent each of Cabernet Sauvignon and Pinot Nero; it is
aged for three years, with eight months in *barriques*. The white is produced
from Trebbiano Toscano, Malvasia, and Ansonica, a varietal that originated in
Sicily. These drinkable wines are a good value in their category.

CASENOVOLE

NUOVA CASENOVOLE   Casenovole   58030   Civitella Paganico
MEAT: ORGANIC BEEF   TELEPHONE 0564 908951   FAX 0564 908912   OPEN Shop: 9:00-13:00,
14:00-18:00; farm visits by appointment   CLOSED Sunday
MAIL ORDER Yes   CREDIT CARDS None   DIRECT SALE Yes, of dried
goods (no meat)   STOCKIST Meat available from Grosseto's Maremma
Market (p 218); Falorni in Greve (p 191)   ENGLISH SPOKEN Yes
DIRECTIONS From the Siena-Grosseto road (SS 223), exit at Casale di
Pari; follow signs to the farm.

Nuova Casenovole is a large biodynamic farm producing organic grains, olive
oil, and, unusually for Italy, organic beef. It is set in some of Tuscany's most
beautiful countryside.

I say unusually because organic meat hardly exists in Italy,
despite the work of some of its European partners. Indeed, the concept of what
constitutes a dignified life for an animal generally leaves a lot to be desired in
Italy. So Nuova Casenovole is a welcome, and important, exception. Ironically,
the farm began with purely commercial objectives. "We didn't make a committed, philosophical choice for this type of system," explained the farm's director,
Riccardo Micheli. "We researched possibilities to make this vast tract of land
profitable, and this solution worked best." Over time, however, the positive
results are converting the unbelievers.

Nuova Casenovole is run using Rudolf Steiner's biodynamic
model. The farm operates as a "closed cycle": crops are grown using only farm-
produced natural fertilizers (manure); in turn, the animals eat only these cereals
as supplements to their grazing pastures. As a biodynamic company, the farm is
under the strict auspices of Demeter, the German organization that controls all
procedures from planting to sales.

The most striking validation of this system is to be found with
the animals themselves. A walk through their barns at feeding time (I visited in
early spring when the cows were calving) shows how completely different their
lives are from their contemporaries'.

The cattle are grouped in "families": each bull living amid a
herd of twenty-five cows. Calves also stay within the group for as long as they
feed from their mothers. Each herd, with its bull, spends most of the year out
at pasture. So there is no stress. You sense this peacefulness immediately. The
animals rarely get sick, as they are contented and have no space restrictions.
This is a boon for both animals and breeders.

"Conventional breeders spend an average of 1.100 lire per day per animal
on veterinary expenses," Micheli said. "Whereas our cost is ridiculously low, at 23
lire per day, including the four dogs that guard the herds. The paradoxical thing
is that veterinary rules for Italian animals are much stricter than other European

countries'. Hormones are forbidden here [unlike in other countries]. Yet when it comes to the animals' living conditions, things are still primitive."

The cattle, of mainly the Limousin breed, are butchered at fourteen to sixteen months near Siena. The meat is not sold on the farm, so I couldn't taste any, but I was assured that the difference between it and conventional beef was "night and day"—it's not hard to believe.

The farm also produces extra-virgin olive oil from its own olives and mill, as well as five types of hard wheat for the making of pasta. These goods are sold on the farm.

FOLLONICA

PODERE S. LUIGI   I Poggetti   58022   Follonica
OLIVE OIL   TELEPHONE 0566 51350   OPEN Sales by appointment only
CREDIT CARDS None   DIRECT SALE Yes   ENGLISH SPOKEN No
DIRECTIONS From Follonica, go toward Massa Marittima. After about 1 km, pass the Metanauto station; at the next curve, take the dirt road between two white arrows in the road to the farm.

When it is well made, Maremman extra-virgin olive oil is sweet and full, qualities conferred to the olives by the mild climate and sea breezes. It is less bitter and less aggressive than the oils made on higher ground, but it still has a satisfying freshness to it. Antonio Perico's oil is some of the best I have found of this type. His 30 hectares (74 acres) of olive groves are located just inland from Follonica, off the country road that leads to Massa Marittima. His olives are hand-picked and pressed in a local modern *frantoio*.

Perico's oil is only available privately: such is the demand that he has no trouble selling it. The family villa is just a few minutes' drive from Follonica, and the charming farm manager will meet clients there by appointment. The oil is available in bottles and 5 kilo/8.8 lb cans.

DA SANTARINO   Piazza 24 Maggio, 21   58022   Follonica
RESTAURANT   TELEPHONE 0566 41665   OPEN Lunch and dinner
CLOSED Tuesday in winter; October   CREDIT CARDS None
ENGLISH SPOKEN A little   RESERVATIONS Recommended
PRICE $$ DIRECTIONS By the covered market in the town center

Santarino's fish trattoria is a local tradition at Follonica. Family-run for over thirty years, it is an unpretentious, informal place. The dining rooms, with their wooden booths and hunting lodge decor, are always bustling.

A prime attraction is the *polpo lesso* (boiled octopus). It comes one to a plate (hand-sized), as tender as chicken, drizzled with olive oil and a hint of hot *peperoncino*. Pasta specials depend on fish availability, but there are always *spaghetti con scampi* (Mediterranean shrimp from Sardinia) or *vongole* (clams), tossed simply with garlic, parsley, and olive oil. Main courses are uncomplicated: the day's catch is broiled, baked *in cartoccio,* or poached. *Orata* (gilt-head bream), *dentice* (sea bream), and *spigola* (sea bass) are popular, as are *astice* (lobster) and *aragosta* (clawless spiny lobster). The house wines are local.

GASTRONOMIA	Via Bicocchi, 85 58022 Follonica
MARRINI	TELEPHONE 0566 40093 OPEN 7:00-13:30, 16:00-20:30
SPECIALTY FOODS,	CLOSED Wednesday afternoon; Sunday in winter; November
PASTA	CREDIT CARDS Amex ENGLISH SPOKEN No OTHER Caters parties
	and weddings DIRECTIONS Via Bicocchi runs parallel to the sea, a few
	blocks inland.

Renzo Marrini's family started producing fresh egg pasta in 1937. Stuffed pasta is made daily, with seasonal fillings of artichokes, asparagus, and pumpkin, with fish in summer. The business has expanded into a complete *gastronomia,* offering both ready-cooked dishes and local specialty foods. A large counter features home-cooked dishes: pastas and regional soups like *aquacotta* and *cacciucco,* pasta sauces, main courses, and desserts. Tuscan *salumi* and cheeses are also available. Packages of dried mushrooms and herbs make attractive gifts to take home. The Marrinis also stock Italian wines from many regions.

Also

Follonica has a lively covered market that is open Monday to Saturday (summer 9:30-13:30, 17:00-20:00; winter 9:30-13:30). It sells everything from bread and cheese to fruit and meat. Many stalls carry local produce: tender salad greens, fava beans (*baccelli*) to eat raw with pecorino, and wild herbs brought from the country. The area is also famous for its spring *carciofini* (tiny artichokes) for preserving in olive oil. Look for Pescheria Pallino, the market's best fish stall.

Gelateria Caribia. Viale Italia, 212. 0566 60059.

Follonica's most popular *gelateria* is not its most central, but it's a nice walk along the beach road. The family-run *gelateria's* specialty is *gelato al forno,* a variation on baked Alaska. They also make refreshing *granite* of fresh fruit, ice cream cakes, and a range of unusual gelato flavors.

GROSSETO

HERBONATURA
HONEY

Via Tripoli, 41   58100   Grosseto
TELEPHONE 0564 417677   OPEN 9:00-13:00 ,16:00-20:00
CLOSED Saturday afternoon in summer; Monday morning in winter
CREDIT CARDS None   ENGLISH SPOKEN A little
OTHER Rossi's workshop is at Viale Caravaggio, 62. Tel: 20459. Honey is
also available from there.   DIRECTIONS The shop is just east of the walls
of the old town, by the Teatro Moderno.

This shop belongs to one of the Maremma's best beekeepers, and sells honeys
and other natural and herbal products. Novaro Rossi and his family travel
around Tuscany with their hives practicing "nomadic" beekeeping.

In Italy, single-flower honeys must contain at least 50 percent of
nectar from the named species. When the chestnut tree flowers in June, any hives
located in a chestnut wood will then produce "chestnut" honey. After the flowers
fade, the hives are emptied and relocated. Maremman species include *erica*
(broom), rosemary and *sulla*, a wildflower in the clover family. An unusual
honey from higher ground is *melata di abete.* In hot humid weather pine trees
"sweat," exuding a sticky resin that attracts the bees. They transform it into an
intense amber honey with a decisive, resinous flavor. Add it to plain yogurt.

Rossi started working with bees as a hobby over twenty-five
years ago. It soon became a way of life. "Working with bees is a labor of love,"
his wife admitted. "But once you get to know them you realize they are better
than most normal families!"

TAVERNA "IL CANTO
DEL GALLO"
RESTAURANT

Via Mazzini, 29   58100   Grosseto
TELEPHONE 0564 414589   OPEN Lunch and dinner; dinner only July
and August   CLOSED Sunday   CREDIT CARDS DC
ENGLISH SPOKEN A little   RESERVATIONS Recommended on weekends
PRICE $$ DIRECTIONS In the old town

Nadia Svetoni's personal little restaurant is located within the town's sixteenth-
century Medicean walls. An ex-ceramicist, she opened it in 1992. She may have
banished tablecloths (she says they intimidate some local young diners) but the
mood is feminine in this unusual vaulted space.

A self-taught cook with a penchant for vegetarian food, Nadia's
menu is based on local specialties. Standard *crostini* of wild boar or chicken
livers complement her selection of vegetable tarts. In winter she favors hearty
soups of *farro* (spelt wheat) or chick-peas. Her pasta is handmade nearby and is
very good. A brown rice risotto with grilled vegetables and wild mint sounded
better than it was. Main courses vary, but include chicken, stewed rabbit, wild
boar, and at least one vegetable dish. A fresh ricotta mousse with wild berries
was a light, fragrant dessert.

Nadia works from a tiny kitchen, prepreparing as many dishes as possible, with slightly uneven results. But her price to quality ratio is good, and the service is friendly and attentive.

MAREMMA MARKET Via Teano, 3   58100   Grosseto
SPECIALTY FOODS: TELEPHONE 0564 23424   FAX 0564 23492   OPEN 8:00-13:00, 16:00-
SUPERMARKET 20:00   CLOSED Wednesday afternoon; Sunday   MAIL ORDER Yes
CREDIT CARDS None   ENGLISH SPOKEN A little
DIRECTIONS From Grosseto's center go toward Scansano on Via
Scansanese. Turn left onto Via Teano at the outskirts of Grosseto.

This is an enterprising modern supermarket selling primarily Maremman products. Formerly a fruit warehouse, the building was modernized in 1993 when a cooperative of about a hundred local food producers launched this new venture. The result is a well-organized store with displays of locally grown fruits and vegetables, cheeses and *salumi*, fresh Maremman meat, wine, olive oil, and dried goods. Many fine producers and cooperatives are represented, including some organic (including Nuova Casenovole p 214). The service is friendly and helpful, and the prices competitive. A great store.

Also

Bar Olimpico. Via Brigate Partigiane, 32. 0564 415325.
A short walk south of the old town, this unassuming bar is known for its homemade gelati. The *creme* assortment is particularly good: creamy and not too sweet. There is a deep, rich chocolate, *panna cotta, cremino*, chocolate mint, and one amusingly called *il dolce della suocera* (the mother-in-law's dessert) with a crumbly crunchy topping.

L'ARATRICE

DISTILLERIA ARTI- Fattoria di Litiano   L'Aratrice   58048   Paganico
GIANA DI NANNONI TELEPHONE 0564 905204   FAX 0564 905580   OPEN 8:00-12:00, 14:00-
GRAPPA, VINEGAR 18:00   CLOSED Saturday, Sunday; August   CREDIT CARDS Visa, MC
DIRECT SALE Yes   ENGLISH SPOKEN No   DIRECTIONS The dark red
distillery is on the road that runs north-south between the Paganico-
Roccastrada and the Civitella-Roccastrada roads, north of L'Aratrice.

Gioacchino Nannoni could be called the father of Tuscany's "designer" grappa. Nannoni, a spirited man with twinkling eyes, learned his craft in northern Italy, where the concept of single-grape variety grappa was not unknown. "Twenty-five years ago," he explained, "nothing of quality was being done in Tuscany. I believed a great grappa could be made from Brunello, as was being produced in Piedmont from Barolo."

The first experiments were made in 1972 in collaboration with Montalcino's Altesino. Fresh *vinacce*, the wine-soaked grape residues left over

from the winemaking process, were distilled; the resulting grappa retained the
perfumes specific to Brunello. Other fine Tuscan estates followed suit.

"Great grappa depends on having high quality, fresh, *vinacce*," he
continued. "The rest hinges on the type of still and the distiller's experience."

The *vinacce* are first distilled directly by steam—in this "tumul-
tuous" process everything is extracted from the grape residues. A second, indi-
rect, distillation is more delicate, allowing the grape's perfumes to remain in
the grappa. The third and final distillation takes place in a copper column 3
meters (about 3 yards) high. The distiller then separates the "heart" of the grappa
from its "head" and "tail" (both the first and last parts of the distillate are full
of impurities and must be discarded). Nannoni revealed his trick for doing
this: "Mother Nature comes to the rescue of distracted distillers," he chuckled.
"At the top of the distilling column is an outlet called the 'mushroom,' covered
over with fine netting, where the vapors escape. When the grappa passes the
'head' and enters the 'heart,' or middle section, a cloud of miniscule flies is
attracted to its sweet, aromatic fumes. When he sees those flies the distiller
knows the good part of the grappa has been reached. He can open a valve
and syphen it into a vat. Once the flies disperse he shuts it off, excluding the
impure 'tail.'"

Grappa, like wine, improves with age. Colorless grappa matures
in the bottle and is sold after seven to eight months. Golden *riserva* grappa is
aged in small wood *barriques* for three to five years and acquires a more complex aroma. Nannoni recommends that grappa be drunk within four to five
months once the bottle has been opened.

From his distillery Nannoni sells named Tuscan estate grappe as
well as his unusual and delicious *aspretti*, under the Rossana Rosini label. These
are fruit vinegars with a difference. The *aspretto di mora*, for example, is made
from 90 percent blackberry juice with 10 percent distilled blackberry spirit
added; the mixture is fermented as vinegar, filtering through beech wood shavings to acquire enzymes. The *aspretti* are matured in small wooden kegs for one
to two years before being bottled. The blackberry *aspretto*, reddish-brown in
color, has a full bouquet of mellow fruit balanced with a hint of acidity.

The vinegars come in several flavors. With their distinctive fruit
accents, *aspretti* are great in cooking: try sprinkling a few drops on meat, poultry, or game before serving. They may even be added to cocktails for a note of
fruity sharpness.

MAGLIANO IN TOSCANA

FATTORIA LE PUPILLE Pereta   58051   Magliano in Toscana
WINE TELEPHONE/FAX 0564 505129   OPEN Monday-Friday 8:00-17:00;
Saturday by appointment; visits and tastings by appointment only
CLOSED Sunday   CREDIT CARDS Visa, MC   DIRECT SALE Yes, subject
to availability   ENGLISH SPOKEN Yes   DIRECTIONS The winery is on
the main road between Scansano and Magliano, 3 kms south of Pereta.

Fattoria Le Pupille is perched up on the top of a dome-round hill, one of two
that are known locally as "the pupils"—*le pupille* seem like eyes staring up at
the sky. The estate has been in the same family since the last century, but its
role as trendsetter in the up-and-coming Maremman wine area of Scansano
began in 1978. Alfredo Gentile was passionate about wine, and it was he who
began aging the local Sangiovese and Alicante in French *barriques* for the
Morellino di Scansano, and he who engaged the interest and services of
Tuscany's most celebrated winemaker, Giacomo Tachis. Together they decided
to experiment with the Bordeaux varietals, Cabernet Sauvignon and Merlot,
and conceived southern Tuscany's finest super-Tuscan, Saffredi. Alfredo, for
whom the wine was named, died in 1985, two years before the wine was first
fermented. It has become an award-winner: an intense, concentrated wine of
structure and elegance that is built to age.

The estate, with over 20 hectares (50 acres) of vineyards, and more
on the way, is now run successfully by Elisabetta Geppetti Gentile, Alfredo's
enterprising young daughter-in-law. In addition to the exemplary Morellino di
Scansano in the good value "normal" and Riserva versions, and small quantities
of a late-harvest Aleatico dessert wine, Le Pupille produces a fine Vin Santo.
Solalto is a late harvest wine of Sauvignon, Traminer, and Sémillon.

MANCIANO

CASEIFICIO SOCIALE Piano di Cirignano   58014   Manciano
MANCIANO TELEPHONE 0564 609137, 609193   FAX 0564 609043
CHEESE OPEN Shop 7:30-13:00; tours by appointment only   CLOSED Sunday
CREDIT CARDS Visa   ENGLISH SPOKEN A little
DIRECTIONS From Albinia take SS 74 toward Manciano. Do not take the
first right turn for the Caseificio, which appears after 18 kms. Continue
for 5 kms, turning right toward Vallerana (across the road from a trattoria).
After 4 kms you will pass a sign saying "Chiarone Scalo 4." Take the second
left turn after it. The Caseificio is a 100 meters down this road on the right.

This 1961 cooperative has 630 members; it pools the resources of local sheep
and cow farmers. The factory combines artisan techniques with modern technology to produce its large quota of cheeses, which are exported to Europe and
the U.S.

Fresh milk is computer-tested and pasteurized before being "transformed" into cheese. The Pecorino Toscano DO (*Denominazione di Origine*) is considered an "eating" cheese when it is matured for 30 to 60 days. The consistency is smooth and compact, with an aromatic sweetness characteristic of sheep's milk. Left to mature for over 120 days, it becomes *stagionato;* still a cheese to eat rather than grate, it remains tender while acquiring a saltier, decisive sharpness. The Maremma's pastures give the sheep's milk a distinctive flavor, more refined and less forceful than its Sardinian counterpart.

Other cheeses include Saturnella, a delicate *caciotta* of mixed sheep's and cow's milk, aged for only two weeks, and a fresh-tasting creamy ricotta of mixed milks.

MANLIO & CLARA VITICOLTORI: LA STELLATA WINE

Via Fornacina, 18   58014   Manciano
TELEPHONE 0564 620190   FAX 0564 620190   OPEN Visits, sales and tastings by appointment only   CREDIT CARDS None
DIRECT SALE Yes   ENGLISH SPOKEN A little   DIRECTIONS La Stellata is on SS 74, about 3 kms from Manciano toward Pitigliano.

Abbiamo fato una scelta di vita e di vite. "We chose our life and our vines." In 1983 Clara Divizia and Manlio Giorni left Rome, moved to the Maremma, and started a vineyard. "We were not wine experts then, just looking for a different way of life. The passion for winemaking has grown on us," admitted Clara.

And they are good at it. Under their label, La Stellata, they produce a Bianco di Pitigliano DOC called Lunaia that is considered the Maremma's most interesting white wine. Relatively *profumato*, it has the slightly bitter aftertaste characteristic of grapes grown on tufa.

"A lot of our decisions are made while the grapes are still on the vine," explained Clara. The *potatura verde,* or green pruning, reduces the quantity of grapes to favor the quality of those that remain. Most of their 5 hectares (12 acres) of vineyards are planted to Trebbiano Toscano, the mainstay of Lunaia. The rest is divided between Malvasia, Grechetto, and Verdello. Clara and Manlio also make grappa and a white *vino da tavola.* They live in a colorful house full of cats and dogs, and they welcome visitors.

MASSA MARITTIMA

LE LOGGE PASTRY

Piazza del Duomo, 11-13   58024   Massa Marittima
TELEPHONE 0566 902256, bakery 901860   FAX 0566 901910
OPEN Winter 6:00-20:30; summer 6:00-1:00 a.m.   CLOSED October
MAIL ORDER Yes   CREDIT CARDS None   ENGLISH SPOKEN No
DIRECTIONS The *pasticceria* and bar is under the arched portico up the hill from the Duomo.

Panpepatus was a medieval delicacy savored by ecclesiastics with Vin Santo at Christmas. They valued the dense confection for the rarity of its ingredients:

nuts and candied fruits, pepper and Oriental spices. Dominated by Siena for three hundred years, Massa Marittima justly makes claims on this Sienese specialty. Giuseppe Schillaci was an experienced *pasticciere* when he began making it. He now uses a recipe from 1300.

Legend dictated that the confection be as hard as glass, softened at a fire before eating. The modern *panforte*, literally strong bread, is made just soft enough to chew. In their small bakery, the Schillacis handmake it in dark (*nero*) and light (*bianco*) versions, using the finest ingredients. The results are excellent: their *panforti* are exquisitely refined—a cut above their Sienese counterparts.

"The recipe for the light *panforte* called for 15 percent almonds," explained Giuseppe's son Paolo. "We increased it to 28 percent of top-quality Pugliese almonds." *Panforte* comes in flat cakes, cut into thin wedges before eating. It is a complex taste experience: the *bianco* features aromatic almonds in a warmly spiced golden paste with highlights of candied citrus; the deeply spiced dark *panforte* includes toasted hazelnuts, cocoa, pepper, cinnamon, and candied melon. Both are delicious. The bakery also makes great *cantucci* and *cavallucci* biscuits.

Le Logge's *panforti* are named for *Il Balestro,* a traditional crossbow contest between Massa Marittima's neighborhoods that is held in Piazza del Duomo, where the *pasticceria* is situated. Schillaci's son Paolo won it in 1995. The *balestra* is held on the first Sunday after May 20, and on the second Sunday of August.

TAVERNA DEL VECCHIO BORGO RESTAURANT

Via Norma Parenti, 12   58024   Massa Marittima
TELEPHONE 0566 903950   OPEN Lunch and dinner
CLOSED Sunday evening except in August; Monday
CREDIT CARDS Visa, MC, Amex   ENGLISH SPOKEN A little
RESERVATIONS Recommended   PRICE $$$ DIRECTIONS From the Duomo go down the small street to the left. The Taverna is on the left.

Claudio Bindi is a devotee of all things Maremman. A fine selection of *salumi* from Monte Amiata, rustic soups of grains and pulses, succulent grilled mountain lamb, stewed boar and rabbit—the classics of this hearty country cuisine—are served with style, accompanied by a fine selection of local vintages. His wife, Grazia Innocenti, is an *appassionata* of the kitchen, a natural cook with a flair for vegetables and desserts. The combination works.

MORIS FARMS
WINE

Fattoria Poggetti   Cura Nuova   58024   Massa Marittima
TELEPHONE 0566 919135   FAX 0566 919380   OPEN Winery sales 8:00-17:00; tastings and visits by appointment   CLOSED Saturday, Sunday   CREDIT CARDS Visa, MC   ENGLISH SPOKEN Yes   DIRECTIONS From Scarlino go toward Massa Marittima; the winery is on the right: follow the avenue of cypresses.

The Moris family has long had large holdings in the Maremma, but until recently their wines were produced for quantity. "We took over my wife's father's farm in 1978," explained Adolfo Parentini. "In 1988 we brought wines to Vinitaly—Italy's prestigious wine fair—and realized we were way behind. We had to greatly improve or close."

They improved: new vineyards were planted, grape yields dramatically reduced, winemaker Attilio Pagli consulted, and modern cellaring methods applied. Beautiful buildings were restored for wine tasting and hospitality. Two *enoteche* selling their wines, bottled and not, were opened in Massa Marittima, Via Butigni, 1 (0566 901599) and Follonica, Via Lamarmora, 30 (0566 40617).

Moris Farms produces a fine Morellino di Scansano DOC and its Riserva; Avvoltore, a forceful Sangiovese-Cabernet super-Tuscan; and an unusual white, Sinfonia. Of 100 percent Ansonica grapes left to dry on the vines for two weeks after being clipped, the must is fermented in French *barriques* for up to eight months before being bottled. These grapes are special to the Maremman coast, Elba, and Giglio, and related to the Sicilian varietal Inzolia. The wine, a deep straw yellow, is dry and rich; it marries well with Tuscan *primi* and pecorino.

A curiosity: At the Cura Nuova farm wild boar are raised. Being bred in captivity seems to have tamed the piglike animal's wildness: I found them snoozing lazily in the sun.

MONTEMERANO

CAINO
RESTAURANT

Via Canonica, 3   58050   Montemerano
TELEPHONE 0564 602817   FAX 0564 602807   OPEN Lunch and dinner   CLOSED Wednesday; Thursday lunch; holidays in January and July   CREDIT CARDS Visa, MC, Amex   ENGLISH SPOKEN No   RESERVATIONS Necessary   PRICE $$$$ DIRECTIONS In the village center

Caino is one of the Maremma's most refined and admired restaurants. Two rooms without views are subtly lit and decorated in discreet-traditional style, with exposed rafters, terra-cotta floors, clean-lined chairs, and fine china. Maurizio Menichetti is a skilled sommelier, his wife Valeria a self-taught chef. Valeria, a warmly attractive, modest woman reminiscent of a Maillol sculpture, cooks everything, aided by two women.

The large menu includes two *degustazione,* or tasting, menus—of "creative" recipes or of classic Maremman dishes. Everything is prepared with care and attention to detail. Many vegetables are homegrown, breads are homemade, and Valeria's *sott'olii* are exceptional.

Valeria's spring sampler began with a hot Mediterranean "pudding" of eggplant, red peppers, and zucchini, accompanied by cold fresh tomato sauce and peppery olive oil. Pigeon terrine looked like a jewel on the plate: rosy pâté was studded with black truffles and pale pigeon breast on a bed of wild leaves. The flavor was refined—gamy, but subtly so.

Pasta dishes were elaborate. *Pappardelle* was sauced with asparagus, pancetta and *formaggio di fossa,* a forceful northern Italian pit-matured cheese. Here the balances seemed less successful. The bacon's salt and the cheese's pungency overwhelmed the delicate asparagus and watery egg noodles. Twin tortelli stuffed with a mousse of guinea fowl and sweetbreads followed, served in a celery sauce dotted with minced vegetables of contrasting colors. The pasta was shaped like candy-wrappers—twisted at both ends around the rich filling. The tastes were interesting, though I prefer my pasta less contrived.

The meat course was memorable. A soft greenish "crust" of finely ground artichokes encased a brilliantly tender loin of lamb, pink-centered with seared edges. The almost caramel-sweet meat went perfectly with its savory coating.

Valeria's golden-topped *crème brulée di ricotta* was fragrant from local ricotta and vanilla. Well executed *piccola pasticceria,* intricate small cookies and candies, ended this interesting meal of complex flavors. The fine wine list includes the Maremma's best.

PITIGLIANO

IL LABORATORIO
DELL'ERBORISTA
HERBAL PRODUCTS

Via Zuccarelli, 31   58017   Pitigliano
TELEPHONE 0564 615450, 619417   OPEN 900-12:30, 16:30-19:00
CLOSED Monday, some Sunday mornings   MAIL ORDER Yes
CREDIT CARDS None   ENGLISH SPOKEN No
DIRECTIONS In the town center

This small herbalist's shop is on the narrow street that leads down through the town's old Jewish ghetto to the newly refurbished synagogue. The enterprising women who run it, Costanza Giunti and Fiorella Campana, complemented their university degrees with long apprenticeships and studies of the local flora. Using pesticide-free plants they have grown or picked themselves, their laboratory distills extracts and tinctures. Their beauty products include carrot cream (for dry skin), sage and thyme skin tonics, and nettle shampoo.

Edible products include local honeys, tomato-based vegetarian pasta sauces, and homemade jams that seemed to me oversweet and overcooked, as is so often the case in Italy.

MACELLERIA
GIOVANNINO
MEAT: SALUMI

Via Roma, 76   58017   Pitigliano
TELEPHONE 0564 616108   Enrico Polidori   OPEN 7:00-13:00, 16:30-19:30   CLOSED Sunday; Monday and Wednesday afternoon
CREDIT CARDS None   ENGLISH SPOKEN No
DIRECTIONS In the town center

Enrico Polidori was hand-twisting a string of little pork sausages as we talked: "My grandmother was famous for these. In those days the shop was run by women; the men did the heavy butchering. Now it's different: I serve in the shop and prepare the meat. I think women like to have a man to talk to when they do their shopping."

His grandmother also made rare *culatello di cinghiale*, prepared from the top round of wild boar's leg. Polidori gets the boar from local hunters, or when some are culled to keep the numbers down. A most unusual *salume* is *prosciutto di tacchino,* a scaled-down version of the familiar salt-cured ham made not from pork but from a turkey's leg.

CANTINA
COOPERATIVA
DI PITIGLIANO
WINE

Vignagrande   58017   Pitigliano
TELEPHONE 0564 616133   FAX 0564 616142   OPEN Shop 8:00-13:00, 15:00-18:00; *cantina* visits and tastings by appointment only
CLOSED Saturday, Sunday   CREDIT CARDS None   DIRECT SALE Yes
ENGLISH SPOKEN Yes   FEATURES Kosher wine produced
OTHER Shop in Via di Sorano, Pitigliano, open Monday to Saturday and Sunday afternoon   DIRECTIONS From Pitigliano, take the SS 74 toward Orvietto. The Cantina is on the right after about 1 km.

Pitigliano was once known as "the Little Jerusalem." An imposing medieval town carved directly from the tufa cliff it sits on, its origins go back beyond the Etruscans to the Bronze Age. Pitigliano's Jewish community, which first settled there around 1500, swelled over the next few centuries to over five thousand, before meeting a violent end at the hands of the Fascists in World War II, despite the resistance of the local people. The town is proud of its Jewish heritage, and in recent years it has refurbished the synagogue and renovated the former "ghetto."

This explains why Pitigliano's large Cantina Cooperativa lists two kosher wines amongst its products, a Bianco di Pitigliano DOC, and a red table wine, *della Piccola Gerusalemme.* The entire winemaking process for these wines is carried out by a Jewish team overseen by a rabbi from Livorno.

The large Cooperativa was founded in 1954 with 11 members; it now comprises 900 local wine growers and 1,250 hectares (3,087 acres) of vineyards. Its annual output is around 12 million liters. The Cantina's signature wine, Bianco di Pitigliano DOC, is a dry white with the *amarognolo*, slightly bitter, aftertaste characterisitc of grapes grown on volcanic tufa. By definition it consists of primarily Tuscan Trebbiano grapes.

Also

Ghiottornia. Via Roma, 41. 0564 616907.

         Lida Manetti's delicatessen features Maremman specialties from local producers: sheep's yogurts from La Parrina (p 213); fresh ricotta and pecorino from Sorano (p 234); *salumi* made by her husband, Enrico Polidori (p 225); *salse* and bottled organic vegetables from La Selva (p 231); plus local wines.

POGGIOFERRO

FRANTOIO ANDREINI   Via Amiatina, 25   58050   Poggioferro
OLIVE OIL   TELEPHONE 0564 511002   FAX 0564 511075   OPEN Always: the family lives upstairs. Sales: year round, no set hours; *frantoio*: November to December   CREDIT CARDS None   ENGLISH SPOKEN No DIRECTIONS The *frantoio* is on the main road through the village. Ring bell in courtyard behind row houses.

Andreini produces excellent Maremman olive oil. Located in a rural village above Scansano, the family-run *frantoio* extracts oil using superior modern Foligno and Sinolea machinery. Andreini cultivates some olives and buys others from trusted growers. He mills for third parties, and bottles two extra-virgin oils under his own label: top-of-the-line Mignola from Scansano olives and Maremma Toscana from olives grown throughout the Maremma.

         Olives are hand-picked and brought to the mill as quickly as possible. Leaves are removed by aspiration, and the olives washed in cold water. In a room that is kept warm at 20°C /68°F, they are slowly crushed to a pulp by stainless-steel hammers. "This may take up to thirty minutes," explained Stefano Andreini. "Olives are a fruit—they must not be handled too aggressively."

         His best Mignola oil, from olives in his Fontelinda grove, then drips out of the mass of pulp by gravity; it is neither pressed nor spun free. This liquid is given a final centrifugal spin to remove the water content. "This is the 'flower' of the oil—the best part," he asserted. Indeed, the green-gold oil's bouquet is as sweet and fresh as newly cut grass. The flavor is full and balanced, with a pleasing taste of olives and a faint peppery aftertaste. Andreini said, "It is fruity but not too arrogant."

Olive oil must be handled carefully. "It is alive. Left in a hot place, it ferments." Keep it cool (but not refrigerated) and stored in the dark. Andreini's oils may be tasted and bought directly, with a range of prices and sizes.

POMONTE

FIORENZO CARLUCCI
CHEESE

On SS 322 at junction for Pomonte   58050   Pomonte
TELEPHONE 0564 599000   OPEN 7:00-19:00 Tuesday to Sunday, from the van   CLOSED Monday   CREDIT CARDS None
ENGLISH SPOKEN No   DIRECTIONS The turnoff to Pomonte is on the main road from Scansano to Manciano. The bar and cheese van are at that junction.

Fiorenzo Carlucci formerly sold his cheeses by driving from town to town. He still makes cheese, selling it from his van, but he no longer travels. The old van now sits beside his daughter Alessandra's bar, and customers drive to him. If there is no one in the van when you arrive, ask in the bar.

Carlucci's cheeses are made of 100 percent sheep's milk from his own herd. *Pecorino fresco*, a young cheese with an aromatic fresh taste, is delicate and creamy. The *semi-stagionato* (half-matured) pecorino is delicious, with a soft, slightly crumbly texture, light salt content, and faint nutty taste. In the mature *stagionato*, the salt is more emphatic, and the texture denser without becoming rubbery—unlike the "Pienza-style" industrial pecorini. Other cheeses include a meltingly fresh ricotta, and walnut- or *peperoncino*-flavored pecorini. They are sold by weight, whole or by the piece.

TRATTORIA DA
VERDIANA
RESTAURANT

58050   Pomonte
TELEPHONE 0564 599184   OPEN 12:30-14:00, 19:00-21:00
CLOSED Wednesday; vacations variable   CREDIT CARDS None
ENGLISH SPOKEN A little   RESERVATIONS Recommended for dinner and weekends   PRICE $$ DIRECTIONS The turnoff to Pomonte is on the main road from Scansano to Manciano. The trattoria is visible from the junction, next to the church.

This reasonably priced country trattoria is run by a mother and her son: Sergio Ciampani hosts and his mother, Miranda, cooks—very well. The menu is unusually imaginative, and not just for rural Tuscany. The Ciampanis have sought out high-quality ingredients and put them to good use. Sergio Ciampani is a keen hunter and expert on game cookery.

In the spring, antipasti included nice salad combinations: goat's cheese with roebuck prosciutto and bitter green radicchio; arugula with fresh porcini mushrooms; and smoked prosciutto of goat with pear, pecorino and arugula. Plus a tempting wild mint frittata. An airy *gnocco* of ricotta and semolina was delicately fragrant and granular; its vivid green sauce was of field

borage and nettle. Chestnut-flour *tortelli* were speckled like bird's eggs. Their
sweetness complemented the stuffing of fennel-scented wild boar. Vegetable-
based soups included artichoke.

    Some rustic game recipes followed: mountain lamb flavored
with marjoram; hare with onions; local venison marinated in apple vinegar and
herbs; and wood pigeon baked with green olives. Vegetarian dishes included
eggplant cooked with thyme and porcini with mint; and baked tomatoes,
stewed zucchini and wild salad leaves. Fresh goat's cheese came with aromatic
chestnut honey. And to finish, a palate-clearing sorbet of pink grapefruit.

    The wine list contains some big reds to match the robust meat
cookery. The restaurant is attractive, airy, and colorful, with peach walls and
mint green shutters. There were bird prints on the walls and wild anenomes on
the tables.

PORTO SANTO STEFANO

IL FORO
RESTAURANT

Banchina Toscana (Galleria Valle)   Porto Santo Stefano   58019
Monte Argentario
TELEPHONE 0564 814138   OPEN Lunch and dinner; dinner only June
through August   CLOSED Monday; January   CREDIT CARDS Visa, MC,
Amex   ENGLISH SPOKEN A little   PRICE $$$ DIRECTIONS From the
seafront at Porto Santo Stefano, take the small slip road along the shore to
the left (with your back to the sea). The restaurant is along that road a little
ways, by the Giannutri ferry ticket office.

This pleasant family restaurant and pizzeria is located near the water's edge.
From the long windowed room you can watch the port as you eat. The food is
just right for the seaside: wholesome platters of pasta tossed with chunky fish
sauces followed by simply cooked local fish.

    Spaghetti with mixed seafood—small calamari, clams, mussels,
and other shellfish—in a light tomato sauce sprinkled with parsley is good. So is
the *fritto misto mare:* shrimp, calamari, and little fish deep-fried in a light batter.
Triglie (red mullet), *San Pietro* (John Dory), and *gallinella* (gurnard) are nicely
cooked over a wood grill and served with big wedges of lemon. The owner is not
keen on the farm-raised fish the markets are full of, like the *spigola* (sea bass).
"They are bland and too expensive." He prefers the less fancy but more flavorful
(and certainly more colorful) "secondary" fish of the Tyrrhenian Sea.

Also

To see some of these weird and wonderful Mediterranean fish, walk along the
seafront to the cluster of fishmongers whose large storefronts extend into the
street. "Da Roberto" is one (open 8:00-20:00, closed Monday. Tel: 0564 812693).

ROCCASTRADA

AZIENDA AGRICOLA   Venturi, 36   58036   Roccastrada
POGGIO OLIVETO   TELEPHONE 0564 577257   FAX 0564 415700   OPEN 9:00-12:30, 14:30-
OLIVE OIL, FRUIT   19:00   CREDIT CARDS No   DIRECT SALE Yes, of fruit in season and oil
ENGLISH SPOKEN Yes   OTHER Rooms available for holiday rental
DIRECTIONS The farm is halfway between Roccastrada and Ribolla. There
is a yellow sign and a short avenue of pine trees to the farmhouse.

This farm is positioned above the Grosseto plains and the sea. There are pretty
buildings, an old well, a tiny chapel, and friendly white Maremman sheepdogs.

The 40 hectares (98 acres) of olive groves use the *lotta guidata*
system of pest control to monitor the olive fly; predators are also used, reducing chemical spraying to a minimum.

The Curatolo family have their own *frantoio,* or mill. From late
October they make and sell fine unfiltered extra-virgin oils. The *frantoio* may
be visited during the late autumn season. This farm also specializes in un-
sprayed strawberries from greenhouse and field, cantaloupes, and watermelons.

ROCCATEDERIGHI

MELETA   Meleta   58028   Roccatederighi
WINE, PIGEON   TELEPHONE 0564 567155   FAX 0564 567146   OPEN Shop 9:00-12:00,
15:00-19:00; *cantina* visits by appointment   CLOSED Saturday afternoon;
Sunday   CREDIT CARDS None   DIRECT SALE Yes
ENGLISH SPOKEN Yes   OTHER Pigeons may be bought directly from
the farm, but it is best to order them ahead.   DIRECTIONS Meleta is
on the road between Roccatederighi and Tatti.

A pigeon feather anchored in a wine cork is this estate's graphic symbol:
Meleta's farming activities are divided between the production of fine wines
and the raising of gourmet eating pigeons. The company was started by a Swiss
couple, Peter Max Suter and his wife, Erica. Until his untimely death in 1994,
Suter had ambitions to produce world-class wines from this largely underval-
ued part of the country. His estate is perched high above the reclaimed swamps
of the Maremma. The vineyards were planted with no expenses spared: Suter
set his sights high. "He wanted to create something that would last," Roberto
Tonini, the farm's director, told me. Suter's wife now runs the estate.

The accent at Meleta is on efficiency and modernity: the colorful wine labels have abstract paintings on them. Suter was advised by Franco
Bernabei, one of Tuscany's best winemakers. Rosso della Rocca is a super-
Tuscan style blend of Bordeaux grape varieties (Cabernets Sauvignon and
Franc, and Merlot) with Sangiovese. Bernabei vinifies and matures each variety
separately for up to two years before assembling the wine. Daniel Thomases
described the 1990 as "large in size and authoritative in character." Other wines

include Pietrello D'Oro, of pure Sangiovese, and Bianco della Rocca, of pure Chardonnay matured in French *barriques* of differing ages.

As for the pigeons, Meleta has become the largest producer of quality eating pigeons in Italy. Many of these go to fine restaurants in Tuscany and beyond (including the Gambero Rosso, see p 160). The meat may also be sent by mail or truck within Europe. Meleta's pigeons compare very favorably to France's famous *pigeons de Bresse*.

The beautiful white birds are kept in airy, computer-controlled coops. The area is pollution-free; the pigeons drink natural spring water and may fly around if they want to. They feed on a rich assortment of whole grains and seeds; the birds are free to select their own diet, which changes during their life cycles. The birds are treated with preventative organic medicines, and even the slaughtering (at thirty days) is done in the most modern, humane way. Pigeon meat is low in fat, tender and well flavored; Meleta's pigeons are among Europe's best.

SAN DONATO

AZIENDA BIO-AGRICOLA LA SELVA
FARM PRODUCE: ORGANIC

Strada Provinciale 81   San Donato   Albinia   58010   Orbetello
TELEPHONE 0564 885799, 885669   FAX 0564 885722
OPEN Shop: 8:00-12:00, 16:00-19:00; Monday-Saturday in summer: Monday, Wednesday, Saturday in winter   CLOSED Sunday; Tuesday, Thursday, Friday in winter   CREDIT CARDS None   DIRECT SALE Yes
ENGLISH SPOKEN Yes   OTHER Six rooms on the farm available for holiday rentals   DIRECTIONS From SS 1 Aurelia turn inland (east) at the Corte dei Butteri bar. The farm is on the left, after 3 kms.

If it is true that we are what we eat, then Karl Egger is the best example anyone could find for converting to organic foods. A large, friendly man with an almost volcanic amount of energy, Egger has for many years been an active, though often isolated, champion of organic fruits and vegetables. A native of Germany, he was among the first to settle in the Maremma and start (in 1980) cultivating and selling this kind of produce.

His beautiful farm of 345 hectares (850 acres) is positioned between the sea and the foothills below Scansano. A seven-year crop rotation system is used on the farm, with no chemical fertilizers or pesticides. In addition to a full range of vegetables and fruits, cattle and sheep are raised—most of this meat is sold by private order. Grapes are grown for making into robust organic wines.

An attractive farm shop is filled with baskets of freshly picked produce. The walls are lined with jars of Egger's preserves and pulses. There is no delay between the picking of the ripe vegetables and their cooking. For the "Tuscan antipasto" line, sliced zucchini, eggplant, and peppers are grilled in a machine that removes up to 75 percent of their water content, then stored in olive oil, ready for eating. La Selva's tomato sauces, some made by the Ciarlo family (p 153), are wonderful, with all the sweetness of the ripe fruit. There are savory eggplant spreads for vegetarian *crostini*, red pepper purées to use on pasta, and cooked chick-peas and *farro*—the spelt wheat Egger said the Romans used to conquer the world.

SATURNIA

BACCO E CERERE Via Mazzini, 4   58050   Saturnia
SPECIALTY FOODS, TELEPHONE/FAX 0564 601235   OPEN Shop: 9:00-13:00, 16:00-19:30;
RESTAURANT   restaurant: in summer lunch and dinner Saturday and Sunday, dinner only Monday, and Wednesday to Friday; in winter lunch and dinner Thursday to Monday   CLOSED Shop: Tuesday; restaurant Tuesday in summer; Tuesday and Wednesday in winter   CREDIT CARDS Visa, MC, Amex   ENGLISH SPOKEN No   FEATURES Garden wine bar   RESERVATIONS Recommended on weekends   PRICE Restaurant: $$-$$$ DIRECTIONS   In the center of Saturnia

Bacco and Cerere (the god of wine and the goddess of grain) are the symbolic figure-heads of this gastronomic center. On the ground floor, Eugenio Piccini has a small wine bar and shop selling selected artisan foods, cookbooks, and handmade kitchen objects. Upstairs, his son Federico runs a restaurant. The shop has been going for over fifteen years.

"Each product tells a story," Eugenio Piccini told me. "I have spent years helping people who still make foods as our grandfathers did." Under his creamy yellow Saturnia label, Piccini sells preserved vegetables, dried mushrooms, jam, honey, cheese, pasta, olive oil (his own), and more. There is a good range of wines, particularly Maremman and Tuscan, and the wine bar offers a chance to taste them. Customers can select from the assortment of cheeses (including Fiorini's pecorini see p 249) and *salumi*, to eat inside or out with local bread and wine.

Upstairs the small, airy restaurant has nice wooden chairs and embroidered curtains. After an antipasto of mixed *salumi* or *crostini,* the menu offers seasonal *primi* of a Maremman character. *Zuppa di ricotta* is a thick spinach soup enriched with sheep's ricotta. Other wholesome starters include soups of fava bean or spelt wheat and handmade pastas.

Meats come from small local suppliers—a *contadino* who might have a few extra chickens or ducks, or a hunter selling native game. They are grilled, roasted, or stewed with wild herbs from the surrounding hills. Wild boar comes well cooked in a spicy sauce. *Agnello in buglione* is a rustic dish of assorted cuts of lamb with rosemary, garlic, hot pepper, tomatoes, and wine. *Buglia* is a local term for "mixture" or "tangle." Desserts are handmade by

Signora Piccini. There are no great local desserts, so her repertoire comes from farther afield.

GROSSETO'S THERMAL WATERS

The Metalliferous Mountains are famous for their sulphur springs, whose waters have healing powers. The natural warm springs in this area were frequented by the Etruscans and Romans, and today they offer full spa facilities. Terme di Saturnia is a modern hotel-spa, with a large natural waterfall nearby. Tel: 0564 601061; fax: 601266. Farther north is the hotel-spa Terme di Petriolo, Civitella Paganico, Pari. Tel: 0564 908871/2; fax: 908712.

SCANSANO

CANTINA COOPERATIVA DEL MORELLINO DI SCANSANO
WINE

SS 322   Saragiolo   58054   Scansano
TELEPHONE 0564 507288   FAX 0564 507785   OPEN Shop: 8:30-12:30, 14:00-18:00   CLOSED Saturday and Sunday   CREDIT CARDS None   DIRECT SALE Yes   ENGLISH SPOKEN A little   DIRECTIONS On the SS 322, 1 km from Scansano going toward Grosseto. The building is set back from the road on the right.

This cooperative began in 1973 when a renewed interest in Maremman wines brought 40 small producers together. They decided to pool grapes and production costs and to organize distribution for the wines. The enrollment fee was 10.000 lire (about $6). Today the members number 168, with over 340 hectares (840 acres) of vineyards. In 1977 the first wines appeared; in 1978 Morellino was granted DOC status.

"A noted red wine was produced here by the Etruscans," explained Benedetto Grechi, the Cantina's president. "We believe it was named Morellino much later—noblemen coming to Scansano to buy wine had horses of the Morello breed." Morellino di Scansano is a red wine of 85 to 100 percent Sangiovese grapes, with the remaining percentage of other black varieties. A deep ruby red, it has a full bouquet, moderate tannins, and austere warmth to its flavor. It is best served at 18°C/65°F and goes well with red meats. Its Reserve spends one year in Slavonian oak barrels. A young version, Vin del Fattore, is designed to be drunk within one year of production. The Cantina has two distinct lines: one for the mass market at economical prices; the other, of higher quality wines, at competitive prices.

ERIK BANTI AZIENDA   Fosso dei Molini 58054 Scansano
AGRICOLA VINOSO   TELEPHONE 0564 508006   FAX 0564 508019   OPEN 8.30-12.30,
WINE   14.00-17.00   CLOSED Saturday and Sunday   DIRECT SALE Yes
ENGLISH SPOKEN Yes   DIRECTIONS The *cantina* is 400 meters outside of Scansano, going toward Manciano.

Erik Banti is considered responsible for having launched Morellino di Scansano as one of Tuscany's key wines. An articulate, extrovert wisp of a man, he was a racing driver, photographer, and travel agent before becoming a winemaker. "I came here from Rome," he recounted in perfect English, "wanting to make a great wine. I took it to the country's top restaurants—including Gualtiero Marchesi and Pinchiorri—and they went for it." He had transformed a *contadino* wine, robust and drinkable but with little finesse, into one fit for an international audience.

Banti owns a few hectares of vineyards and rents the rest. He also buys selected grapes from around Scansano. His best wines are *crus,* single vineyard Morellinos named Ciabatta and Aquilaia which are made only in great years. Ciabatta is matured for thirteen to eighteen months in Slavonian oak barrels and sold three years after harvesting. (The 1985 Ciabatta was voted one of Italy's top thirty-two wines by the Gambero Rosso). Aquilaia is sold after two years; it spends twelve to fifteen months in French oak *barriques.* The "normal" Morellino is a wine to drink young—though all of Banti's wines may be cellared successfully for at least five years. At their best, his wines have great concentration and body while remaining deliciously drinkable.

Also

Panificio Pasticceria Gualtiero Bernardini, Via xx Settembre, 40.

I found several unusual breads in this bakery, including a crusty small *schiacciata,* oval and flat, with a central slash to keep it crunchy. *Schiacciata con ricotta* has soft cheese blended into the dough. *Pane fritto con zucchero* was just that: deep-fried crusty bread sprinkled with sugar—simple but delicious. It is special to Scansano.

SORANO

CASEIFICIO SOCIALE
COOPERATIVO
SORANO
CHEESE

Via La Fratta, 54   58010   Sorano
TELEPHONE *Caseificio* 0564 633002, shop 0564 633748
FAX *Caseificio* 0564 633093   OPEN Shop: summer 8:30-13:00, 17:00-
19:30; winter 8:30-13:00, 16:00-19:00   CLOSED Shop: Wednesday
afternoon; Sunday   MAIL ORDER Yes   CREDIT CARDS Visa, MC
STOCKIST The cheeses are sold in grocery stores throughout the Maremma.
ENGLISH SPOKEN A little   DIRECTIONS The Caseificio's cheeses are sold
from their shop in Via Pitiglianese, on the road from Sorano to Pitigliano,
on the right after less than 1 km.

This dairy cooperative was formed in 1963, and now numbers 700 members,
producing sheep's and cow's milk from local pastures. The wild herbs and
grasses the animals eat gives the milk an aromatic quality that is maintained
in the cheeses.

This *caseificio* makes very fine eating (as opposed to grating)
pecorino: perfectly smooth, it has a slight sweetness to complement the distinctive sheep's milk flavor. It is sold *da taglio* (matured for thirty to ninety days
before eating), and *da serbo* (for eating or grating, a semihard version that may
be matured from four to twelve months). The large modern dairy makes excellent, delicate *ricotta* of pure sheep's milk, or mixed cow's and sheep's milk.
Stracchino is a fresh, slightly acid spreadable cheese of cow's milk.

BANDARIN
TABLE CRAFTS:
POTTERY

Via Roma, 7   58010   Sorano
TELEPHONE 0564 633143   OPEN 9:00-13:00, 14:30-18:30 or later
CLOSED Almost never   CREDIT CARDS Visa, MC
ENGLISH SPOKEN No   DIRECTIONS Via Roma is the main street in the
old part of Sorano.

In 1980 Beatrice Bandarin, a ceramicist and art school teacher, opened this potter's studio. In 1984 her students Moreno Migliorelli and Laura Corsini took
the business over. They decorate and sell a range of colorful hand-painted
plates, bowls, and mugs with delicate flowers and leaves. Half-glazed terra-cotta
pitchers spattered with green are remakes of the rustic peasant ware once used
in the local kitchens, now sadly so hard to find.

Also

Salumificio SA.SO. Via La Fratta, 57. 0564 633185.
        Giuliano Fratini salt cures pork products. His fine *capocollo*
(boned shoulder) is aged for forty days; many of his prosciutti are sent to be
aged near Parma; *salame Toscanello* is made of ground lean shoulder of pork,
with 30 percent belly fat added.

SOVANA

LA TAVERNA
ETRUSCA
RESTAURANT

Piazza del Pretorio, 16   58010   Sovana
TELEPHONE 0564 616183   FAX 0564 614193   OPEN Lunch and dinner
CLOSED Monday; holidays in winter   CREDIT CARDS Visa, MC, Amex
ENGLISH SPOKEN Yes   FEATURES Outdoor terrace
RESERVATIONS Recommended   PRICE $$ OTHER Hotel rooms
available   DIRECTIONS In the village center

La Taverna Etrusca is in Sovana's only square, the unspoiled medieval village located near an important Etruscan burial ground. The restaurant, on the ground floor of a 1241 building, has recently been restored with stylish simplicity. Amparo Hurtado left Colombia thirty years ago. She was a regular customer at the restaurant when the former owners offered it to her. "I was known for my cooking, which is simple in keeping with local traditions. I had a small farm nearby and made all my own preserves."

She serves seasonal food rooted in the Maremma's specialties. A coarsely chopped nettle soup contains a slice of country bread, and is sprinkled with pine nuts and piquant pecorino. *Pici* are thick handmade local spaghetti; *gnocchetti* are made of chestnut flour and ricotta. Amparo serves simple grilled sausages, meats, or *baccalà*, and game when available. Desserts are homemade, including ricotta mousse with wild berries. The wine list features the Maremma's best.

TORNIELLA

SALUMIFICIO
SILVANO MORI
MEAT: SALUMI

Via S. Girolamo, 1 58030   Torniella
TELEPHONE/FAX 0564 575436   OPEN 8:00-13:00 Tuesday, Thursday,
Friday; 8:00-13:00, 16:00-19:00 Saturday   CLOSED Monday, Wednesday,
Sunday; July.   MAIL ORDER Yes   CREDIT CARDS None
DIRECT SALE Yes   ENGLISH SPOKEN Yes   DIRECTIONS The shop is
in Torniella's main square.

"Wild boar, *cinghiale*, is a difficult meat to work," Silvano Mori explained. "It is very lean. Without enough fat, *salumi* tend to toughen. But it is a traditional Maremman specialty." Mori's *salumi* are some of the best I tasted in Tuscany. His small boar sausages, *salsicce di cinghiale*, are excellent: tight-grained and peppery, with a good meaty flavor that is strong without being gamy. They require no cooking and are best sliced finely with unsalted Tuscan bread. They are sold loose or preserved in jars of sunflower oil—to stop them from drying out. I also liked Mori's *salamella*. This narrow pork *salame* is evenly spiced and made without an excess of fat. His *finocchiona* is large, unusually compact, and peppery; it is matured for two months or more. Mori also makes a fine *prosciutto Toscano*—tender and not overly salty.

Silvano Mori, a friendly, spirited artisan, keeps scrupulously clean workshops that conform to E.U. requirements; his products may be exported. He uses no additives or preservatives.

VALPIANA

LA NOVELLA   Via Massetana   Valpiana   58020   Massa Marittima
SPECIALTY FOODS   TELEPHONE 0566 919005   FAX 0566 919194   OPEN 8:30-12:30,
16:00-19:30   CLOSED Sunday; Wednesday afternoon in winter
MAIL ORDER Yes   CREDIT CARDS Visa, MC, Amex
ENGLISH SPOKEN A little   DIRECTIONS The shop is in the ex-Cantina Sociale on SS 439, the main road between Follonica and Massa Marittima.

When Valpiana's Cantina Sociale, or cooperative winery, closed down in 1985, four of its young employees decided to save the building. They took it over and sought out the area's best food products: olive oils, *salumi*, and wines. Starting as a distribution network, they supplied restaurants and food shops.

Their shop offers a fine selection of specialty foods: *pecorini* and *salumi* from the hills around Massa, preserved vegetables and fruits, sauces, and vinegars. La Novella's own label, *La Ceppaia*, appears on many items made for them by local food artisans. Local olive oil is well represented; buyers can choose between *La Ceppaia's* modern extraction system oil, and the more traditional stone-ground types. La Novella has not forgotten its enological roots: they sell inexpensive but drinkable local wine *sfuso* (unbottled), for those who bring their own containers, as well as a selection of reasonably priced Maremman labels.

CHAPTER 10

Mount Amiata

*M*ount Amiata is southern Tuscany's highest mountain. On a clear day it can be seen from points north of Arezzo—a distinctive group of four soft peaks over 1,000 meters above sea level. The highest of these, Monte Labbro, reaches 1,193 meters (3,914 feet). Of volcanic rock and clay, the wide-based mountains straddle two provinces: Grosseto and Siena. Once famous for its mercury mines, Amiata's economy slumped when, in the 1960s, the mines' closing coincided with the disbanding of the *mezzadria* sharecropping system. Thousands of hectares of cultivated holdings were abandoned as the *contadini*, or peasants, left the hillsides to seek work in the industrial cities.

Now, many years later, Mount Amiata's economy is being revived. An area of great natural beauty and resources, the mountain's unspoiled countryside and picturesque towns are attracting tourism throughout the year. In summer the statuesque beech and chestnut forests offer a cool respite; the autumn woods abound with wild mushrooms, chestnuts, and game; winter snow brings skiing; in spring the hedgerows are thick with wildflowers. There are wonderful paths for trekking or biking.

Sheep graze in herds in the sloping pastures; Amiata is famous for its herb-sweet sheep's cheeses. Mushrooms, from the celebrated *fungo porcino* to the rarer *ovolo* are prepared in a myriad of ways. Rustic mountain *salumi* of wild boar are made here, as are bitter herb liqueurs from medieval recipes. The unusual local olive oil is used in many hearty dishes of the mountain's *cucina povera*—a cuisine of seasonal ingredients simply cooked to enhance their decisive natural flavors.

Azienda di Promozione Turistica dell'Amiata
Via Mentana, 97
53021 Abbadia San Salvatore
Siena
0577 778608, fax: 0577 779013

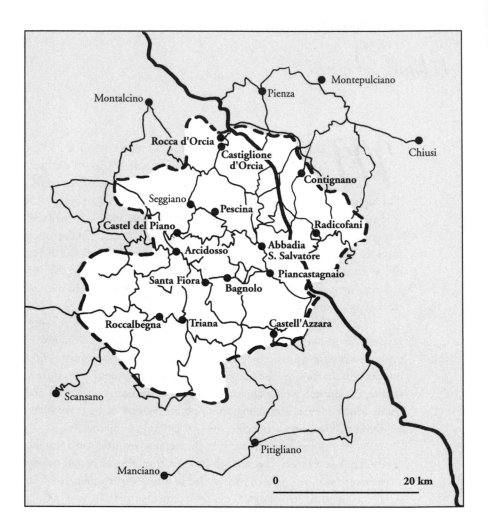

Town names in **bold** indicate towns that are included in this chapter.

ABBADIA SAN SALVATORE

FORNO BAFFETTI   Viale Roma, 32   53021   Abbadia San Salvatore   Siena
& CONTORNI   TELEPHONE 0577 778298   OPEN 7:00-12:30, 16:00-19:30
BREAD   CLOSED Wednesday afternoon, Sunday   CREDIT CARDS None
                        ENGLISH SPOKEN No   DIRECTIONS In the town's central square

This busy bakery offers an assortment of baked goods. *Biscotti all' anice* are a surprisingly tasty salty-sweet combination. Anise seeds are added to a salted bread dough that is shaped like a pretzel and boiled like a bagel before being baked.

"They are good for the digestion," explained baker Luigina Baffetti. "Anise helps settle the stomach. We eat them as snacks—plain or dunked in wine."

Schiacciata, or *ciaccia* as it is called here, is flat crusty bread sprinkled with coarse salt and oil before baking. Here it is topped with *i friccioli,* little pieces of pork fat which become brown and crunchy in the oven. I also liked the rosemary version.

Abbadia's special cake, *la ricciolina,* is an elaborate affair of meringue, chocolate, almonds, and pastry. It is gooey, terribly sweet, and madly popular with the locals.

LOMBARDI   Zona Artigianale 'La Miniera'   Via Amman, 51   53021
& VISCONTI   Abbadia San Salvatore   Siena
HERBAL PRODUCTS: TELEPHONE 0577 777092   OPEN 10:00-12:00, 17:00-19:00 mid June
LIQUEURS   to September   CLOSED October to May   MAIL ORDER Yes
                        CREDIT CARDS None   STOCKIST Liqueurs also sold at Bar dei Tigli,
                        Piazza 20 Settembre, 37, in Abbadia   ENGLISH SPOKEN No
                        DIRECTIONS From Abbadia go toward Monte Amiata; after 1 km turn
                        left into La Miniera.

The tradition of transforming aromatic herbs into liqueurs to stimulate the digestion dates at least to the Middle Ages. The Italians are fond of these often very bitter alcoholic drinks (called *amari*) and like to collect them. They come in decorative bottles and make an interesting addition to the liquor cabinet, primarily for use as after-dinner "digestives."

This small artisan company makes liqueurs from dried herbs, without artificial colors or extracts. Each liqueur contains different herbs, which are grown on an herb farm in northern Italy. Stilla, made to a recipe first used by Abbadia's monks, comprises five types: Asiatic Karkadé (a kind of hibiscus), *Mentha piperita, melissa* (balm), *Artemisia absinthium* (Roman absinthe), and rhubarb. The resulting liqueur is bright yellow-gold, fairly sweet in its fiery herbal impact, with a pleasantly bitter aftertaste. Elisir Lucrezia is altogether a lighter affair: made from just basil and sage, it is a refreshing, perfumed *digestivo* for a summer's lunch. Sage, or *salvia,* is known for its healing properties; its bitterness is tempered by the basil's peppery sweetness.

To make the liqueurs, dried herbs are macerated in a mixture of alcohol and water for five to fifteen days. The herbs are filtered out and the liquid is blended with distilled water and sugar. The resulting mixture is fairly cloudy. It is clarified through *farina fossile,* a ground stone powder, and then through carbon filters used in winemaking. The liqueurs, with an average alcohol content of 30 percent, are then aged for several months.

Dried mushrooms, herbal mixes, and honey are also on sale from the shop in the Miniera complex, in what was once the town's famous mercury mine.

IL CANTINONE
RESTAURANT

Via Asmara, 14-16   53021   Abbadia San Salvatore   Siena
TELEPHONE 0577 776552   OPEN Lunch and dinner
CLOSED Wednesday in winter   CREDIT CARDS Visa, MC
ENGLISH SPOKEN No   RESERVATIONS In summer and on weekends
PRICE $$ DIRECTIONS Near Piazza della Repubblica

Il Cantinone was formerly an inn. It is a large space with the dark wood beams characteristic of mountain architecture. The kitchen, run by Maurizio Bisconti, serves uncomplicated country fare with some refinements. Our spring *primi* were wholesome and satisfying. *Zuppa di verdura* was a thick mix of seasonal vegetables with beans and rice. Homemade *tortelli* were stuffed with fragrant sheep's ricotta and spinach, and topped with Parmesan and torn arugula. Wide *pappardelle* noodles came with a sauce of tender artichokes. The best season for wild mushrooms is autumn, particularly for the prized porcini, though some do grow in spring and summer.

Meats were grilled or deep-fried, like the *coniglio* (rabbit), or *agnello* (lamb chops). Others were stewed simply with wine. Everything was well salted, as is the custom in rural Tuscany. For dessert there was thick home-made *panna cotta* (baked cream pudding), and a bowl of fresh fruit. The house wine is an uncomplicated red from Montalcino, served in pitchers. The service is relaxed but attentive.

PINZI PINZUTI
SPECIALTY FOODS,
WINE, OLIVE OIL

Via Cavour, 30   53021   Abbadia San Salvatore   Siena
TELEPHONE 0577 778040   OPEN Shop: 8:30-13:00, 16:00-20:00;
wine bar: 9:00-13:00, 16:00-20:00, 21:00-23:00 in summer
CLOSED Wednesday afternoon; Sunday in autumn and winter
CREDIT CARDS Visa, MC   ENGLISH SPOKEN A little
DIRECTIONS Near the abbey

Take one step into Marcella Pinzuti's treasure trove of a store and you will be overwhelmed by the quantity of bottles, jars, and assorted curiosities cohabiting in such a tiny space. There are hundreds of wines, grappe, olive oils, and liqueurs as well as unfilled, decorated bottles. There are vegetables in oil and nuts in honey; jams made from quince, figs, or chestnuts; and packages of pasta, cookies, dried herbs, and spices.

This is more than a provision store: it is a personal, hand-picked accumulation, and a very feminine one. Marcella Pinzuti is a soft-spoken woman of great delicacy, and this is her domain. Among the bottles are traditional baskets and rare woven flasks, made especially for her by a few elderly *contadini*. There are dried flower arrangements, carefully assembled gift boxes . . . and much more.

Marcella's father, Lido, makes wine and olive oil, and runs his own *frantoio*. I was very impressed by him. A courteous white-haired man, he seemed much younger than his years, thanks to his passionate commitment to his land.

"In my childhood it was still the Middle Ages," he recounted. "The men worked in the mine all day and then came home to work the land. Each family had a little strip planted with a few vegetables, vines, and olives. If you were lucky, you had a donkey to help with the loads. It was backbreaking. But most of the land here was cultivated then. It looked very different with all those well-tended terraces. I have never forgotten it."

In the 1960s everything changed. People left the countryside to seek employment in the industrial cities. The *mezzadria*, or sharecropper, system collapsed. Nobody wanted to work the land anymore.

For years Lido Pinzuti nurtured a dream to recultivate a large piece of a devilishly steep hillside whose nickname in Italian means "hell." "It took me ten years to coax all the families who owned the strips into selling them to me," he asserted. "Some of the old-timers only agreed because they too wanted to see the land come alive again." Walking around Pinzuti's steeply terraced vineyards and thriving olive groves you would never guess what went into taming the wildness of the terrain. Some of the biggest boulders had to be blasted with dynamite.

Pinzuti's vines and olives are grown organically, without chemical fertilizers or pesticides. He has built a *frantoio* with traditional stone wheels for grinding the olives. It's an amazing achievement, of interest to anyone who cares about the land, its present and its past. Appointments to visit the *frantoio* and farm may be made through the shop.

Also

Fattoria Cortevecchia. Via Case Nuove, 16. 0577 779358.

This butcher shop sells meat from animals raised on its large farm nearby. Pork, chicken, beef, and eggs are also available, as is game, which must be ordered.

ARCIDOSSO

RISTORANTE AIUOLE   Aiole   Via Provinciale   58031   Arcidosso   Grosseto
RESTAURANT   TELEPHONE 0564 967300   FAX 0564 966747   OPEN Lunch
and dinner   CLOSED Monday   CREDIT CARDS Visa, MC, Amex
ENGLISH SPOKEN A little   RESERVATIONS Recommended
PRICE $$ DIRECTIONS The restaurant and hotel is on the main road
between Arcidosso and Santa Fiora, 3.2 kms from Arcidosso.

I had a really enjoyable meal at this restaurant because of its convivial atmos-
phere and the excellent home-cooking of Signora Rossana Bargagli Quattrini.
The restaurant, on the ground floor of their thirty-room hotel, is run by
Rossana with her family and son, Ugo. Rossana's cooking celebrates the
bounty of the woods and fields, against the backdrop of Monte Amiata's
unspoiled verdant landscape.

"I love to go searching for wild mushrooms or herbs," explained
the vivacious Rossana. "Even after working in the kitchen it relaxes me." What-
ever she comes back with—be it spring *prugnoli*, the first mushrooms of the
year, earthy porcini, young nettle shoots, or wild aparagus tips—she transforms
in simple but delicious ways.

In spring an antipasto "salad" of creamy beige *prugnoli*, with
their delicate, cucumberlike flavor, is served with shavings of Parmesan, lemon
juice, and fragrant olive oil. There are *crostini* toasts topped with frail asparagus
or mushrooms, and a bowl of the little black *olivastra Seggianese* olives. Used
primarily to produce oil in the nearby town of Seggiano, some of the olives
are dried near the fireplace in wicker baskets and then soaked in garlic- and
orange-flavored water before eating. They are unlike any other olive, an intense
mixture of sweet and bitter.

The restaurant is hosted by Ugo, whose nickname is "Pampini."
He is tall and distinguished with his bushy moustache and an expert on
Tuscany's *cucina povera* and on local artisan foods. Let him advise you about
the day's *primi*—like Rossana's fine *fiocchi di neve*, or snowflakes. These exquis-
ite little balls are made of potato, local sheep's ricotta, and eggs. They are
floured and poached but remain incredibly light, served simply with grated
cheese and butter. Her pasta is hand-rolled, and as fine as any I've had: *tortelli*
are stuffed with ricotta and nettle, and served with a little meat sauce; noodles
are married to woodsy mushrooms.

Main courses feature meat and game, including some classics
of Tuscan country cooking: *capriolo in salmì*, stewed roebuck, tender but still
moist in a rich reddish sauce; delicately seasoned roast suckling pig; wild boar;
local sausages; chestnut polenta; and meats grilled simply, *alla brace*.

Save room for cheese. Orange-crusted, delicately salted local
pecorino is perfectly married to lemon-infused honey, while creamy sheep's

ricotta is coupled with a purée of sweet chestnuts. "We call these dishes *compa-natico*—literally to go with bread—because in the old days that was all you had," explained Ugo. "If you were lucky there was cheese or honey to accompany it, which acted as main course and dessert."

Desserts are homemade. The wine list is extensive. Ugo bottles their Montalcino house red. The extended Quattrini family eats at a big table in the dining room, and, in the off-season at least, it is lovely to see Rossana sit down afterward to play cards with her friends.

BAGNOLO

MULINO IMPERO Via Fratelli Rosselli, 43   58037   Bagnolo   Grosseto
BELLINI TELEPHONE 0564 953003   OPEN 8:00-12:30, 15:00-19:00
FLOUR MILL CLOSED Wednesday afternoon, Sunday; June.   CREDIT CARDS None
DIRECT SALE Yes   ENGLISH SPOKEN No   DIRECTIONS In the village of Bagnolo, on the main road from Santa Fiora to Piancastagnaio

For anyone interested in the past, this old-fashioned, fully operational flour mill is worth visiting. Opened in 1928 by the present millers' grandfather, it still uses postwar machinery and some original stone grinding wheels. The Bellini brothers, Luciano and Lorenzo, mill flour for local bakeries using an ingenious machine that reminded me of *Charlie and the Chocolate Factory.*

The Maremman grain undergoes eight procedures while being sped along pneumatic tubes and hoisted on pulleys. After cleaning it is wetted to raise the moisture content before grinding, or the delicate inner kernel, *il fiore,* would be scorched. The grain is cracked, separated from the bran, and ground to "O" or "OO" for use in baking or pasta-making. Coarser grinds are used for animal feed.

The two original stone mills are now used only for grinding corn, chestnuts, and organic grain. The large French stone wheels each have a different configuration of grooves hand-chiseled on their flat sides that determine the thickness of the grind once the grain is crushed between the top and bottom stones. These "canals" are hammered by hand once a year to remove any impacted grain. The chestnuts, once a staple food of the mountain population, were smoke-dried until hard enough to be ground.

The miller, an open-faced patient man who looks the part, will sell small amounts of the flours directly. He is justly proud of his machinery and happy to show it when he is not too busy.

CASTEL DEL PIANO

CASEIFICIO CIOLO
CHEESE

Via Cellane   Zona Artigianale   58033   Castel del Piano   Grosseto
TELEPHONE 0564 956225   FAX 0564 955108   OPEN 8:00-13:00
CLOSED Sunday   CREDIT CARDS None   DIRECT SALE Yes
ENGLISH SPOKEN A little   DIRECTIONS The Zona Artigianale is south
of the town, on the road to Arcidosso. The Caseificio is signposted.

This privately owned *caseificio*, or cheesemaker, "transforms" sheep's milk from
the surrounding provinces into pecorini and ricotta. About 350 quintals (34
tons) of sheep's and cow's milk is pasteurized before being made into cheese
each day. Interestingly, sheep's milk is twice as fat as cow's and produces double
the amount of cheese per quintal of milk.

"We make two types of pecorino here: the *Pienza* and the
pecorino tipico," Ciolo's manager Claudio explained. Pienza is a nearby town in
the province of Siena famous for its sheep's cheese." Each is worked differently.
The *Pienza* is eaten within twenty days of being made. It is whiter and a bit
saltier when young. If you come up here to buy it, it also costs half the price!

"The *pecorini tipici* are sold either fresh or matured. The milk is
given more rennet for a longer fermentation, and the cheese loses some of the
acidity it has when fresh."

The formed cheeses are brined before being laid on angled
wooden boards to mature. Cedar is used as it imparts a slightly resinous flavor
to the cheeses. Maturation lasts from one to several months. The cheeses' crusts
are hand-colored using natural substances. The orange color is tomato-based
while the browny black comes from *morchia,* the dark fatty sediment from
olive oil. Some cheeses are given a black plastic covering. The *caseificio's*
pecorini are available in 1 kg, 2 kg and 2.5 kg sizes.

CORSINI BISCOTTI
PASTRY

Via Marconi, 2   58033   Castel del Piano   Grosseto
TELEPHONE 0564 955250 store, 956787 factory   FAX 0564 956615 factory
OPEN 7:30-13:00, 17:00-19:30   CLOSED Tuesday; Sunday afternoon
MAIL ORDER Yes   CREDIT CARDS None   ENGLISH SPOKEN A little
OTHER   Corsini has a store in Grosseto, Via Matteotti, 12-14
DIRECTIONS In Piazza Garibaldi, the town's central square

Corsini's bakery has been a fixture in Castel del Piano since 1921.

"My mother and father started making and selling bread,"
explained Ubaldo Corsini. "I took over when I was seventeen and although
I liked bread-making, I preferred baking cookies and cakes."

Corsini, with his sons, now runs a profitable cookie business
as well as the bakery. From their two factories, built in the sixties and eighties,
the Corsinis successfully blend traditional and modern techniques.

I visited the factory and saw croissants being hand-rolled and
bread being kneaded by old machines that are as slow as manual motion. Their

yeast "mother" (which one of Corsini's four sons described as "the fifth brother") is over thirty years old. Every four hours, 365 days a year, it is "freshened" with water and flour, allowed to rise, and then divided. It has its own special room.

I sampled several of the fifty or more products Corsini makes. The cookies are substantial, short, and not too dry, with good biting texture. Whole-wheat flour *biscotti integrali con yogurt,* shaped like an oval O, are flecked with bran, with a moist firmness in the crumb. Ridged *torciglioni* are the closest thing to shortbread: buttery in taste and crumbly in texture. *Biscottoni al latte* are thin finger cookies with a fine crumb and buttery sweetness.

Corsini manages a lot better with their *crostata,* a flat jam tart, than most Italian housewives do. Italian women invariably bake these tarts for parties and fairs, and just as invariably they turn out leaden, dry, and indigestible.

I found myself eating a whole package of *pizza croccante.* About the size of an Italian railway ticket, these crisp flat breads are salted and flavored with olive oil—a cross between a cracker and focaccia. They are great alone or with cheese or olives. Some of Corsini's products are available in the United States under the name of "Bellino."

FUNGOAMIATA	Pian di Ballo 58033 Castel del Piano Grosseto
SPECIALTY FOODS:	TELEPHONE/FAX 0564 956214 OPEN 8:00-12:00, 14:00-18:30
VEGETABLE PRESERVES	CLOSED Sunday CREDIT CARDS None DIRECT SALE Yes
	ENGLISH SPOKEN A little DIRECTIONS On the main road between Seggiano and Castel del Piano

"Come in," cried Gastone Angeli merrily. "You have caught us at a good moment. We are waging war on the baby artichokes!"

The scene did resemble a battle: young workers were surrounded by mountains of small purple artichokes in various phases of "transformation." The factory floor was deep in discarded outer leaves. Much of this work is done by hand. "Just think," the *simpatico* Angeli continued, "in thirty days in late spring we trim and cook over one million artichokes. Then the season ends."

In fact, that was why I was there. I tracked Fungoamiata down after tasting their *carciofini sott'olio*—baby artichokes in olive oil. Unlike many vegetables preserved in oil—which often taste more of sharp vinegar than vegetables—Fungoamiata's let the artichoke's natural flavors dominate. There is a light tang of lemon to complement the fruity olive oil, a hint of herbs and peppers, but the star is the vegetable.

"Our artichokes are grown nearby, at Venturina by the coast. We use the dark *morello Toscano* variety. They are smaller and more flavorful." The tiny artichokes are simmered for a few minutes with water, fresh herbs, lemon juice, and vinegar. Batches are tasted and seasoned individually. They are pulled off the heat when just tender and still almost crunchy in the center. "Only someone who isn't normal would do this," joked Angeli.

The Angeli family use no chemical fertilizers when growing their vegetables, and no preservatives, citric acid, ascorbic acid, colorings, or antioxidants when preserving them.

As the company's name indicates, mushrooms are featured. "Many types grow wild in the Amiata woods," Angeli explained. "The volcanic terrain naturally gives a better flavor." *Funghi* of all shapes and sizes are preserved under oil, pickled, sauced or dried. I liked the soft gray *Pleurotos ostreatus*. They are meaty without being slimy, their delicate flavor enhanced by the fragrant preserving oil.

Fungoamiata sells many products under its own label. It also produces them anonymously for many Tuscan shops. If you see a small white rectangular sticker on the back of the jar saying "prodotto e confezionato da Az.Agr PI 0094 . . . C. Piano (GR)," you'll know it's theirs.

Also

Cerboni's *salumificio* is one of the best on the Amiata. They do not sell directly to the public, but their products are easily found at COOP supermarkets in the Amiata section and in other local specialty shops.

Vittorio and Augusto Cerboni specialize in boned *prosciutto Toscano,* three types of pork *salame* (lean, "sweet," and hot); and other salt-preserved pork products. "Our *salumi* contain less garlic than the Sienese," explained Signor Cerboni, "so they don't leave a strong aftertaste." The Cerbonis also work wild boar, making small deeply flavored *salsiccie* (sausages).

CASTIGLIONE D'ORCIA

OLEIFICIO SOCIALE COOPERATIVA DI CASTIGLIONE D'ORCIA OLIVE MILL   La Fonte   53023   Castiglione d'Orcia   Siena   TELEPHONE/FAX 0577 887184 in winter; 887535   OPEN November to early January   CLOSED Mid-January to October   CREDIT CARDS None   DIRECT SALE Yes, during milling season   STOCKIST The cooperative's oil is available from Pane e Companatico under the tower in the village center   ENGLISH SPOKEN No   DIRECTIONS Coming from Siena on the SS 2, go toward Castiglione d'Orcia, turning right at the fork before Castiglione d'Orcia. After about 4 kms, the *frantoio* is on the left.

This 1960s cooperative olive mill has 200 private members from the Orcia Valley. In 1993 they installed a modern extraction system and began selling their oil under the cooperative's label. During the winter olive season the *frantoio* may be visited and the new oil bought.

The *ciclo continuo* double-centrifuge system may be less picturesque than the old stone mill, but it provides a more hygienic, versatile way of producing oil. Temperatures at different stages of the process may be controlled. The stainless-steel containers are easily cleaned and guarantee less contamination between batches of members' olives.

The cooperative's oil is very low in acidity; it is made from hand-picked Leccino, Frantoiano, and Moraiolo olives. In a blind taste test I carried out with some friends, this fruity green-gold oil, with its artichoke-like bitterness, was a favorite.

CONTIGNANO

**CASEIFICIO COOPER-
ATIVA VAL D'ORCIA
CHEESE**

Strada dell'Orcia   Contignano   53040   Radicofani   Siena
TELEPHONE 0578 52012   FAX 0578 52085   OPEN 7:30-13:00,
15:00-17:00   CLOSED Wednesday and Saturday afternoons, Sunday
CREDIT CARDS None   DIRECT SALE Yes   ENGLISH SPOKEN No
DIRECTIONS The *caseificio* is on the outskirts of Contignano, on
the road which skirts the village going north toward Chianciano and
Montepulciano.

This cheese cooperative has an interesting history. In the 1950s Tuscany's feudal estates were broken up and many farm workers moved to industrial cities. The *contadini* left the land they had worked for generations, including much of the Val d'Orcia and Crete Senesi hills. Meanwhile, a number of Sardinian shepherds, struggling to make a living in Sardinia, came across to the mainland. Some brought their herds. They began to reclaim the abandoned land, which was well suited for grazing. They made sheep's cheeses, as they had in Sardinia.

In the early 1960s these independent cheese producers had difficulty competing with large private monopolies. In 1964 a priest from Contignano, Don Oscar Guasconi, helped the shepherds form a cooperative. It began with ten members and today has over ninety, though fewer are now Sardinian.

In 1995 the factory was remodeled to European Community standards. The modern cooperative now works 320 quintals (about 31 tons) of milk daily. The product line includes eleven types of cheese, from fresh ricotta to matured grating pecorini. Some are made from mixed sheep's and cow's milk.

This *caseificio* specializes in Pienza-style pecorini. Their youngest (matured one month) has a creamy white interior. The flavor is delicate with a light sweetness. Barely salted, it has only a faint taste of sheep's milk. The mottled orange skin pecorino is colored with tomato paste. Matured for longer, its flavors and salt are more emphatic; smooth-textured, it is less moist than the younger cheese. The black-skinned pecorino, matured for over two months, is drier and saltier. There is a real sheep's milk character to its crumbly interior, yet some sweetness remains. There is a sales point behind the factory.

PESCINA

SILENE
RESTAURANT

La Pescina 58038 Seggiano Grosseto
TELEPHONE 0564 950805   FAX 0564 950553   OPEN Lunch and
dinner   CLOSED Monday; November.   CREDIT CARDS Visa, MC,
Amex   ENGLISH SPOKEN Yes   RESERVATIONS Recommended
PRICE $$$ DIRECTIONS The restaurant is signposted from Pescina.

Situated a short drive from Amiata's peak amid monumental forests, this
restaurant specializes in wild mushrooms. This family-run hotel, formerly an
inn, was founded in 1830. The walls of the large, semimodernized restaurant are
hung with botanical mushroom prints. Dried flowers and floating candles
adorn each table. The owner, Maurizio Landi, is a gregarious, energetic man
who brings the place alive.

Pasta is homemade, served with toppings that include porcini
mushrooms, truffles, meat sauce, and in spring, wild asparagus. I sampled sev-
eral. Very thin noodles, *taglierini,* were sauced with asparagus, onion, ham,
cream, and Parmesan, and enclosed in a slice of Parma ham. There was even
black truffle in this highly seasoned, complicated dish. Tagliatelle noodles were
tender and well made, though in summer their peppered mushroom sauce
lacked the intensity of autumnal porcini. *Tortellini,* tiny pasta squares stuffed
with pigeon, were well-flavored.

A nice salad of sliced *prugnoli* mushrooms with shavings of
Parmesan cheese was dressed with the unusual olive oil from Seggiano. These
delicate spring mushrooms taste of woods, peat, and cucumber.

Main courses are mountain fare. They include roebuck and
wild boar, deep-fried lamb chops, grilled porcini caps, local snails, and beef
tagliata—always popular with Italians. Thin slices of raw beef are flash-cooked
on a hot griddle. Here they were topped with arugula and balsamic vinegar or
porcini and truffles.

The *semifreddo* of lemon mousse and strawberry jelly was elabo-
rate; fresh strawberries served with balsamic vinegar was a lighter option. The
wine list features Tuscany with a limited but well-selected group from Montal-
cino, Montepulciano, and Chianti.

PIANCASTAGNAIO

Bottega del Buongustaio, Viale Gramsci, 79. 0577 786052.
This specialty food shop carries a good selection of wines, spirits
and artisan foods. Locals include *salumi* from Cerboni (p 246) and vegetable
preserves from Fungoamiata (p 245).

ROCCA D'ORCIA

CANTINA IL BORGO
RESTAURANT

53023   Rocca d'Orcia   Siena
TELEPHONE/FAX 0577 887280   OPEN Lunch and dinner
CLOSED Monday; January and February   CREDIT CARDS Visa, MC,
Amex   ENGLISH SPOKEN Yes   FEATURES Three rooms available for
holiday rental   RESERVATIONS Recommended on weekends
PRICE $$ DIRECTIONS The restaurant is up in the village center.

Cantina Il Borgo is situated in a picturesque medieval village, commanding
great views of the wide Orcia Valley. The *borgo* is tiny, with just forty-seven
residents. The restaurant faces inward: its outdoor terrace overlooks the *borgo's*
intimate piazza and restored antique well. The vaulted dining room is in a
1700s carriage house. The furnishings are stark but tasteful: a terra-cotta floor
has been uncovered; walls are refreshingly bare; a massive wood counter recalls
the medieval style.

The menu, too, is pared down but interesting. The Tanganelli,
a cultured family from Rome, are the owners and hosts; a local woman does the
cooking. The family have sought out fine pecorini from Vergelle (p 281) and
produce wonderful olive oil. This stars in a plate of *pici con le briciole*—hand-
rolled ropes of pasta tossed with sautéed breadcrumbs, garlic, *peperoncino,* and
oil. Ricotta and spinach *tortelli* are tossed with butter and sage: fresh sheep's
ricotta always imparts a fragrance of summer fields. *Ribollita,* the twice-cooked
Tuscan vegetable soup, is also available.

Main courses are meat-based and uncomplicated. *Scottiglia* is
three meats stewed together: rabbit, chicken, and pork. There are steaks, roasts,
and a mixed grill. I was offered crisply fried sage leaves and a delicious *sformato
di carciofi*—a kind of artichoke pudding.

Here pecorini are served alone or with honey and walnuts.
Desserts are homemade: I liked a dense apple and nut cake. There is a short
but decisive Tuscan wine list: Montalcino, Montepulciano, Chianti, San
Gimignano. Plus the house's own Bianco and Rosso del borgo.

ROCCALBEGNA

**CASEIFICIO IL
FIORINO**
CHEESE

Zona Artigianale   Paiolaio   58053   Roccalbegna   Grosseto
TELEPHONE 0564 989059   FAX 0564 989067   OPEN 8:00-12:30,
14:30-18:00   CLOSED Sunday   CREDIT CARDS None
DIRECT SALE Yes, for whole cheeses   ENGLISH SPOKEN No
DIRECTIONS From Roccalbegna go toward Triana. After 500 meters, turn
right onto a dirt road across from a group of cypress trees. The *caseificio*
is pinky beige.

Il Fiorino is a private, family-run *caseificio*. Working with all local sheep's milk,
Duilio Fiorini makes some of the area's best pecorini. The factory transforms

about 10 tons of milk per day. Some of this is cow's milk used in Il Fiorino's ricotta and *marzolino,* both of which are mixed-milk cheeses. Fiorini described his *pecorini* as "old-fashioned, traditional style." He explained that the difference between cheeses has less to do with the milk than with the fermentation process. "Starting with the same milk there are over twenty ways to work it," he said.

I tried the *stagionato,* matured for a minimum of six to seven months. It has a pronounced but fine sheep's milk flavor, good texture, and a well-balanced salt content—one of the best I've tasted. The cheeses are available in the traditional round forms, usually weighing between 800 g to 1.5 kg.

SANTA FIORA

PANIFICIO MANNI   Via della Ripa, 24 (Piazza 12 Giugno)   58037   Santa Fiora   Grosseto
BREAD   TELEPHONE 0564 977141   OPEN 8:00-13:00, 17:00-19:30
CLOSED Wednesday afternoon; Sunday; June; November.
CREDIT CARDS None   DIRECT SALE Yes   ENGLISH SPOKEN A little
DIRECTIONS Off Piazza 12 Giugno

Hidden in the heart of the old town, this family-run bakery produces sweet and savory breads and cookies unique to Monte Amiata, if not to Santa Fiora. Much of their flour is ground by the mill at Bagnolo (p 243).

Biscotti dell'ascensione were originally made to celebrate the Ascension, but are now a year-round staple. Looking like a double-tiered bracelet, these delicious crisp biscuits are made of bread dough with added egg, sugar, olive oil, lemon, and aniseed. They make good snacks because they are not too sweet, but have a refreshing taste of anise. Other sweet items include the *stinchi di morto,* crisp meringue-based biscuits with ground hazelnuts; yellow butter cookies made with granular corn flour; and *schiaccia di pasqua,* an Easter ring cake of yeast dough flavored with aniseed.

Some savory breads are unusual: *biscotto salato lessato* is a salted bread dough seasoned with olive oil and aniseed, boiled then baked in a pretzel shape. The *schiacce salate* are flat yeast breads mixed with fresh ricotta and olive oil or finely chopped pork rind, *friccioli.* They are baked in individual-sized oval loaves with a couple of central slashes to keep their edges crisp. The most unlikely combination is the *schiaccia con friccioli e zucchero*—a salty dough blended with pork rind and sprinkled with sugar before baking.

Also

Scala d'Oro. Piazza Garibaldi. 0564 977021.

This lively bar, know locally as "da Beppe," is open till late. It makes its own gelati using fresh dairy products, and they are some of the Amiata's best.

TRIANA

OSTERIA DEL   Via della Chiesa, 2   Triana 58050 Roccalbegna Grosseto
VECCHIO CASTELLO TELEPHONE/FAX 0564 989192   OPEN Lunch and dinner
RESTAURANT   CLOSED Wednesday; holidays variable   CREDIT CARDS Visa, MC, Amex
ENGLISH SPOKEN Yes RESERVATIONS Necessary PRICE $$$
DIRECTIONS In the village center

Sometimes wonderful restaurants exist in unexpected places; Osteria del
Vecchio Castello is one. Triana, in Amiata's rural hinterland, is a tiny cluster of
buildings: a few rustic houses, a mechanic's lawn dotted with tractor parts like
sculptures, and the stone *osteria*.

Step inside and you enter the personal world of two people and
their passions—Alfredo Sibaldi Bevilotti, connoisseur and lover of wines, and
his wife, Susanna Fumi, devotee of fine cooking, present and past. The house,
for it feels like one, is diminutive. A small room is dedicated to wine; it has soft
sofas, specialized books, and some tentlike drapery. The intimate, feminine
dining room contains a handful of lace-topped tables, an open fireplace, small
windows too high to see out of. And everywhere, on shelves, on ledges, stacked
in corners or along wood sideboards, are bottles of wine. Great bottles. Historic
bottles. Wines to savor and discuss. You read in their presence. You eat in their
company.

"Ten years ago we opened a *spaghetteria* here," recounted the
young Susanna, "with two local wines, a red and a white. We quickly outgrew
them." The cooking, too, became more ambitious and creative. "Our restau-
rant is still evolving," explained Alfredo. "This year we introduced new plates
to enrich the visual aspect of the meal. We collect old recipe books to learn
about how people ate."

Their food is the fruit of this research. Susanna Fumi uses local
ingredients, cultivated or wild, with imagination, as a late spring *degustazione*
menu revealed.

A *sformato* of nettle (*ortiche*) was served with a warm pecorino
sauce. The delicate green mousse, less sweet than spinach but less sour, had
sharper accents of parsley. It was meltingly soft. The airy cheese sauce
confirmed the sensations of fresh-scented pastures.

In contrast, the next courses were earth-inspired. Fawn chest-
nut-flour ravioli were stuffed with pork and aromatic rosemary; sheep's-ricotta
gnocchi came with shavings of pungent truffles and field mushrooms. The
wine, a rare Morello aged in chestnut wood from Franceschini at Scansano
complemented these deep, woodsy flavors. The meat course came from an
antique cookery book: a favorite dish of Brunelleschi's, *pepposo* dates back
to 1430. Made of Chianina beef, salt, garlic, wine, and abundant pepper, it
requires six hours of marination, six hours of cooking, and a day to rest. The

resulting rectangles of highly stewed beef are very salty, very peppery. Quite
interesting. After I had finished there were fifty peppercorns left on my plate.

A remarkable cheese platter followed. It included a lighter-
than-air goat's *ravaggiolo;* nearby Fiorino's pecorino (p 249) aged under ash
for a slight smokiness; a satisfyingly salty goat's cheese from Ville di Corsano
(p 281) served here with sweet fig jam; and a very ripe cow's cheese reminiscent
of Camembert. These were matched with a deliciously clear-tasting 1975
Marsala. Fragrant homemade sorbets and other desserts followed.

A word about the wine list. Containing over six hundred wines,
it is itself something to read on a soft sofa. Alfredo Sibaldi describes and tells
stories about many wines—an informative, affectionate account of a personal
love affair.

CHAPTER 11

Siena and the Crete Senesi

*S*iena is a territory rich with history, culture, and gastronomy. A medieval Ghibelline rival to Guelf Florence, Siena spent centuries battling to retain its independence from Tuscan and foreign domination, with limited results. It is visited today for its fine examples of Gothic art and architecture and for the Palio. This bare-backed horse race is run twice per year, on July 2 and August 16. The evening before the race each *contrada*, or town ward, holds an elaborate banquet in its streets. Places at these tables may sometimes be obtained by visitors. The beautiful town is known for its sweet baked goods, especially *panforte*—a medieval spiced confection of honeyed paste studded with nuts and candied fruits. At its best this is a rich, perfumed sweetmeat for eating after dinner; more popular versions are oversweet and cloying.

Few areas of Tuscany are as suggestive as the Crete Senesi, the rounded limestone hills to the south of Siena likened to moonscapes. These barren hills are fit for little cultivation, but offer fine grazing pastures to the flocks of sheep whose milk is made into pecorino.

Siena is also the territory of some of Tuscany's greatest wines. Half of Chianti Classico (p 177) lies within the province of Siena, as do Montepulciano, San Gimignano, and Montalcino (see next chapter, p 283).

Azienda Promozione Turistica
Piazza del Campo, 56
53100 Siena
0577 280551, fax 0577 270676

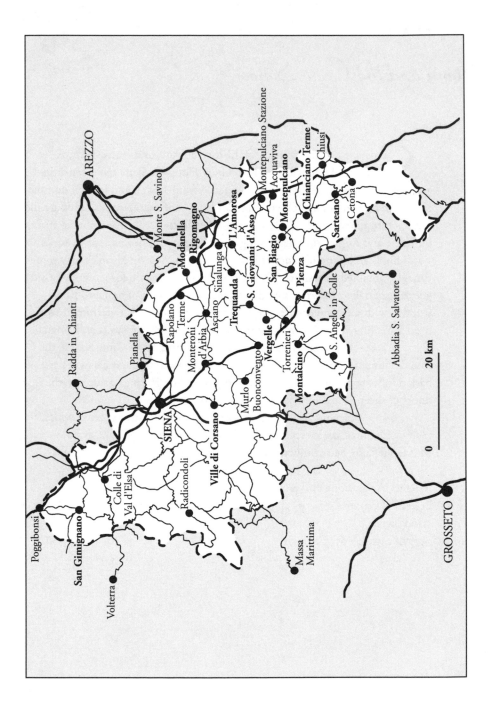

Town names in **bold** indicate towns that are included in this chapter.

CETONA

LA FRATERIA DI
PADRE ELIGIO—
MONDO X
RESTAURANT

Convento di S. Francesco   53040   Cetona
TELEPHONE 0578 238015, 238261   FAX 0578 238015   OPEN Lunch
and dinner   CLOSED Tuesday; January 12 through February
CREDIT CARDS Visa, MC, Amex   ENGLISH SPOKEN Yes
FEATURES Special diets catered for with advance notice
RESERVATIONS Necessary   PRICE $$$$$ DIRECTIONS From Cetona
go uphill toward Sarteano. After less than 1 km, turn left to Mondo X.
The Frateria is up on the right. Park up beyond it.

In 1975 a beautiful but derelict eleventh-century Franciscan convent was given
to Father Eligio, a Franciscan monk, to house one of his Mondo X communities of young people with pasts of drug-abuse and abandonment. "Even then
its exceptional qualities of peace and spiritual well-being were apparent,"
asserted its chef, Walter Tripoli.

Painstakingly, over many years, the buildings and grounds were
restored. Today not a stone, not a flower is out of place. The convent, with
exquisite cloisters and chapels in the Gothic and Romanesque styles, has been
brought back to life with a rare sense of beauty and culture. Perfectly tended
grounds contain scented herb terraces, orchards, vegetable patches, and rose
gardens. Mondo X, with communities throughout Italy, is almost self-
sufficient, producing cheeses, organic vegetables and fruits, meats, and fish.

The remarkable setting is now matched by wonderful food,
thanks to Tripoli. "I learned to cook here, after joining the community," he said.
"Padre Eligio organized high-level cooking classes, bringing in master chefs in all
categories. Since then I have developed my own style." The restaurant was started
to raise money for the communities; it has since built a reputation on its merits.
The hand-illustrated tasting menu changes daily, offering a long and interesting
succession of courses using Tuscan ingredients with refinement but simplicity.
The spare, elegant room overlooks the formal gardens.

After an artistically presented *aperitivo*, my September meal
began. Perfect shrimp on a soft bed of stewed onions came with a mustard-
yellow *timballino* of puréed onion. Tender rabbit fillet was topped with pine
nuts, rosemary, and golden raisins plumped in Vin Santo; it went well with
an earthy medley of potato, porcini mushrooms, and onion. Spinach leaves
enclosed a creamy filling of barley, yellow peppers, and sweet walnuts.

Primi were vegetable-based: soft noodles with a broccoli sauce,
and a painterly risotto of zucchini flowers, zucchini, and tomato. Partridge
braised in red wine was served with rosemary-scented sauce and garden vegetables. Desserts, too, were delicious. A lacy butter biscuit cup, crisp with hazelnuts,
contained an iced chestnut cream. For anyone who still had room, there were
petits fours small enough for a doll's house served on an alabaster plate. The

restaurant offers fine wines and impeccable service. The set-price menu (exclusive of wines) may not be cheap, but it provides a unique dining experience.

CHIANCIANO TERME

Il Telaio. Piazza Italia, 70. 0578 60593.

  This linens shop has striking window displays featuring pretty tablecloths, hand towels, sheets, and more, in jacquards, linens, and cottons. Inside are tea towels with Renaissance designs, napkins, and place mats in myriad colors and a good range of bolt fabrics for making tablecloths or curtains, which the shop will sew to order.

Also

Chianciano Terme has been built around its thermal baths and waters, and is one of Italy's most important spas. For information contact
Azienda Promozione Turistica
Piazza Italia, 67
53042 Chianciano Terme, Siena
0578 63167, fax 0578 63277

L'AMOROSA

LOCANDA DELL'AMOROSA RESTAURANT

53048 Sinalunga
TELEPHONE 0577 679497   FAX 0577 632001, 678216
OPEN Lunch and dinner   CLOSED Monday, Tuesday lunch; January 10 through February   CREDIT CARDS Visa, MC, Amex
ENGLISH SPOKEN Yes   FEATURES Outdoor tables in summer
RESERVATIONS Necessary for dinner   PRICE $$$$$
DIRECTIONS From Sinalunga, go toward Torrita; after 2 kms follow signs to L'Amorosa.

Locanda dell'Amorosa is one of the loveliest restaurants in Tuscany. It occupies the vaulted stables of a fortified medieval *borgo* of the same name, which is also a fine hotel. These quintessentially Tuscan buildings are reached along an avenue of cypress trees. The dining rooms are comfortable without being stuffy, the food is delicious, the service formal; in summer you eat in a picturesque courtyard. The restaurant's chef, Walter Redaelli, is committed to using Tuscany's specialties as a springboard for lighter dishes with a modern feel (and less salt than usual). His menu includes versions of rustic bread soups and frittate or, in late autumn, dishes devoted to the new season's olive oil.

  I arrived in early summer, and vegetables were plentiful: a fresh-tasting *bavarese* of tomato with tarragon was a set *coulis*, beautifully red, served with herbed vegetable strips. A zucchini flower stuffed with a cloud-light ricotta mousse was balanced with a hot compote of cherry tomatoes, olives, and basil. *Ceci e farro* was a refined chickpea and spelt wheat soup, drizzled with fragrant olive oil. *Stracci alle mille erbe,* irregular "rags" of handmade pasta, were tossed with aromatic garden herbs. Speckled gnocchi made with porcini mushrooms and black truffles was excellent, lighter and more woodsy than its potato namesake.

Main courses were divided between fish and meats (the restaurant serves only Chianina beef). Fillet of turbot (*rombo*), was spiced with fresh ginger and served with grilled vegetables. A fanned duck breast was accompanied by a sauce of balsamic vinegar and acacia honey and by caramelized onions.

A soufflé tart of Amorosa's lemons was nicely sharp, with its decorative salad of berries topped with caramel brûlée; it was well matched with Malvasia delle Lipari, the Sicilian dessert wine. The restaurant's wine list contains over 130 wines, with emphasis on fine Tuscans. L'Amorosa even makes a few wines of its own.

MODANELLA

CASTELLO DI   Modanella 53040 Serre di Rapolano
MODANELLA   TELEPHONE 0577 704604, 704553   FAX 0577 704740
WINE   OPEN 8:30-13:00, 14:30-19:00; group visits and tastings by appointment
only   CLOSED Saturday and Sunday in winter; Sunday in summer
CREDIT CARDS Visa, MC   DIRECT SALE Yes   ENGLISH SPOKEN Yes
OTHER Houses available for holiday rentals DIRECTIONS Modanella is
signposted from the SS 326; look for the northeast turnoff to Modanella
near Serre di Rapolano.

Modanella is a handsome twelfth-century castle with Gothic-arched vaults and a dramatic inner courtyard, and a cluster of secondary buildings and church. It once belonged to the powerful Piccolomini family of Pope Pius II.

The estate, with 25 hectares (62 acres) of vineyards, has adopted an interesting policy of winemaking. "When my company took over in 1987," explained Gabriella Cerretti, its director, "we decided to abandon Chianti and concentrate on single-variety wines." Modanella now boasts a group of six: three red, three white. The grape varieties are Sangiovese, Cabernet Sauvignon, and Canaiolo; Chardonnay, Sauvignon, and Malvasia. Each varietal is vinified and bottled separately. Most are modern-style, aged in small French oak casks.

The farm is becoming increasingly organic. "With the wine institute of Arezzo," she continued, "we experimented by reducing chemical treatments. This has been possible for the Sangiovese and Malvasia, but our Canaiolo vines are very old and need some fertilizing." Modanella also sells Vin Santo, olive oil, and organic produce.

MONTALCINO

For listings, see Chapter 12, page 283.

EARLY SUMMER IN MONTEPULCIANO

Montepulciano in June is divine: the fields are cropped of their first hay, golden but not yet parched. The olives are just flowering, the vines freshly green with still unpruned tendrils and their first miniature *grappole*. If the surrounding countryside is sun-soaked, the town, with its warm peachy stone, is the perfect respite: hot in the sun, away from the hill breezes, cool in the shade, and almost bone-chilling in the dark interiors.

Midweek few people were there, mostly foreigners, and we gently wandered up and up, diverted on either side by enticing boutiques of local foods. Here wine is king but it is also culture; there need be no apologies for so many wine stores and *cantine*, one after the other, on the way up.

The main street is wide enough to be zig-zagged from side to side, but its charm lies in its steady ascent, unfolding one section at a time—you never see the whole stretch at once. Nor do you more than glimpse the extraordinary sweep of countryside as you peer past arched openings or slits between palazzi, until you reach the top, when the whole magnificent panorama is revealed.

MONTEPULCIANO

FORMAGGI SILVANA CUGUSI CHEESE

SS 146 per Pienza   Via della Boccia, 8   53045   Montepulciano
TELEPHONE 0578 757558   OPEN 8:00-13:00, 15:00-19:30
CLOSED Never   CREDIT CARDS None   DIRECT SALE Yes, for whole or half cheeses   STOCKIST Cugusi's shop is in Via di Gracciano nel Corso, 31, in Montepulciano   ENGLISH SPOKEN No
DIRECTIONS The *caseificio* is off the main road between Montepulciano and Pienza, 3 kms from Montepulciano, 10 kms from Pienza.

This cheesemaker is located amid the extraordinary rounded Crete Senesi hills. The Cugusis make some of the finest sheep's cheeses in Tuscany, and their story is interesting. Rafaele Cugusi was one of the first Sardinian shepherds to bring his flock (and eight children) from Sardinia in the early 1960s to land abandoned after the sharecropping system was disbanded. It was suited for grazing sheep; its wild herbs and grasses lent the milk a distinctive fragrance. The

Cugusis bought it for little and began making pecorino as they had at home. Today, several decades later, the business is run by Silvana, an attractive, energetic young woman, and her siblings.

The Cugusis still handmake their cheeses, using milk now pasteurized to conform to E.U. standards. Their exquisite ricotta is exceptionally delicate and creamy—the secret is in its whole-milk enrichment. Ricotta is made from the whey that remains after pecorino is made. It is steam heated to 75°-80°C/ 167°-176°F in a large cauldron, while Silvana's sister Giovanna spins it constantly by hand, for "it must never stay still." The small ricotta curds are formed by heat alone; no rennet is needed to make them set. A little salt and whole milk are added, and that is all.

The Cugusis make a range of pecorini (the real Pienza pecorini) in different stages of maturation of up to six months. All the cheeses are turned by hand as they mature; some are rubbed once a week with *la morchia*, the murky residue from a vat of olive oil. This thick oil prevents cracking and gives a brownish crust. Sometimes ash is sprinkled over the cheeses; they may be rubbed with tomato paste, or packed under walnut leaves—each element imparting a slight but particular flavor.

A rare cheese is fresh *ravaggiolo*. This is the "first curd": one solid curd, uncut, of whole milk, placed in a small mold and left to set. It is like eating soft, set milk, and must be consumed within a few hours of being made. Sprinkle it with salt, pepper, and a little good oil and eat with fragrant fresh bread.

IL FRANTOIO DI MONTEPULCIANO OLIVE MILL

Via di Martiena, 2   53045   Montepulciano
TELEPHONE Mill 0578 716305; shop 0578 758732   FAX 0578 758732
OPEN Shop 10:00-13:00, 16:00-19:30; mill may be visited in winter during operation   CLOSED Wednesday afternoon and Sunday in summer. The shop is closed during the milling season, when oil is sold from the mill. CREDIT CARDS Visa, MC, Amex   DIRECT SALE Yes   STOCKIST Shop in Piazza Pasquino, 9   ENGLISH SPOKEN No   DIRECTIONS The shop is within the town walls; the mill is just outside them.

Montepulciano's *frantoio* (olive oil mill) belongs to a large cooperative of olive growers with 650 members in the *comune* of Montepulciano. The *frantoio* presses their olives and sells oil from the cooperative's shop. Many growers also produce wine, as the olive harvest begins in early November after the grapes are finished.

The recently modernized mill uses stainless-steel Alfa-Laval and Rapanelli machines. These may be less picturesque than stone wheels and presses, but they offer a more hygienic and flexible system, since members can control temperatures at each stage. There is also far less danger of contamination from one batch of olives to the next.

After being washed and freed of their leaves, the olives are effectively cut up (rather than hammered) between flat discs covered with blunt *lamelle* (little blades). The *gramola* (paste) is then lightly heated in a double-boiler system to 25° or 30°C (77° or 86°F). Without some heat, the olives will not readily render their oil, but compared to industrial methods, in which the paste is worked at very high temperatures, this still constitutes "cold" extraction, the mill's director explained. The paste is then pushed against a series of blunt blades like a comb, which gently draw the oil and olive water out by drops. For every 100 kgs of olives, only 14 kgs of oil are made. The oil and water mixture is separated by centrifuge, and may be cotton-filtered.

The *frantoio* sells several grades of oil, in sizes from 5 liters to 250 ml. Their best oil has a vivid, cut-grass flavor with the decisive "peppery" finish that characterizes Tuscany's finest oils.

CAFFÈ POLIZIANO
RESTAURANT, CAFÉ

Via Voltaia nel Corso, 27   53045   Montepulciano
TELEPHONE 0578 758615   OPEN 7:00-1:00 a.m.   CLOSED Never
CREDIT CARDS Visa, MC   DIRECT SALE Yes, of wines
ENGLISH SPOKEN Yes   DIRECTIONS On Montepulciano's main street

Caffè Poliziano is a Montepulciano landmark. The café, with its Italian art nouveau-style decor, first opened in 1868. Its celebrated clientele has included Carducci, Pirandello, and Fellini. It went through several transformations—from *café chantant* to movie house—before its refurbishment in 1992. It is a pretty place, with lofty rooms commanding exceptional views of the valley below, and a handy one—you can have coffee, lunch, snacks, afternoon tea, or a glass of wine. There are six *primi* to choose from for lunch, plus salads and sandwiches. Set menu dinners are held downstairs several times per week. Prices are fair—no cover or service charges are added.

DIVA & MACEO
RESTAURANT

Via Gracciano nel Corso, 92   53045   Montepulciano
TELEPHONE 0578 716951   OPEN Lunch and dinner
CLOSED Tuesday; three weeks in July   CREDIT CARDS None
ENGLISH SPOKEN No   RESERVATIONS Recommended, especially
in summer   PRICE $$ DIRECTIONS On Montepulciano's main street

This is a cheerful, unpretentious little trattoria offering good-sized portions at modest prices. The menu's pastas include local *pici all' aglione* (thick spaghetti in garlicky tomato sauce), and baked *cannoli*—a cross between cannelloni and lasagne. Meats are fried, stewed, or roasted simply with rosemary. In spring baby artichokes are quartered and sautéed in fruity olive oil. Desserts are baked locally. The waitresses are great: old pros who have seen it all without losing their sense of humor.

MONTEPULCIANO'S NOBLE WINE

Vino Nobile di Montepulciano is a red wine from primarily Prugnolo Gentile grapes (a local clone of Sangiovese similar to that of Chianti), with Canaiolo Nero and Mammolo. A small percentage (up to 10 percent is still allowed) of white grapes was traditionally added, but progressive wineries have mostly eased them out. The DOCG (granted in 1980) regulations stipulate the wine be aged for two years in wood, three for a Riserva.

As in Montalcino, a "younger brother" exists for the Vino Nobile: Rosso di Montepulciano DOC. This uses the same grapes as Vino Nobile, but is aged less and sold sooner.

Prugnolo Gentile (named for its tiny, plum-shaped grapes) affords the wine good structure and concentration of flavor, while Mammolo confers the characteristic hint of violets that distinguishes Vino Nobile from Chianti. Like all big red wines, Vino Nobile will benefit from a few years of extra cellaring.

As for the name, it may have been a case more of pomp than circumstance, but in 1685 the poet Francesco Redi declared that "Montepulciano, of all wines, was king." From royal to noble, the concept stuck—with today's wines coming closer to their lofty title than ever before.

Consorzio Del Vino Nobile di Montepulciano
Via delle Case Nuove, 15
Palazzo Cervini
53045 Montepulciano, Siena
0578 757812, fax 0578 758213, e-mail nobile@bcc-mp.it

AVIGNONESI	Via di Gracciano nel Corso, 91 53045 Montepulciano
WINE	TELEPHONE 0578 757872/3/4, restaurant 724008 FAX 0578 757847
	OPEN Shop: Monday-Friday 9:00-13:30, 14:30-20:00 from March to November; Saturday in August; Sunday from mid-April to mid-July and from September to November; winery or cellar visits by prior written request only CLOSED December to February CREDIT CARDS Visa, MC, Amex DIRECT SALE Yes, subject to availability ENGLISH SPOKEN Yes RESERVATIONS Required for restaurant PRICE $$$ DIRECTIONS Shop is on Montepulciano's main street

Avignonesi is what you would think of if you closed your eyes and imagined a quintessential Tuscan wine estate. The country villa—with its courtyards of sweet *tiglios*, grouped buildings, cypress avenue, herb garden, *vinsantaia*, and its surrounding sea of vineyards—has a style and beauty that is perfect yet natural. The *cantina* slopes ever downward underground, with room upon room of *barriques:* it is immaculately kept and quite spectacular. In town, an elegant sixteenth-century palazzo with antique cellars houses the winery's shop.

Ever since the three Salvo brothers merged lands to create Avignonesi, they have invested it with passion and ambition. The estate boasts a list of fourteen fine wines, from Vino Nobile and its Riservas to modern single-variety wines aged in *barriques:* Pinot Nero, Merlot, Aleatico, Il Vignola (Sauvignon), Il Marzocco (Chardonnay). They make lovely extra-virgin olive oil and Occhio di Pernice, Vin Santo so rare hardly anyone has tasted it.

Avignonesi has recently opened a new communal table restaurant at the farm. A fixed-price four-course meal does not include wines, but these are priced as in their shop. An opportunity not to be missed for Avignonesi admirers—admission is by advance booking only. Call to make an appointment to visit the cellars while you are there.

BINDELLA
WINE

Vallocaia   Via delle Tre Berte, 10/A   53040   Montepulciano
TELEPHONE 0578 767777   FAX 0578 767255   OPEN 8:30-16:00; *cantina* visits by appointment only   CLOSED Saturday and Sunday   CREDIT CARDS Visa, MC   DIRECT SALE Yes   STOCKSIT Wines also available from shop in Montepulciano: Terra Toscana, Via Ricci, 14. 0578 757708   ENGLISH SPOKEN A little   FEATURES Apartments available for holiday rentals   DIRECTIONS From Montepulciano Stazione, go through Acquaviva toward Tre Berte, passing over the *autostrada*. After about 1 km turn right to Bindella and Fattoria del Cerro.

Rudolf Bindella, a Swiss wine importer, owns Terre di Bindella comprising this Vallocaia estate, with 16 hectares (40 acres) of vineyards, and Borgo Scopeto in Chianti. His style is modern, technologically advanced, even experimental. His large ship-shape *cantina* exemplifies a progressive attitude to winemaking.

Vineyards are planted at high density (over eight thousand plants per hectare, with grass beneath them as a natural deterrent to the vines' natural vigor. Cellar temperatures are controlled against summer and winter extremes. The estate's best wines are its Vino Nobile di Montepulciano (reserve and normal) and Vallocaia, an unfiltered super-Tuscan of selected Prugnolo Gentile grapes matured in *barriques*—a powerful, elegant wine set to improve with time.

CONTUCCI   Via del Teatro, 1   53045   Montepulciano
WINE   TELEPHONE/FAX 0578 757006   OPEN 9:00-12:30, 14:30-18:30 for sales
                      and tastings; groups by appointment only   CREDIT CARDS Visa, MC
                      DIRECT SALE Yes   ENGLISH SPOKEN Yes
                      DIRECTIONS In the town center

A visit to the Contucci cellars is de rigueur for anyone interested in Montepulciano's Vino Nobile. All the atmosphere and history is there, in those almost
spooky cellars in the bowels of a sixteenth-century palazzo in the heart of town.
Apron-clad male attendants act as guides on the tour, friendly and full of talk
of waning moons and their importance for a wine's development.

Count Alamanno Contucci's family has played a key role in the
town's history for seven hundred years. He is president of the Vino Nobile consortium. A traditionalist by tradition, he seems recently to be veering toward
modernity: far from the tourist track of picturesque red-and-black painted old
barrels, he is experimenting with small new oak—with optimistic results. "You
need common sense in these matters," he told me. "We are finding that old
and new ideas work well together."

Contucci makes three types of Vino Nobile: a *cru,* from the
vineyard called Pietra Rossa, a "normal" and, in good years, a reserve. The
best grapes go to Vino Nobile; the rest are used for the younger Rosso di
Montepulciano. Contucci also produces Vin Santo: rich and raisiny in taste,
golden amber in color.

FATTORIA DEL CERRO   Via Grazianella, 5   Acquaviva di Montepulciano   53040   Montepulciano
WINE   TELEPHONE 0578 767722, 767700   FAX 0578 768040
                         OPEN Visits and tastings by appointment only   CREDIT CARDS None
                         DIRECT SALE Yes   STOCKIST Shop in Piazza Grande, Montepulciano
                         ENGLISH SPOKEN Yes   RESERVATIONS Groups of fifteen or more may
                         eat lunch or dinner in the *cantina* by previous appointment only.
                         DIRECTIONS From Montepulciano go toward Chianciano; after 5 kms
                         turn left at big curve; Fattoria is after 6 kms, signposted.

Fattoria del Cerro is a large force in the winemaking landscape of Montepulciano. It is one of the biggest estates, with over 140 hectares (345 acres) of
vineyards, belonging to Saiagricola, a giant insurance company with holdings
throughout Italy. (Italian law dictates that insurance companies must invest in
property assets). Its catalog of wines includes those geared for mass distribution; the top labels, including a fine Vino Nobile, win awards.

The large complex is efficiently and intelligently run (the estate
participates in many winemaking experiments), but, like all corporations, it
remains anonymous. Those wanting to taste or buy its wines should go there:
the countryside and views are exceptional.

PODERI BOSCARELLI
WINE

Via di Montenero, 24   Cervognano   53045   Montepulciano
TELEPHONE 0578 767277, 767608   FAX 0578 767277
OPEN Monday-Friday 8:00-13:00, 15:00-20:00; weekends by
appointment; tastings and *cantina* visits by appointment only
CREDIT CARDS None   DIRECT SALE Yes   STOCKIST Shop in
Montepulciano at Via Ricci, 42 (off Piazza Grande)
ENGLISH SPOKEN Yes   DIRECTIONS From the center of Aquaviva,
across from the tobacconist, take the small Via delle Vecchie Mura
toward Cervognano. The *cantina* is on the right after about 1.5 kms.

"Our winery began in the sixties," explained Marchese Luca de Ferrari Corradi,
"because my mother, Paola, remembered the taste of wines drunk at Montepulciano with her grandfather and wanted to recreate them. Much local land was
abandoned then, and most wines were pretty awful."

This passionate hobby became a full-time commitment for
Paola and her sons. Poderi Boscarelli is an intimate setup: a country house shel-
tered by an oak wood, with cellars that have now outgrown their original small
room. The atmosphere is relaxed, personal. The family live as winemakers and
are proud of the recognition their wines have achieved in collaboration with
Maurizio Castelli, one of Tuscany's finest winemakers.

The estate's 16 hectares (40 acres) of vineyards produce a small range
of wines. The award-winning Vino Nobile Riserva, in both the normal and *cru*
(del Nocio) versions, is made only in great years. These are concentrated, rich
ruby wines of elegance and warmth. Boscarelli is a modern-style wine of pure
Prugnolo Gentile grapes aged in small French casks. Vino Nobile, Rosso di
Montepulciano, Chianti Colli Senesi, and extra-virgin olive oil are also produced.

POLIZIANO
WINE

Via Fontago, 11   Montepulciano Stazione   53040   Montepulciano
TELEPHONE/FAX 0578 738171   OPEN 8:00-12:00, 12:30-18:00; tastings
and cellar visits by appointment only   CLOSED Saturday and Sunday;
August   CREDIT CARDS None   DIRECT SALE Yes
STOCKIST Enoteca Poliziano in Piazza Grande, Montepulciano, open
from April to October   ENGLISH SPOKEN A little
DIRECTIONS Reached from the Montepulciano Stazione-Nottola road,
or the Gracciano-Montepulciano Stazione road, along symmetrical
cypress avenues

Federico Carletti is Poliziano, and vice versa. Described affectionately as "the
volcano," Carletti's passion for his wine is contagious. The estate is big, with
over 120 hectares (296 acres) registered to DOC and DOCG wines, but Carletti's
personal involvement renders it intimate.

When he took over from his father in the early eighties, Carletti
selected the best clones of the local Prugnolo Gentile grape and replanted or
grafted any weak plants. His best wines now consistently win top accolades.
His stars are two *crus*, made only in exceptional years: Vigna Asinone and
Vigneto Caggiole. Both are Vino Nobile di Montepulciano Riservas of choice

grapes from the respective vineyards. The wine matures for two years in large casks or small *barriques;* batches are then blended. "You have to move with the times," he exclaimed enthusiastically. "*Barriques* are the future, and it is as well to understand them. For me, the sweeter taste conferred by the French oak is better suited to Vino Nobile; the Slavonian seems bitterer."

His *cantina* is at ground level and not much below. Everywhere the old wooden *botti* with their red-and-black trim are giving way to raw-looking, purple-stained *barriques*. They may have less character, but they do afford a thrill when you think of the winemaking revolution they are part of.

TENUTA TREROSE Villa Belvedere   Via della Stella, 3   Valiano   53040   Montepulciano
WINE TELEPHONE 0578 724018, 724103   FAX 0577 849316   OPEN 8:00-12:00, 14:00-18:00; tastings possible for retail buyers; cellar visits and groups by appointment only   CLOSED Saturday and Sunday   CREDIT CARDS None   DIRECT SALE Yes   STOCKIST Wines also on sale at the *borgo*   ENGLISH SPOKEN Yes   OTHER The medieval *borgo* has holiday accomodation   DIRECTIONS From the Val di Chiana exit on *autostrada* A1, go toward Perugia. Take the second exit, for Cortona, then go toward Montepulciano. After 6 kms go toward Pozzuolo; the winery is after 1 km.

Tenuta Trerose is now owned by the pharmaceutical Angelini family, whose holdings in Tuscany include the prestigious Val di Suga winery at Montalcino and San Leonino in Chianti. The family is investing heavily in them, refurbishing the buildings and maintaining a high standard of winemaking. The estate's former owner, Lionello Marchesi, modernized the winery by planting at high density in 11 hectares (27 acres) of the 55 hectares (135) of vineyards. (Lasers were used to keep the rows straight). A spacious *cantina* was built adjacent to the attractive sixteenth-century villa.

The estate makes Vino Nobile and its reserve, and La Villa and Simposio of selected Prugnolo Gentile grapes. The Tenuta has also planted non-Tuscan vines. Three interesting white wines, Salterio (Chardonnay), Flauto (Sauvignon), and Liuto (Viognier) are the fruit of this policy. Each wine is made of single-variety grapes and aged in small *barriques*.

VALDIPIATTA Via della Ciarliana, 25/A   53040   Montepulciano
WINE TELEPHONE 0578 757930   FAX 0578 717037   OPEN 9:00-18:00; guided tastings and cellar visits by appointment   CLOSED Saturday and Sunday   CREDIT CARDS Visa, MC, Amex   DIRECT SALE Yes   STOCKIST Wines also on sale at Caffè Poliziano, in Montepulciano   ENGLISH SPOKEN Yes   OTHER Holiday accommodation available   DIRECTIONS From Montepulciano, follow green *autostrada* signs. After 3.7 kms, take unpaved road to right signposted to winery, following it down for 1 km.

Tenuta Valdipiatta was taken over in 1990, and the new owners have already made a name for themselves. The setting is rural, in a valley surrounded by vineyards. The offices and vinification areas are plain, but the aging *cantina* is spectacular. It has been hewed horizontally from the hillside, like an outdoor stage setting. Inside, an avenue of large casks leads to an inner *degustazione*, or tasting, room sitting right under the mountain. This *cantina* is modern but not characterless, reflecting the forward-thinking philosophy of the estate's three young partners.

"We determined to make fine wines as ecologically as possible," explained Lauretta Bernini, the serious young agronomist. "We use no chemical herbicides and fight pests with the *lotta guidata*, or 'guided struggle,' system of natural predators and minimal spraying."

Working with Bernini and winemaker Paolo Vagaggini, Valdipiatta's owner Giulio Caporali has replanted select clones of Prugnolo Gentile and restored existing vineyards. The emphasis is on quality: even the Rosso di Montepulciano, often considered Vino Nobile's poor cousin, is made of select grapes and matured partly in French *barriques*. The result is a more concentrated wine than usual. Valdipiatta's Vino Nobile Riserva, made only in excellent years with the estate's best grapes, has also won high praise.

ENOTECA
OINOCHÓE
WINE STORE

Via di Voltaia nel Corso, 82   53045   Montepulciano
TELEPHONE 0578 757524   OPEN 9:00-19:00   CLOSED Sunday;
January and February   MAIL ORDER Within Europe
CREDIT CARDS Visa, MC, Amex   DIRECT SALE Yes
ENGLISH SPOKEN No   DIRECTIONS In the town center

"The ancient Etruscans poured their wine into a clay *oinochóe*," explained Grazia Giunta, the shop's owner, "and the word inspired us when we decided to sell wines." The shop stocks all of Montepulciano's Nobile wines and a good selection of Brunello di Montalcino, Chianti, and super-Tuscans. The owners of the shop, which doubles as an antique store, are knowledgeable and friendly. A good place to stock up on your favorite noble wines.

PIENZA

TRATTORIA LATTE
DI LUNA
RESTAURANT

Via San Carlo, 2-4   53026   Pienza
TELEPHONE 0578 748606   OPEN Lunch and dinner (last orders at 21:30)
CLOSED Tuesday; February and July   CREDIT CARDS Visa, MC
ENGLISH SPOKEN No   RESERVATIONS Always recommended
PRICE $$ DIRECTIONS In the town center, near the Porta al Ciglio gate

This small family-run trattoria, with summer tables out in the piazza, is always packed. The menu is uncomplicated but appetizing: rustic soups, pastas with a choice of sauces (meat, tomato, truffle), including local *pici all' aglione*—thick spaghetti in a garlicky tomato sauce. Meats are roasted or grilled: steaks, suckling pig, country sausages, duck with olives. Daily specials (ask for these) include unusual vegetable dishes like *sformato di zucchine*—a soufflé-like pudding of zucchini. Frozen *semifreddi* are a specialty here. I sampled a great orange-flavored one encased in Swiss roll. Portions are generous, prices fair, wines local, and the service friendly. Sounds good, doesn't it?

PIENZA'S CHEESES

In Italy the name Pienza is synonymous with pecorino, sheep's cheese. It is considered among the country's finest, due to the fragrant pastures the local sheep graze on. The pretty village is stuffed with food boutiques professedly selling local artisan cheeses, often displayed maturing in ash or walnut leaves. But be warned: many are Sardinian or industrial southern Italian cheeses masquerading as local pecorini (they may be good cheeses, but are rarely worth such high prices). Read the small print on the labels for production information, and be wary of any without labels—the really small peasant producers do not sell their cheeses through these shops.

Several of the good local sheep's cheese producers (*caseificio*), who are nearby and sell to the public are Belsedere (p 280), Crete Senesi (p 281), Cugusi (p 258), Putzulu (0577 669744), SOLP (0578 748695), and Val d'Orcia (p 247).

**LA CORNUCOPIA—
CLUB DELLE
FATTORIE
SPECIALTY FOODS**

Piazza Martiri della Libertà, 2   53026   Pienza
TELEPHONE/FAX 0578 748150, 748491   OPEN 9:30-13:00, 14:30-19:30
CLOSED Tuesday, Wednesday morning in November, January and
February   MAIL ORDER Yes   CREDIT CARDS Visa, MC, Amex
ENGLISH SPOKEN Yes   DIRECTIONS In the town center, on Pienza's
main street

Alberto and Mara del Buono were among the earliest champions of Italy's artisan foods. Their Club delle Fattorie, literally "farm club," is a mail-order business, which is a rarity, as Italian mail is notoriously undependable. It offers selected gourmet foods at good prices to subscribers. "You could call us the soul and palate of the business," exclaimed the genial Alberto del Buono. "We personally travel and taste each product—and never sell anything we don't eat or drink ourselves."

Their lively shop is filled with rare honeys and pastas, sauces and patés, biscuits and cheeses, oils and wines . . . a cornucopia of gourmet treats. Definitely worth a food lover's detour!

Also

Ceramiche della Mezzaluna. Via Gozzante, 67. 0578 748561.

Dino and Fabrizio are friendly potters with a workshop under Pienza's fifteenth-century hanging gardens (ask to see these gardens' brick supports). They specialize in ceramic tiles and objects with clean geometric lines and modern colors. The short walk down to it from the Duomo offers breathtaking views of the Val d'Orcia.

RIGOMAGNO

BOSSI & TURCHI
SALUMI

Rigomagno Scalo   53040   Sinalunga
TELEPHONE 0577 663550   FAX 0577 663592   DIRECT SALE Due to begin in 1998   STOCKIST Antonio Miccoli, Via di Città, 93. Siena; Bazar dei Sapori, Via S.Giovanni, 8. San Gimignano
ENGLISH SPOKEN A little   DIRECTIONS The factory is by the train track at Rigomagno Scalo.

Bossi & Turchi produce game *salumi*, bottled game sauces for pasta and *crostini*, and other gourmet foods. They specialize in salt-cured hams, air-dried meats (*bresaola*), sausages, salami, and more. Most game comes from ex-Eastern block countries, with some from Tuscany. Many meats are sold presliced in "modified atmosphere" packages—inert gasses replacing the oxygen—with prolonged shelf lives and maroon-and-white striped labels. When I visited, the factory direct sales point was not yet open.

I sampled a selection of game products: The small roebuck (*capriolo*) sausages have a smoky, peppery taste, and a close-grained texture; they are better than the venison (*cervo*) which, though highly seasoned, has less taste. Presliced wild boar (*cinghiale*) prosciutto has a strong pepper aftertaste, and is decisively flavored and smoky. The venison is less successful, tasting bitter and of blood. The turkey (*tacchino*) *bresaola* is a pleasant surprise, as is the horse (*cavallo*) *bresaola*, which is tender and less spiced than the rest. In a private taste test, it was voted the best of this group.

SAN BIAGIO

LA GROTTA
RESTAURANT

San Biagio   53045   Montepulciano
TELEPHONE/FAX 0578 757607   OPEN Lunch and dinner
CLOSED Wednesday; January and February   CREDIT CARDS Visa, MC,
Amex   ENGLISH SPOKEN Yes   FEATURES Garden terrace
RESERVATIONS Recommended for dinner   PRICE $$$
DIRECTIONS San Biagio is the church below Montepulciano (to the west,
off the road to Pienza, 1 km from town). Drive down the avenue of
cypresses to restaurant facing the church.

This restaurant is beside the lovely San Biagio church. Its spacious dining room
has walls of stone and stucco and a big fireplace; in summer you eat in the
shady garden. The style is sophisticated but not stuffy. The wine list features
Montepulciano (with twenty-three wineries), Tuscany, and beyond.

My June lunch began with excellent *panzanella*, the quintessen-
tially Tuscan summer salad: soaked bread combined with tomatoes, olives, aru-
gula, capers, celery, red radicchio, and a little onion, then chilled. *Crostini* were
also far from banal: a fine, warm calves' liver paté came with a Vin Santo sauce as
pure as nectar. I began to suspect an unusually creative hand was in the kitchen.

Homemade *raviolini* were stuffed with fresh sheep's *ricotta*
mousse (you tasted its tangy sweetness), basil, and pine nuts and topped with
Parmesan flakes and herbed oil. Rabbit in sweet and sour sauce, *in agrodolce*,
had Indian colors: the tender rabbit was dressed in an ochre sauce of soft
onions with an edge of vinegar. Beside it a dark oak lettuce leaf held spicy rata-
touille of eggplant, peppers, potato, and zucchini. The food was light and
fresh-tasting. (Even the garnishes were intelligent!)

For dessert, a berry tart resembled a soft *clafouti*, served with
a *crème Anglaise*—with an unmistakably French touch. The waiter explained
that, indeed, his mother, Pierrette Matthieu, was French and had run this
restaurant for over ten years: the marriage of French technique and Tuscan
inspiration works!

SAN GIMIGNANO

OFFICINALIA
HONEY,
ORGANIC FRUIT

Cortennano, 46   53037   San Gimignano
TELEPHONE/FAX 0577 941867   OPEN Always, but best to phone ahead
CREDIT CARDS None   DIRECT SALE Yes   ENGLISH SPOKEN A little
DIRECTIONS From San Gimignano go toward Poggibonsi. After about 5
kms, take left fork toward Poggibonsi; after 150 meters turn left toward
Villa di Pietrafitta, up the dirt road. Officinalia is the first house uphill
on right.

Luciano Pasolini and Olga Balducchi produce wonderful organic honey and
grow stone fruit: apricots, plums, cherries, nectarines. I discovered their honey
on Elba (p 169), where Pasolini had taken his hives for the eucalyptus flowers.

Moving the bees to follow the flowering cycles of different plants is called
"nomadic" beekeeping.

In May Volterra's hills are crimson with wild *sulla* (*Hedysarum
coronarium*) flowers; its delicate, sweet honey has a faint lemony aftertaste. The
deeply flavored, dark amber chestnut honey (*castagne*) is from higher ground.
Mille fiori (one thousand flowers) is made in spring and summer, when many
flower species bloom simultaneously. The spring version is clearer and more
delicate than the aromatic summer honey.

Pasolini and Balducchi belong to the biodynamic movement.
Luciano Pasolini explained: "Like organic farmers, we are committed to not
using chemical fertilizers or pesticides, but the Steinerian biodynamic model is
unique in its use of *preparati,* or natural preparations, sprayed onto crops to
boost growth."

In the case of beekeeping, *preparati* are being used against
varroa, the parasite that is attacking the world's bee population, diminishing
honey yields without affecting the honey. "We are having quite a lot of success
against varroa with essential oils and lactic acid," he admitted. "But the solution may come from the bees, once they learn to defend themselves."

LA BUCA DI   Via San Giovanni, 16   53037   San Gimignano
MONTAUTO   TELEPHONE/FAX 0577 940407   OPEN 8:30-21:00 in summer; 10:00-19:00
MEAT: SALUMI   in winter   CLOSED Tuesday in winter   CREDIT CARDS Visa, MC
    ENGLISH SPOKEN Yes   DIRECTIONS In the town center

As you might guess by the wild boar "guarding" the door, this shop specializes
in *salumi di cinghiale.* The farm-reared boar are transformed into sausages,
hams, and salami. The meat has a more pronounced taste than pork and
always seems more peppery, due to spices used in the curing. A close-textured
salame is delicately scented with truffle (*al tartufo*); the deep-colored, lean cured
fillet is tender and not too salty; and the little sausages in strings make ideal
antipasti—just slice them into rounds and serve with a glass of Chianti. There
are saffron-flavored boar *salumi* and locally produced saffron (see next entry).

The attractive shop is manned by the lively Signora Capezzuoli.
The shop will vacuum-pack its meats for easy conservation during inter-
European travel.

L'ASSOCIAZIONE   Casella Postale, 17 (for mail)   53037   San Gimignano
"IL CROCO"   TELEPHONE 0577 940986   OPEN Not open to the public
SAFFRON   DIRECT SALE No   STOCKIST Various food shops in San Gimignano
    ENGLISH SPOKEN A little

"It began lightheartedly," recounted Brunello Bertelli, president of
L'Associazione "Il Croco," the "crocus" association. "In 1990 a group of us

decided to try growing saffron, as centuries ago San Gimignano had been famous for it. It was even used as currency here until its cultivation was lost as an art." They got advice from the University of Firenze about how to grow the bulbs. But what exactly is saffron?

"Saffron is the red-colored stigma from the purple autumn-flowering crocus, *Crocus sativus*," explained Bertelli. "Each flower has just three of these filaments, plus three yellow ones without flavor. A productive bulb may produce up to seven flowers, so at best it will yield twenty-one saffron strands. The flowers are picked in October, just before they would have opened. They are unwrapped by hand and the three precious stigmas are removed and dried over a wood fire."

Saffron's current market value is 50 million lire per kilo, about $13,000 per pound; 125 flowers yield just 1 gram of saffron. Still, a little goes a long way, and it is a delicious spice. "Yes," he agreed, "it can transform many dishes, and goes well with our famous wine, Vernaccia."

CESANI
WINE

Pancole 82/D   53037   San Gimignano
TELEPHONE/FAX 0577 955084   OPEN Visits and tastings by appointment only   CREDIT CARDS None   DIRECT SALE Yes, but best to phone first   ENGLISH SPOKEN Yes   OTHER Three rooms available for holiday rentals   DIRECTIONS From San Gimignano go northwest toward Certaldo. Go to Pancole, under its church and straight on the unpaved road. The house is on the right 500 meters after the church.

Vincenzo Cesani began working his small farm in the 1950s, and planted his first half hectare vineyard in 1964. A warm, friendly man more at home driving a tractor than sitting behind a desk, he explained that sharecropping families were able to buy their own land after the *mezzadria* system was disbanded. "My family had always worked the land," he explained simply. "We moved from Le Marche when I was a child, settling in these beautiful hills. At that time there was no demand for Vernaccia—local wines were sold unbottled."

The vineyards have since increased to 9 hectares (22 acres): the once-humble farm now boasts a sophisticated *cantina* and the assistance of winemaker Luca D'Attoma. Cesani makes two Vernaccias: a selection called Sanice that includes some Chardonnay, aged partly in *barriques,* and the affordable "normal," that is very pleasant to drink. It has a flowery bouquet, and is fresh-tasting and less bitter in the finish than some Vernaccias. Other wines include a red Chianti Colli Senesi and a rosé. I asked Cesani how he became so interested in wine: "When we were children, after the war, there were no snacks—we dunked our bread into wine. I suppose that was how it started."

GUICCIARDINI
STROZZI
WINE, APPLES

Fattoria Cusona   53036   Poggibonsi
TELEPHONE 0577 950028   FAX 0577 950260   OPEN 9:00-12:00,
15:00-18:00; cellar visits and tastings by appointment only
CLOSED Winery: Saturday and Sunday; Shop: Tuesday
CREDIT CARDS Visa, MC   DIRECT SALE Yes   STOCKIST Shop in Piazza
Sant'Agostino, 3/A, San Gimignano   ENGLISH SPOKEN Yes
DIRECTIONS From San Gimignano, go toward Poggibonsi. After about
10 kms, but before Poggibonsi, turn left toward Ulignano and Cusano.
The winery is on the left after 4 kms.

Vernaccia di San Gimignano is one of Italy's oldest white wines, and it has been loved by popes, poets, and pilgrims. Dante mentioned it in *The Divine Comedy:* Pope Martin IV was infamous for having avidly eaten eels drowned in Vernaccia. Prince Girolamo Strozzi's Fattoria di Cusona is Vernaccia's historic home: in 1994 it celebrated its thousandth year. In 1966 Vernaccia was the first Italian wine to gain DOC status, followed in 1993 by DOCG: all wines bearing this name must be made of Vernaccia grapes grown and vinified within San Gimignano.

The wine sung by the poets was different from today's Vernaccia, a dry white wine with a nuttiness to its fruit and a signature light bitterness to its aftertaste. Modern wines are made using soft presses and sophisticated cooling systems.

Prince Girolamo Strozzi, a professor of international law, produces five types of Vernaccia on his large estate, including San Biagio—a single vineyard wine given some contact with the skins and consequently better structured, more elegant, and fuller in flavor than the "normal"—and the Riserva, made from selected ripe grapes aged partly in *barriques.* Reds include a young, drinkable Chianti and Sòdole, a well-structured super-Tuscan of pure Sangiovese.

Vineyards and orchards surround the stately villa with its *parterre* gardens. The cellars are suitably atmospheric, with long underground tunnels now lined with *barriques.* In autumn, the estate also produces wonderful apples, sold directly from the farm. They were sweet and perfumed— I happily ate mine on the long drive home.

MONTENIDOLI
WINE

53037   San Gimignano
TELEPHONE 0577 941565   FAX 0577 942037   OPEN Tastings, visits,
sales by appointent only   CREDIT CARDS None   DIRECT SALE Yes
ENGLISH SPOKEN Yes   OTHER A villa available for holiday rentals
DIRECTIONS Take the road beside San Gimignano's Carabinieri station
over 2 kms to the farm (it becomes unpaved).

"A wine cellar is a place of culture," affirmed Elisabetta Fagiuoli, the driving force behind Montenidoli, one of San Gimignano's most interesting and beautiful wineries. Indeed, you see it in the marble sculptures that people Montenidoli's cellars; you enjoy it in the art of Fagiuoli's conversation; you taste it in the wines. Elisabetta Fagiuoli is a warm, creative woman who has given San Gimignano's native wines a very personal stamp.

"When I arrived in 1965, there was nothing on top of this hill—no road, no electricity, no water. Just an old farm with very overgrown vineyards and a stunning view of San Gimignano." She dug a well, struck water, and began to fashion her winery—"Sono Montenidoli" (I am Montenidoli) proclaims one of her wines. "Vernaccia is a white wine from a land of red wines, unlike the white wines from Friuli or Germany," she said. "A great white wine, even a dry one, should become *meloso*—honeylike." Her 1990 Vernaccia Fiore, tasted in 1996, does have a wonderful, honeyed richness to it, with full and complex *profumi*. She specified that her Vernaccias are wines that can age well and may be drunk over time; three of her nine wines are Vernaccias.

"I believe that each patch of vineyard, each vine, has a distinct character. Grapes are like flour to a baker, they give us something to work with, but it is up to us to learn how to interpret them. In my mind I have an ideal wine—and I will undoubtedly keep working toward it until I attain it."

TERUZZI & PUTHOD
WINE

Fattoria Ponte a Rondolino   Casale, 19   53037   San Gimignano   TELEPHONE 0577 940143   FAX 0577 942016   OPEN 8:00-12:00, 14:00-18:00; visits by appointment only; no tastings   CLOSED Saturday and Sunday   CREDIT CARDS None   DIRECT SALE Yes, twelve-bottle minimum, subject to availability   ENGLISH SPOKEN Yes   DIRECTIONS From San Gimignano go toward Certaldo; turn right almost immediately beyond San Gimignano. Ponte A Rondolino is signposted from there.

If Guicciardini Strozzi represents Vernaccia's historical past, Teruzzi & Puthod has revealed its future potential: in twenty years Enrico Teruzzi, the company's dynamic founder, has put Vernaccia squarely on the international wine-market map. An ex-jockey whose father made his fortune patenting light switches, Teruzzi and his French ballerina wife, Carmen Puthod, have created a wine empire from the simple farm they bought in 1974.

Grapes are grown on the estate's 65 hectares (160 acres) of vineyards, or bought locally. "The methodology required for white wines is very different from that needed for reds," explained the charismatic Teruzzi. "The French have a saying: red wine is made in the vineyard; white wine is made in the cellar. I believe it's true." The Vernaccia grape is difficult to work, tending to oxidize easily. "It is not enough to do an honest job with it," he said. "You need to stabilize and control it." To do this, Teruzzi built one of Italy's most avant-garde *cantine*. Looking rather like a moon base, this impressive "cellar" is a network of outdoor "islands" of stainless-steel tanks fed by miles of underground tubing and commanded by the latest microtechnology and computers.

"I spend 70 percent of my time planning for the future," he admitted. "Most of the day-to-day decisions I leave to my staff." Indeed, the company is run along American lines, with a young workforce given plenty of responsibility.

Teruzzi & Puthod's best-known wines are its Vernaccia di San Gimignano, in the "normal" and Terre di Tufi versions, Carmen Puthod, a modern-style blend of white Tuscan grapes, and Peperino, a red wine of pure Sangiovese. These last three spend time maturing in small French oak *barriques* and have achieved a loyal international following.

Also

Bottega D'Arte Povera. Via San Matteo, 83. 0577 941951.

The Calonaci's tourist shop sells *arte povera*, or poor art—handmade baskets, olive wood bowls and boards, terra-cotta cooking pots, recycled glass from Empoli. Look for local chestnut baskets with wide ribbon weave, *cesti da olive* (semicircular waist baskets for olive-gathering), and flat tear-drop baskets for drying figs.

SAN GIOVANNI D'ASSO

San Giovanni d'Asso hosts an annual truffle fair each November (usually the third Sunday of the month). The Fiera del Tartufo is organized by the Associazione Tartufai Senesi, whose members hunt for the truffles in the surrounding hills, with the help of specially trained dogs. *Tuber magnatum pico*, the white truffle, is the most sought-after variety; it can be bought directly from its finders at the fair. For more information, call Associazione Tartufai Senesi, 0577 823213.

SARTEANO

FRANTOIO TISTARELLI
OLIVE MILL, OIL
& WINE STORE

Viale Europa, 106   53047   Sarteano
TELEPHONE/FAX 0578 265425   OPEN 8:00-13:00, 16:00-20:00. Sunday by appointment only   MAIL ORDER Yes   CREDIT CARDS Visa, MC   ENGLISH SPOKEN Yes   DIRECTIONS On the main road from Sarteano to Chianciano Terme

Mario Tistarelli is an olive oil expert. He runs a *frantoio* and shop selling his company's oils, selected wines, and specialty foods. An experienced connoisseur with a fine palate, he is an outspoken advocate for "real" extra-virgin oil.

"All this hype today about cold-pressed means nothing," he asserted. "Olive oil freezes at 8°C/46°F, and for the stone-ground system of extraction to work the temperature in the *frantoio* must be at least 15°C/59°F. Without some heat the olives will not even release their oil."

Tistarelli holds that the best oil is made using this stone-ground, mechanical press system, but only under certain conditions. "This system is more vulnerable than the modern," he explained, "and requires more attention to avoid the oil being tainted." For example, to avoid contamination, *fiscoli*, the round woven mats used in the press, must be changed frequently, and absolutely no defective olives must be accepted into the machinery. Tistarelli explained why this system is best. "The slow crushing movement and soft rhythm of the stone wheels is less stressful on the olives than high-powered modern machinery, so the oil remains sweeter."

Of Tistarelli's three types of oil, the finest, Cinque Monti, is made from local olives picked as they change color from green to black (*invaiatura*). The result is a clear green oil with a fragrant olive perfume and a well-balanced taste of artichoke. Reticchio is a blend of Tuscan olives grown at fairly high altitudes. Decisive in taste, it has the elegant bitterness that characterizes many Tuscan oils. Tistarelli's most economical line is named for his grandfather: "Signor Olio," or Mister Oil, as he was known. It is a blend of olives bought from central Italy.

SIENA

FORNO DEI GALLI—
SCLAVI
BREAD

Via dei Termini, 45   53100   Siena
TELEPHONE 0577 289073   OPEN 7:30-13:15, 17:00-19:30
CLOSED Saturday afternoon in summer; Sunday
CREDIT CARDS In some of the shops   DIRECT SALE Yes
ENGLISH SPOKEN A little   OTHER Sclavi's other bakeries include:
Panificio Moderno, Via Montanini, 84; Forno Indipendenza, Piazza
Indipendenza, 27; Forno Antiporto, Via Vittorio Emanuele, 85; Forno
Da Penny, Via Massetana Romana, 41.
DIRECTIONS Via dei Termini is north of the Campo

"Our *pane basso* is so good," the elderly lady at the cash desk announced proudly, "that I eat it in the street on my way home!" It is very good. The "low bread" is given two risings; it remains deliciously crisp outside and soft inside. Other specialties from this historic Sienese bakery are the *schiacciate*, (flat yeast breads) dotted with raisins or olives or, in autumn, baked with grapes in them. A crunchy, crumbly version, *ciaccina friabile*, is baked in large flat sheets—a great snack for touring the city. There are breads of all types, including some using organic flours. Sclavi produces pastries, cakes, and cookies, including the Sienese classics *panforte* and *ricciarelli*.

ANTICA TRATTORIA
BOTTEGANOVA
RESTAURANT

Strada Chiantigiana, 29 (SS 408)   53100   Siena
TELEPHONE 0577 284230   FAX 0577 271519   OPEN Lunch and
dinner   CLOSED Monday   CREDIT CARDS Visa, MC, Amex
ENGLISH SPOKEN Yes   RESERVATIONS Recommended for dinner
PRICE $$$-$$$$ DIRECTIONS The restaurant is between Siena and
Pianella on SS 408, the main road into Chianti.

This restaurant is located a few hundred yards from Siena's gates. It has recently been taken over by two young men attentive to detail in both the kitchen and dining room. The atmosphere is fairly formal with careful service. Guido Bellotti and Michele Sorrentino propose two tasting menus in addition to the main list: the shorter offers four full courses, includes wines, and is a good value.

During my February visit, the seasonal menu featured winter vegetables and game—though good T-bone steaks (*la Fiorentina*) are always available. My lunch began with a tartare of ground sea bass with blood orange, lemon, and fennel. I preferred the *cappelletti* stuffed with Tuscan winter cabbage (*cavolo nero*), sautéed with oil, garlic, and chili pepper. The pasta was tender, the filling unusual and good, and it went well with a sauce of puréed beans. A second pasta was successful, though rich: *tortelli di pecorino*, pasta stuffed with sheep's cheese, was served on a searingly hot plate, topped with truffle-scented melted Parmesan just browned at the edges.

The young chef likes layering unusual flavors, as in the breaded *mazzancolle* (large shrimp), served on a bed of onions braised in red wine. Quail breast *alla grappa* might have been named *au poivre*, for its demiglace was thick with aromatic crushed pepper. It was, however, carefully cooked and tender. Fruity olive oil was liberally drizzled over it. The fine dessert was beautifully presented: *semifreddo* (frozen cream) of nougat and rum was served with a decorative caramel sauce. The wines, from various Tuscan zones, were well matched to the foods. The list read very much like the selection in this book.

IL GHIBELLINO
RESTAURANT

Via dei Pellegrini, 26   53100   Siena
TELEPHONE 0577 288079   FAX 0577 40775   OPEN Lunch and dinner
CLOSED Monday   CREDIT CARDS Visa, MC, Amex
ENGLISH SPOKEN Yes   FEATURES Additional fish menu Thursday
and Friday   RESERVATIONS Recommended weekend evenings
PRICE $$ DIRECTIONS Via dei Pellegrini runs from the Campo
to the Duomo.

Il Ghibellino is perfect for a plate of pasta and a glass of wine after a morning's sightseeing. A cross between an *osteria* and a trattoria, Il Ghibellino offers a relaxed mood, reasonable prices and uncomplicated local dishes. The *osteria* influence is apparent in the attention to detail and the slightly more creative cooking. The interior is spare but quite stylish: marble-topped tables are set with butcher-paper mats, the napkins are linen, the floors traditional terracotta tile, the white walls framed by original wood beams.

The food is best when it stays within the range of *cucina povera*, the simple, hearty foods of Tuscany's countryside. *Zuppa di farro* is a well-seasoned soup of spelt wheat, and *rustici con melanzane* a satisfying bowl of handmade curlicued pasta in a tomato and eggplant sauce. I was less convinced by some of the antipasti: the fresh vegetable tart and the cheese and tomato strudel are nice ideas, but both suffered from having under-cooked pastry; the red pepper mousse seemed a bit flat.

The varied meat *secondi* menu includes local favorites, rabbit and tripe; on Thursday and Friday Il Ghibellino also features a fish menu. The desserts are homemade, ambitious and quite successful. The wine list features Tuscany and is well priced. The amiable young owners take turns on the floor, so the service is intelligent and attentive.

OSTERIA DEL FICOMEZZO RESTAURANT

Via dei Termini, 71   53100   Siena
TELEPHONE 0577 222384   OPEN Lunch and dinner (last order 23:00)
CLOSED Sunday; July   CREDIT CARDS Visa, MC, Amex
ENGLISH SPOKEN Yes   RESERVATIONS Recommended for weekend dinner
PRICE Lunch $, dinner $$ DIRECTIONS Via dei Termini runs north of the Campo.

This small, unpretentious restaurant has an intelligent quick lunch formula, well-suited to the busy visitor: it offers eight "combinations" at very reasonable prices. These take the classic three-course form (starter, main course, dessert) or its variations (mixed salad, pasta, dessert). The recipes range from simple grilled meats with potatoes to more ambitious vegetable-based crèpes or pies, to country soups or pastas with meat or vegetable sauces. Service is included in the price. (The dinner menu offers an à la carte menu.) There is a limited range of wines.

Cinzia Minucci and Carlo Petrucci's menu changes weekly. Most of their produce is grown by Cinzia's father, and many of the dishes reflect this commitment. The vegetable-based *zuppa di farro* is satisfying and wholesome, with aromatic vegetables to set off the plumped spelt wheat grains. *Torta di verdura*, like a vegetable quiche, is filled with zucchini and leafy greens; its short crust pastry happily cooked right through. Desserts, too, have a nice homemade feel to them.

ANTICA DROGHERIA MANGANELLI 1879 SPECIALTY FOODS, PASTRY

Via di Città, 71-73   53100   Siena
TELEPHONE 0577 280002   FAX 0577 349389   OPEN Summer 9:00-20:00; winter 9:00-13:00, 15:30-19:30   CLOSED Wednesday afternoon in winter   CREDIT CARDS Visa, MC, Amex   DIRECT SALE Yes
ENGLISH SPOKEN Yes   DIRECTIONS Via di Città runs beside the Campo

This shop is a gourmet treasure trove. Its antique wood cabinets are stacked to the ceiling with edible (and drinkable) goodies of all description. Here, in the rarified spice-perfumed interior, you find everything from "designer" olive oils to truffle-scented polenta. There are herbed vinegars from Volpaia (p 209), Martelli's pasta (p 123), Falorni's *salumi* (p 191), jams and honeys, sauces and *sott'olii*—vegetables preserved in oil that make great antipasti. One room is devoted to wines, liqueurs, and grappas. A perfect place for presents and personal indulgences.

Manganelli bakes its own traditional Sienese pastries from "very old" recipes—the store has been going since 1879. It makes two types of *panforte:* Margherita is the paler; its thick paste has a strong presence of cinnamon and is studded with toasted almonds and green melon *canditi.* The darker version, also full of nuts, tastes of mixed Tuscan spices and is slightly more bitter. The *ricciarelli,* made of ground almond dough, are wonderful: moist and sticky with real almond flavor.

**CONSORZIO
AGRARIO SIENA
SPECIALTY FOODS**

Via Pianigiani, 9   53100   Siena
TELEPHONE 0577 222368, 44251   FAX 0577 280378
OPEN Winter 7:45-13:00, 16:30-19:30; summer 7:45-13:00, 17:00-20:00
CLOSED Sunday; Wednesday afternoon in winter, Saturday afternoon
in summer   CREDIT CARDS Visa, MC   DIRECT SALE Yes
ENGLISH SPOKEN A little   DIRECTIONS Near Piazza Matteotti

This supermarket features foods from the province of Siena. It is run by the Consorzio Agrario (farmer's consortium), an organization under the auspices of the Ministry for Agriculture. It was founded in 1901 and now has four thousand members. The consortium helps producers promote their goods, and sells them seeds, fertilizers, and equipment.

The supermarket stocks a range of pecorini, the area's famous sheep's cheeses, *salumi,* grain and honey, olive oil and wine. Many of its producers are mentioned in this book. Under the brand name Granducato, it sells members' oil and wine at reasonable prices. The consortium has a modern-system oil mill at Pianella; this may be visited during November and December. This consortium has several shops in the province, at Montalcino, Pienza, Buonconvento, and Chianciano Terme.

**GASTRONOMIA
MORBIDI 1925
SPECIALTY FOODS:
DELICATESSEN**

Via Banchi di Sopra, 73-75   53100   Siena
TELEPHONE 0577 280268, 282257   FAX 0577 285077   OPEN 8:00-
13:15, 17:00-20:00   CLOSED Saturday afternoon and Sunday
CREDIT CARDS Visa, MC   DIRECT SALE Yes   ENGLISH SPOKEN A little
OTHER A second shop is in Via Banchi di Sotto, 27. Catering facilities
available   DIRECTIONS On the main street leading into the north side
of the Campo

Gastronomia Morbidi has offered quality foods in Siena since 1925. Armando Morbidi began as a cheese resaler. His granddaughter Patrizia said he had been the first to introduce certain cheeses to Siena. The family now run the Salcis *caseificio* near Pienza, selling their excellent pecorini in the shops.

The present shop, with its clean white vaulting, is modern and attractive. A long counter holds dairy foods, *salumi,* and a fabulous array of home-cooked foods to take out—the *gastronomia.* Recipes change daily, but there are always ready-to-eat antipasti (including seasoned olives, vegetables preserved in oil, sweet and sour onions), *primi* (pastas and thick soups), and *secondi* (roast meats, aspics, herbed fish dishes). These are sold in containers, by weight or by the piece, and make great picnic foods. There is even a wine cellar downstairs.

ENOTECA ITALIANA
WINE STORE, WINE BAR

Fortezza Medicea, 1   53100   Siena
TELEPHONE 0577 288497   FAX 0577 270717
INTERNET http://www.agriline.it/wol/enosiena   OPEN Monday
12:00-20:00, Tuesday-Saturday 12:00-1:00 a.m.   CLOSED Sunday
CREDIT CARDS Visa, Amex   DIRECT SALE Yes   ENGLISH SPOKEN Yes
DIRECTIONS The fortress is at the top of Siena. The *enoteca* is on the left as you enter it.

The underground cellars of a Medicean fortress are the dramatic setting for one of Italy's most important wine stores. Enoteca Italiana is state run; its mandate is to promote wines from all of Italy's regions. Its vaulted brick cellars house permanent displays of over 750 types of quality wines. A team of professional wine tasters constantly tastes and grades Italian wines to maintain the Enoteca's high standards. Only those attaining a score of over seventy-five points are chosen.

At the upstairs wine bar over eight hundred selected wines may be tasted by the glass, at modest prices. This exceptional opportunity invites comparisons between regions, grape varieties, or neighboring producers. (You can just as happily sit with a glass or bottle of wine and have lunch or a snack.) Wine may also be bought to take away.

Enoteca Italiana organizes many events and activities: guided wine tastings at all levels of expertise, concerts, exhibitions of wine-related art, a Wine Week in June, and buffets and banquets. Groups can be accommodated by prearrangement. A must for wine lovers.

TREQUANDA

MACELLERIA RICCI
(FONDO PENSIONE
CARIPLO)
MEAT

Azienda Agricola Trequanda   Via Traversa dei Monti, 4
53020   Trequanda
TELEPHONE 0577 662252   FAX 0577 662001   OPEN Tuesday-
Wednesday 9:00-13:00; Thursday-Saturday 9:00-13:00, 17:00-20:00
CLOSED Monday, Sunday; variable winter holidays
CREDIT CARDS Visa, MC, Amex   ENGLISH SPOKEN A little
OTHER The farm may be visited by appointment.   DIRECTIONS On the
main Sinalunga-Montisi road at Trequanda

This butcher's shop belongs to the pension fund of one of Italy's biggest banks. Ricci specializes in pure Chianina beef, one of the world's finest breeds, raised nearby in Trequanda. The Chianina have been known since Etruscan times. They are the pale cattle with dark eyes seen pulling the plough in old Tuscan photographs. A consortium called 5R controls this and four other pure cattle breeds.

"Our beef comes from our own farm," explained Enrico Ricci, the butcher. "So there is an absolute consistency of quality. We know what the animals have been eating, so there is no danger of disease." Chianina make the best steaks for the *Fiorentina,* the Tuscan T-bone traditionally grilled over a wood fire. The ultra-clean shop also sells fresh and salt-cured pork from the same farm, and wine and other products from Fondo Cariplo producers.

AZIENDA AGRICOLA
BELSEDERE,
DE GORI AVANZATI
MEAT, SALUMI, CHEESE

53020   Trequanda
TELEPHONE/FAX 0577 662307   OPEN 9:00-13:00, 15:00-19:00
CLOSED Never   MAIL ORDER By courier within Europe
CREDIT CARDS None   DIRECT SALE Yes   STOCKIST The farm's products are on sale in their shop in Siena at Via Camollia, 29.
ENGLISH SPOKEN A little   OTHER Several villa apartments for holiday rentals   DIRECTIONS From Trequanda go toward Belsedere and Asciano. The farm is signposted along that road. Ask for sales assistance at the villa.

This farm is nestled in the beautiful rolling hills to the west of Trequanda. It has long been noted for its fine handmade *salumi,* farm-reared meats, and pecorini. "This land has been in our family since 1200," explained Silvia De Gori. "My father-in-law decided to raise sheep and pigs thirty years ago, when most people were leaving the land to work in industry. It was a way of saving his patrimony—the buildings and the land."

She and her husband built their reputation on their genuine artisan foods. "We could never have stayed in business if our products had not been of very high quality," she continued. "The competition from industrial food companies is fierce."

The farm, which also produces grain, is certified to organic standards. Fresh pork and lamb are sold. Most lamb sold in Italy is very small and scrawny, with a different flavor than American or British lamb. Signora De Gori explained that Sardinian lambs, bred throughout Italy for milk, are small by nature, and their young are butchered before they have time to develop. Sheep bred for meat, such as Belsedere's, are larger; their lambs remain with the mothers until they are eating grass.

Belsedere makes a full range of excellent pork *salumi,* from hand-salted *prosciutto* to lean sausages, pancetta, *salame,* and *finocchiona,* the fennel-scented sausage. Due to the very small percentage of preservatives these cured meats contain, they cannot be considered organic, even if the original animals are.

VERGELLE

CRETE SENESI
CHEESE

Vergelle 53020 San Giovanni d'Asso
TELEPHONE 0577 834046, 834431   FAX 0577 834046   OPEN 8:00-20:00
CLOSED Never   CREDIT CARDS None   DIRECT SALE Yes, for whole
cheeses   ENGLISH SPOKEN A little   DIRECTIONS From the Torrenieri–
San Giovanni d'Asso road follow yellow signs up the cypress avenues to
Vergelle. The road is unpaved but good. The caseificio is in the village

This *caseificio* makes pasteurized sheep's cheeses. The beautiful area around
Pienza is famous for pecorino cheeses, and this family-run business is one of
several owned by Sardinian shepherds who came to Tuscany in the early 1960s.

The Cosseddu family makes unusual pecorini weighing about
500 grams (1 lb) flavored with herbs—mixed dried tarragon, rosemary, sage,
and juniper, blended into the milky mass before the cheeses set. Other varieties
include arugula (made with fresh leaves), hot pepper, dried porcini mushrooms, saffron, and olive. Pecorini are also preserved in jars of oil: sunflower
for the herbed and olive oil for the truffle-scented cheeses. These keep for
several months and make attractive presents.

VILLE DI CORSANO

AZIENDA AGRICOLA
S. MARGHERITA
GOAT'S CHEESE

50010 Ville di Corsano
TELEPHONE/FAX 0577 377101   OPEN 14:00-19:00   CLOSED Never
CREDIT CARDS None   DIRECT SALE Yes   ENGLISH SPOKEN Yes
DIRECTIONS Coming from Siena or Monteroni D'Arbia, go to Ville di
Corsano, through the village to the cemetery (look for group of cypresses).
The main road curves to the right, but go straight ahead. Follow until the
road turns right, but go straight ahead again. There is a signpost from
there. Follow to the end of this road, going left at the fork.

Maria De Dominicis is an active defender of Italy's artisan food makers, struggling to survive in an ever more industrialized society. She herself makes some
of Tuscany's finest goat's cheeses, from milk produced by her organically
certified herd.

"The most important thing is to enable your animals to lead
dignified lives," she asserted. "If you allow them freedom, light, and sunshine,
they almost never get sick and, by extension, neither do we."

I visited her farm (located in exquisite countryside) in late
February, when many of her 130 goats were about to give birth. Maria keeps
them in the barn at this time because of wolves and other predators who
would attack the pregnant females and newborn kids. As we talked in the

sweet-smelling barn (she described it as her *salotto*, or living room), she moved knowingly among the animals. "This one is about to give birth," she said. And, sure enough, she did—with help from Maria. "Goats are funny," she observed. "They willingly rely on humans to help them." Within minutes the baby kid was awake and mewling.

Maria started making cheese because no one wanted the goats' milk. She makes French-style cheeses that she learned to make by reading books. These fresh, white, smooth-textured *caprini* are then flavored with herbs or toasted sesame seeds, and matured in wood ash or walnut leaves. She sells them directly from the farm (a future project is to open a small organic shop there) and to some of the area's best restaurants and food shops (including La Galleria, p 202).

CHAPTER 12

Montalcino and Its Wines

*T*he medieval hill town of Montalcino merits a chapter of its own: this one *comune* has 160 registered producers of Brunello di Montalcino, one of the world's greatest wines. Montalcino is a wine lover's mecca. Many wineries are visitable; the unspoiled town has wine shops and wine bars. There are restaurants but few hotels. The steep town with its monumental 1300s fortress commands spectacular views.

Although each winery has its own distinct character—big or small, traditionalist or forward-thinking, of noble family or humble—the producers are bonded by a commitment to do justice to their famous wine. These estates are wonderful to visit. Usually a phone call in advance is all that is needed. Many offer informal tours of the cellars or vineyards. In most, wines may be tasted and bought. Many also produce fine extra-virgin olive oil.

A selection of Montalcino's resturants, wine stores, and specialty food shops is included at the end of this chapter.

The Brunello Consortium is very friendly and helpful; they have excellent maps of the region with the producers marked. They are housed in the ground floor of Montalcino's *comune* building, in the town's center.

Consorzio Del Vino Brunello Di Montalcino
Costa del Municipio, 1
53024 Montalcino Siena
0577 848246
fax 0577 849425
Open Monday-Friday 8:30-13:00, 15:00-18:00

Azienda Promozione Turistica
Costa del Municipio, 8
53024 Montalcino Siena
tel/fax 0577 849331
Open Tuesday-Sunday 10:00-13:00, 15:00-19:00

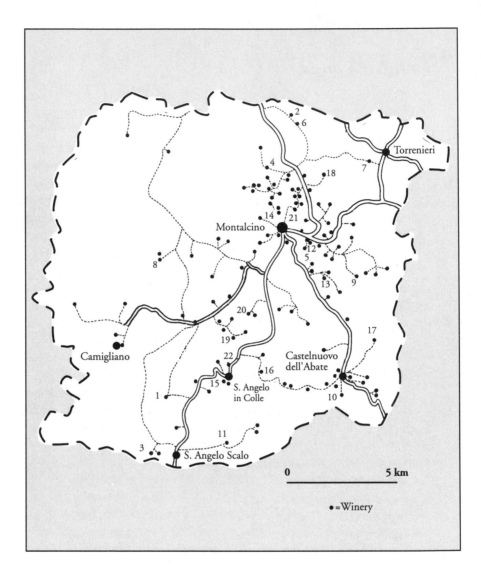

Torrenieri

Montalcino

Camigliano

Castelnuovo
dell'Abate

S. Angelo
in Colle

S. Angelo Scalo

0   5 km

•=Winery

SELECTED WINE PRODUCERS KEYED TO THE MONTALCINO MAP

1   ARGIANO
2   AZIENDA AGRICOLA ALTESINO
3   BANFI
4   BARICCI—COLOMBAIA DI MONTOSOLI
5   BIONDI-SANTI
6   CAPARZO
7   CASANOVA DI NERI
8   CASTELGIOCONDO
9   CERBAIONA
10 CIACCI PICCOLOMINI D'ARAGONA
11 COL D'ORCIA
12 CONTI COSTANTI
13 FATTORIA DEI BARBI
14 FULIGNI
15 IL POGGIONE
16 LISINI
17 MASTROJANNI
18 SIRO PACENTI
19 PIEVE DI SANTA RESTITUTA
20 POGGIO ANTICO
21 SALVIONI—LA CERBAIOLA
22 TALENTI—PODERE PIAN DI CONTE

Brunello di Montalcino DOCG

Brunello was Italy's first wine to be granted DOCG status (*Denominazione di Origine Controllata e Garantita*) in 1980, but its story began long before. During the town's siege of 1555, Montalcino's commander Marshal Montluc "reddened his face with a robust vermilion wine" in order to appear less pale and food-deprived. Brunello's birth came in the 1880s when Ferruccio Biondi Santi first made a wine from just one local grape type, Sangiovese Grosso. This fruit turns dark violet, earning it the name *brunello*. Biondi Santi was ahead of his time: nineteenth-century Tuscan wines were blends of red and white grapes, made to drink young. Biondi Santi wanted to produce a wine to age. He succeeded: in 1988 Brunello celebrated its hundredth birthday. It was toasted with a rare, still drinkable, Biondi-Santi Brunello from the vintage of 1888. Brunello is one of Italy's most prestigious wines, whose fame is linked to its longevity; it is a concentrated, complex red wine with powerful structure. At its best it is packed with fruit and has smoky or spicy flavors and balanced tannins.

What Makes Brunello So Special?

In part, the terrain: Montalcino's hills are situated in a zone with several distinct microclimates and soil compositions. Vines are planted at 300 to 500 meters on soils ranging from limestone to clay. Wines produced to the southeast are rich and robust, whereas vineyards to the northeast make more elegant wines.

Brunello's regulations allow a maximum yield per hectare of 80 quintals (8.8 tons) of Sangiovese grapes—and some producers go much lower. This means better but fewer bunches per plant, at the cost of pruning away half a vine's production.

Finally, the vinification and cellaring. Here again DOCG regulations are very strict. Brunello must be aged a minimum of four years, of which at least three and a half must be in wood casks. One additional year of aging and the wine becomes a Riserva. Traditionalists want to maintain the status quo, with the risk that much Brunello will be drunk before it is fully mature, while reformers are pushing for an "accessible" Brunello that is drinkable sooner.

Rosso di Montalcino DOC

Montalcino's second wine is considered "Brunello's younger brother" (*vino* is masculine in Italian). Rosso di Montalcino—literally Montalcino's Red—is made of the same grapes as Brunello: 100 percent Sangiovese Grosso aged for one year. Grapes may be designated for it while still on the vine, or the immature Brunello may be "declassified" to Rosso after one year in wood. In poor vintages some producers make little or no Brunello, putting all their grapes into Rosso for a quick turnover of cellar space and cash; in great years there is no obligation to produce it. A ready-to-drink, fruity red wine, Rosso di Montalcino provides wine lovers with a chance to taste some of Brunello's flavors at a third of the price.

Moscadello di Montalcino DOC

This sweet white wine is Montalcino's oldest wine, known in a different form in the Middle Ages. It is found in lightly bubbly, still or *passito* versions.

BRUNELLO: THE CONSORTIUM'S RATINGS SINCE 1970

After each vintage Brunello is given a rating from one to five stars.
1970 ***** 1971 *** 1972 * 1973 *** 1974 ** 1975 ***** 1976 * 1977 ****
1978 **** 1979 **** 1980 **** 1981 *** 1982 **** 1983 **** 1984 * 1985 *****
1986 *** 1987 *** 1988 ***** 1989 ** 1990***** 1991 **** 1992 ** 1993 ****
1994 **** 1995 ***** 1996 ***

BRUNELLO'S OWN GLASS

"A few years ago Brunello di Montalcino's consortium decided to have a
glass custom designed for its wine," explained Stefano Campatelli, its
director. "The glass often used for mature red wines was the large spherical
ballon, but it did not bring out Brunello's best."

Brunello is made for extended aging, and is characteristi-
cally high in tannins. The *ballon* shape's low, wide aperture let too many of
Brunello's *profumi* escape and accentuated the astringency of the wine's
tannins and its acidity. "Each area of the mouth responds to different taste
sensations," explained Campatelli. "Acidity is sensed by the sides of the
tongue, as are tannins, using taste buds in the sides of the mouth. So when
you drink from a glass with a very wide aperture, the wine is pushed
towards the outer edges of the mouth, heightening these acid sensations."

A group from the consortium, including Piero Talenti,
Andrea Costanti, Nuccio Turone, and Giulio Gambelli—reputed to have
the greatest palate in Tuscany—went to Austria to the crystal firm of
Riedel to develop a better form. "We brought a supply of Brunellos and
tasted them in differently shaped glasses," he continued. "A wide high
tulip shape worked well: its narrow top trapped the bouquet released when
the wine was swirled, and focused the wine's entry toward the mouth's
center, where its mellow fruit is better appreciated. Using a large glass is
a valid alternative to decanting or opening wines hours ahead."

WINERIES

ARGIANO
WINE

S. Angelo in Colle   53020   Montalcino   Siena
TELEPHONE 0577 864037   FAX 0577 864210   OPEN Visits by
appointment only   CLOSED Saturday and Sunday   DIRECT SALE No
STOCKIST Enoteca Franci in Montalcino   ENGLISH SPOKEN Yes

Argiano is a restrained, handsome 1482 castle built around three sides of a courtyard and set amid perfect vineyards and olive groves. The castle's recent history has been checkered. Rescued from bankruptcy in 1980 by a marriage into the Cinzano family, the property was taken over by Countess Noemi Marone Cinzano after her father's death in 1990.

Determined to improve the winery's 25 hectares (62 acres) of vineyards, the young countess appointed the equally young Sebastiano Rosa as manager, entrusting the winemaking to the brilliant enologist, Giacomo Tachis. "When Tachis arrived," explained Sebastiano Rosa, "we tasted everything in the cellars. He liked the wines' bouquets, but found them too aggressive. Our goal was to create modern wines—a Brunello that was drinkable sooner."

Grape yields were dramatically reduced and older vineyards replanted. Small French oak *barriques* are now used judiciously in conjunction with traditional larger casks. "Brunello's regulations stipulate three years' aging in wood," Sebastiano explained keenly as we toured the castle's underground cellars. "Tachis feels that this is too long, so we balance the older casks' neutrality with the characterful new wood of the *barriques.*"

In addition to the fine Brunello and its Riserva, Argiano produces Rosso di Montalcino and Solengo (lone wild boar in Tuscan dialect), a brand-new table wine. An unusual blend of Sangiovese, Merlot, Syrah, and Cabernet, Solengo seems bound to follow in the footsteps of Tachis's other sensational super-Tuscans: Sassicaia, Tignanello and Solaia.

AZIENDA AGRICOLA
ALTESINO
WINE

53028   Montalcino   Siena
TELEPHONE 0577 806208   FAX 0577 806131   OPEN Visits and tastings
Monday-Saturday, best by appointment; group tastings by appointment
only and with fee   CLOSED Sunday   CREDIT CARDS Visa, MC, Amex
DIRECT SALE Yes   ENGLISH SPOKEN Yes

Altesino is a sizable estate exemplifying one facet of present-day Montalcino. In 1969 it was bought by Milanese entrepreneurs who invested heavily in remodeling the existing buildings, planting vineyards, and creating a modern winery. They also invested in an image they hoped would appeal to a sophisticated international audience. A restored 1400s palazzo sits in perfectly manicured grounds with grazing thoroughbred horses. In 1982 Altesino officially became part of a conglomerate owning a restaurant chain with outlets through-out northern Italy.

A lengthy list of wines, both red and white, is produced from Altesino's own and subcontracted local vineyards. The best exposure and ter-rain are on the hillside named Montosoli; several of the company's high-end wines originate there.

BANFI
WINE, MUSEUM

Castello di Poggio alle Mura   53024   Montalcino   Siena   TELEPHONE 0577 840111   FAX 0577 840205, 840444   E-MAIL castellobanfi.com   OPEN Visits by appointment only, made at least two days ahead. Reservations made from the U.S. must be re-confirmed two days ahead.   CREDIT CARDS Visa, MC, Amex   DIRECT SALE Yes   ENGLISH SPOKEN Yes   RESERVATIONS Required for restaurant   OTHER Glass Museum

There is nowhere quite like the Banfi winery. If you want to visit an intimate, family-run *cantina*, this is not the place for you. If instead you are attracted to the grandeur of modernity, to the marriage of industry and integrity—this is it! Banfi is a giant. Literally. Its vast steel tanks and architect-designed glass struc-tures are on such a mighty scale that they make Montalcino and its personal-ized estates recede to dwarfdom. You can't help but marvel at it.

Banfi is an American creation, the brainchild of leading wine importers John and Harry Mariani. The Italian American brothers bought a feudal domain and, with the great enologist Ezio Rivella, transformed it into one of the world's most innovative wineries. If an average Montalcino winery has 2 to 12 hectares (5 to 30 acres) of vineyards growing Sangiovese, Banfi has 148 (365 acres), with another 600 (1,480 acres) producing Cabernet, Chardonnay, Sauvignon Blanc, Moscadello, and other grape varieties. Its hold-ings stretch for miles around the medieval Castello Banfi.

Banfi's wine list reads like a catalog. It includes the prestigious Brunello Riserva Poggio all'Oro, a single-vineyard *cru* aged in large *botti* in the estate's model cellars; Centine, a fresh, fruity Rosso di Montalcino; Summus, a modern-style table wine of Sangiovese, Cabernet, and Syrah aged in *barriques;* "B," a late-harvest dessert wine of Moscadello grapes; and many more. The level is consistently high.

Worth visiting are the spectacular cellars, the shop in the twelfth-century *borgo*, the restaurant and the Glass Museum—a fascinating collection from Roman times to the present. All in all, a multicultural experience.

BARICCI—AZIENDA   Montosoli   53028   Montalcino   Siena
AGRICOLA   TELEPHONE/FAX 0577 848109   OPEN Daily; appointments preferred
COLOMBAIA DI   CREDIT CARDS None   DIRECT SALE Yes   ENGLISH SPOKEN A little
MONTOSOLI
WINE   My first visit to a Montalcino wine producer was to Nello Baricci. I couldn't
have found a better place to begin. Any apprehension about the possibility of
a snobbish reception by some of the world's finest winemakers was dispelled by
Nello's lovely wife, Ada Nannetti. She was wearing an enormous straw hat and
a flowery dress and had just come in from the vineyard.

"We were checking the vines for damage," she said, a little out
of breath, "after last night's hailstorm." Nello himself appeared, mopping his
brow from the heat. "We have always worked the land," he explained simply,
"but there's no beating the weather."

Until the mid-1950s Nello was a landless *contadino*, or peasant,
working the farm of a local landowner. When the *mezzadria*, or sharecropping,
system ended, he was given the opportunity to buy a plot. "It was a big change
for us," said Nello. "But at that time there were sponsored mortgages for people
in our situation." They bought a 15-hectare (37 acre) farm on the hillside of
Montosoli, now a choice wine-growing zone. Then it comprised fields of mixed
crops, a few animals, and some vines. "We went along that way until 1967,
when an agrarian reformer, Dr. Ciatti, taught us how to prune the vines
to make better wine." Nello smiled as he thought back. "The rest is history."

In 1967 Nello was one of eighteen founding members of the
Brunello Consortium, and in 1971 he bottled his first Brunello. His Brunello
and Rosso di Montalcino have gained high praise from wine critics; there is
never enough to go around. "We now have three hectares registered to
Brunello. Even if I wanted to I couldn't increase my plantings, as the land permitted to produce Brunello is strictly limited. I could only do it by buying out
someone else's rights."

BIONDI-SANTI   Il Greppo   53024   Montalcino   Siena
WINE   TELEPHONE 0577 848087   FAX 0577 849396   OPEN 9:00-11:00, 15:00-
17:00 appointment preferred; groups pay a limited fee for tastings
CLOSED Saturday and Sunday   CREDIT CARDS Visa, Amex
DIRECT SALE Yes, for available vintages going back to 1891
ENGLISH SPOKEN Yes

The approach to Il Greppo, the Biondi Santi estate, is along an extended
avenue of cathedral-high centennial cypresses. Here even the notion of time
has shifted and a wine's life is conceived in decades, if not centuries. The stately
vine-covered villa is a house of distinguished style, but it is comfortable and
accessible, just like its owner, Franco Biondi Santi, a tall, elegant man now in
his seventies.

"To make a really long-living wine you must have perfect grapes," he asserted. "You must always keep the future life of your wine in mind, and not submit the grapes to anything that could adversely affect the wine in years to come." Franco Biondi Santi represents the fifth generation of professional winemakers in a family credited with Brunello's birth. Clemente Santi won prizes with a Vino Rosso Scelto (Brunello) of the 1865 vintage. His grandson Ferruccio Biondi Santi, an enologist, identified a local clone of Sangiovese, named it Sangiovese Grosso, and by 1890 had grafted it throughout his vineyards. Its wine was called Brunello. Franco's father, Tancredi Biondi Santi, established a methodology for producing Brunello and began making the wine known in Italy and abroad.

By harvest time each stalk in the 20 hectares (49 acres) of vineyard is left bearing just one perfect bunch of grapes. The best of these go for Brunello, the second-best for Rosso. "Our grapes are also selected by age," Franco Biondi Santi explained. "The Brunello Riserva is produced from vines over twenty-five years old. The normal Brunello uses plants of ten to twenty-five years, while the white label Rosso is made from vines under ten years of age. The Rosso di Montalcino's red label signifies a year in which no Brunello has been produced."

Despite the modern technology in the historic cellars, each stage of the winemaking process is performed with personal attention. Bottles are corked, labeled, and numbered by hand. If over time (meaning decades) a customer finds the level in a well-cellared Brunello has dropped, Biondi Santi will recork it, topping it up with wine of the same vintage.

The Biondi-Santi Brunellos have always been expensive symbols of prestige, collector's items representing the absolute guarantees of tradition and quality. Burton Anderson, in the introduction to his 1988 book on Biondi-Santi, describes his first tasting, in 1971, of the 1964 Riserva:

"It was young and aggressive, robust in constitution and rich in color, with the extract and tannins that would maintain it proudly for decades. But already it had those niceties of bouquet, those sensations of flavor, those intricate traits revealing what the experts refer to as race or breed which even an inspired amateur might recognize though perhaps not venture to explain. After years of tasting through the region's wines . . . this was a revelation. I wrote in my notes: 'At last, a Tuscan *grand cru!*'"

CAPARZO   Torrenieri   53028   Montalcino   Siena
WINE   TELEPHONE 0577 848390, 847166   FAX 0577 849377   OPEN 9:00–
                     12:00, 14:30–18:00 for visits and tastings; groups by appointment only
                     CLOSED Saturday and Sunday   CREDIT CARDS Visa, MC, Amex
                     DIRECT SALE Yes   ENGLISH SPOKEN No

Giulio Consonno was one of the businessmen who bought Altesino and, in
1970, Tenuta Caparzo, then a run-down country house with a few barns and
vineyards. By 1981 the estate had grown to 65 hectares (160 acres), of which 32
(79 acres) were vineyards. The choice 7-hectare (17-acre) vineyard, La Caduta,
was added in 1991. The Milanese Nuccio Turone now runs the successful business in an atmosphere of innovation and experimentation. With winemaker
Vittorio Fiore as consultant, vineyards were planted, including Montalcino's
first Cabernet Sauvignon, and a sophisticated cellar established.

"We were the first in Montalcino to use *barriques*," recalled
Turone, "for our Sangiovese/Cabernet blend, Ca' del Pazzo, presented in 1982.
And we were criticized for it." But Turone and Fiore were attuned to the
demands of a changing international wine market. Their white wine, Le
Grance, is considered one of Tuscany's most convincing barrel-aged Chardon-
nays. Also containing small amounts of Traminer and Sauvignon grapes,
Le Grance was Caparzo's answer to the need for a white wine to be aged.

Their single-vineyard Brunello *cru*, La Casa, matures in barrels
of differing sizes, from small *barriques* to large Slavonian casks. Three years is
too long for the wine to remain in small casks, Turone explained. The fine La
Caduta, of Sangiovese Grosso grapes aged for one year, is sold as a Rosso
di Montalcino.

CASANOVA DI NERI   Torrenieri   53028   Montalcino   Siena
WINE   TELEPHONE 0577 834029   FAX 0577 834455   OPEN 8.00–12.30,
                       14.30–19.30; cellar visits and tastings by appointment only
                       CLOSED Sunday   CREDIT CARDS None   DIRECT SALE Yes
                       ENGLISH SPOKEN Yes

Giacomo Neri belongs to the new generation of Brunello winemakers. He
learned about winemaking from his father, Giovanni, who bought his first
Montalcino vineyards in 1971. "My father's intention here was always to make
high-quality wines." Within a few years Giovanni Neri added more vineyards
in strategic positions, for a current total of 20 hectares (49 acres). Ever-better
clones of the local Sangiovese grape were developed.

"He spent years researching and experimenting with smaller,
more intensely flavored fruit," continued Giacomo, a strapping young man
with a relaxed, friendly manner. "The individual grapes had to be widely
spaced within the bunch to avoid mildew." By the mideighties this selection
process and the modernized cellars were paying off.

"After tasting many great foreign wines," he said, "we were convinced that without compromising Brunello's traditional qualities, it could become more approachable: a more elegant wine with softer tannins and respect for its fruit. A wine to drink now that would last."

When Giovanni died in 1991, Giacomo—by now a winemaker in his own right—took over the estate. In addition to the Brunello and Rosso di Montalcino, in great years Neri produces a rich, concentrated Riserva— Cerretalto, a single-vineyard *cru*. He also makes a delicious, atypical, olive oil from *olivastra* olives.

CASTELGIOCONDO Castelgiocondo 53024 Montalcino Siena
WINE TELEPHONE 0577 848492 FAX 0577 849138 OPEN Visits and tastings only for groups of four to six by appointment only CLOSED Saturday and Sunday CREDIT CARDS None DIRECT SALE Yes, subject to availability ENGLISH SPOKEN No OTHER For larger groups or other enquiries call Frescobaldi's head office in Firenze: 055 2381400

Castelgiocondo is the Marchesi de' Frescobaldi's holding in Montalcino (see p 107), and one of the area's largest, with over 200 hectares (494 acres) of vineyards, of which 140 (345) are registered to Brunello. Set in the expansive countryside south of Montalcino, the austere but impeccably run estate is deservedly gaining recognition after a period of change and renovation.

"Castelgiocondo is part of the Frescobaldi group, but is run autonomously," the estate's manager, Gilberto Cosci, explained. A large modern *cantina*, highly efficient but without much character, has been built. New vineyards—including some with higher density planting—have been created with the winemaker Niccolò D'Afflitto.

The estate's wines include a classic-style Brunello, with an excellent, concentrated Riserva in great years, which may be aged briefly in *barriques*. Unusually, the Rosso di Montalcino Campo ai Sassi is a single-vineyard wine. Newer additions to the list are Lamaione, of pure Merlot, and the white Vergena, of pure Sauvignon, which also spends some time in the small oak barrels. A recent joint venture sees Robert Mondavi as partner.

Castelgiocondo also produces olive oil. During the season hand-picked olives are trucked every two to three days in special aerated cages to the Frescobaldi's in-house stainless-steel mill near Firenze (see Laudemio p 116).

CERBAIONA 53024 Montalcino Siena
WINE TELEPHONE/FAX 0577 848660 OPEN Visits by appointment preferred; tastings only when owners present CREDIT CARDS None DIRECT SALE Yes, subject to availability ENGLISH SPOKEN Yes

"This has always been a place for friends," the hospitable Diego Molinari said as he showed me Cerbaiona's tiny *cantine*. "But right now I wish I had a crystal ball to see into the future. We are getting older and finding it harder to manage all the work."

Cerbaiona is in one of Montalcino's most stunning positions, with a spectacular panorama of the Crete Senesi. The beautiful villa and its striking *giardino all'Italiana* have an intimacy the larger estates lack. "When we bought the place," Molinari explained, "an old *contadino* still lived here, in the almost slavelike conditions imposed by the sharecropping system." Diego and Nora Molinari came from Rome, where he had been a senior pilot for Alitalia. They planted new vineyards, and in no time were winning top marks with their great Brunellos.

"I was never that interested in the Rosso di Montalcino," Molinari confided. "So recently I decided to try an experiment." He planted what he described as "a bit of salt and pepper" to add to the Sangiovese: Cabernet, Merlot, Syrah, Aleatico. "For me Sangiovese alone is no longer mysterious. I like the idea of creating a new wine. It's fun. It will be something to talk to our friends about."

CIACCI PICCOLOMINI D'ARAGONA **WINE**	Via Borgo di Mezzo, 62 Castelnuovo dell'Abate 53020 Montalcino Siena TELEPHONE 0577 835616 FAX 0577 835785 OPEN 9:00-12:00, 15:00-19:00; *cantina* visits and tastings by appointment only CLOSED Saturday and Sunday CREDIT CARDS None DIRECT SALE Yes, from the side of the palazzo, appointments preferred ENGLISH SPOKEN Yes

"Come down to the *cantina* and taste the wines directly from the barrel. That's the best way. A bottle doesn't necessarily need to be opened in a room with a view," said Roberto Cipresso, the genial young winemaker of Tenuta Ciacci Piccolomini d'Aragona. The aging cellars turned out to be wonderfully atmospheric, dug deep below medieval Castelnuovo. The palazzo, formerly a bishop's seat, dates back to the 1500s, but the cellars are older.

Once the property of the Countess Elda Ciacci Piccolomini, the palace and its holdings were bequeathed in 1985 to the estate's then manager Giuseppe Bianchini. Under the management of Bianchini and Cipresso, the domain has earned a reputation as one of Montalcino's best.

We tasted the young 1995 wine, still some years away from being released. Cipresso declared enthusiastically, "1995 has the potential to become one of the century's greatest vintages for Brunello. The wines will be big but elegant, with great structure and complexity. A balanced, opulent wine for the year 2000."

Many of the estate's 20 hectares (49 acres) of vineyards are planted to Sangiovese Grosso, the grape variety of Brunello and Rosso di Montalcino. Ten more have been recently planted with Sangiovese, Merlot,

Cabernet Sauvignon, and Syrah. Cipresso is fascinated by new genetic grape varieties and is researching the best clones of Sangiovese.

In addition to its Brunellos and Rosso, the farm produces a super-Tuscan table wine with the provocative name of Ateo—or atheist— of Cabernet and Sangiovese grapes, with added Merlot and Syrah. Why this name? Roberto Cipresso smiled before answering. "Ateo came from a desire to go against the current. I don't believe in the dogma or god of Brunello— I believe in our Italian grape varieties, but the challenge to do something new with them is exciting."

COL D'ORCIA S. Angelo Scalo   S. Angelo in Colle   53020   Montalcino   Siena
WINE TELEPHONE 0577 808001   FAX 0577 864018   OPEN Monday-Saturday 8:30-12:30, 14:30-19:00, Sunday 8:30-12:30; limited tastings possible in estate shop; guided tastings, cellar visits, and large groups by appointment only   CREDIT CARDS Visa, MC   DIRECT SALE Yes, of wines and oil   ENGLISH SPOKEN Yes

Count Francesco Marone Cinzano's estate, Col d'Orcia, is one of Montalcino's largest. It includes 79 hectares (195 acres) of Sangiovese Grosso grapes for Brunello, and a further 21 (51.8 acres) of other varieties. Its attractive villa and shipshape modern *cantine* are set in landscaped gardens.

The estate's star wine is Poggio al Vento, a Brunello Riserva of selected grapes from a single vineyard; complex and elegantly structured, it is made only in exceptional years. Olmaia, a Cabernet Sauvignon super-Tuscan, is aged for eighteen months in French *barriques*. Lovers of meditation wines will appreciate Pascena, a late-harvest sweet Moscadello di Montalcino wine. "To make this wine the white Muscat grapes are left to dry on the plant until mid-October," explained Giuliano Dragoni, the estate's agronomist. A slow fermentation in *barriques* is followed by a year in wood.

Col d'Orcia participates in viticultural experiments with the University of Firenze. "The program covers all aspects of the winemaking process," explained Dr. Dragoni. "A key factor in vine growing is the vigor of the plant." Grapevines should not be too vigorous, or the plant's energy is spent making foliage rather than in enriching the fruit. "Planting in stony, dry soil is one way of reducing its vigor; another is to grow grass between the rows, providing competition for the vines."

Some techniques being experimented with are common organic practices. "We have borrowed many of their ideas to improve production— using fewer chemical fertilizers or pesticides definitely helps."

CONTI COSTANTI
WINE

Colle al Matrichese   53024   Montalcino   Siena
TELEPHONE 0577 848195   FAX 0577 849349   OPEN Visits and tastings
by appointment only; groups charged a per-glass fee for tastings
CLOSED Saturday and Sunday   CREDIT CARDS None
DIRECT SALE Yes, subject to availability   ENGLISH SPOKEN A little

The Costantis, one of Montalcino's oldest families, are based in Colle al
Matrichese, a stately villa with box-hedged gardens. "First accounts of winemak-
ing in my family are from 1550, although no one did it professionally until this
century," said Andrea Costanti, who runs the estate. "In 1870 Count Tito
Costanti presented two wines named Brunello at an exhibition in Siena. One
was five years old, and the other two, just like present-day Brunello and Rosso."
Andrea Costanti, who is the current president of the Consorzio del Brunello di
Montalcino, is an articulate member of the new generation of growers.

"What I find interesting about Brunello," continued Costanti,
"is that it constituted a revolution in winemaking terms. Never before in Italy
had a single grape variety been used to produce a wine of prestige. Tito
Costanti's generation had traveled and seen the wines of Bordeaux. They too
wanted to produce a red wine that could age."

Andrea Costanti trained as a geologist but took over the estate
in 1983. "I took the plunge, learning as I went along." He was advised by winemaker Vittorio Fiore, but always took an active part in the decision making:
"After all, my name is on the bottles."

"All three of my wines are made from Sangiovese," he asserted.
"The Brunello matures for three years in Slavonian oak. It used to be a wine for
long aging, but it is becoming more immediate. The Rosso is an easier wine:
with ten months in French *barriques*, it's about youth and wood and is drinkable right away." The third wine, Vermiglio, is between the two: made of
Sangiovese, it spends two years in large oak barrels and six months in *barriques*.
Two fine Brunello Grappas and a decisive, fresh-tasting extra-virgin olive oil are
also made. Andrea Costanti is a generous, affable young man who believes that
meeting the people "behind" the wine is important. "You get right to the person," he declared. "And they to you. After all, drinking a glass of wine together
is very nice."

FATTORIA DEI BARBI
WINE, CHEESE, SALUMI

Fattoria dei Barbi e del Casato   53024   Montalcino   Siena
TELEPHONE 0577 848277   FAX 0577 849356   OPEN Monday-Friday
9:00-13:00, 15:00-18:00; Saturday-Sunday 14:30-17:30; guided tastings and
groups by appointment only   CREDIT CARDS Visa, MC, Amex
DIRECT SALE Yes   ENGLISH SPOKEN Yes   FEATURES Restaurant
OTHER Vacation apartments available, call 0577 849421

A tour of the Fattoria dei Barbi's cellars is a multimedia experience. The underground labyrinth illustrates various stages of the winemaking process, as well as

the history of the Colombini Cinelli family and their wines. Amid the barrels are paintings, murals, family trees, soil samples, maps, fables, and even a few videos. It has all been done with a kind of fanciful pedagogy—like a teacher thinking up amusing ways to interest and educate a class of children. I suspect a lot of this is Donatella Colombini's idea—she has a charming air of whimsy about her. The acting secretary of the Movement for Wine Tourism, she has long been a keen promoter of Italian wines.

The Colombini family traces itself back to 1200 and beyond, punctuating its history with an eccentric cast of characters. Of these, the brigand Bruscone and the blessed Beato Giovanni have had wines named after them. Of the classic Montalcino wines, the Fattoria's stars are the *cru* Brunello di Montalcino Vigna del Fiore Riserva, made of selected grapes from one vineyard, and the Brunello Riserva, made only in great years. These elegant, structured wines have benefited from the recent collaboration with the enologist Luigi Casagrande. The estate has 42 hectares (103 acres) given over to Sangiovese Grosso.

Fattoria dei Barbi, headed by Donatella's mother, Francesca Colombini Cinelli, hosts a restaurant specializing in local cuisine, and sponsors an annual literary prize. The estate is also noted for its pecorino cheeses and the excellent *salumi* it produces from farm-raised pigs, both of which can also be purchased here.

HOW TO DRINK BRUNELLO

Brunello di Montalcino is matured for four to five years before being sold, but additional aging should take place in a horizontal position in a cool dark cellar, where it may remain for years. If you intend to drink an older vintage soon after buying, it is best to let it settle for a few days, ideally in a horizontal position. The wine should be drunk at 18°-20°C /64°-68°F. Open the bottle at least one hour before drinking. Or slowly decant the wine, thereby also eliminating any sediment deposited during its aging. Any remaining wine will keep for around twenty-four hours in a corked bottle unless rubber vacuum corks are used. Both Brunello and Rosso di Montalcino are full-flavored red wines that go best with red meats, game, and cheese. Brunello also makes a fine meditation wine for sipping slowly after dinner.

FULIGNI
WINE

Via S. Saloni, 33   53024   Montalcino   Siena
TELEPHONE/FAX 0577 848039   OPEN Visits and sales by appointment
only   CREDIT CARDS None   DIRECT SALE Yes, by appointment sales
possible from farm or villa   ENGLISH SPOKEN Yes

"Our father came here from Verona in 1925 with the Grand Duke of Tuscany, when the *mezzadria* system was still in operation. We have stuck to the traditional pairing of grapes and olives. Since his death, all six of us brothers and sisters have run the estate," said Signorina Maria Flora Fuligni.

She and her sister Matilde, both retired teachers, were showing me their vineyards. Like colorful Frank Capra characters, the two ladies carried on a spirited discussion about old times and new, stopping here and there to point out features in their beloved landscape. "Our land is very stony. But the earth is rich," explained Maria Flora. "They say that olives born on rocky soil make the best oil," interjected Matilde. "Before 1985, before the terrible winter that killed almost all our great old olive trees," continued Maria Flora, "we picked the olives using a tall ladder with thirty-two rungs. Some of those trees were two hundred years old. It was heartbreaking when they died."

They cut their trees down to the ground and waited for them to regenerate. They are now producing oil again. Maria Flora is justly proud. "I am not a big wine drinker, but I love our oil. I use it every day. We particularly like it for *bruschetta*, drizzled onto toasted unsalted bread." Their extra-virgin olive oil is milled locally in the La Spiga *frantoio* (see p 305).

The Fulignis' atmospheric wine cellar is under their pleasantly crumbling 1400s palazzo in town. Alongside the large oval *botti* containing the estate's admired Brunello and its Riserva are some of the new *barriques* they use for aging their Rosso di Montalcino, Ginestreto. "This comes from a very arid, rocky vineyard of the same name. Leopardi called *ginestra* (broom) "the flower of the desert," added Maria Flora. "And we liked the name."

IL POGGIONE
WINE

S. Angelo in Colle   53020   Montalcino   Siena
TELEPHONE 0577 864029   FAX 0577 864165   OPEN Cellar visits and
tastings by appointment only   CREDIT CARDS None   DIRECT SALE Yes,
from the *cantina*   ENGLISH SPOKEN Yes

The Franceschi family's Il Poggione is inextricably bound to Pierliugi Talenti (p 303). Since its creation in 1959, Talenti has managed the estate, its acclaimed wines, and their policy of reasonable pricing. In recent years he has worked with Fabrizio Bindocci, director of the estate's 90 hectares (222 acres) of vineyards.

"Although Il Poggione's Brunellos will age well, they are made to be drunk now, rather than to be kept as collector's items," explained Bindocci. Talenti believes that *barriques*, the small French oak casks used for many modern wines, are not for Montalcino's classic reds. "When you drink

Montalcino's wines you should taste the fruit of the Sangiovese, not the wood," he asserted. "For me, too much wood is a defect. Great red wines are made on the vine." Grape yield is reduced by pruning, and clones of Sangiovese Grosso are selected in an ongoing search for better quality.

The estate was one of the first to reintroduce Moscadello di Montalcino, a slightly bubbly sweet amber wine with origins in the medieval Moscadelletto. "I was fascinated by Montalcino's oldest wine," Talenti recalled. "I sought out old vines of Moscato di Canelli for it, which is more aromatic than the Moscato di Montalcino." It should be drunk soon after being bought.

Il Poggione makes a fine Vin Santo of combined Malvasia and Trebbiano grapes. It also has its own *frantoio*, or olive mill. The estate's olives are pounded by steel hammers before being cold-pressed in a more traditional way.

LISINI
WINE

Fattoria di S. Angelo in Colle   S. Angelo in Colle   53020
Montalcino   Siena
TELEPHONE 0577 864040   FAX 0577 864219   OPEN *Cantina* visits by appointment only (no tastings)   CLOSED Saturday and Sunday
CREDIT CARDS None   DIRECT SALE Yes, if available
ENGLISH SPOKEN Yes

Set in untamed countryside on the scenic unpaved road between S. Angelo in Colle and Castelnuovo dell'Abate, the Lisini estate is among Montalcino's oldest. Farm buildings include a tower dated 1300 and an arched brick *loggia* in the Sienese style. The family's 11 hectares (27 acres) of vineyard include some of Montalcino's finest terrain.

"Since great wine is made with great grapes," explained Lorenzo Lisini Baldi, "we prune and select them as they grow and harvest only the finest." Each vineyard and type of grape is vinified separately. The Brunello/Rosso division is decided in the cellar, once the grapes have been made into wine. This allows for a lot of flexibility: in a lesser year they may make no Brunello (as in 1992) and come out with only the Rosso. All the wines are matured in different-sized chestnut and oak casks, but not in the smaller French oak *barriques*.

"Our wines are very *fruttato*, so we really have had no need of *barriques*, which might overemphasize their qualities," Lorenzo Lisini added. Lisini's excellent Brunello Riserva, made only in exceptional years, is called Ugolaia, after its vineyard. Lisini also produces a decisively fragrant olive oil, extracted at Montalcino's Frantoio La Spiga (see p 305).

MASTROJANNI Poderi Loreto e S. Pio   Castelnuovo dell'Abate   53024
WINE   Montalcino   Siena
                 TELEPHONE 0577 835681   FAX 0577 835505   OPEN *Cantina* visits
                 and tastings by appointment only   CREDIT CARDS None
                 DIRECT SALE Yes, if available   ENGLISH SPOKEN A little

The Mastrojanni estate is located in beautiful countryside. A dirt road climbs
up from Castelnuovo to the crest of the hill, revealing sweeping views of Monte
Amiata and its valleys. The farm was bought in 1974 by a Roman lawyer for his
son, and for years its 18 hectares (44 acres) of vineyards produced good but not
exceptional wines. In 1992 winemaker Maurizio Castelli was brought in to
work with Andrea Machetti, the young expert running the estate; recent wines
have been very well received.

In addition to the "regular" and reserve Brunellos, Mastrojanni
produces an award-winning Brunello *cru*, in which only small perfect grapes
from a vineyard named *schiena d'asino* (the shape of a donkey's back) are used.
Rosso di Montalcino and San Pio, a super-Tuscan table wine of 75 percent
Sangiovese and 25 percent Cabernet Sauvignon grapes, complete the estate's list
of reds.

"Rather than make a Vin Santo," Machetti went on, "we liked
the challenge of a *passito*." This is an intense dessert wine made from sun-dried
grapes. Golden in color and highly perfumed, Mastrojanni's is a blend of
Malvasia, Moscato, Riesling, Chardonnay, and Candia grapes. The winery's
aromatic Brunello grappas are made from very lightly pressed grapes, the
amber grappa spending three years in wood.

SIOR PACENTI Pelagrilli   53024   Montalcino   Siena
WINE   TELEPHONE/FAX 0577 848662   OPEN *Cantina* visits and tastings by
                  appointment only   CREDIT CARDS None   DIRECT SALE Yes, for
                  small amounts   ENGLISH SPOKEN A little

"I believe in the rapport between a wine's drinker and its producer," asserted
Giancarlo Pacenti, the talented young man now at the helm of this winery.
"That's why we are happy to receive visitors when we can. It breaks down the
barriers and helps people understand what wine really is."

A committed campaigner for progressive reforms in the often
traditionalist seas of Montalcino, Pacenti, with other young producers, is trying
to bring a change to Brunello's strictly prescribed DOCG code. "We feel that individual producers should be allowed a bit more leeway in deciding how to age
their Brunellos," Pacenti stated. "To many of us three years in wood seems too
long—two years in wood followed by two in the bottle would be better."

Like many of his contemporaries, Giancarlo Pacenti has traveled
abroad and become familiar with new trends and methods in winemaking.
"We would like to produce wines that are approachable and drinkable when

they go onto the market. We also want them to age well, but one should not cancel out the other. There seems no sense in selling a Brunello to a restaurant and saying: this wine is all right now but will be better in five years' time."

The rules about aging the Rosso di Montalcino are more elastic. "I am free to experiment, and have had great results using *barriques* for my Rosso," he added. His Rosso, like the Brunello, is a blend of selected Sangiovese Grosso grapes from the estate's two vineyards. The northern exposure gives the wines elegance and finesse. The southern is less refined, but adds tannins and structure. Pacenti feels optimistic about the future. "The *consorzio* is functioning well. Big and little producers are working together for change. It's an exciting time."

PIEVE DI SANTA RESTITUTA WINE	Chiesa di Santa Restituta 53024 Montalcino Siena TELEPHONE 0577 848610 FAX 0577 849309 OPEN Not open to the public DIRECT SALE No STOCKIST *Enoteche* Fortezza and Franci in Montalcino ENGLISH SPOKEN Yes

Although this lovely estate is not open to visits from the public, its recent history is having a significant impact on Montalcino, and I include it for those interested in what lies behind its fine wines.

In 1972 Roberto Bellini bought the land from the adjacent church of Santa Restituta, transforming its 18 hectares (44 acres) from the mixed-crop system into top-quality vineyards. But Bellini did more than simply modernize: his passion for wine created a cultural environment for its making, as his poetic underground cellar-stairway will attest. Then, in 1994, he sold it.

Its new owner-partner, Angelo Gaja, is one of Italy's most brilliant wine producers, a legendary figure in Piemonte thanks to what Robert Parker has described as his "fanatical commitment to excellence." That he should be spreading his interests to Montalcino has caused a stir in winemaking circles.

Fabrizio Moltard, the estate's young new manager, explained the direction it was taking. "Clearly, Angelo Gaja shares Bellini's ideals of quality," he affirmed. "He wanted to study Tuscan methods before making any radical changes, so things are evolving naturally." There will be no Brunello Riservas, as three years in wood are felt to be too long. But in good years two Brunellos will be produced, matured partly in small oak casks: Sugarille, a single-vineyard *cru*, and Rennina, of grapes from three plots.

"We don't think of *barriques* as a means of imparting a vanilla flavor to wine," stated Moltard, "but to help it grow: increasing its range of aromas and perfumes, and stabilizing its color. There is no mystery about this: you must respect tradition, but not become its prisoner." The *simpatico* Moltard concluded, "After all, successful innovation in time becomes tradition."

And other wines? "Brunello is Sangiovese's maximum expression, so there seems no point in producing a Rosso di Montalcino," he explained. "Our new 'table wine,' Promise, of 90 percent Sangiovese and 10 percent Cabernet Sauvignon will give us the flexibility to absorb more Sangiovese in less good Brunello vintages."

POGGIO ANTICO
WINE

Poggio Antico   53024   Montalcino   Siena
TELEPHONE/FAX 0577 848044   OPEN Shop: 8:00-20:00 daily; *cantina* visits: Monday-Friday 9:00-20:00, appointment preferred; tastings only for groups of 10 or more, with nominal fees   CLOSED Shop: never; *cantina:* Saturday and Sunday   CREDIT CARDS None   DIRECT SALE Yes   ENGLISH SPOKEN Yes   OTHER For Poggio Antico's restaurant, see p xxx

Paola Gloder's office is right in the heart of this estate: we talked against a background of soft clinking from the bottling line. This attractive, energetic young woman is herself the heart of Fattoria Poggio Antico, one of the most dynamic of Montalcino's "younger" wineries.

When her father, a Milanese stockbroker, bought the estate in 1984 Paola was a student in her twenties. He offered her the chance to run it. She was amazed: "He said, 'You are very young. You are a woman. You know no one in Montalcino. But it would be all yours for the making.' I thought it over. It meant giving up my whole life in Milan. But I loved this place, and hoped I could turn it into something great. I accepted."

She had everything to learn, but threw herself into it, winning the respect of the locals with her determination and hard work. The *fattoria* was overhauled, new *cantine* were built, and the restaurant refurbished (see p 307). Everything was created with style, from the handsome wine labels to the "library" of old vintages in the immaculate cellars. Massimo Albanese, formerly a wine consultant to the consortium of Brunello, remained as winemaker. Together they created some of Montalcino's better wines, which Paola personally sold around the world.

Poggio Antico's Brunellos are characterized by an elegance imparted by the vineyards' high position, at 450 to 520 meters. With 20 hectares (49 acres) given over to Sangiovese, and 9 (22) more recently planted, the *fattoria* concentrates on Montalcino's traditional wines, giving them a modern character. Alongside the estate's Brunello, Riserva, and Rosso di Montalcino is its "table wine," Altero, of Sangiovese Grosso grapes; they deserve their international following.

SALVIONI	Piazza Cavour, 19 53024 Montalcino Siena
LA CERBAIOLA	TELEPHONE/FAX 0577 848499 OPEN Visits by appointment only
WINE	CLOSED Saturday and Sunday CREDIT CARDS None
	DIRECT SALE Yes, subject to availability ENGLISH SPOKEN A little

Giulio and Mirella Salvioni make celebrated Brunellos. Yet they started making wine as a hobby, in their spare time. The land, which they inherited, is fortuitously positioned at 420 meters with southeasterly exposure, conferring perfect aromas and elegance to their Sangiovese-based wines. Luckily their very small vineyard is being expanded, so their winemaking capacity will double.

"If we have obtained top results," asserted the loquacious Giulio Salvioni, "it is because we believe in a drastic selection of the grapes when they are still growing on the vine." During July the Salvionis work with their enologist Attilio Pagli to carry out a "green harvest," leaving only two bunches per plant, one big and one smaller. At the beginning of September the vines are cleared of lower leaves, giving the grapes a maximum exposure to sun and air. Only the healthiest bunches are left, in readiness for the harvest. Two *vendemmie* (harvests), are carried out: for Brunello all the smallest bunches, plus the top *orecchiette* (literally ears) on the bigger bunches are picked. The remaining bigger bunches are then gathered for making Rosso di Montalcino.

"If we have done our job correctly, the smaller grapes are more mature and a better color than the larger ones," Salvioni explained. "In fact they may contain a half degree more alcohol." From then on the vinification process is identical for the two batches.

Salvioni also makes a limited amount of extra-virgin olive oil from trees he has planted, milled in the nearby *frantoio* La Spiga (p 305).

TALENTI—PODERE	S. Angelo in Colle 53020 Montalcino Siena
PIAN DI CONTE	TELEPHONE 0577 864004 FAX 0577 864043 OPEN Visits and tastings
WINE	by appointment only CREDIT CARDS None DIRECT SALE Yes
	ENGLISH SPOKEN A little

For over fifty years Pierluigi Talenti was Il Poggione's guiding light (p 298). He still is, but in 1980 its owners gave him a farm at Pian di Conte as a present. He has since enlarged it to 11 hectares (27 acres) of vineyards and won high acclaim for his classic Brunellos.

Pian di Conte is a very pretty place, with its handsome round tower and cluster of cypresses. It is a fittingly dignified seat for one of modern Montalcino's founding fathers. "I began to learn about wine as a boy," explained the elderly but sprightly Talenti. "My father ran a restaurant in Romagna, and occasionally brought me to Tuscany when he chose his wines."

Blessed with a perfect palate, the lively eyed Talenti is a charter member of the Brunello Consortium and is still one of its main tasters. He is critical of wineries that, in order to win top ratings from wine critics, produce "special" barrels of exceptional wine only for wine fairs or tasters' samples. "Only a very scrupulous critic who double-checks by anonymously buying a bottle and tasting it can spot the difference, if there is one," Talenti concluded, shaking his head in disapproval.

"Now that I am of a certain age I have to watch my health," he admitted. "But I am very excited about my new super-Tuscan wine Talenti, a blend of Sangiovese, Canaiolo, and Syrah." His extra-virgin olive oil, made exclusively from Corregiolo olives, has a sweet, somewhat almondy flavor. Extracted in Il Poggione's in-house olive press, the oil drips simply through a cotton filter before being bottled.

RESTAURANTS, WINE STORES, AND SPECIALTY FOOD SHOPS

CAFFÈ 1888
FIASCHETTERIA
ITALIANA
CAFÉ, WINE BAR

Piazza del Popolo, 6   53024   Montalcino   Siena
TELEPHONE 0577 849043   FAX 0577 847137   OPEN 7:30-24:00
CLOSED Thursday in winter; February   CREDIT CARDS Visa, MC, Amex
ENGLISH SPOKEN No   Directions In the town center, by the *comune*

"This is one of only five *fiaschetterie* left in Italy with original nineteenth-century decor," Gianfranco Tognazzi told me proudly. It is a gem: red velvet banquettes, marble tables, Thonet chairs, and mirrored walls set the mood in Montalcino's favorite café. In warm weather tables spill out into the piazza, in the shadow of the historic commune building. It is the place for a morning cappuccino and *brioche* (croissant), or an *aperitivo* any time of the day.

Being Montalcino, it features wines. (It was orginally opened by Tancredi Biondi Santi). Many Brunellos are sold by the glass, and the back room is like a wine bar, with snacks to accompany a bottle of the town's historic wine.

APICOLTURA
FRANCI E TASSI
HONEY

Capanna   53024   Montalcino   Siena
TELEPHONE 0577 848546, 848205   OPEN 9:00-13:00, 15:00-20:00
CLOSED Wednesday afternoon in winter   CREDIT CARDS None
DIRECT SALE Yes   STOCKIST Franci's shop faces the fortress
ENGLISH SPOKEN No   DIRECTIONS From Montalcino, go toward Torrenieri. About 500 meters after the Siena fork, turn left at the big curve. There is a sign. Follow the central dirt track for 100 meters to the warehouse shop.

"I am eighty-six and a half years old," Guido Franci told me proudly. "I have been a beekeeper for sixty-one years." A small, wiry man with lively eyes, Franci is the "grandfather" of Tuscan apiculture. "When I started the country-side was full of wildflowers; there were no pesticides, so the bees were never sick. But working for a *padrone*, we couldn't travel much." By the 1940s he had his own business and was practicing "nomadic" beekeeping. "You bring the hives to each type of flower as it blooms. When those flowers finish, you remove the honey and go elsewhere."

Franci, with his son-in-law Tassi, sells local and non-Tuscan honeys like Sicilian orange blossom. *Sulla,* made from a crimson clover found in southern Tuscany, is a delicately flavored sweet honey with a whiff of wheat fields; eucalyptus has a deeper character and a lingering aftertaste. Other single-flower honeys are chestnut, acacia, clover, heather, and *marruca.*

Sadly, Franci's old age has been spent battling a parasite called varroa, which kills bees but does not affect the honey. "I'm still hopeful that we will find a strain of bees strong enough to resist. Each year I carry out experiments but it's slow work. And you need a lot of time," he said, smiling a little wistfully.

FRANTOIO LA SPIGA
OLIVE MILL,
WINE STORE

Via Circonvallazione, 212   53024   Montalcino   Siena
TELEPHONE/FAX 0577 848611   OPEN Shop: 9:00-13:00, 14:30-19:30; *frantoio*: November and December   CLOSED Thursday
CREDIT CARDS Visa, MC, Amex   DIRECT SALE Yes
ENGLISH SPOKEN No   DIRECTIONS The shop and mill are on the outer road circling Montalcino, halfway up the hill

La Spiga is a modern-style olive mill, or *frantoio*. Being Montalcino, it is also a wine shop—La Spiga's olive growers are mostly wine producers. Their oil and wine are available at reasonable prices. Several grades of oil are sold with La Spiga's label. The cooperative has about 110 members and was formed in 1952.

In November and December the freshly picked olives arrive in airy plastic crates. The leaves are sucked away and the olives rinsed. In a large stainless-steel Sinolea machine they are pounded and churned at a maximum temperature of 25°C/77°F. A system of tiny metal blades enables oil to drip free of the mass. The final centrifuge separates oil from water. All parts are stainless steel, easy to clean and hygienic. The oil may be drip-filtered before bottling. During the milling season the *frantoio* runs twenty-four hours a day, and may be visited.

FORNO LAMBARDI
PASTRY, BREAD

Via S. Saloni, 54   53024   Montalcino   Siena
TELEPHONE 0577 848084   OPEN 8:00-13:00, 17:15-1:30
CLOSED Wednesday afternoon, Sunday   CREDIT CARDS None
DIRECT SALE Yes   ENGLISH SPOKEN No
DIRECTIONS   In the town center

Lambardi, an old-fashioned bakery, is tucked into the narrow street leading to Montalcino's *comune*. It specializes in bread, pastries, and handmade pasta, but is famous for its dried biscuits.

Montalcino's classic cookies are *ossi di morto* (dead man's bones). Bite into one, and you will see why. These brittle biscuits are light as a feather, despite being studded with chewy almonds. They are so good it's impossible to eat just one. Other Sienese favorites are honey-enriched *cantucci*, *ricciarelli*, and *panforte*.

Along with salted and unsalted (*sciocco*) Tuscan bread, I found unusual *schiacciatine con uvetta*. Crusty flat rounds of oiled bread with raisins, they are best eaten in the morning, as they dry out fast.

BOCCONDIVINO Via Traversa dei Monti 53024 Montalcino Siena
RESTAURANT TELEPHONE 0577 848233 FAX 0577 848340 OPEN Lunch and dinner CLOSED Tuesday; November CREDIT CARDS Visa, MC, Amex ENGLISH SPOKEN Yes RESERVATIONS Recommended on weekends PRICE $$ à la carte, $ pizza DIRECTIONS Coming from Siena and the north, on the left 1 km before Montalcino

This family-run restaurant and pizzeria overlooks Montalcino's vineyard-covered slopes and, farther north, the Crete Senesi hills. There is a breezy outdoor terrace in summer. The menu offers casual pizzas and a wider selection of dishes. The food includes some ambitious fare. *Carabaccia*, a "hymn to the onion" as the chef described it, is a thick oniony soup with a crust of cheesy bread. Eggplant-stuffed ravioli comes with a tangy fresh tomato sauce, while homemade *tagliolini* noodles are dressed with butter and truffles. In the main courses, *scaloppine* are paired with balsamic vinegar, lamb with artichokes, marinated wild boar with little toasts.

BocconDivino means a sip of wine and a divine mouthful; its interesting international wine list encourages comparisons between Montalcino's and foreign wines.

L'OSTERIA Via Traversi dei Monti, 214 53024 Montalcino Siena
COLLINA D'ITALIA TELEPHONE 0577 847134 OPEN Restaurant: lunch and dinner;
RESTAURANT, shop: 9:00-20:00 daily CLOSED Restaurant and bar: Monday
WINE STORE CREDIT CARDS Visa, MC, Amex DIRECT SALE Yes ENGLISH SPOKEN Yes RESERVATIONS Recommended at weekends PRICE $$ DIRECTIONS Coming from Siena or the north, Collina d'Italia is on the last big curve before reaching Montalcino.

This restaurant and wine shop is part of the Altesino estate's chain. It has a modern feel, clean and functional, with paper place mats and light wood furniture. The kitchen, run by an Englishwoman, is flexible: there is no obligation to have many courses. In summer there is a salad bar. The menu, though geared for tourists with non-Tuscan dishes like *vitello tonnato* and *cotoletta alla Milanese*, has a few local specialties: the *zuppa di fagioli* is a thick bean soup of chard and bread, drizzled with olive oil. The wine shop has a good selection of Brunellos.

OSTERIA DI PORTA
AL CASSERO
RESTAURANT

Via della Libertà, 9 and Via Ricasoli, 32   53024   Montalcino   Siena
TELEPHONE 0577 847196   OPEN 9:00-24:00   CLOSED Wednesday;
January   CREDIT CARDS Visa, MC, Amex   ENGLISH SPOKEN No, but
an English menu is available   RESERVATIONS Recommended at peak
times   PRICE $ DIRECTIONS Near the fortress

This unpretentious family eating house is furnished simply with attractive
marble tables and wooden chairs. In summer, tables are in an awning-covered
courtyard. Service can be haphazard when the restaurant is full, but food is
available all day, so time your meal before or after peak times.

Homemade soups and pastas are good, including local *pinci*—
thick hand-rolled spaghetti. The menu offers assortments of cheese, *salumi*,
salads, or grilled vegetables, and a few hot egg or meat dishes. Desserts are
cantucci with Vin Santo or home-baked tarts. Pitchered wine is red or white.
This is a low-pressure, inexpensive but friendly place—the kind welcomed by
many travelers.

RISTORANTE
POGGIO ANTICO
RESTAURANT

Poggio Antico   53024   Montalcino   Siena
TELEPHONE/FAX 0577 849200   OPEN Lunch and dinner
CLOSED Monday; January   CREDIT CARDS None
ENGLISH SPOKEN Yes   RESERVATIONS Necessary   PRICE $$$$
DIRECTIONS In Poggio Antico winery (see map p 284)

This is Montalcino's best restaurant, the only one worthy of a detour. Located
in the landscaped grounds of Poggio Antico estate, with great views of the Val
d'Orcia, it is reached along a quintessentially Tuscan avenue of cypress and
maritime pines. Inside, the elegant clean-lined interior has a terra-cotta floor
and modern picture windows. The service is attentive and not too formal; the
gracious Patrizia Leonardi, wife of chef Roberto Minnetti, explains the dishes
and, in her role of sommelier, serves the wines.

The food is quite elaborate, with a modern feel despite traditional roots. The normal and tasting menus change seasonally; there is no
obligation to have numerous courses. My June tasting-menu lunch was accompanied by lovely freshly baked rolls.

Minnetti's *panzanella* salad was bready and cool. An unexpected
flavor made the taste buds sit up: Was it fish? The next dish looked like a flower
on the plate: paper-thin slices of cured pork loin (*lombo*) were arranged around
a kind of apple-fig chutney; the sweet spicy fruit complemented the strong,
salty meat. A very rich "parfait" of duck and goose liver was voluptuous and
velvety, with a honey-sweet sauce of reduced Moscadello, Montalcino's historic
sweet wine. *Gnocchetti*'s "white" wild boar sauce contained not tomato but
grated zucchini and carrot. This elaborate dish lacked the depth of flavor
expected from game. Pigeon with herbed beef stuffing and Vin Santo vinegar
was succulent and successful. The desserts were refined and fresh-flavored.

As for the wine list: I expected, in Montalcino's only fine restaurant, to find a stimulating selection of Brunellos. Instead, the list's only Brunellos were Poggio Antico's, with a token pair of Montalcino "table" wines—a limitation imposed on the restaurant by the mother estate. This is a shame. To preclude the possibility of comparison or choice seems shortsighted, no matter how good the estate's own wines are.

ENOTECA LA FORTEZZA
WINE STORE,
WINE BAR

Piazzale Fortezza   53024   Montalcino   Siena
TELEPHONE/FAX 0577 849211   OPEN Winter 9:00-13:00, 14:00-16:00;
summer: 9:00-13:00, 14:30-20:00   CLOSED Monday in winter
CREDIT CARDS Visa, Amex   DIRECT SALE Yes   ENGLISH SPOKEN Yes
FEATURES Tickets for the fortress' ramparts are on sale from the *enoteca*
DIRECTIONS The shop is inside the fortress. Enter through the large gate
in the piazza.

A fourteenth-century fortress is a dramatic location for a wine bar, and it is a perfect place to sample or buy Montalcino's great wines. The bar and shop are within the walls of the 1362 monument, situated at the top of the town. On nice days you can sit in the peaceful inner courtyard sipping wine and listening to medieval music. What could be nicer?

In the warm, vaulted brick interior over one hundred Brunello producers are represented—a breathtaking array. Wine is sold by the glass from many bottles (not Riservas or other premium wines), so you can compare producers, or choose a favorite before investing in a few bottles to take home.

To accompany the wines, Mario Pianigiani and Marzio Giannelli have selected excellent local cheeses and *salumi*. These are sold whole or served in sandwiches. The *enoteca* carries locally produced olive oils, honeys, and biscuits. There are tables inside and out.

Also

Osteria Basso Mondo at Castelnuovo dell'Abate is a great place to get sandwiches filled with pecorino cheese or *salumi* made locally by Vasco Sassetti, which are also sold by Enoteca La Fortezza at Montalcino. I found the adjacent restaurant overpriced, and recommend a picnic in the vicinity of the exquisite Romanesque church Sant'Antimo, very nearby.

Pieve di San Sigismondo. Poggio alle Mura. 0577 866026.
Situated between Villa Banfi and Montalcino, this recently opened trattoria is located amid vineyards. The room is cheerful, the atmosphere informal, and the menu straightforwardly Tuscan: it holds no surprises, but is fine if you are in the mood for a pleasant lunch in the country.

CHAPTER 13

Arezzo, Its Hills and Valleys

A rezzo is one of Tuscany's largest provinces, dominated geographically by three wide valleys: Val di Chiana, Valdarno, and Casentino. The latter two are valleys of the River Arno, separated by the monumental Pratomagno mountain range. The landscape is varied, with the Casentino providing unspoiled mountain scenery, while the reclaimed valley of the Chiana canal is flat, but punctuated by remarkable hill towns that were once strategic Etruscan holdings: Cortona, Arezzo, and Chiusi to the south. The Casentino's rural villages offer hearty country cooking with goat's and sheep's cheeses, wild mushrooms, and herbs.

The Val di Chiana is a key industrial and agricultural plain, with fruit orchards, crops, and cattle raising—especially of the sought-after Chianina breed. I expected to see a lot of these animals in this area, but most are reared indoors, with little possibility of outdoor grazing. The lower slopes around the central valleys are planted with olive groves for making fine extra-virgin oil. There are organic growers of vegetables and the Aretino's yellow bean, *zolfino*.

Art lovers will associate this province with Piero della Francesca. Indeed, the Piero "tour" includes Sansepolcro, his birthplace, Monterchi, site of the extraordinary *Madonna del Parto* fresco, and Arezzo, where in the 1450s Piero painted his great masterpiece, the *Legend of the True Cross* fresco cycle.

Azienda Promozione Turistica
Piazza Repubblica, 22
52100 Arezzo
0757 377677, fax 0575 377676

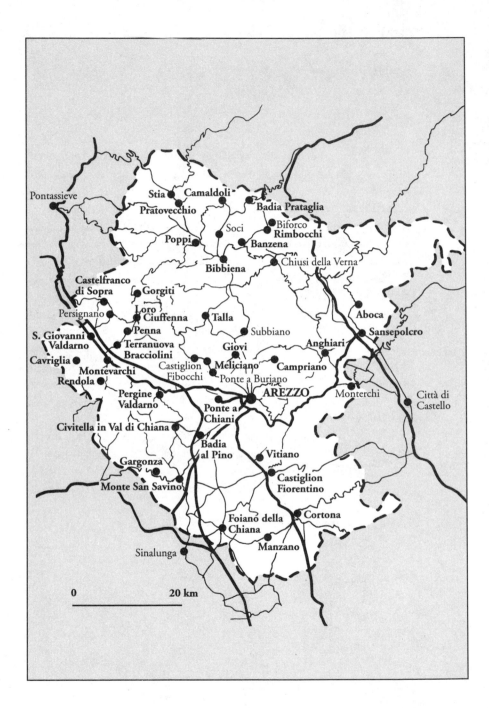

Town names in **bold** indicate towns that are included in this chapter.

ABOCA

ABOCA
HERBAL PRODUCTS

SS 258   Aboca   52037   Sansepolcro
TELEPHONE 0575 7461   FAX 0575 749130
E-MAIL commerciale@aboca.it; www.aboca.it   OPEN Shop: 9:00-13:00,
16:00-19:00   CLOSED Monday morning; Sunday except before Christmas
MAIL ORDER Yes   CREDIT CARDS None   DIRECT SALE Yes
ENGLISH SPOKEN Yes   DIRECTIONS From Sansepolcro take SS 258 toward
Aboca. L'Erboristeria di Aboca is on the left after about 6 kms.

Of the many places I visited for this book, Aboca is among those that most
impressed me. Set in virgin countryside, Aboca is an extensive farm producing
organically grown herbs for medicinal and culinary use. If the Italians are not
often very informed about the organic movement, they do widely believe in the
curative use of herbs. One has only to look at the vast number of *erboristerie* to
see they are almost as likely to resort to herbal remedies as pharmaceutical ones.

Valentino Mercati's Aboca is a large farm comprising the growing fields for over ninety varieties of herbs and flowers, the laboratories for
"transforming" them, as well as a sophisticated center for research. The herbs
are sold dried (for use in teas) or as essential oils, tinctures, or concentrates.
Many are combined in "complex" capsules—such as the Energo (energy-
giving) formula that includes the essential oils of sage and rosemary with
cinnamon, ginseng, royal jelly, seaweed, pollen, and wheat germ. There are
herbal products to aid dieting, energy, sleeping, and toning.

The company's shop sells much of the range. A resident herbalist gives advice about the products (they can also provide an English-speaking
expert). Aboca also produces wonderful honey—gathered by the bees that pol-
linate the fields of beautiful flowers.

ANGHIARI

LOCANDA AL
CASTELLO DI SORCI
RESTAURANT

Via San Lorenzo, 21   Sorci   52031   Anghiari
TELEPHONE 0575 789066, 1678 67089   FAX 0575 788022
OPEN Lunch and dinner   CLOSED Monday evening
CREDIT CARDS Visa, MC, Amex   ENGLISH SPOKEN A little
RESERVATIONS Recommended on weekends   PRICE $$ adults (including
wine), $ children   OTHER Houses available for holiday rentals; banquets
and receptions catered   DIRECTIONS From Anghiari go toward
Monterchi; after 3 kms turn right to Castello.

The medieval Castello di Sorci is dramatically positioned above a wide valley.
Its nearby *locanda*, or inn, houses a big, lively restaurant. The style is a nicely
done rustic; this is a great place to come in a group or family. There is a special
reduced price for children, and the adult's fixed price is both reasonable and all-
inclusive, comprising a four-course menu of traditional local recipes. All the
pasta is handmade. There are no freezers.

A typical dinner begins with platters of *crostini,* Tuscan canapés, spicy tomato *bruschetta* on country bread, and mixed *salumi. Primi* include tagliatelle noodles, potato gnocchi, *ribollita,* or risotto. Main courses feature mixed roasted meats and seasonal vegetables. For dessert a local cake, *torcolo,* is eaten with Vin Santo. Red and white wine and water are on the tables and included in the price.

Primetto Barelli is a lively, elderly gentleman with twinkling eyes. His father was a shoemaker, and he was a farmer before buying the Castello over twenty-five years ago. "It took fifteen years to fix it up," he admitted, "but I have revolutionized the restaurant trade by my all-inclusive price. It has meant that entire families can afford to eat out, and well."

The Castello is also a cultural center, housing musical concerts and a study center for the culinary traditions of the central Apennine mountains.

BUSATTI
TABLECRAFTS: LINENS

Via Mazzini, 14   52031   Anghiari
TELEPHONE 0575 788424 store; 788013 office   FAX 0575 789819
OPEN Summer 9:00-13:00, 16:00-20:00; winter 9:00-13:00, 15:30-19:30
CLOSED Monday morning   MAIL ORDER Yes   CREDIT CARDS Visa, MC   ENGLISH SPOKEN Yes   DIRECTIONS Off Corso Matteotti, in the town center

Anghiari is an unspoiled medieval hill town of particular interest to linen enthusiasts. After spotting the Busatti's shop in Arezzo (p 316), I determined to see their mill, which also sells to the public.

"Weaving natural local fibers has been a tradition in Anghiari for centuries," explained Signora Busatti Sassolini, whose family has run the business since 1842. "My family created a niche for itself producing high-quality linens for the table, bed, and bath."

The Busatti palazzo comprises an attractive shop, offices, and the looms in the basement. I was taken down to see these, crowded into a large, deafeningly noisy room worked by local women. Some of the fascinating machinery predates World War II.

Upstairs, the shop sells mainly Busatti fabrics (with others from neighboring regions), finished as hand- or dish-towels, tablecloths, napkins, and more. Many have elaborate woven borders in medieval designs, knotted fringes, or open-worked hems. Fabrics may also be bought by the meter (about one yard) for anyone who wants to make their own—wide enough for bedspreads, tablecloths, or curtains.

AREZZO

PANE E SALUTE　　　Corso Italia, 11　52100　Arezzo
BREAD　　　　　　　TELEPHONE 0575 20657　OPEN 7:30-13:00, 16:30-20:00
　　　　　　　　　　　CLOSED Sunday; Wednesday afternoon in winter; Saturday afternoon
　　　　　　　　　　　in summer; August　CREDIT CARDS None　ENGLISH SPOKEN No
　　　　　　　　　　　DIRECTIONS In the town center

This is a hundred-year-old bakery on the street leading up to Piazza Grande. You'll know it by the delicious smell of baking bread that wafts out into the street. The *forno* used to be wood-burning until a health regulation some years back made them convert to modern ovens. "Now they have decided that wood ovens are not dangerous after all," explained Iride Magnani, the shop's owner, "but we can't keep ripping out our ovens every time the bureaucratic wind changes."

One of her specialties is the *pan di romarino*, a bread dough studded with rosemary and raisins. The *schiacciata* also reigns here: flat, crunchy, and salt-topped, it marries perfectly to cheese and *salumi*. Eat it early in the day— by nightfall it has already lost its sparkle. I also spotted Irish soda bread, dried rounds of bread for *bruschetta*, and loaves of soya, corn, and hard wheat flours.

TORREFAZIONE　　　Via Vittorio Veneto, 125　52100　Arezzo District
CAFFÈ DONATELLO　TELEPHONE 0575 907067　OPEN 9:00-13:00, 16:00-20:00
COFFEE　　　　　　CLOSED Wednesday afternoon; Sunday　CREDIT CARDS None
　　　　　　　　　　　ENGLISH SPOKEN A little　OTHER Home delivery
　　　　　　　　　　　DIRECTIONS Via Vittorio Veneto is the continuation of Corso Italia,
　　　　　　　　　　　southwest of the town center.

Maurizio Sestini is a coffee roaster. He buys green coffee beans from the equatorial countries, and roasts them in a propane gas oven that leaves no residual odors. The coffee is sold in his quaint shop by the kilo, ground to order. The range goes from 100 percent Arabica (the most expensive) to 100 percent Robusta (which costs less but is closer to industrial), or any combination in between. Water-decaffeinated coffees are available.

Stand up at the tiny bar for *un caffè*, freshly ground and irresistibly aromatic. There is a choice of exotic teas, herbal candies, and local specialty foods on sale. Sestini also runs a local delivery business from a catalog, a rare enterprise in Italy.

L'ERBA SALVIA   Via Vittorio Veneto, 98   52100   Arezzo
HEALTH FOODS   TELEPHONE 0575 907261   OPEN 9:00-13:00, 16:00-20:00
                           CLOSED Wednesday afternoon; Sunday   CREDIT CARDS None
                           ENGLISH SPOKEN Yes   DIRECTIONS Via Vittorio Veneto is the
                           continuation of Corso Italia, southwest of the town center.

This health food shop always has a wide selection of fresh organic produce,
local when seasons allow. It is on one of the main roads leading into Arezzo,
so parking is quite easy. It also sells organic breads, tofu, oils, honeys, dairy
products (including sheep's and goat's cheeses), and wonderful stone-ground
polenta flour. Many items are approved by Demeter, the stringent European
biodynamic organization.

UN PUNTO   Piazza San Gemignano, 1   52100   Arezzo
MACROBIOTICO   TELEPHONE 0575 302420   OPEN Shop: 9:00-13:00, 17:00-20:00;
HEALTH FOODS   restaurant lunch Monday-Friday 12:00-14:00, dinner Thursday-Saturday
RESTAURANT   20:00-21:30   CLOSED Sunday; two weeks in August
                          CREDIT CARDS None   ENGLISH SPOKEN A little
                          PRICE $ DIRECTIONS Near Piazza S. Agostino

Un Punto Macrobiotico has been a mainstay in the Italian macrobiotic movement since the eighties. The shop in Sansepolcro opened in 1991, this one in
1994. At lunchtime there is a nice mix of people in the small restaurant: families with children, elderly people, office workers, students. Everyone is welcome, macrobiotic or otherwise.

For a modest sum you can have the set lunch, usually a soup
and a mixed vegetable and pulses platter—Italian style, of course. There are
daily pastas and a few desserts. Foods are strictly seasonal and, whenever possible, local. The shop sells a variety of macrobiotic and other health foods:
unpasteurized miso, rices and grains, natural jams and juices. The center also
organizes macrobiotic cooking classes.

IL GELATO   Via dei Cenci, 24   52100   Arezzo
ICE CREAM   TELEPHONE 0575 23240   OPEN 10:30-13:10, 13:45-23:30; till 20:30
                          in winter   CLOSED Wednesday; November or January
                          CREDIT CARDS None   ENGLISH SPOKEN A little
                          DIRECTIONS Off Corso Italia, in the town center

Il Gelato makes the best gelati in the area. Only fresh milk, eggs, sugar, and
fresh or frozen fruits are used. Of the custard-based gelati, I liked the *crema di
riso*. This is textured with grains of rice boiled in milk before being sweetened.
A hint of lemon spices this grown-up child's dessert. Best summer fruits
include fig and mixed berries.

PASTICCERIA
MIGNON
PASTRY SHOP,
TEAROOM

Via Tolletta, 20   52100   Arezzo
TELEPHONE 0575 29860   OPEN Shop: 6:45-13:15, 15:30-20:00; tearoom:
13:00-14:30, 16:00-20:00   CLOSED Monday; two weeks in August
CREDIT CARDS None   DIRECT SALE Yes   ENGLISH SPOKEN Yes
DIRECTIONS Off Via Madonna del Prato

This elegant pastry shop runs a dainty tearoom of the type my grandmother took me to as a child. At lunchtime there are "tasty little bites," *primi*, sandwiches, and quiches. Afternoon tea features pastries, crêpes, and hot chocolate. The shop sells Italian regional cakes with a French influence. The *pasticceria mignon*, (*petits fours*), are finely made and good. The soft *pan di Genova* is denser than *panettone* (it rises only once before baking) and is studded with raisins, pine nuts, and candied citrus peel. There are ricotta cheesecakes, apple tarts, and pastry shells filled with rice pudding. The store makes its own sugared flowers (violets, rosebuds, mimosa, and mint leaves) and sugar-coated *confetti*.

ANTICA OSTERIA
L'AGANÌA
RESTAURANT

Via Massini, 10   52100   Arezzo
TELEPHONE 0575 25381   OPEN Lunch and dinner
CLOSED Monday; June   CREDIT CARDS Visa, MC, Amex
ENGLISH SPOKEN No   RESERVATIONS None accepted
PRICE $$ DIRECTIONS In town center, off Corso Italia

L'Aganìa is full of local color—it's the only phrase that springs to mind. Run by a group of very friendly women who have worked there for years, the *osteria* serves the Italian equivalent of "down-home cooking." The dining room is just below street level. It is painted a warm reddish brown and decorated with a motley mix of old pictures, pitchers, photos, wine bottles, and strings of peppers and garlic. In autumn, each table held a vase containing rosemary, bay, sage, and one pink rose.

At lunchtime there is a lively atmosphere. No reservations are taken, so get there early for the first sitting. The food is unpretentious and appetizing: an antipasto platter of cold cuts with homemade meatballs; nourishing soups of chick-peas, *farro* wheat, or vegetables; pasta, polenta, or gnocchi with a good choice of sauces; simply roasted meats, like rabbit scented with wild fennel and served with roast potatoes, or local favorites of tripe or sausages; and for dessert, fresh fruit, a pie, or some *cantucci* biscuits.

MORINI
TABLE CRAFTS:
KITCHENWARES

Piazza San Jacopo   52100   Arezzo
TELEPHONE 0575 23277   FAX 0575 33231   OPEN Summer 9:00-13:00,
16:00-20:00; winter 9:00-13:00, 15:30-19:30   CLOSED Sunday; Monday
in winter, Saturday afternoon and Monday morning in summer; August
MAIL ORDER Yes   CREDIT CARDS Visa, MC   ENGLISH SPOKEN Yes
DIRECTIONS At the beginning of Corso Italia

Morini is a top contender for my best kitchen and tablewares shop. It covers the whole range, from basic kitchen tools through specialist equipment, fine china, and crystal. You can tell by looking at the stylish window displays that the shop has a serious commitment to the art of the table.

Morini's has been a fixture in Arezzo since the 1930s. The basement is the cook's paradise: you'll find everything from high-tech utensils to pressure cookers, from French gratin dishes to Alessi's stainless-steel-lined copper saucepans (expensive but fabulous). There are oven thermometers and Parmesan graters, Tuscan bean pots and picnic baskets. China and glass departments feature world leaders and fine Italian design objects, such as Alessi (including the wooden Twergi range), Aldo Rossi's lighthouse, and Fornasetti.

"ABBRACCIO"
TABLE CRAFTS: LINENS

Piazza Grande, 10   52100   Arezzo
TELEPHONE No   OPEN 10:00-13:00, 16:00-19:30
CLOSED Sunday, Monday   CREDIT CARDS None
ENGLISH SPOKEN A little   DIRECTIONS Piazza Grande is at the
top of Arezzo.

In her very personal shop, Diana De Mori has garnered linens—old and new—yarns, tablecloths, and the like. She has a great eye and has chosen beautiful, rare, and simple fabrics of natural materials. Here you can find the rust-printed kitchen linens from Emilia Romagna, with their bold stenciled designs, and other artisan weaves. Some of the rarest items are costly, but worth the money for their quality. There is no name to the small shop, but if it is not raining she hangs a few fabrics up outside the door. The shop is always open the first Sunday of the month, when the antique market is in town.

BUSATTI
TABLE CRAFTS: LINENS

Corso Italia, 48   52100   Arezzo
TELEPHONE 0575 355295   OPEN 9:00-13:00, 15:30-19:30
CLOSED Sunday; Monday morning; one week in August
CREDIT CARDS Visa, MC, Amex   ENGLISH SPOKEN Yes
DIRECTIONS In the town center

Linen lovers should make a pilgrimage to this store. Renaissance griffins, floral arabesques, and simple stripes are woven from natural cotton and linen, wool and hemp (*canapa*) in the subtlest shades. Most come from the Busatti artisan loom in Anghiari (p 312). Fabrics are also sold by length for home sewing at lower prices. So treat yourself (or a friend) to an original piece of Italian style.

ACETIFICIO ARETINO
VINEGAR

Via Romana, 76   52100   Arezzo
TELEPHONE 0575 903244   FAX 0575 900925   DIRECT SALE No
STOCKIST Local wine stores and Esselunga supermarkets

There are few vinegar makers in Tuscany—a separate building and license are now required to produce it. This *acetificio* is a semi-industrial plant that transforms Chianti wine into wine vinegar; white wine vinegar is made from the local Bianco Vergine Valdichiana. The vinegars are good quality and less expensive than the "designer" vinegars that use the traditional system.

"We work with Chianti that has spent six months in wooden casks," explained Signor Verdi, one of the brothers who runs it, "which gives the vinegar a richer flavor."

Air (which naturally contains vinegar bacteria) is pumped into the wine; it is then kept in continuous motion for twenty-four hours to distribute these bacteria, at temperatures below 40°C /104°F. Since wine contains many trace elements of metals (iron, copper, zinc) that would cause the vinegar to oxidize, it is filtered. The top-of-the-line red Chianti vinegar is then aged for one year in wooden casks before being bottled. "Our system is less picturesque than the old-fashioned methods," he continued. "But it is more hygienic and more stable—our vinegars do not have problems with oxidization or fermentation; they remain crystal clear for at least one year."

Acetificio Aretino does not sell directly to the public, but it is not difficult to find its vinegars locally. Its best "Chiantigiano" products come in tall square-sectioned bottles.

Also

Panetteria Tavanti. Borgo Santa Croce, 15-17.

This small grocery store sells wonderful bread *cotto a legna*—baked in a wood oven. It is in an unspoiled part of town that is fun to explore.

Elena Caccialupi. Via Madonna del Prato, 25.

This old-fashioned shop sells seeds to eat or plant, dried beans, ground polenta, pulses, and grains.

On Saturday morning, Arezzo's large street market includes a small local farmer's market. It is in a car park across Viale Mecenati from the Esselunga supermarket, and it is the place to find homegrown vegetables, fruit, eggs, and other country sundries.

Whenever wild mushrooms are to be found in the woods and fields in early summer and fall, the mushroom collectors gather on the corner of Via Garibaldi and Corso Italia to sell them from cardboard boxes or baskets. There are many types on display; even if you can't cook them, it makes for an interesting scene.

BADIA AL PINO

BOSCOVIVO TARTUFI
SPECIALTY FOODS:
TRUFFLE PRODUCTS

Via dei Boschi, 34   Badia al Pino   52040   Civitella in Val di Chiana
TELEPHONE 0575 410696, 410388   FAX 0575 410381
OPEN 9:00-13:00, 14:30-19:00   CLOSED Saturday and Sunday; August
MAIL ORDER Yes   CREDIT CARDS Visa, MC, Amex   DIRECT SALE Yes
ENGLISH SPOKEN Yes   DIRECTIONS From the Arezzo exit of A1 *autostrada*,
take first right toward Badia al Pino; the company is after 4 kms.

"We started small," recounted Franca Bianchini Landucci. "I was a teacher and my husband had a full-time job, but we loved going searching for truffles. Then we began selling them: fresh, preserved and in sauces." That was back in 1982. Signora Landucci now has a small factory employing 26 people and a worldwide client list.

Boscovivo has a large catalog: truffle-scented pastes and oils, meat and game sauces for *crostini*, plus preserved vegetables and honeys bought from other suppliers. Boscovivo's Tuscan specialties use the brand name "Le Ricette di Caterina." These include rich pasta or canapé sauces of chopped liver or game. Gift packs are also available.

As for the truffles, several types are used: white, *Tuber magnatum pico;* white spring truffle, *Tuber albidum pico;* black, *Tuber melanosporum vitt.;* summer, *Tuber aestivum vitt.* They come from various parts of Italy. "The white is the most delicate—the best for *primi*," she explained. "Whereas the black is more pungent, and better for use with meats."

Boscovivo also sells excellent Chianina beef, bred locally by registered breeders. It must be specially ordered.

BADIA PRATAGLIA

PASTICCERIA ANNA
SNACK BAR, PASTRY

Via Nazionale, 35   52010   Poppi
TELEPHONE 0575 559121   OPEN Summer: 8:00-13:00, 15:00-1 a.m.;
winter: 8:00-13:00, 15:30-20:00   CLOSED Tuesday
CREDIT CARDS None   ENGLISH SPOKEN No
DIRECTIONS On the main road through the village

After a nice hike in the pure mountain air, you'll be in the mood for a slice of pizza or a *schiacciata* with mushrooms on it. This little Swiss-style snack bar also makes some great *tortelli di patate*, the potato-stuffed pasta famous in this area. There is also a range of pastries.

BANZENA

IL BIVIO
RESTAURANT

Bivio di Banzena, 65   Banzena   52010   Bibbiena
TELEPHONE 0575 593242   OPEN Lunch and dinner   CLOSED Monday;
holidays variable   CREDIT CARDS None   ENGLISH SPOKEN A little
RESERVATIONS Recommended for dinner and on weekends   PRICE $$
DIRECTIONS From Bibbiena, take SS 208 for La Verna. The restaurant is
after 9.5 kms.

A *bivio* is a fork in the road, and Il Bivio is located at one on the road that
winds up the hillside to the Franciscan sanctuary of La Verna. Il Bivio doubles
as a simple country bar; travelers can stop in for a coffee or snack. Behind this
bar is an interesting restaurant.

With his wife and her family, Lorenzo Giuliani has created a
fine menu of local dishes, *cucina tipica,* with recipes that are traditional in ori-
gin yet modern in feel. It offers many reasonably priced choices. The wine list
features some of the less well known wines of the area; Giuliani is a qualified
sommelier and author of a book about the wines of Arezzo. "Part of the work
of a sommelier," he explained, "is to *abbinare,* or match, each dish with a wine
that best complements it."

The restaurant, with its light wood and exposed stone interior,
is a mixture of informal and formal. The customers include serious food lovers
and locals on a night out; Giuliani is a fine host to all.

In autumn, I began with a pastry tart filled with artichoke and
potatoes. A *pappa* of yellow pumpkin and *farro,* spelt wheat, was a thick golden
soup, both sweet and fiery, thanks to its fresh basil and *peperoncino.* Delicate
ravioli contained a vivid green filling of wild herbs and ricotta, and came with
truffle-speckled cream. *Svaccheroni col pizzichino* used a local curate's recipe from
1637: *maccheroni* was served with a very "stinging," matured pecorino cheese
sauce. This was apparently popular on fasting days, when meat was forbidden.

Main courses include roasted meats and steaks and stewed wild
boar. Duck was moist and flavorful, with a good crispy skin; guinea fowl was
braised with rosemary. Giuliani explained that these game birds were free-range
and reared locally. Pastries were fine: a golden-topped ricotta tart on biscuit
crust was studded with nuts and raisins; lemon *torta* was sharp and dairy-free.
Homemade *semifreddi* blended fresh fruits into a frozen cream base.

BIBBIENA

APICOLTURA   Via del Artigiano, 10/12   52012   Bibbiena
CASENTINESE   TELEPHONE 0575 560916   OPEN 8:00-12:00, 14:00-18:00
HONEY   CLOSED Sunday   CREDIT CARDS None   DIRECT SALE Yes
                        ENGLISH SPOKEN A little   DIRECTIONS From Bibbiena, go toward
                        Soci; after 2 kms follow signs for Zona Industriale Ferrantina, where the
                        company is located.

This company sells twelve typically Tuscan honeys. It owns two thousand
hives; other honey is bought locally or from the south of Italy. Alberto Ricci,
the company's young director, explained about some of the by-products from
beekeeping.

Flower pollen is a complete substance. "All life starts here," said
Ricci. It is rich in amino acids, minerals, and vitamins. Royal jelly is the queen
bee's food. Ricci described propolis as "the first miracle of beekeeping." A
resinous gluelike material obtained by bees from the buds of some plants (such
as poplars), propolis is used by them to seal the cracks in their hives and to dis-
infect them. Propolis is an anti-inflammatory agent and a natural antibiotic;
the Egyptians used it for embalming mummies.

The company moves its hives around for "nomadic" collection—going to an area when a particular type of plant is in flower. Ricci
explained that it was difficult to guarantee that honey was organic "as you can
never know what a peasant has sprayed his fields with." However all the honeys
are analyzed before being sold.

I was particularly struck by the *melata di abete*. This deep amber,
runny honey has an intense resinlike taste and great richness of flavor. It is made
by the bees from the *abete*, an evergreen in the pine family. The bees are attracted
to the resin released by the trees and produce this "honey" from it. Other typically Tuscan honeys are acacia, chestnut, *sulla*, *erica*, sunflower, and clover.

CAMALDOLI

ANTICA FARMACIA   52010   Camaldoli
DEI MONACI   TELEPHONE 0575 556143   OPEN 9:00-12:30, 14:30-18:00
CAMALDOLESI   CLOSED Wednesday in winter   CREDIT CARDS None
SPECIALTY FOODS   ENGLISH SPOKEN No   DIRECTIONS Camaldoli is signposted from Poppi.

A winding drive up into the Casentino forest leads to Camaldoli, the
monastery founded in the eleventh century by St. Romuald. Some of the
monks chose to take vows of silence and live as hermits here, isolated from
the rest of the world in tiny cells. Others established an important pharmacy
and hospital, making herbal cures and liqueurs.

The pharmacy, with its original walnut paneling, is from 1543. The monks' alembics and other equipment are on view in the atmospheric rooms, which are still intact, serving today as the monastery's gift and souvenir shop. Here you can find a range of herbal products, honeys, and jams packaged for the monks by local producers. There are also some of the bitter herbal elixirs that the monks once made.

CAMPRIANO

LA CAPANNACCIA
RESTAURANT

Antecchia, 51   52100   Campriano
TELEPHONE 0575 361759   OPEN Lunch and dinner   CLOSED Sunday evening; Monday; August   CREDIT CARDS None
ENGLISH SPOKEN A little   FEATURES Outdoor terrace in summer
RESERVATIONS Recommended at lunchtime and weekends   PRICE $$
DIRECTIONS From Campriano, the restaurant is signposted. Take the winding road to La Capannaccia, a thatched stone building set back from the road.

La Capannaccia is a lively country trattoria. Its large picture windows overlook the beginning of the Casentino hills; in summer there is a vine-covered terrace. This is the only thatched restaurant I have seen in Tuscany. This rustic trattoria is popular and does a busy lunchtime trade. The atmosphere is informal, the helpings generous, the food wholesome, and the prices reasonable.

My autumn lunch began with mixed *crostini* topped with liver paste, ham and spicy tomato sauce. *Primi* included fluffy polenta heaped with mushrooms, wide *pappardelle* noodles with a well-seasoned sauce of coarsely ground hare, penne with a piquant *arrabbiata* sauce, and a compact risotto with *funghi porcini.* Second helpings were available.

Meat-lovers will appreciate the main courses. There were platters of grilled chicken, steak, sausages, rabbit, and ribs cooked in the giant open fireplace. To accompany them were *fagioli*—white Tuscan beans stewed with sage—or fried potatoes.

Desserts included satisfyingly sweet tiramisù, *affogato al caffè*— ice cream with hot expresso coffee poured over it—and *cantucci* biscuits dunked in Vin Santo. Anyone wanting help digesting all of this should have an *amaro,* the bitter herbal liqueur favored by the Italians as a *digestivo.*

CASTELFRANCO DI SOPRA

IL VICOLO DEL CONTENTO RESTAURANT

Mandri, 38   52020   Castelfranco di Sopra
TELEPHONE 055 9149277   FAX 055 9149906   OPEN Wednesday-Saturday dinner only, Sunday lunch and dinner; lunch other days possible by prearrangement   CLOSED Monday, Tuesday; holidays variable   CREDIT CARDS Visa, MC, Amex   ENGLISH SPOKEN Yes   FEATURES Outdoor terrace   RESERVATIONS Recommended   PRICE $$$$ DIRECTIONS From Castelfranco di Sopra go toward Pian di Sco. The restaurant is after about 1 km, on the left.

Set in beautiful countryside, Il Vicolo del Contento is known for its fish cookery. Angelo Redditi, owner and chef, told me that 70 percent of his fish comes from the markets of Firenze and Paris, France, with specialties like scallops arriving from Scotland. Redditi is keen on the cooking of Italy's south: "For me, it is the best cuisine of all, but you have to apply a bit of technique to it," he asserted.

The restaurant has an outdoor terrace for warm weather. Indoors the decor is an eclectic mix of new and old—rather spare with just a few choice objects. Modern architectural elements, glass bricks, and wood-grained cement are used unusually in a traditional context. China, crystal, and silverware are well selected.

My February dinner from the tasting menu (which includes a daily suggestion of honestly priced wines) began with warm boiled *mazzancolle* (large shrimp), served with an aromatic olive oil and basil mayonnaise. They had been sliced in half to expose the coral. A fillet of *cernia* (grouper) showed the southern influence Redditi mentioned. The firm-fleshed fish went well with black olives (baked and almost crunchy), capers, sweet cherry tomatoes, and basil olive oil. These are the decisive flavors of the Mediterranean.

Taglierini con funghi e gamberetti was a nest of thin noodles (cooked more al dente than is usual with egg pasta) richly topped with chunks of fresh shiitake mushrooms (from Paris) and shrimp in a garlicky, buttery sauce—an interesting marriage of land and sea. Short *trofie* pasta was tossed with *piccante* strips of *calamari*, the plate decorated with a dramatic border of black squid's ink. No other food so captures the essence of the sea as this salty, intense ink. A roasted fillet of *branzino* (sea bass) was arranged on a bed of oiled spinach and bright green beans. There are also always several "land" dishes available for those not wanting fish.

A sampler of desserts included an airy berry *bavarese* with a tart raspberry *coulis*, a mixed chocolate terrine with good depth of flavor, served very cold, and a white chocolate mousse. Signora Redditi is happy to suggest wines for the guests, but there is of course a studied wine list.

CASTIGLION FIORENTINO

COOP PRO.AGRI.A.   Via Cosimo Serristori, 53   52043   Castiglion Fiorentino
MEAT   TELEPHONE 0575 680226   OPEN 8:00-13:00, 16:30-19:30
CLOSED Wednesday afternoon; Sunday   CREDIT CARDS None
ENGLISH SPOKEN A little   DIRECTIONS From Castiglion Fiorentino
take SS 71 toward Arezzo. After about 2 kms turn left toward Manciano,
Lucignano, and green *autostrada* sign. The shop is on the right after about
300 meters, set back in its own car park.

Produttori Agricoli Associati is a small cooperative run by two farming families.
They raise (but do not breed) cattle, pigs and sheep for meat they butcher and
sell at this shop. On their farm, 5 kms away, they also grow the grains for the
animals' feed.

"We kept hearing about the meat that was being imported from
other countries," explained Tiziana Palazzoni. "It was full of hormones, and
now we know that even the animals' feed may not be very trustworthy. It made
us quite angry, so we decided to form this cooperative and supply fine meats to
the local population whose provenance we could guarantee."

That was five years ago, and the cooperative is now going
strong. They buy young calves of the Chianina or Charollais breeds and raise
them for from eight to twelve months before butchering. As members of the
Carni Bovine DOC consortium, their meats are rigorously checked; no hormones are used. In the cheerful shop homemade *salumi* are sold in addition to
the fresh meats. There are artisan-made cheeses and other local products—olive
oil, honey, and wine.

AZIENDA AGRICOLA   Via Montecchio, 301B   Pievuccia   52043   Castiglion Fiorentino
"IL MORO"   TELEPHONE 0575 651370   OPEN 8:00-19:00   CLOSED Saturday
PRODUCE: ORGANIC   and Sunday   CREDIT CARDS None   DIRECT SALE Yes
STOCKIST L'Erba Salvia, Arezzo (p 314)   ENGLISH SPOKEN A little
OTHER One simple apartment available for holiday rentals
DIRECTIONS From Castiglion Fiorentino, go toward Cortona. Turn left
toward Pievuccia at third set of traffic lights. Go through S.Lucia, over a
hump-backed bridge and continue about 1 km to the church on the
right. Four hundred meters after the church at Pievuccia, cross the green
bridge on the right, then take two right turns to the cream-colored house
on the right.

Alberto Bennati is a certified (AIAB) organic grower. On his small farm he produces broccoli, beets, celeriac, potatoes, melons, pumpkins, and strawberries.
In keeping with organic regulations, he uses no chemical sprays or fertilizers.
"When it comes to the bugs," he said, "either we pick them off by hand (as in
the case of the cabbage caterpillars) or else we spray with the so-called Bordeaux
mixture used for the vines, of copper and sulphur. The amazing thing is that
within just a few years of the land being worked organically, both diseases and
pests have radically diminished."

In addition to crop rotation, the earth is enriched with animal manure and with "green manure." Here plants such as annual lupins or comfrey are grown over the winter. As soon as they flower they are cut and left on the ground for two to three days before being dug under. This is one of the best fertilizers: the plants' roots fix nitrogen in the ground, and the green stems offer organic material for gradual breaking down in the soil. It is not too easy to find this rural farm, but it will be worth it to anyone who wants to taste great vegetables.

Also

Nearby to the Il Moro farm, the Materazzi family (tel: 0575 651095) produce organic wines, olive oil, and *farro*, spelt wheat.

CAVRIGLIA

LA LOCANDA CUCCUINI RESTAURANT

Aia   52022   Cavriglia
TELEPHONE 055 9166419   OPEN Lunch and dinner
CLOSED Sunday for dinner; Monday; holidays in winter
CREDIT CARDS None   ENGLISH SPOKEN Yes
FEATURES Summer terrace   RESERVATIONS Recommended
PRICE $$ OTHER Two rooms for holiday rentals
DIRECTIONS From Cavriglia, follow signs for Aia; the Locanda is signposted.

Stefano Cuccuini worked in Paris before coming home to open this restaurant in 1996. His country house now hosts a friendly, informal, but cultured restaurant, with an outdoor terrace for hot weather. Cuccuini is bright and refreshingly well traveled. "In Paris in the 1980s everybody was interested in Franco-Italian restaurants," he recalled. "But now I think we want a return to the kinds of foods our grandmothers prepared." Indeed, he has dedicated his restaurant to his grandmother. It was she who inspired both the Locanda's cooking and its spirit of hospitality.

I loved the food at this restaurant. Cuccuini's is a cuisine of clear flavors and fine ingredients; it is modern and pure, yet authentic. He proposes a very reasonably priced "combination" of three or four courses that includes the service charge, with a choice of five or six dishes for each course. The menu keeps up with the seasons.

In November, the antipasti were *bruschetta* toasts topped with eggplant and olives, Tuscan *salame* and figs, or warm fillets of herring served with cold parsleyed potatoes.

"For us Italians," he exclaimed, "pasta is hot bread in search of a flavoring." His was wonderful. A *semplicissimo* plate of speckled buckwheat spaghetti (*grano saraceno*) came dressed only with freshly pressed olive oil and garlic. It was aromatic, uncluttered, and delicious. His grandmother's *tortellacci* had a delicate pale orange filling of pumpkin, buttery and sweet. Other *primi* included a risotto of radicchio and local sausage meat, and noodles cooked with hare.

Main courses went from *baccalà* (salt cod) to tripe, grilled cheese with vegetables to anchovy-scented steak. I tried a tender chicken fricassee with a yellow egg and lemon binding, and a more decisive duck (*anatra muta*) stewed in wine, served with braised *rochietti*, a kind of celery. Dessert was frothy, sharp lemon curd on a piece of very flaky pastry. The wines are local and good. I look forward to going back.

CIVITELLA IN VAL DI CHIANA

RISTORANTE   Via Trove, 27   52040   Civitella in Val di Chiana
DEI LAGHI   TELEPHONE 0575 448031   OPEN Lunch and dinner
RESTAURANT   CLOSED Wednesday; August   CREDIT CARDS Visa, MC
                 ENGLISH SPOKEN Yes   FEATURES Trout fishing; children's playground
                 RESERVATIONS Necessary on weekends   PRICE $$
                 DIRECTIONS From Civitella, go toward Badia Agnoano. The restaurant
                 is clearly signposted after 4 kms.

This hunting-lodge style restaurant is set in the woods and surrounded by small lakes and streams—with trout fishing available. There is a large outdoor garden with dining terrace and kids' playground. The rustic interior is dominated by an enormous copper-hooded open fireplace that warms the whole room in winter. Here the restaurant's owner acts as grill chef, cooking meats and local mushrooms. The Del Cucina family has run this restaurant for over twenty-five years; I imagine the collection of stuffed game birds that decorates the dining room dates back that far.

This is a great place for mushroom-lovers. In autumn there were excellent *crostini di funghi:* charcoal-scented toasts topped with fine slices of raw mushrooms. The rare *ovoli* were sprinkled with coarsely grated Parmesan cheese, fruity olive oil, and black pepper; the stronger porcini had a garlic-rubbed toast. These number among the best *crostini* I tasted in Tuscany. In addition, there were *funghi fritti, alla brace,* or *trifolati*—fried, grilled, or stewed. Mushrooms appeared in pasta sauces too.

The restaurant's other specialty is, not surprisingly, meat cookery. A basket next to the fireplace holds logs cut to size for the imposing *camino*. Diners are provided with sharp knives. The fresh, quality meats—fillet steaks, chops, ribs, and *la Fiorentina*, the T-bone—are brushed with herbed oil and salted before being broiled. It is a spectacular scene, with the glowing red embers and the appetizing aroma of roasting meat. Juicy porcini mushroom caps are given the same treatment and are a delicacy. Some game is also prepared, including wild boar and pheasant. There are seasonal vegetable accompaniments.

Most diners seem to drink the house red but other wines are available. When the dinner service is finished, the friendly family leaves the kitchen and settles in the dining room to eat its meal.

CORTONA

AZIENDA AGRICOLA Via Santa Margherita, 9   52044   Cortona
RISTORI TELEPHONE 0575 603571, 0584 23261, 075 5725260   OPEN Sales by
OLIVE OIL appointment only   CREDIT CARDS None   DIRECT SALE Yes
ENGLISH SPOKEN A little   OTHER Holiday rentals available
DIRECTIONS In the town center

Silvio Ristori has long been an important personage in the food and wine world of Arezzo. He is a qualified sommelier and oil expert (he helps run local oil courses), and produces fine extra-virgin olive oil from his olive groves around Cortona of the classic Tuscan blend of Frantoiano, Leccino, and Moraiolo olives, processed in a *frantoio* nearby.

"The oils from these regions," he explained, "are very forceful: green, *fruttato*, and with a pleasant, characteristic bitterness. They go well with thick rustic soups like the *ribollita,* or on fresh salads—but not with fish, which they tend to overpower."

On what was once some of Ristori's property in the hills beside Cortona, a young German friend is now making oil. It too is available for private sales: call Michele Geyer 0575 62536.

CASTEL GIRARDI Castel Girardi, 61   52044   Cortona
RESTAURANT TELEPHONE 0575 691030   OPEN Lunch and dinner
CLOSED Tuesday   CREDIT CARDS Visa, MC   ENGLISH SPOKEN A little
FEATURES Outdoor summer terrace   RESERVATIONS Recommended
in summer   PRICE $$; pizza $ DIRECTIONS From the top of Cortona
go toward Città di Castello. The pizzeria is on the main road after 5 kms.

On a clear day you really can see for miles from this modest family-run trattoria. Perched high up on a hill above Cortona the panorama extends across the Val di Chiana into Umbria. Children are welcome (there is a little playground) and there is no problem about having just pizzas or pasta—the menu even offers a reasonably priced *tris* of three pastas.

Some daily specials do not appear on the menu. In spring and fall local wild mushrooms are featured in "salads"—sliced raw and served with shavings of Parmesan, oil, and pepper. These may be porcini, or the rarer *ovoli:* firm-fleshed, orange-skinned mushrooms that taste wonderfully peaty. Pizzas have paper-thin crusts in these parts, and come with many toppings. Although they are in no way Tuscan specialties, they are popular with kids (and with whoever is paying the bill). The restaurant also offers mixed vegetables grilled over wood embers, the usual assortment of meat dishes, a good range of desserts, and some local wines.

IL FALCONIERE
RESTAURANT

San Martino, 43   52044   Cortona
TELEPHONE 0575 612679   FAX 0575 612927   OPEN Lunch and dinner
CLOSED Wednesday in winter; November   CREDIT CARDS Visa, MC,
Amex   ENGLISH SPOKEN Yes   FEATURES Summer outdoor terrace
with view   RESERVATIONS For dinner and on weekends   PRICE $$$$
OTHER Il Falconiere, a relais, has eleven rooms to rent within the villa's
grounds   DIRECTIONS The restaurant is off SS 71 between Castiglion
Fiorentino and Cortona, about 3 kms north of Cortona. It is clearly sign-
posted from the main road.

Il Falconiere is one of this area's most elegant restaurants: a picturesque 1600 villa set in perfectly manicured grounds with cypress trees and flowers. The rest-aurant is in the *limonaia*, once used for wintering lemon trees. The summer dining terrace offers painterly views of Cortona and its vineyard-covered hillsides.

Il Falconiere's owners are strikingly young. Within a few years of inheriting the property, Silvia and Riccardo Baracchi have brought the complex up to relais (a luxurious small country hotel) standards. The well-appointed dining rooms have vaulted brick ceilings, warm terra-cotta floors and are deco-rated with fine murals and paintings. "We wanted to create a refined, comfort-able environment," explained the attractive Silvia. "One where the food matched its setting."

Being both a wine sommelier and a talented cook, she is ambi-tious about the restaurant's scope. The cuisine is based on Tuscany's native ingredients—wild herbs, local game, seasonal produce—but they are elaborated creatively. The autumn antipasti included a delicate *baccalà* tartlet with a purée of rosemary-scented chick-peas. A soufflélike hot *budino* of breadcrumbs and cheese came with a cool sauce of sweet pears. A mold of cardoons and sun-dried tomatoes was served with a creamy onion sauce. Quite a few of the *primi* were fish-based. A slice of corn polenta was topped with mixed shellfish and wild mushrooms. I preferred the woodsy colors and aromas of pumpkin-stained pasta filled with a savory pheasant stuffing and sauced with red wine and juniper.

Main courses were again divided by sea and land. A fine fillet of turbot (*rombo*) was topped with crunchy deep-fried celery and porcini mush-rooms. The boned rabbit, rolled around pistachios and carrots, was highly salted, but the rosemary lamb with its purée of garlic was wonderfully tender. Other *secondi* featured pheasant, pigeon, beef, and locally gathered porcini.

Desserts are elaborate and beautifully presented. A rich hot choc-olate pudding came with an airy chocolate mousse. A rustic frozen *semifreddo* had crunchy breadcrumbs and chocolate chips in it, and it was surrounded by a voluptuous vanilla sauce. Much of the extensive wine list is Tuscan, with a complement of foreign wines. The service, as would be expected in a restaurant of this caliber, is excellent.

L'ETRURIA
TABLE CRAFTS:
POTTERY

Piazza Signorelli, 21   52044   Cortona
TELEPHONE 0575 62360   OPEN 9:00-13:00, 15:30-20:00
CLOSED Monday in winter   CREDIT CARDS Visa, MC
ENGLISH SPOKEN A little   DIRECTIONS In the town center

Cortona has several little shops selling terra-cotta tableware. They all claim that the pieces are locally made, but I have my doubts (the nearby Umbrian town of Deruta supplies china shops all over the country with this kind of rustic ware). But that doesn't stop them from being pretty enough to take home. This shop has some good garlic pots pierced with airholes, a range of *zabaglione*-colored dinnerware with olive-green trim, and a series of plates with indigo borders around central scenes of rabbits or birds. Years ago I bought a small, one-handled pottery colander here; it was glazed off-white and punched full of draining holes, and just perfect for rinsing berries. I have it still.

ENOTECA ENOTRIA
WINE BAR,
SPECIALTY FOODS

Via Nazionale, 81   52044   Cortona
TELEPHONE 0575 692007   OPEN 9:30-13:30, 16:00-20:00 (later in summer)   CLOSED Tuesday   CREDIT CARDS Visa, MC
DIRECT SALE Yes   ENGLISH SPOKEN No
DIRECTIONS In the town center

This *enoteca* is one of Cortona's principal meeting places for locals. Since 1985, Imola, the owner, has run this friendly, informal wine bar and shop, selling a selection of reasonably priced Tuscan wines and local artisan foods. You can sit at the little counter or at one of the tables in the back while you drink a glass of wine (interested buyers can taste the wines before purchasing a bottle) or eat a *panino* filled with one of her well-selected food finds. She sells wild boar *salumi* and pecorini and ricotta from Mateassi (see next page) to eat with *ciaccia*—local slang for *schiacciata*, a flat crusty bread—and other breads made nearby in a wood-burning oven.

FOIANO DELLA CHIANA

CASEIFICIO
MATEASSI
CHEESE

Via di Cortona, 66A 52045 Foiano della Chiana
TELEPHONE/FAX 0575 649101 OPEN 8:00-13:00, 15:00-19:30
CLOSED Sunday CREDIT CARDS None DIRECT SALE Yes, for whole
cheeses ENGLISH SPOKEN No DIRECTIONS From Foiano, go toward
Cortona. The *caseificio* is on the right, 500 meters after the stop junction.
It is behind a beige private house.

This family-run *caseificio* makes cheeses from sheep's and cow's milk. In early
summer the sheep provide a lot of milk, so the company's pecorini are 100 percent sheep's; later in the year some cow's milk may be added into it. All the
sheep's milk comes from Tuscany and nearby Umbria. Mateassi's pasteurized
pecorini are sold fresh, semi-seasoned (one month) and fully seasoned (three to
six months). They also produce a delicate sheep's milk ricotta that is sold on the
day it is made, as well as the milder but less sweet cow's milk ricotta. Other
cheeses vary with the seasons.

When I visited them there was no company sign visible from
the road even though the small factory shop is well frequented; they said they
are planning to put one up soon.

GARGONZA

CASTELLO DI
GARGONZA
RESTAURANT, WINE

Gargonza 52048 Monte San Savino
TELEPHONE 0575 847021; La Torre restaurant: 0575 847065
FAX 0575 847054 OPEN Restaurant: lunch and dinner
CLOSED Restaurant: Tuesday; January and February
CREDIT CARDS Visa, MC, Amex DIRECT SALE Yes, wine and oil
available from the castle reception ENGLISH SPOKEN Yes
RESERVATIONS Recommended PRICE $$$
OTHER Apartments available for holiday rentals DIRECTIONS From the
top of Monte San Savino take SS 73 toward Siena. Gargonza is 7 kms up
the hill, signposted.

In 1304 the Castle of Gargonza hosted a gathering of Ghibellines that included
the poet Dante Alighieri. One hundred and thirty years later a Florentine
decree ordered that the walls of some of the Val di Chiana castles taken as war
booty from the Aretines be knocked down, Gargonza among them. And so
they were, though parts of the original structure were left. Subsequently, the
castle and the buildings within its circular walls were rebuilt and used for agri-
cultural purposes. It now belongs to the Florentine count Roberto Guicciar-
dini. He has, in recent years, set about fixing it up, revitalizing its vineyards
and olive groves, and creating a restaurant and a well-appointed "residence."

The Castello commands breathtaking views of the Val di
Chiana—after all, castles were built to that end. The restaurant is on the long
approach close to the castle. It is a nice setting, with a pretty courtyard for eating

outside in summer. Inside, I spotted some of Rampini's beautiful hand-painted platters from Chianti (see p 203). The count's idea for the restaurant is to return to the uncomplicated but satisfying country fare that Tuscany is famous for. "The Mediterranean diet is increasingly popular," he affirmed. "The basic elements of olive oil, wine, simple meats, and seasonal vegetables: these are the building blocks of this healthy home-cooked cuisine."

The restaurant, which had only been going for a short time under the new management when I visited, offers a range of pastas and soups, followed by meats (including Chianina beef) grilled over wood embers. There is a nice choice of side dishes, including grilled mixed vegetables, stewed peppers or haricot beans, and various salads. Cheeses and desserts follow, accompanied by the Chianti Putto of the castle, though there is a fuller wine list.

GIOVI

ANTICA TRATTORIA AL PRINCIPE RESTAURANT

52010   Giovi
TELEPHONE 0575 362046   OPEN Lunch and dinner
CLOSED Monday; holidays in summer   CREDIT CARDS Visa, MC, Amex
ENGLISH SPOKEN No   RESERVATIONS Recommended Thursday
and weekends   PRICE $$$ DIRECTIONS From SS 71 about 8 kms
north of Arezzo, follow signs to Borgo a Giovi and Giovi. The restaurant
is in the center of the old village.

Don't be put off by the "suburb" you must drive through to get into the old part of Giovi. At its heart is a medieval square, remarkably intact, with a Romanesque church and a cluster of what were once coach houses for the travelers stopping between the Casentino and Arezzo. Then this small square had enough passing trade to fill three restaurants. Al Principe is the only one left. It is the oldest trattoria in Arezzo, founded over 180 years ago. Inside, a series of small rooms has been opened up to form the dining rooms, as a patchwork of beamed ceilings reveals.

At lunchtime the trattoria is filled with local businessmen and farmers, many of whom spend a good part of the meal talking about food. There is nothing unusual in that: Italian men love discussing the foods they love.

I arrived in November, and the new season's olive oil was being pressed throughout the surrounding hills. As each group of diners sat down they were offered a bottle of thick green oil, a peppermill, and a basket of bread. They took a slice, drizzled on some oil, and ground pepper over it. With this *fettunta* (and no further ado) the meal had begun.

Along with the classic Tuscan starters of *crostini* and *affettati* (platters of cured meats), the season afforded the rare *ovoli* mushrooms, served raw. There was a choice of meat- or fish-based *primi* and *secondi*. My neighbors started with a creamy risotto with mixed *frutti di mare,* followed by an unusual dish of squid, celery, and *cannellini* beans. My *passato di fagioli* was a creamy purée of beans and vegetables with a handful of very fine pasta thrown in. A little "raw" oil and two large scallions went with it. Handmade pastas included *maccheroni,* which here were noodles almost as wide as *pappardelle,* with a hearty meat and mushroom sauce.

Main courses went beyond the usual grilled meats, *alla brace.* The unusual *anguilla al coccio* came bubbling hot in a terra-cotta pot—tender eel in a spicy tomato sauce. It was served with *cannellini* beans boiled with sage. There was a good selection of fresh seasonal vegetables, including braised artichokes and stewed *coste* (Swiss chard). The desserts are homemade. The wine list includes a lot of big names as well as a drinkable local *sfuso.*

GORGITI

FORNO COCOLLINI
BREAD

Gorgiti   52024   Loro Ciuffenna
TELEPHONE 055 9704001   OPEN 8:00-20:00   CLOSED Wednesday
CREDIT CARDS None   DIRECT SALE Yes   ENGLISH SPOKEN No
DIRECTIONS From Loro Ciuffenna, follow signs to Gorgiti.

Anyone who has had the pleasure of reading Burton Anderson's book *Pleasures of the Italian Table,* about Italy's artisan foods and their makers, will remember his evocative description of a predawn visit to this bakery to watch Carlo Cocollini making bread in his wood-burning oven. The *pane Toscano* is worth a trip to the tiny village; the informative book is worth reading.

LORO CIUFFENNA

COOPERATIVA
VECCHIO
FRANTOIO
"IL FONTINO"
OLIVE MILL

Via Setteponti Levante, 30   52024   Loro Ciuffenna
TELEPHONE 055 9172259   OPEN End of October to end of December;
sales by appointment only rest of the year   CREDIT CARDS None
DIRECT SALE Yes   ENGLISH SPOKEN No   DIRECTIONS On the
Setteponti road between Loro Ciuffenna and San Giustino; the mill is on
the right, 1.2 kms after Loro.

In late autumn, when you see the olives being hand-picked from the trees by men and women on ladders, you can take your clean empty bottles and buy the new season's extra-virgin oil directly from this small mill. It is always a wonderful spectacle to see the giant stone wheels grinding the olives to a paste: the air is filled with a fragrant mist of oil.

This cooperative has about twenty members—all independent olive cultivators within a two-kilometer radius of the mill. The olive harvest is a joyous time; visitors to the *frantoio* can sample the just-pressed spicy green oil on slices of country bread, washed down with a little local wine.

Mulino Parigi. Under Loro Ciuffenna's high bridge at the entrance to the town, there is a miller who still uses the powerful river water to drive his grinding wheels. This seventeenth-century mill was sadly on the verge of closing when I last visited it, but if it is still open, it is well worth seeing for anyone interested in the history of Tuscan foodmaking. Chestnut and other flours are on sale, freshly ground.

MANZANO

FATTORIA DI MANZANO WINE

Via Manzano, 15   52042   Camucia
TELEPHONE 0575 618667   FAX 0575 618411   OPEN Sales 9:00-12:00, 15:00-19:00; tastings and visits by appointment only   CLOSED Never
CREDIT CARDS Visa, MC, Amex   DIRECT SALE Yes
ENGLISH SPOKEN Yes   DIRECTIONS On the road between Camucia (Cortona) and Foiano della Chiana

"This is an area without winemaking traditions," explained Massimo d'Alessandro, "so we have been free to create our own." One of three Roman brothers who own the Fattoria di Manzano, d'Alessandro is an architect who, since the early 1980s, has become increasingly involved with winemaking. The estate, with over 50 hectares (125 acres) of vineyards and a remarkable eighteenth-century villa, is beautifully positioned on a small rise in the Chiana plain. Their father bought the estate in 1967, planting it all to Sangiovese and Trebbiano, Tuscany's classic red and white grapes. The results were mediocre.

"When I took over we did some experimentation," he continued," and discovered that the modern system of high-density planting of hot-climate grape varieties—especially Syrah and Chardonnay—gave great results here." The vineyards were replanted: from sixteen hundred plants per hectare, they increased to seven thousand. If before, each plant produced 10 kgs (22 lbs) of grapes, it now produces only 800 grams (less than 2 lbs). "The French have a saying: one plant, one glass of wine. This way there is incredible concentration of flavor in the fruit, as all the plant's energy goes into it."

Indeed, Manzano's wines are praised for their terrific intensity. The estate's primary red, Podere Il Bosco, of 100 percent Syrah, is a wine of elegance and structure. Podere di Fontarca is Manzano's modern-style Chardonnay with Viognier; aged in *barriques*, it, too, is a powerful, harmonious wine. Others include Podere Il Vescovo, of Gamay grapes, Le Terrazze, of primarily Sauvignon Blanc, and a lovely sweet Vin Santo. There is also a range of less costly wines.

Manzano's investments have included the cellars. They are now filled with legions of small French oak *barriques;* a distillery has been installed for the making of grappa. There are plans for a really modern *cantina* designed by d'Alessandro—if he can get planning permission.

MELICIANO

FATTORIA LA VIALLA   Via di Meliciano, 26   52029   Meliciano
OLIVE OIL,   TELEPHONE 0575 364372   FAX 0575 364623   OPEN 9:00-12:30,
SPECIALTY FOODS   15:00-18:00   CLOSED Saturday and Sunday   CREDIT CARDS Visa
DIRECT SALE Yes   ENGLISH SPOKEN Yes   OTHER Rooms to rent
DIRECTIONS From Castiglion Fibocchi go towards Meliciano. The farm is on the left after about 4 kms.

This interesting and large organic farm produces extra-virgin olive oil in its own stone mill. The small mill building is in a rural setting: an unpaved road barely reaches it. The hand-picked olives—black *morellina*, green *raggiaia*, and mottled *frantoiana*—are ground and pressed the day they are picked. If the air in the mill is too chill, a small wood-burning stove is lit in the corner.

"If the olives are allowed to go below 6°C /42°F they freeze," explained Piero Lo Franco, the farm's owner, "and oil extraction is difficult under 15°C /59°F. So some heat must be applied, if only to the room."

The farm's wines, jams, vegetable preserves and other products are on sale from its pleasant shop.

MONTE SAN SAVINO

MACELLERIA ALDO   Piazza Gamurrini, 31   52048   Monte San Savino
MEAT: PORCHETTA   TELEPHONE 0575 844098   OPEN 8:00-13:00, 16:00-19:30
CLOSED Wednesday afternoon; Sunday; first two weeks of July
CREDIT CARDS None   ENGLISH SPOKEN No
DIRECTIONS In the town's central square

Monte San Savino is known for *porchetta*—whole roasted pig. This is a very popular food in Tuscany: even the smallest markets have stalls selling the crispy-skinned meat sliced from the animal which is proudly on show, head and all. This cheery butcher's shop, run by Aldo Jacomoni and his wife Giorgina, makes the finest *porchetta* in Monte San Savino. Signora Jacomoni explained how it was done.

"We start with large animals weighing around 75 kilos (165 lbs). The pig is washed and the skin pricked at intervals, to let the hot fat out as it cooks. The major bones and organs are carefully removed from inside, leaving the skin intact. The cavity is stuffed with our special mixture of seasonings that includes wild fennel and garlic, and is then sewn up."

Meanwhile, the huge wood-burning oven is prepared. Branches of dried broom (*erica*) are stacked in the oven to start the fire; they will confer a particular aroma to the meat. The refractory brick oven is heated for about two hours, until it reaches 300°C/572°F. Then the prepared pig is placed inside. "The first half hour is crucial," she continued. "You have to make sure the temperature is right. Then you leave the pig to roast for ten hours, until it is beautifully browned on the outside and cooked right through."

The shop features homemade *salumi* and fresh meats, including Chianina steaks vacuum-packed for anyone who has far to go. Monte San Savino holds its annual *sagra della porchetta*—roasted pig fair—in September.

RISTORANTE Bano, 226   52048   Monte San Savino
BELVEDERE   TELEPHONE 0575 849588   FAX 0577 844262   OPEN Lunch and dinner
RESTAURANT CLOSED Monday   CREDIT CARDS Visa, MC, Amex
ENGLISH SPOKEN A little   FEATURES Summer terrace, minigolf, children's playground   RESERVATIONS Necessary on weekends
PRICE $$, pizza $ DIRECTIONS From Monte San Savino, take the road up toward Gargonza. The restaurant is signposted.

Positioned way up above the Val di Chiana, this spacious family-run restaurant and pizzeria is a relaxed place to take the whole family. Not only is it very reasonably priced, but parents can let their kids play outside while they linger over a nice bottle of wine. The restaurant offers free minigolf for its clients and other outdoor games.

Massimo Rossi, the Belvedere's young owner, is a qualified sommelier and an active champion of local artisan-made foods and olive oils. He organizes tastings and has researched a fine selection of wine and oil for the restaurant, with a smaller mark-up than usual.

The full menu includes a range of pizzas. Try a platter of mixed *crostini* to start—most Tuscans do. The egg pasta is homemade; baked *ricotta gnocchetti* are a house special. Meats grilled over a wood fire (*alla brace*) are always good. *Stracetti* (little rags) are thin strips of beef cooked with softened onions and balsamic vinegar. There is a wide choice of desserts (important for kids), including homemade gelati.

LUIGI LAPUCCI Corso Sangallo, 8-10   52048   Monte San Savino
TABLE CRAFTS: TELEPHONE 0575 844375   OPEN 9:00-13:00, 15:00-19:30; other times
POTTERY   ring bell for sales   CLOSED Saturday and Sunday in winter
CREDIT CARDS None   ENGLISH SPOKEN No
DIRECTIONS Off Piazza Gamurrini

Working with red and white clay from Empoli, the Lapuccis and Chelis create unusual ceramics traditional only to Monte San Savino. The clay is cut away by hand (*traforato*) to look almost like lace, and then glazed white or colored. The work is very detailed; the objects—bowls, plates, vases—are precious yet rustic enough to look handmade. *Scaldini* are earthenware pots with high handles that held glowing embers; they served as hand warmers. In November a *festa* in the town is dedicated to them.

MONTEVARCHI

LA BOTTEGA
DI PATERNA
FARM PRODUCE:
ORGANIC

Le Logge, 11   52025   Montevarchi
TELEPHONE 055 982391   OPEN 8:00-13:00, 17:00-20:00
CLOSED Sunday; Saturday afternoon in summer, Wednesday afternoon
in winter   CREDIT CARDS None   ENGLISH SPOKEN No
DIRECTIONS Under the portico in Piazza Mazzini, near the station

This wonderful shop is the outlet for the Paterna farm at Terranuova
Bracciolini (p 346). It sells fresh organic produce, preserved vegetables and
fruits (including Sandra Masi's fine range), pulses, organic wine, and some
organic dairy foods—from farm to consumer, without middlemen. The staff
are friendly; the vegetables and fruit are delicious—and it's all good for us!

PASTICCERIA
BONCI
PASTRY, BAR

Viale Diaz, 49   52025   Montevarchi
TELEPHONE 055 982308 shop   FAX 055 981225 fax and tel of bakery
OPEN 7:00-13:30, 16:00-20:00   CLOSED Monday; Sunday afternoon
in summer; August   CREDIT CARDS None   ENGLISH SPOKEN Yes
DIRECTIONS On SS 69 *circonvallazione*, or ring road, through outer
Montevarchi, by Via Piave

This attractive pastry shop is run by the Bonci family. They have their own
bakery nearby producing pastries, cakes, *panforte*, chocolates. The Bonci's *panforte* weighs 500 grams (1 lb); it comes in a pretty wrapping and makes a good
present to take home. This version is lightly-spiced, soft and fresh-tasting, with
almonds and candied melon rind in it.

The chocolates are made by the young Michele Mezzasoma,
who was trained in the Piemontese manner of cream and liquid fillings. There
are candied fruits and *confetti*—the hard candy-covered seeds of coriander,
anise, cumin, and cardamom that make nice breath-fresheners.

PERGINE VALDARNO

"PERGENTINO"
OIL COOPERATIVE
OLIVE OIL

Piazza della Chiesa, 10   52020   Pergine Valdarno
TELEPHONE 0575 896020   FAX 0575 897045   OPEN November-
January and June-August 17:30-19:00; the rest of the year and other times
by appointment only   CREDIT CARDS None   DIRECT SALE Yes
ENGLISH SPOKEN Yes   OTHER The cooperative's *frantoio* is at Pieve
a Presciano. It may be visited in November and December.
DIRECTIONS The shop is in the center of the village.

The lovely hills around Pergine are terraced with olive groves, and the town's
extra-virgin olive oil is considered to be among Tuscany's finest. This small
cooperative was formed in 1983—just two years before the winter that froze
most of central Italy's olive trees. It was not until 1991 that the group was able
to begin production.

"Despite 1985, we are lucky here," explained Arturo Ghezzi, a member of the cooperative. "This area is north-facing, so the most serious olive parasite gets killed off in winter. Consequently, we do very little spraying."

Each tree yields about 15 kgs (33 lbs) of olives, which translates into only about 2 kgs (4½ lbs) of oil—just two or three bottles per plant. The olives are picked by hand before being taken to the nearby modern-style *frantoio*. The oil has very low acidity. Unfortunately I visited Pergine only a couple of weeks before the harvest, so I was unable to taste the new season's oil (and the old, after a year, had lost a lot of flavor).

The cooperative has produced an artist-designed bottle for their gift-packs; it comes in its own wooden carrying box. The oil is available in regular bottles, too. Artichoke hearts preserved in oil are also on sale from the little shop.

PONTE A CHIANI

FRANTOIO E CANTINA Ponte a Chiani, 57F   52040   Ponte a Chiani
VINI TIPICI ARETINO TELEPHONE 0575 363038   FAX 0575 363950   OPEN Shop 8:00-12:30,
OLIVE MILL, WINE   14:30-18:00   CLOSED Saturday afternoon; Sunday
CREDIT CARDS None   DIRECT SALE Yes   ENGLISH SPOKEN No
DIRECTIONS On the main road between Ponte a Chiani and Indicatore

This Frantoio and Cantina Sociale produces oil and wine for its many small members from the surrounding *colline Aretine*. The two modern buildings, the oil mill and the wine cellar, are side by side, and they share a shop selling their reasonably priced oils and wines. The *cantina*'s range of wines includes the local white Bianco Vergine Valdichiana DOC.

The *frantoio* is of the modern type, with steel hammers to pound the olives to a pulp and centrifugal separators. In November, when the harvest is on, the parking lot is full of *api*, the three-wheeled vehicles so popular in the countryside. Inside, the farmers watch over their olives like anxious parents as the bitter green and black fruit is so mysteriously transformed into golden oil.

POPPI

AZIENDA AGRICOLA   Filetto, 21   52014   Poppi
MULINO ROSSI   TELEPHONE 0575 500163   OPEN Sales by appointment only
CHEESE: GOAT'S   CREDIT CARDS None   DIRECT SALE Yes   STOCKIST From Easter to
October at Ponte a Poppi market on Tuesday mornings
ENGLISH SPOKEN A little   OTHER Organic produce in summer
DIRECTIONS From Ponte a Poppi, cross the bridge toward Poppi. After the
bridge turn right toward Quorle. After 700 meters take right toward
Quorle for 2 kms. After a small stone bridge, take the right fork toward
Filetto (yellow sign). The road becomes unpaved, and after a very sharp
left bend, the house is on the left after another km.

If you are a fan of goat's cheese and like to explore the countryside, you will enjoy
the drive up into the hills above Poppi to this small farm. The views are spectacular and the dirt roads are passable if your car is not too low off the ground.

Arianna Adani and Angelo Rossini have a herd of thirty-five
goats grazing the pastures around their house. Their creamy, unpasteurized
organic cheeses are made in the French style, as Arianna explained: "Unlike
pecorino-style cheeses, which are made in about one hour at fairly high heat
[30°C/86°F], *caprino* goat's cheese requires a *cagliatura* [addition of rennet] at
lower temperatures of 18°C /64°F, which must be sustained for a full twenty-
four hours." She explained that goat's milk is closer to human milk than cow's,
and has a lower fat content.

Arianna makes a fresh curd *caprino* that resembles Quark as well
as herbed and matured cheeses. She also sells her cheeses at Firenze's Fierucola
and Fierucolina markets (see p 93).

PLATEAU PASTA   Via dei Guazzi, 8   Ponte a Poppi   52014   Poppi   Arezzo
PASTA   TELEPHONE 0575 529504   OPEN 8:30-19:00   CLOSED Saturday
afternoon; Sunday   CREDIT CARDS None   DIRECT SALE Yes
ENGLISH SPOKEN No   DIRECTIONS From Bibbiena, go toward Poppi,
turning right toward Cesena before Poppi; the factory is on the right after
20 meters.

This small, semi-industrial pasta factory makes handy packages of vacuum-
packed pasta that keep in the refrigerator for up to two months. The *tortelli di
patate,* a favorite Casentino recipe, are stuffed with a delicious potato filling.
There are a range of tagliatelle noodles as well as *ravioli* filled with nettle
(*ortica*) and ricotta, or truffle-scented ricotta.

PRATOVECCHIO

**L'OSTERIA
DI GIOVANNI
PETRAGLIA
SNACK BAR**

Via Roma, 57　52015　Pratovecchio
TELEPHONE 0575 58843　OPEN Monday, Wednesday-Saturday 6:00-22:00; Sunday 8:00-13:30, 15:00-22:00　CLOSED Tuesday; August
CREDIT CARDS None　ENGLISH SPOKEN A little
DIRECTIONS Just beyond Pratovecchio, on the road to Stia

For the past ten years Giovanni Petraglia's bar has provided a stopping place for people journeying to and from the Casentino. They come in for a coffee or a glass of wine, or for one of his sandwiches made from fragrant, unsalted local bread and his special *prosciutto affumicato al ginepro.* This lightly smoked ham is seasoned with salt, pepper, chili, and garlic before being smoked over a fire of juniper branches. It is then matured for eight months. The prosciutto is wonderfully moist and tender (not overly salty) with a slight sweetness from the smoke.

"In the old days this was a common *salume* in these parts," he told me. "People used to hang up their hams near the fireplace to dry out, and they took on this smoky flavor." Giovanni also stocks a few cheeses, including those made by the Talla Cooperative on the Pratomagno (p 345).

RENDOLA

**OSTERIA
DI RENDOLA
RESTAURANT**

Via di Rendola　Rendola　52025　Montevarchi
TELEPHONE 0575 9707491　OPEN Lunch and dinner
CLOSED Wednesday; holidays in winter　CREDIT CARDS Visa, MC
ENGLISH SPOKEN Yes　RESERVATIONS Recommended on weekends and for dinner　PRICE $$$　DIRECTIONS From Montevarchi, go south toward Mercatale Valdarno. Rendola is signposted from there.

This *osteria* has a rural setting, overlooking olive groves and vineyards. It is within the grounds of the Fattoria di Rendola, in what were the blacksmith and carpentry workshops. The buildings were refurbished when the restaurant opened in 1993. The interior has been tastefully stripped to reveal wood beams, brick, and stone. There is a large open fireplace.

The menu has been devised in a similar way: traditional and contemporary dishes have been selected with care and pared down to accentuate their primary flavors. The chef, Francesco Berardinelli, whose experience includes a stint at San Domenico's in New York, has sought out fine local ingredients.

In autumn, my lunch began with slices of home-smoked tuna served with a compote of Mediterranean vegetables—eggplant, peppers, beans—and a garlicless basil pesto. A *fonduta di finocchio* was a well-seasoned stiff purée of fennel seasoned with newly pressed olive oil. It was garnished with grilled shrimp. Other, more typically Tuscan, options included local *salumi* and *crostini.*

A very fine *passato* (puréed soup) of *fagioli* beans was scented with rosemary and given texture by plumped grains of *farro*, and tiny diced pieces of pancetta bacon. It was drizzled with oil and nicely peppered. Smoky-sweet *pappardelle* noodles were made with chestnut flour and topped with a chunky wild boar sauce. Stewed rabbit was served here with an aromatic *bramata* (medium grind) polenta enhanced with fresh herbs. A *feuilleté* tart of pears had a surprising rosemary accent. There are well-chosen wines to accompany these well-cooked foods.

RIMBOCCHI

AZIENDA AGRICOLA
GABRIELE MATEUCCI
CHEESE

Canvecchio, 26   Biforco   52011   Rimbocchi
TELEPHONE 0575 599261   OPEN Telephone appointment preferred for sales   CREDIT CARDS None   DIRECT SALE Yes
ENGLISH SPOKEN No   DIRECTIONS From Bibbiena, go toward Chiusi della Verna, and then follow signs for Rimbocchi. From Rimbocchi take the road for La Verna. The farm is on the right after about 3 kms. It is the first cluster of buildings after Montefatucchio.

A drive up the mountain to this cheesemaker reveals some spectacular scenery. Gabrielle Mateucci and his lovely wife, Gina, overlook a landscape of unusual striated rock formations that change continually as the light moves across them. Their flock of 180 sheep grazes in sloping fields full of wild herbs.

"Our pecorino is so flavorful because of these aromatic pastures," he said. "The biggest problem we have are the wolves. They are a protected species and are increasing in number. We guard our flock with big Maremman sheepdogs. Otherwise our sheep would be killed off."

As well as her prize-winning fresh and semiaged (aged from three to eight weeks) pecorini, Gina makes a small amount of fragrant ricotta, which should be preordered due to the high demand. The cheeses, on sale directly from the farm, are at their most plentiful from April through October. The couple are always there, but it is best to phone before going up, preferably at meal times.

SAN GIOVANNI VALDARNO

IVV
TABLE CRAFTS:
GLASSWARE

Lungarno Guido Reni, 60   52027   San Giovanni Valdarno
TELEPHONE 055 942619   OPEN 9:00-13:00, 16:00-19:30
CLOSED Sunday, Monday   CREDIT CARDS Visa, MC
ENGLISH SPOKEN Yes   DIRECTIONS On the east bank of the Arno River, (across from the town) 1 km from the Valdarno *autostrada* exit.

This glass factory has updated its image and now produces some stylish colored glass pieces at affordable prices. Glasses, vases, and other objects are blown or blown and then pressed into molds. There are good discounts on many items.

Shoppers at Williams Sonoma, Pottery Barn, and Barney's will recognize some of the pieces, as IVV produces glassware for them.

SANSEPOLCRO

**UN PUNTO
MACROBIOTICO
HEALTH FOODS,
RESTAURANT**

Via Giordano Bruno, 48/A   52037   Sansepolcro
TELEPHONE   0575 735544   OPEN Lunch Monday-Saturday, dinner
Thursday-Saturday   CLOSED Sunday   CREDIT CARDS None
ENGLISH SPOKEN A little   DIRECTIONS In the town center,
near Porta Fiorentina

Like its sister store in Arezzo (see p 314), Un Punto Macrobiotico sells macrobiotic and other health foods, and offers a reasonably priced restaurant serving vegetarian meals made with organic produce.

**CARNI SHOP
MEAT**

Via dei Lorena, 32   52037   Sansepolcro   Arezzo
TELEPHONE 0575 742924   OPEN 7:30-13:00, 15:30-19:30
CLOSED Wednesday afternoon in winter; Monday in summer; August
CREDIT CARDS None   ENGLISH SPOKEN No
DIRECTIONS On the main road into Sansepolcro from Anghiari and
the *superstrada*

Antimo Buzzichini's butcher's shop has specialized in Chianina beef for nearly twenty years. This local breed is considered to be among the finest beef in the world. "The Chianina are very low in fat, so their meat is lean and tender," explained Antimo. "You can tell by looking at a raw steak: the Chianina's color is less deeply red than other beef, and has a nice layer of pure white fat around its edge. Recently even the Americans have been importing them to breed at home. In Italy the animals are controlled by veterinary inspectors who also ensure that no hormones have been administered. We know exactly what they eat, so there is no danger of disease."

The most popular cut is the *Fiorentina*, a T-bone, but others are available from the shop, which also sells a small range of ready-to-cook meats.

**MACELLERIA
MARTINI
MEAT**

Via XX Settembre, 95   52037   Sansepolcro
TELEPHONE 0575 742310   OPEN 8:00-13:00, 16:00-20:00
CLOSED Sunday; Monday in summer; Wednesday afternoon in winter; July
CREDIT CARDS None   ENGLISH SPOKEN A little
DIRECTIONS In the town center, by Piazza Torre di Berta

Aldo Martini is the quintessential butcher: red-faced, robust, and cheery. The attractive tiled shop he runs with his family is full of enticing goodies, some of which are special only to Sansepolcro.

Martini and his sons, Ivano and Marcello, produce an excellent *lombo di suino sott'olio*—lean loin of pork that is salt-cured before being sliced thick and preserved in herb-scented extra-vigin olive oil. It is sold in jars and makes a fine antipasto. There is chopped chicken and pigeon liver paste for topping *crostini,* a rich goose sauce (*sugo d'oca*) for pasta, well-flavored *prosciutto Toscano,* and a range of *salami,* some of which are preserved in oil.

The fresh meat counter features Chianina steaks and locally bred pork. A true Casentino rarity is the stuffed goose or chicken's neck (*collo ripieno*). It is filled with a mixture of ground veal, bechamel, liver, and egg, and baked in meat sauce or broth.

ROSA GORI
PASTA

Via del Prucino, 2E   52037   Sansepolcro
TELEPHONE 0575 742606   OPEN Winter 8:00-13:00, 16:30-19:30; summer 8:00-13:00, 17:00-20:00   CLOSED Monday; holidays in summer
CREDIT CARDS None   ENGLISH SPOKEN A little   DIRECTIONS The *pastificio* is located outside of the old part of town, to its west.

Fresh pasta is popular in this part of the Aretino, and this *pastificio* has been a fixture in Sansepolcro since 1968. It sells a range of egg pastas—flat noodles and stuffed. Ravioli are filled with herbs, ricotta and Parmesan; *agnolotti* with mixed ground meats, such as *mortadella,* veal, and pork with Parmesan; and *cappelletti* with ground beef or pork. For an easy dinner there are oven-ready cannelloni and lasagne, potato or spinach gnocchi, and sauces. *Bringoli* are a local eggless pasta—like thick spaghetti—of durum wheat and water. They are traditionally served with *sugo finto* (fake sauce), which is made of vegetables, offcuts of meat and offal, and cheese.

PASTICCERIA
CHIELI
PASTRY

Via Fraternità, 12   52037   Sansepolcro
TELEPHONE 0575 742026   FAX 0575 735507   OPEN 8:00-13:30, 16:30-20:00   CLOSED Monday   CREDIT CARDS None
ENGLISH SPOKEN A little   OTHER Chieli's other *pasticceria* is on Via XX Settembre, 8; the dessert wine shop is on Via Fraternità, 5
DIRECTIONS Off Piazza Torre di Berta, in the town center

Rosangela Chieli runs the finest pastry shops in Sansepolcro. I was struck by her lively intelligence. It was refreshing to meet such a positive modern food artisan. "The *pasticceria* was started by my father in 1948," she explained, "with the local repertoire of butter cream tarts, 'dry' biscuits and fried *bomboloni.* He lacked formal training, but used fine ingredients, and his pastries were a success." Now, fifty years later, the future of the family business lies with Rosangela's brother Daniele and her son Alessio Conti.

"These days there are many options for young pastry chefs wanting to master the specializations. We wanted our son to benefit from them." Alessio attended courses on chocolate, yeasts, candied fruits, and sugar sculpture. The Chielis also invite *maestri* to work in Sansepolcro. The day I was there a *marron glacé* specialist was giving a workshop. "Our clients now appreciate many northern specialties, like fine chocolates or French-style mousses. And of course we still prepare all the local favorites."

The elegant shop is filled with tempting confections. There are *pinoli*-studded ricotta tarts and puff-ball cakes called *cartoccio*, with jam and almond paste in their batter. Small cookies include the light, chewy *brutti ma buoni* (ugly but good) almond macaroons. There are fine chocolates in the Piemontese or Belgian tradition, with sumptuously sweet *fourré* fillings of nut, cocoa, or liqueur creams and contrasting decorative casings.

Fresh fruits are "transformed" into jams, jellies, and preserved in syrup. Herbed jellies of *melissa* (balm) and mint are fragrant pastes for spreading on toast. Anyone who hankers after the aniseed balls of their youth should try *confetti*, the hard sugar balls whose centers contain aromatic seeds. Across the street, the Chielis have opened a small showcase of (mainly) dessert wines to go with their pastries.

DA VENTURA
RESTAURANT

Via N. Aggiunti, 30   52037   Sansepolcro
TELEPHONE 0575 742560   OPEN Lunch and dinner
CLOSED Saturday; January and August   CREDIT CARDS Visa, MC, Amex
ENGLISH SPOKEN Yes   RESERVATIONS Recommended Sunday and
holidays   PRICE $$ OTHER Da Ventura also has a few rooms to let
DIRECTIONS In the center of town, down the street from the museum

Da Ventura is a family-run restaurant popular on the Piero della Francesca "circuit." Situated on one of Sansepolcro's main walking streets, it has lovely terracotta ceilings with old beams and carved wainscoting. As you step down from the sidewalk, you are greeted by mounds of fresh noodles drying on the entrance table. During the meal, the hot pasta and a choice of sauces is served from an amusing trolley. Each diner can determine how much of each they want.

Trolleys return throughout the meal. One appears with mixed antipasti of preserved and pickled vegetables, *lombo di maiale sott'olio* (slices of lean pork loin preserved in oil), and other *salumi*. Later, a *secondi* trolley brings roasted meats and wonderful accompanying vegetables. A final dessert *carrello* comes laden with sweets.

FIORENTINO
RESTAURANT

Via Luca Pacioli, 60   52037   Sansepolcro
TELEPHONE 0575 740350   FAX 0575 740370   OPEN Lunch and dinner
CLOSED Friday; early July   CREDIT CARDS Visa, MC
ENGLISH SPOKEN Yes   RESERVATIONS At weekends   PRICE $$
DIRECTIONS The restaurant is in the Hotel Fiorentino, one flight up from
the street, in the town center, off Via xx Settembre.

Though I have eaten many good meals since my last dinner at Fiorentino, I cannot forget the quality of this restaurant's food. It is like when a wonderful cook invites you over for dinner and prepares special dishes for the occasion that reveal the sensibility of a true artist. The artists in this case are an elderly woman, Signora Uccellini, and her friend. They maintain a tradition of home cooking few are lucky enough to grow up with.

The restaurant, upstairs in Sansepolcro's oldest hotel, is full of character. And so is its host, the signora's son, Alessio Uccellini. This portly gentleman, sporting a bow tie and colorful waistcoat, moves around the dining room with feline dexterity. A man of wit and culture, he dominates the lofty salons of the historic building's *piano nobile*. The brightly lit rooms, with their decorated, timbered ceilings, are filled with an eclectic array of treasures and trophies.

The menu resembles many others I have read; the difference is the quality. *Salumi* for antipasti are Martini's (see p 340). Here, when a simple meat broth is offered, you can be sure it is the real thing—served plain or with a handful of pasta or beans. The homemade egg pasta is excellent. In autumn, I tried tender noodles of a palpably fine texture served with a meltingly soft, savory artichoke sauce. Broad *pappardelle* were paired, as usual, with *lepre*. But this freshly cooked hare sauce had a meaty depth, a tenderness to it that was neither greasy nor heavy. There are no freezers in this kitchen.

An abundant choice of *secondi* included lamb baked with tomato and olives, turkey breast studded with truffles, veal stuffed with artichokes, pork liver with bay, and kidneys with sage. Plump wood pigeon were stewed with big green olives in a liver-enriched sauce, while tender rabbit was cooked with ripe tomatoes and rosemary. There was an unusual *caponata* of carrots, celery, potato, and yellow pepper, and caramelized sweet and sour onions. Everything was fresh, justly seasoned, light and appetizing—Tuscan cooking at its best.

A memorable tiramisù had a froth-light egg yolk sauce. Crème caramel mousse was voluptuous with toasted almonds folded into it. The dish of prickly pears *(fichi d'India)*, persimmons *(cachi)*, pomegranates, and figs was painterly. Delicious food, fine wines, an unhurried, convivial atmosphere—my ingredients for a favorite restaurant.

Also

Those who were brought up in the United States on good-tasting Buitoni macaroni may be interested to find that some of Sansepolcro's most important streets are named after the Buitonis. I discovered that Sansepolcro was the home of this mighty pasta producer: Buitoni was the town's principal employer and author of many philanthropic deeds at the beginning of the century. In 1939 Giovanni Buitoni went to the United States and founded this favorite American food empire. (Another started Perugina, the chocolate-makers famous for Baci, or kisses). A Buitoni factory still exists on the outskirts of town, now part of the multinational Nestlé.

Panificio La Spiga. Via Santa Caterina, 76. 0575 740522.

Using a wood oven fired with oak, beech, broom, and juniper, the young Valerio Caroscioli has made a name for himself baking Tuscany's classic breads. The shop is in the semibasement of a beautiful 1400s building, complete with arched *loggia*, within Sansepolcro's historic walls.

Gelateria Ghignoni. Via Tiberina Sud, 85. Dogana. 0575 741900.

In 1994, this *gelateria* won a national gelato competition with its *pinolata* flavor. Since then it has really expanded its repertoire and now boasts thirty-three flavors, including shrimp, salmon, porcini, and truffle. More palatable flavors include a nicely deep chocolate, and *cavallucci,* named for the popular Tuscan cookies. The *gelateria* is at Dogana, 1 km from Sansepolcro's center, on the road towards Città di Castello (Perugia).

STIA

FILETTO   Piazza B. Tanucci, 28   52017   Stia
RESTAURANT   TELEPHONE 0575 58631   OPEN Lunch and dinner in summer; lunch
                     only in winter   CLOSED Saturday in winter; November and June
                     CREDIT CARDS None   ENGLISH SPOKEN No
                     RESERVATIONS Recommended on Sunday
                     PRICE $$ DIRECTIONS In Stia's top piazza

This old-fashioned trattoria is strategically placed in Stia's highest and prettiest square, Piazza Tanucci, by the Romanesque church. In summer a few tables are set outside. The Francalanci family has run it for four generations. Next door, Filetto's *tabaccheria* also sells local *salumi*.

The dining area occupies a series of low rooms on the square. There are terra-cotta floors, pitchers of spring water, and a kitchen with a large open wood fire. The food is simple but satisfying. Meals start with mixed *salumi,* or at weekends, *crostini* canapés. In autumn, the abundantly portioned homemade *primi* included *pappardelle* noodles with wild boar sauce, tagliatelle, ravioli, and the local specialty, *tortelli di patate*—tender squares of egg pasta enclosing a pale orange filling of potato, garlic, cheese, parsley, and tomato. They are best eaten simply with melted butter. *Penne strascinate* (dried pasta quills in a piquant meat sauce), were served from a Tuscan terra-cotta pot. When it is available, *la zuppa ripiena* is a hearty peasant soup made from chicken innards.

Filetto is known for its succulent meats, roasted or grilled over wood embers. For those who prefer vegetables, there are stewed *fagioli,* chickpeas, peppers, or spinach. Ask for their own olive oil to drizzle over the vegetables. Desserts include tender *panna cotta* with sweet blackcurrant sauce, creamy mascarpone pudding, and *cantucci* biscuits dipped in Vin Santo.

TALLA

Cooperativa Zootecnica del Pratomagno Terra di Petrarca. Via di Bicciano.
Talla. 0575 597680.

I was not personally able to visit this artisan cheesemaker on the
Pratomagno mountain, but its sheep's cheeses are excellent. Its shop hours are
8:00-13:00, 15:00-17:30; closed Saturday afternoon and Sunday. Wines and
salumi from other Aretino cooperatives are also on sale.

ZOLFINO: THE BEAN COLUMBUS DIDN'T FIND

"Christopher Columbus brought many bean varieties back to Europe
from the Americas," explained Marco Noferi, an organic grower from the
Paterna cooperative, "but a few were indigenous to Europe, including the
zolfino. It probably formed part of the genetic dowry of legumes used by
the Etruscans and Romans centuries earlier."

The *zolfino* is pale yellow in color (*zolfo* means sulphur in
Italian) and is famous for its creamy texture, richness of flavor, and almost
imperceptibly thin skin, making it easier to digest than other beans.

"These beans are strange," Noferi added. "It's as if they dis-
dained any but the ground here in the Valdarno—all efforts to grow them
elsewhere have failed. They are quite tricky to cultivate: they don't like
anything but rainwater, and rot if you try irrigation."

Ten years ago the *zolfino* had all but disappeared, cultivated
only by a handful of growers. After a mention on a television food program, they became all the rage among wealthy Florentines and fancy
restaurants—and their wholesale price tripled.

"Our beans are naturally dried [as opposed to kiln-dried]
and need no soaking before cooking. You just boil them until tender and
eat them with some good olive oil; their *profumo* fills the table—we
wouldn't think of eating any other kind."

TERRANUOVA BRACCIOLINI

COOPERATIVA AGRI-
COLA VALDARNESE
FARM PRODUCE:
ORGANIC

Paterna   Via Setteponti, 96   52028   Terranuova Bracciolini
TELEPHONE/FAX 055 977052   OPEN 8:00-13:00, 17:00-20:00
CLOSED Sunday   MAIL ORDER Yes   CREDIT CARDS None
DIRECT SALE Yes   ENGLISH SPOKEN No   OTHER Paterna has an outlet
store in Montevarchi (p 335).   DIRECTIONS On Setteponti road between
Loro Ciuffenna and San Giustino Valdarno

The Valdarno Cooperative, Paterna, began over fifteen years ago and is one of
Tuscany's most important organic producers. Its 40 hectares (100 acres) of land
are under the auspices of the Tuscan branch of AIAB, the Italian organic growers' association.

"Paterna brought people together who believed in the possibility
of reversing the bad habits of Tuscany's post-war farmers," explained Marco
Noferi, its dynamic young director. "Much of the land was cultivated by uned-
ucated *contadini,* peasants. They were pushed into buying and using chemical
pesticides and weed-killers by promises of better yields, and unfortunately the
mentality was often the more, the better. So the land really took a beating."

The association requires that land be left for five years after it
has been chemically treated before it can be called chemical-free, or organic
(*biologico*). On-site controls are carried out yearly.

Paterna produces organic vegetables and fruits, extra-virgin
olive oil, wines, pulses, and grains, including chestnuts and wheat ground at
Loro Ciuffenna's water mill (see p 332). Paterna's produce is sold fresh or preserved under oil or vinegar or as jam. The farm's shop is lined with jars: baby
artichokes, sliced zucchini or eggplant in olive oil, chestnut purées, fruit jams,
tomato sauces.

Noferi is actively safeguarding the Valdarno's indigenous, but
almost extinct, plant species, including the *zolfino* bean; he successfully
brought organic produce to the area's kindergardens. The farm and its shop
are lovely to visit, and the cause is undoubtedly worth supporting.

OSTERIA "IL CANTO
DEL MAGGIO"
RESTAURANT

Penna Alta, 30/D   Penna   52028   Terranuova Bracciolini
TELEPHONE 055 9705147   OPEN Summer: dinner Tuesday-Sunday and
Sunday lunch; winter: dinner Thursday-Sunday and Sunday lunch; snack
lunches in wine bar all year   CLOSED Monday; Tuesday and Wednesday
in winter; ten days in October, one week in January
CREDIT CARDS Visa, MC, Amex   ENGLISH SPOKEN Yes
FEATURES Outdoor summer terrace   RESERVATIONS Recommended
PRICE $$-$$$ OTHER The *osteria* has rooms for holiday rentals.
DIRECTIONS From Terranuova Bracciolini, go toward Loro Ciuffenna.
Penna Alta is on the left after 1 km. The *osteria* is signposted; park at the
top of the drive.

Mauro Quirini describes his *osteria's* delicious cuisine as "the happy encounter
between the poor food of Arezzo and the rich food of Firenze." His country

cooking features fine artisan-made ingredients and seasonal produce. Many vegetables and herbs are homegrown; he has built a room for aging *salumi* and a pit for maturing cheeses—all in the tiny hamlet that is Penna Alta, which, until Quirini arrived, had been abandoned since the 1950s.

Il Canto del Maggio is situated in the small rooms of a small house. There are many personal touches: sculptures and decorative objects are tucked on door ledges or into niches. The menu offers some of the area's culinary rarities: home-cured *salame*, thin-skinned yellowish *zolfino* beans (see p 345), country *prosciutto* aged for over two years—twice that of its commercial counterparts.

In autumn the antipasti included this full-flavored, peppered prosciutto, thin slices of *capocollo* (salt-cured pork shoulder) served with orange-scented butter, Quirini's coarsely ground *finocchiona*, and slices of *salame* accompanied by a paste of crushed figs and nuts. Toasted bread was topped simply with Tuscan black cabbage and fragrant new olive oil. The flavors were pure and decisive—an excellent start to the meal.

The *zuppa di fagioli* was a thick purée of herbed beans, with whole beans and chopped scallions added for texture. Herb *strozzapreti* were like the filling to ravioli without the pasta: tender green dumplings under a blanket of melted, truffled *fonduta* cheese. Wide *pappardelle* noodles were sauced with a coarsely-chopped *battuto grosso* of vegetables and chicken livers. Capon came with fried cardoons, the bitter vegetable in the artichoke family. Duck was tender and served in a jelly dominated by citrus zest.

For dessert, a chilled chestnut mousse was soft, creamy, and smoky from the chestnuts' drying; white chocolate mousse was more compact. A well-selected wine list completed this fine gastronomic experience.

OSTERIA COSTACHIARA RESTAURANT	Badiola 52027 Terranuova Bracciolini TELEPHONE 055 944318 OPEN Lunch and dinner CLOSED Tuesday; second half of August CREDIT CARDS Visa, MC ENGLISH SPOKEN No RESERVATIONS Always recommended PRICE $$ DIRECTIONS From the Valdarno exit of the *autostrada* A1 go left toward San Giovanni Valdarno for 3.5 kms. Turn right into Badiola. Go straight through the village, cross a river, then turn right toward Montemarciano and Persignano. The restaurant is on the right after 800 meters.

This *osteria's* cuisine is *cucina contadina*—peasant cooking. The setting is certainly rural: a large *casa colonica* (farmhouse) situated in a garden over the river from San Giovanni Valdarno. With his family, the affable Aldo Betti has run this lively, atmospheric restaurant since 1991. He is a great host: dressed in his white half apron he describes the foods as if he himself couldn't resist them.

And you can't help feeling hungry seeing his big display of unusual homemade antipasti. There are bowls of olives and *sott'aceti* (pickled vegetables), steamed greens, boiled *fagioli,* twists of crispy pork fat (*ciccioli*), tomatoes stuffed with tuna and capers. Meats include sliced tongue, a deep pink country *prosciutto Toscano* on the bone, and a range of locally cured *salumi.*

Primi are rustic and appetizing. Betti's *"bella" zuppa di fagioli* comes steaming hot in an earthenware bowl. A fine, *piccante* purée of beans, it is thickened with thin noodles, *taglierini. Pici,* like thick spaghetti, is topped with a meaty sauce of pigeon and guinea fowl flavored with rosemary, without tomato.

Meats grilled over the wood fire are a specialty: chops, steaks, and sausages. Whole pork livers (*fegatelli*) are spit-roasted with bay (*alla Fiorentina*) or fennel (*all'Aretina*). Aldo Betti told me that Giorgio Vasari, the Renaissance painter and author of the 1550 *Lives of the Painters,* was born in Arezzo and was very partial to these *fegatelli.* Home-killed wild boar is served with corn-yellow polenta, stewed in a peppery sauce with sage. This is robust country cooking that is best enjoyed with a group of friends and some good Tuscan wine.

VITIANO

Frantoio Oleario Giancarlo Giannini. Vitiano, 227 A. 0575 97370.

This modern-style *frantoio,* or olive mill, may be visited during the olive pressing season—November and December. Oil may be bought directly from the mill during the harvest season. At other times, phone ahead for an appointment to visit.

Tuscan Market Days

These are weekly or monthly market days for each town listed. Some of these markets have large food sections; others may only have a few stalls. Most big towns also have at least one or more permanent covered markets, usually open every morning except Sunday.

Lunigiana and Versilia (CHAPTER 1)

AULLA   Saturday morning

BAGNONE   Monday morning

CAMAIORE   Monday morning, Friday morning

CARRARA   Monday morning

FIVIZZANO   Tuesday morning

FORTE DEI MARMI   Wednesday morning

MASSA   Tuesday morning, Friday morning

PIETRASANTA   Saturday morning

PONTREMOLI   Wednesday morning, Saturday morning

SERAVEZZA   Saturday morning

VIAREGGIO   Piazza Santa Maria, daily

VILLAFRANCA IN LUNIGIANA   Friday morning

Lucca and the Garfagnana (CHAPTER 2)

ALTOPASCIO   Thursday morning

BARGA   Friday morning

CAPANNORI   Friday morning

CASTELNUOVO DI GARFAGNANA   Thursday morning

LUCCA   Mercato del Carmine daily except Wednesday and Sunday; antique market third Saturday and Sunday of each month

MASSAROSA   Tuesday morning

PIAZZA AL SERCHIO   Tuesday morning

PIEVE FOSCIANA   Saturday morning

PORCARI   Saturday morning

Pistoia and Mount Abetone (CHAPTER 3)

AGLIANA   Thursday morning
CUTIGLIANO   Tuesday morning
LAMPORECCHIO   Saturday morning
MONSUMMANO TERME   Monday morning
MONTECATINI TERME   Thursday morning
PESCIA   Saturday morning
PISTOIA   Wednesday and Saturday mornings
PONTE BUGGIANESE   Friday morning
QUARRATA   Saturday morning
SAN MARCELLO PISTOIESE   Thursday morning

Firenze (Florence), Prato, and Their Provinces (CHAPTER 4)

BAGNO A RIPOLI   Wednesday morning
BORGO SAN LORENZO   Tuesday morning
CALENZANO   Wednesday morning
CAMPI BISENZIO   Saturday afternoon
CASTELFIORENTINO   Saturday morning
CERTALDO   Wednesday morning
EMPOLI   Thursday morning
FIGLINE VALDARNO   Tuesday morning
FIRENZE VIALE LINCOLN   Tuesday morning, and see p 94
FUCECCHIO   Wednesday morning
IMPRUNETA   Saturday morning
TAVARNUZZE   Wednesday morning
INCISA VAL D'ARNO   Friday morning
MONTELUPO FIORENTINO   Saturday morning
MONTESPERTOLI   Tuesday morning
POGGIO A CAIANO   Thursday morning
PONTASSIEVE   Wednesday morning
PRATO   Monday morning
REGGELLO   Saturday morning
RÙFINA   Saturday afternoon
SCANDICCI   Saturday
SESTO FIORENTINO   Saturday
SIGNA   Friday morning
VICCHIO   Thursday morning
VINCI   Wednesday morning

Pisa and Its Hills (CHAPTER 5)

BIENTINA   Tuesday morning

CAPANNOLI   Tuesday morning

CASCINA   Thursday morning

CASTELFRANCO DI SOTTO   Monday morning

CASTELNUOVO VAL DI CECINA   Wednesday morning

PISA   Piazza Duomo daily, and see p 129

POMARANCE   Thursday morning

PONSACCO   Wednesday morning

PONTEDERA   Friday morning

SAN GIULIANO TERME   Tuesday morning

SAN MINIATO   Tuesday morning

SAN ROMANO   Wednesday morning

SANTA CROCE SULL'ARNO   Saturday morning

VOLTERRA   Saturday morning

Livorno and Its Coast (CHAPTER 6)

CECINA   Tuesday morning

COLLESALVETTI   Thursday morning

DONORATICO   Thursday morning

LIVORNO   Via dei Pensieri Friday morning, and see p 155

MARINA DI BIBBONA   Wednesday morning in summer

PIOMBINO   Wednesday morning

ROSIGNANO SOLVAY   Monday morning

SAN VINCENZO   Saturday morning

The Island of Elba (CHAPTER 7)

CAMPO NELL'ELBA   Wednesday morning

PORTOFERRAIO   Friday morning

RIO MARINA   Monday morning

Chianti Classico and Its Wines (CHAPTER 8)

CASTELLINA IN CHIANTI   Saturday morning
CASTELNUOVO BERARDENGA   Thursday morning
GAIOLE IN CHIANTI   second Tuesday afternoon of the month
GREVE IN CHIANTI   Saturday morning
PANZANO   Sunday morning
POGGIBONSI   Tuesday morning
RADDA IN CHIANTI   fourth Monday afternoon of the month
SAN CASCIANO VAL DI PESA   Monday morning
STRADA IN CHIANTI   Tuesday morning
TAVARNELLE VAL DI PESA   Thursday morning

Grosseto and the Maremma (CHAPTER 9)

CAPALBIO   Wednesday morning
CASTIGLION DELLA PESCAIA   Saturday morning
FOLLONICA   Friday morning
GROSSETO   Thursday morning
MANCIANO   Saturday morning
MASSA MARITTIMA   Wednesday morning
ORBETELLO   Saturday morning
PITIGLIANO   Wednesday morning
PORTO ERCOLE   Monday morning
PORTO SANTO STEFANO   Tuesday morning
RIBOLLA   Tuesday morning
ROCCASTRADA   Wednesday morning
SCANSANO   Friday morning

Mount Amiata (CHAPTER 10)

ABBADIA SAN SALVATORE   Monday-Saturday mornings
CAMPIGLIA D'ORCIA   first Tuesday morning of the month
CASTEL DEL PIANO   first Wednesday of the month
CASTIGLION D'ORCIA   fourth Saturday morning of the month
PIANCASTAGNAIO   alternate Saturday mornings
RADICOFANI   alternate Thursday mornings

Siena and the Crete Senesi (CHAPTER 12)

BUONCONVENTO Saturday morning

CETONA Saturday morning

CHIANCIANO TERME Wednesday morning

CHIUSI SCALO Monday morning

COLLE DI VAL D'ELSA Friday morning

MONTEPULCIANO Thursday morning

MONTERONI D'ARBIA Tuesday morning

PIENZA Friday morning

RAPOLANO TERME Thursday and Friday mornings

SAN GIMIGNANO Thursday morning

SAN QUIRICO D'ORCIA alternate Tuesday mornings

SARTEANO Friday mornings

SIENA Wednesday morning

SINALUNGA Tuesday morning

TORRITA DI SIENA Friday morning

TREQUANDA first Thursday afternoon of the month

Montalcino and Its Wines (CHAPTER 12)

MONTALCINO Friday morning

Arezzo, Its Hills and Valleys (CHAPTER 13)

ANGHIARI Wednesday morning

AREZZO Saturday morning, and see p 317

BIBBIENA Thursday morning

CAMUCIA Thursday morning

CASTELFRANCO DI SOPRA Friday morning

CORTONA Saturday morning

FOIANO DELLA CHIANA Monday morning

LORO CIUFFENNA Monday morning

MONTE SAN SAVINO Wednesday morning

MONTEVARCHI Thursday morning

PIEVE SANTO STEFANO Monday morning

POPPI Tuesday morning

PRATOVECCHIO Friday morning

SAN GIOVANNI VALDARNO Saturday morning

SANSEPOLCRO Saturday morning

STIA Tuesday Afternoon

TERRANUOVA BRACCIOLINI Friday morning

Glossary

ACCIAIO INOSSIDABILE stainless steel

ACCIUGA, ACCIUGHE (pl) anchovy

ACETO vinegar

ACQUACOTTA rustic Maremman soup of vegetables and egg

ACQUAVITE brandy

AFFETTATI sliced cured meats, a common antipasto

AFFOGATO AL CAFFÈ a popular dessert: ice cream "drowned" in espresso coffee

AGNELLO lamb

AGRITURISMO holiday rentals on farms or in country houses

ALIMENTARI grocery store

ALLA BRACE cooked over wood embers

ALLEVAMENTO animal breeding; farm

AMARETTO macaroon made with bitter and sweet almonds

AMARO bitter; a herbal liqueur used as a *digestivo*

ANGUILLA eel

ANNATA year of vintage

ANTIPASTO hors d'oeuvre, the appetizer course of a meal

APERITIVO predinner drink

APICOLTURA beekeeping

ARAGOSTA clawless spiny lobster

ARRABBIATA a spicy hot tomato-based pasta sauce (literally, "angry")

ASTICE lobster

AZIENDA AGRICOLA farm

AZIENDA company, business

BACCALÀ salt cod

BAR bar serving coffee, alcoholic beverages, and snacks

BARRIQUES small barrels usually of French oak popular in modern winemaking. American oak *barriques* impart a stronger taste

BIANCO white

BICCHIERE glass

BORGO village, especially medieval

BOTTARGA DI TONNO dried tuna roe

BOTTE, BOTTI (pl) large wooden barrels, usually of Slavonian oak or chestnut

BOTTIGLIA bottle

BRACE wood embers

BRANZINO   sea bass; it may be wild or farmed (*di allevamento*)

BRIOCHE   generic Italian name for breakfast pastry, including croissant

BRUSCHETTA   grilled bread usually rubbed with garlic and drizzled with olive oil

BUDINO   sweet or savory "pudding"

CAFFÈ   coffee; if you order *un caffè*, you will be served an espresso

CANNELLINI   white beans popular in Tuscany

CANTINA   cellar, wine cellar or winery

CANTUCCI, CANTUCCINI   hard almond biscuits often dunked in Vin Santo

CAPONATA   sweet-and-sour Sicilian vegetable dish, usually with eggplants

CAPPERI   capers

CAPPUCCINO   espresso coffee with steamed milk

CAPRINO   goat's cheese

CAPRIOLO   roebuck

CARATELLO   small wooden cask used for making Vin Santo

CARCIOFI   artichokes

CARDO   cardoon, a vegetable in the thistle family

CARNE   meat

CARPACCIO   as commonly used, the word means very thinly sliced raw meat or fish with a lemon and oil marinade

CARTA DEI VINI   wine list

CARTOCCIO   a method of baking in paper or foil

CASEIFICIO   cheese factory

CASTAGNA   chestnut

CERVO   venison

CHIANINA   a breed of cattle formerly used to pull the plough, now regarded as the finest eating beef

CHIODINI   two types of small edible wild mushrooms *Armillariella mellea* or *Clitocybe tabescens*

CICLO CONTINUO   modern style of olive oil mill (literally, "continuous cycle")

CINGHIALE   wild boar

COMPANATICO   "to go with bread"

CONFETTI   hard sugar candies

CONIGLIO   rabbit

CONSORZIO   consortium of food or wine producers; it oversees production and sales

CONTADINO   peasant, farmworker, or tenant farmer

CONTORNO   used on menus to signify side dishes

COTOLETTA ALLA MILANESE   breaded veal chop popular in Milan

COULIS   a thick purée or sauce, usually of fruit

CROSTATA   open-faced tart, especially fruit- or jam-filled

CROSTINO, CROSTONE   canapés

CRU   French term used in Italy to indicate a superior single vineyard and its wine

CUCINA POVERA   simple, peasant cookery, literally "poor cooking"

CULTURA PROMISCUA   the traditional style of interplanting crops with vines and olive and fruit trees

DAMIGIANA   demijohn, large glass wine flask

DEGUSTAZIONE   tasting (of wine or food)

DIGESTIVO   digestive, liqueur to aid digestion

DOC, DOCG   denominations used in wine zones, see p 27

DOLCE   sweet, dessert

DOLCI   desserts, sweets

DROGHERIA   grocery store selling imported spices and other specialized ingredients

ENOLOGIST   winemaker

ENOLOGO   enologist, winemaker

ENOTECA   wine bar, wine collection, usually for sale, as in a wine shop

ERBE   herbs, grasses, or wild leaves

ERBORISTERIA   shop selling herbal products

ETICHETTA   label

ETTARO   hectare; measure of land used in farming, equivalent to 2.47 acres

FAGIANO   pheasant

FAGIOLI   beans

FAGIOLINI   string beans

FARAONA   guinea fowl

FARRO   spelt wheat, *Tritticum dicoccum*, see p 49

FATTORIA   farm or estate

FAVA   fava or broad bean

FETTUNTA   like *bruschetta*, grilled bread drizzled with olive oil

FIASCHETTERIA   wine bar and shop

FIASCO   flask, as in the old-style, half straw-covered Chianti bottles

FINOCCHIONA   a salt-cured sausage of coarsely ground pork scented with wild fennel seeds, in Tuscany usually eaten fresh

FIORENTINA   T-bone steak, at its best when of Chianina beef

FIRENZE   Florence

FOCACCIA, FOCACCINA   flat crusty yeast bread, often topped with salt, olive oil and other savory toppings

FRANTOIO   olive oil mill

FRITTATA   Italian slow-cooked omelette, often eaten at room temperature as a snack or antipasto

FRITTO MISTO   mixed fried food

FRIZZANTE   lightly fizzy

FRUTTATO   fruity, of wine

FRUTTI DI BOSCO   wood fruits, especially berries

FRUTTI DI MARE   seafood

FUNGO, FUNGHI   mushrooms

GALLINELLA   Mediterranean fish in the gurnard family

GANACHE   a chocolate and whipping cream filling for chocolates

GELATERIA   ice cream parlor

GELATO   ice cream

GIOVANE   young

GNOCCHI, GNOCCHETTI   small dumplings, usually of potato and flour, eaten
   as a *primo*

GOVERNO TOSCANO   fermentation method once popular in Tuscan winemaking,
   see p 63

GRAMOLATRICE   a machine used to churn ground olive paste before the oil can
   be extracted

GRAPPA   distilled spirit made from the grape residues after the winemaking process

GRAPPOLO   grape bunch

GRIGLIATA MISTA   mixed grill (of meats, etc.)

HECTARE   see *ettaro*, a measure of land used in farming equivalent to 2.47 acres

INTEGRALE   whole wheat (of bread or pasta)

INVAIATURA   the changing of color of grapes or olives

INVECCHIAMENTO   aging, of wine

INVECCHIATO   aged, of cheese or wine

LATTE   milk

LEGNO   wood

LEPRE   hare

LITRO   liter (1.065 U.S. quarts)

LOMBO   loin

MACCHIA MEDITERRANEA   scrub, the stunted plants that grow wild around the
   Mediterranean basin

MACINE   stone wheels, especially for grinding olives

MALLEGATO   blood sausage

MANZO   beef

MARE   sea

MASCARPONE   Italian cream cheese

MEDITATION WINE   a "contemplative" wine that is drunk by itself, without food

MEZZADRÌA   system of sharecropping common in Tuscany until after World War II

MIELE   honey

MINESTRA   soup or first course

MISTO mixed

MORBIDO mellow, about wine

MOSTARDA sweet-and-hot fruit preserve from Cremona

MUFFA mould

NORMALE the basic DOC wine, as opposed to the *riserva*

OLIO oil

OLIVA olive

OLIVASTRA a variety of olive tree found especially on Mount Amiata

ORATA gilt-head bream

ORECCHIETTE small "ear-like" bunches at the top of bunches of grapes; type of short pasta

ORTICA, ORTICHE (pl) stinging nettles

OSSI DI MORTO literally "dead men's bones," very brittle egg white and almond biscuits

OSTERIA inn, now commonly used for informal restaurants

OVOLO delicious orange-capped wild mushroom, *Amanita caesarea*

PADRONE landlord, owner

PANCETTA salt-cured pork belly, like bacon

PANE SCIOCCO unsalted Tuscan bread

PANETTIERE baker

PANFORTE medieval spiced honey confection studded with fruits and nuts, typical of Siena

PANNA COTTA baked cream pudding

PANZANELLA bread and vegetable salad

PAPPA AL POMODORO rustic bread and tomato soup

PAPPARDELLE wide egg noodles

PARAGO, PAGELLO Mediterranean fish in the bream family

PARFAIT in Italian used for pâté-like savory dishes as well as desserts

PASSATA, PASSATO purée, especially of tomato

PASSITO, PASSITI (pl) semi-dried grapes and the sweet wine made from them

PASTICCERIA MIGNON petits fours or bite-size pastries

PASTICCERIA pastry shop, pastry

PASTICCIERE pastry chef or baker

PECORINO cheese made from sheep's milk

PEPERONCINO hot chili pepper

PERNICE partridge

PESCE fish

PESCE SPADA swordfish

PESTO Genovese ground basil, garlic and cheese sauce for pasta

PIAZZA place, square

PICCANTE hot, spicy

PICCOLA PASTICCERIA petit fours, bite-size pastries

PINCI, PICI   thick handmade pasta like spaghetti

PINOLI   pine nuts

PODERE   farm

POGGIO   hill

POLENTA   ground cornmeal and the dish made from it

POLLO   chicken

POLPO, POLIPO   octopus

POMODORO   tomato

PORCINO, PORCINI (pl)   wild mushroom, *Boletus edulis*

POTATURA VERDE   "green" pruning, carried out during the plant's growing season

PRIMI   first courses

PRODOTTO   product, produced

PRODUTTORE   producer

PROFUMO   bouquet, perfume, scent

PROSCIUTTO CRUDO   salt-cured ham

PROSCIUTTO   ham

PROSCIUTTO TOSCANO   Tuscan salt-cured ham, usually saltier and more robust in flavor than the Parma

QUINTALE   quintal, equivalent to 100 kgs

RAGÙ (Bolognese)   meat sauce for pasta

RETROGUSTO   aftertaste

RIBOLLITA   twice-cooked hearty Tuscan soup of vegetables, pulses, and bread (literally, "reboiled")

RICCIARELLI   soft marzipan cookies of Siena

RICOTTA   soft curd cheese made from whey, usually of cow's or sheep's milk

RIMONTAGGIO   the action of pumping the must over the "cap" in winemaking

RIPIENO   filling

RISERVA   reserve, applies to DOC or DOCG wines

RISO   rice

RISOTTO   rice dish

RISTORANTE   restaurant

ROMBO   turbot or brill

ROSATO   rosé wine

ROSSO   red

ROVERE   oak

SALAME, SALAMELLA   salt-cured salami

SALE   salt

SALSICCIA, SALSICCE   sausages

SALUMI   ready-to-eat salt-cured meats, usually of pork, including prosciutto

SALUMIERE   maker of *salumi*

SALUMIFICIO   factory producing *salumi*

SALVIA   sage

SAPORE   flavor

SCAMPO, SCAMPI (pl)   large shrimp or Dublin Bay prawn

SCHIACCIATA (also *ciaccia*)   see focaccia

SCIOCCO   see *pane sciocco*

SECCO   dry

SECONDO   second or main course

SEMIFREDDO   dessert frozen after it has been made

SFUSO   loose; refers to unbottled about wine or liquids

SOMMELIER   wine waiter or expert; French word used in Italy

SOPPRESSATA   head cheese, also known as *biroldo*

SOTT'ACETO, SOTT'ACETI (pl)   preserved under vinegar, usually vegetables

SOTT'OLIO, SOTT'OLII (pl)   preserved under oil

SPALLA   shoulder

SPIGOLA   sea bass (also called *branzino*)

SPUMANTE   sparkling (wine)

STOCCAFISSO   stockfish

SUPER-TUSCAN   modern-style wine, see p 30

TABACCHERIA   tobacconist's shop

TAGLIATELLE, TAGLIATELLINE, TAGLIOLINI   egg noodles

TAPPO   cork, bottle top

TARTUFO DI MARE   shellfish in the clam family

TARTUFO   truffle, also an ice cream

TAVOLA CALDA   informal eatery selling hot foods

TENUTA   farm or estate

TERROIR   French word that denotes an area in winemaking

TIMO   thyme

TIRAMISÙ   a coffee and mascarpone based dessert, literally "pick me up"

TONNO   tuna fish

TORTELLI   a type of stuffed pasta

TORTELLI DI PATATE   potato-filled egg pasta squares

TOTANO   long-bodied "flying" squid

TRATTORIA   a family-run country restaurant

TRIGLIA   red mullet

TUFO   tufa, a yellowish volcanic soil

UVA   grape

UVETTA   dried raisin

VASSOIO   tray

VECCHIO   old

VENDEMMIA   harvest, or grape harvest

VERDURA   vegetable

VIGNA, VIGNETO   vineyard

VIN SANTO   a Tuscan dessert wine, see p 28

VINO DA MEDITAZIONE   a contemplative wine that is drunk by itself, without food

VINO DA TAVOLA (vdt)   table wine

VINO PASSITO   usually sweet wine made from semidried grapes

VINO   wine

VINSANTAIA   room used to store *caratelli* of Vin Santo. It is often under the roof.

VITE   vine

VITELLO TONNATO   thinly sliced veal with tuna sauce, usually served cold

VITICOLTORE   grape grower

VITIGNO   grape variety or type

ZABAGLIONE, ZABAIONE   egg and sweet wine custard

ZAFFERANO   saffron

ZONA ARTIGIANALE, INDUSTRIALE   industrial or artisanal zones (of a town)

ZUPPA INGLESE   a kind of Italian trifle

ZUPPA   soup

Index